Human Rights and Minority Rights in the European Union

The end of the Cold War has ushered in a restructuring of the institutions of the European Community, culminating into its enlargement to Eastern Europe, under the aegis of economic integration, democracy and human rights.

This book examines the development and role of human rights in the European Union, from its inception as an economic cooperation project to an organisation of European states with a political agenda that goes beyond its borders. It argues that human rights have become an important component of the foreign policy of the European Union and that this role has grown from the inception of the Union through the Cold War and thereafter onto the process of enlargement of the Union. The book goes on to analyse the EU's policy on minorities, as a particular example of human rights. It considers the level of their protection within the EU and the framework of international law, and compares minority rights in the older Member States including France, Germany and the UK, with newer Eastern European states.

Kirsten Shoraka has a Ph.D. in law from the London School of Economics and worked as legal adviser for Fair Trials International, Office of Fair Trading, German Institute of Human Rights, the German Foreign Office and the Social Democrat Party in the German Parliament.

Routledge Research in EU Law

Available titles in this series include:

Centralized Enforcement, Legitimacy and Good Governance in the EU
Melanie Smith

EU External Relations and Systems of Governance
The CFSP, Euro-Mediterranean Partnership and migration
Paul James Cardwell

New Governance and the European Strategy for Employment
Samantha Velluti

Forthcoming titles in this series include:

The Evolving EU Counter-Terrorism Legal Framework
Maria O'Neill

Local Government in Europe
The 'Fourth Level' in the EU Multi-Layered System of Governance
Carlo Panara and Michael R. Varney

Criminal Law and Policy in the European Union
Samuli Miettinen

Human Rights and Minority Rights in the European Union

Kirsten Shoraka

Routledge
Taylor & Francis Group
LONDON AND NEW YORK

First published 2010 by Routledge
2 Park Square, Milton Park, Abingdon, Oxon OX14 4RN

Simultaneously published in the USA and Canada
by Routledge
270 Madison Avenue, New York, NY 10016

Routledge is an imprint of the Taylor & Francis Group, an informa business

Typeset in Baskerville by Taylor & Francis Books
Printed and bound in Great Britain by CPI Antony Rowe,
Chippenham, Wiltshire

British Library Cataloguing in Publication Data
A catalogue record for this book is available from the British Library

Library of Congress Cataloging in Publication Data
Shoraka, Kirsten.
Human rights and minority rights in the European Union / Kirsten Shoraka.
p. cm.
ISBN-13: 978-0-415-49125-9 (hbk)
ISBN-10: 0-415-49125-8 (hbk)
ISBN-13: 978-0-203-84924-8 (ebk)
ISBN-10: 0-203-84924-8 (ebk)
1. Minorities–Legal status, laws, etc.–European Union countries. 2. Human rights–European Union countries. I. Title.
KJE5144.M56S54 2010
342.2408'73–dc22
2009051850

ISBN 10: 0-415-49125-8 (hbk)
ISBN 13: 978-0-415-49125-9 (hbk)

ISBN 10: 0-203-84924-8 (ebk)
ISBN 13: 978-0-203-84924-8 (ebk)

Contents

Table of cases

European Court of Justice cases

European Court of Human Rights cases

Decisions of the European Commission of Human Rights

Decisions of the UN Treaty bodies

German cases

Slovenian cases

UK cases

ICJ/PCIJ cases

Table of legislation

Documents by the European Union

EU primary legislation

EU secondary legislation

Documents by the European Commission

Documents by the European Parliament

Documents by the European Court of Justice

Documents by the European Council

CFSP Council decisions

CSCE/OSCE documents

Council of Europe documents

UN documents

Legal materials of the Member States

Estonia

Germany

Lithuania

Slovakia

Act No. 365/2004 Coll. On Equal Treatment in Certain Areas and Protection Against Discrimination ... 270
Temporary positive measures with the aim of training the necessary number of teachers for teaching in the Roma language, No. CD-2004-7613/14980–81: 097 of 28 June 2004 ... 270
Fionnuala Sweeney (16.04.2004) 'Slovakia seeks help on Roma issue' CNN available at http://edition.cnn.com/2004/WORLD/europe/04/14/eu.slovakia.roma/ ... 270–271
Treaty on Good-neighbourly Relations and Friendly Cooperation between the Republic of Hungary and the Slovak Republic of 19 March 1995 ... 271

Slovenia

Constitution of the Republic of Slovenia, 23 December 1991, Official Gazette No. 1/91 ... 209, 271
Law on Local Self-Government, Official Gazette No. 72/93 ... 271
Ombudsman Act, Official Gazette 7/1993 and 15/1994 ... 271
Law on the Office of the State Prosecutor of 29 September 1994 ... 271
Notary Act of 21 February 1994 ... 271
Law on Court Rules of 24 March 1994 ... 271
Public Administration Act of 20 October 1994 ... 271
Law on Self-Governing Ethnic Communities of 5 October 1994 ... 271
Slovenia, Declaration of 25 March 1998 on the application of the FCNM, available at www.interculturaldialogue.eu/web/files/33/en/CFCPNM-R.pdf, last accessed on 2 December 2009 ... 272
Agreement on ensuring the special rights of Slovenians in Hungary and of the Hungarian ethnic population in Slovenia, available at www.un.int/slovenia/foreign.html, last accessed on 2 December 2009 ... 271

United Kingdom

Race Relations Act 1976 ... 218–219
Welsh Language Act 1993 ... 222
Race Relations (Northern Ireland) Order 1997 ... 218
Race Relations (Amendment) Act 2000 ... 219, 224
Racial and Religious Hatred Act 2006 ... 219, 223
Crime and Disorder Act 1998 ... 219, 223
Equality Act 2006 ... 219–220, 227
Human Rights Act 1998 ... 220, 225
Education Act 1996 ... 221, 272
Housing Act 2004 ... 225, 227
Gaelic Language Act 2005 ... 221
St Andrew's Agreement of 13 October 2006 ... 222
Report of the Commission for Racial Equality inquiry in England and Wales, 15 May 2006 ... 273
Delivering for Scotland's Gypsies/Travellers, June 2004 ... 220
Scottish Executive's Equality Strategy and Race Equality Scheme 2000 ... 220
ODPM Circular 01/2006, Office of the Deputy Prime Minister ... 273

France

Miscellaneous (in order of chapter)

Chapter 2

CFR–CDF/Conclusions 2005, EU Network of Independent Experts in Fundamental Rights 2005, Report on the Situation of Fundamental Rights in the European Union and its Member States 241, 242
EU Network of Independent Experts in Fundamental Rights, Thematic Comment No. 3, the Protection of Minorities in the European Union, 25 April 2005 259
International Association for Impact Assessment, at www.iaia.org 45–46, 242

Chapter 3

Leading by Example – A Human Rights Agenda for the European Union for the Year 2000, European University Institute (October 1998). Report commissioned by the EC on the occasion of the 50th anniversary of the UNDHR 248
Treaty on Understanding, Cooperation and Good Neighbourliness between Hungary and Romania of 16 September 1996, reprinted in 36 ILM 340 (1997) ... 250

Chapter 4

Human Rights Watch Report of 9 October 2005 'Serbia Fails to Curb Violence against Minorities', available at www.hrw.org/en/news/2005/10/09/serbia-fails-curb-violence-against-minorities, last accessed on 2 December 2009 251
First EU Roma Summit of 16 September 2008 available at http://ec.europa.eu/news/employment/080916_1_en.htm, and 'NGOs want results from first EU Roma Summit', last accessed on 2 December 2009 251
The European Roma Rights Centre Calls on the EU to Reaffirm Human Rights Standards in Policies on Roma available at www.errc.org/cikk.php?cikk=2983, last accessed on 2 December 2009 251
EU Network of Independent Experts in Fundamental Rights, Thematic Comment No. 3, the Protection of Minorities in the European Union, 25 April 2005 259
Sixth Framework Programme FP6, an EU programme for research and technological development, available at http://ec.europa.eu/research/fp6/index_en.cfm, last accessed on 2 December 2009 259
Report on Social Inclusion 2005: An analysis of the National Action Plans on Social Inclusion (2004–6) submitted by the 10 new Member States' framework for national strategy development as well as for policy coordination between the Member States on issues relating to poverty and social exclusion available at http://ec.europa.eu/employment_social/spsi/vulnerable_groups_en.htm, last accessed on 2 December 2009 260

List of abbreviations

ACP	African, Caribbean and Pacific (countries)
AJIL	*American Journal of International Law*
APPG	All Party Parliamentary Group
ASEAN	Association of South East Asian States
BVerfGE	Bundesverfassungsgerichtsentscheidung
BYIL	British Yearbook on International Law
CAHMIN	Ad Hoc Committee for the Protection of National Minorities
CARDS	Community Assistance for Reconstruction, Development and Stabilisation
CD	Collection of Decisions of the European Commission of Human Rights
CEECs	Central Eastern European countries
CEHR	Commission for Equality and Human Rights
CERD	International Convention on the Elimination of All Forms of Racial Discrimination
CFI	Court of First Instance
CFSP	Common Foreign and Security Policy
CHD	Conference on Human Dimension
CIO	Chairman in Office (of the OSCE)
CMLR	Common Market Law Review
CoE	Council of Europe
COR	Committee of the Regions
CPRSI	Contact Point for Roma and Sinti issues
CRC	Convention on the Protection of the Rights of the Child
CRE	Commission for Racial Equality
CSCE	Conference on Security and Cooperation in Europe
CSCE/OSCE	Conference on Security and Cooperation in Europe/Organization for Security and Cooperation in Europe
DCAL	Department of Culture, Art and Leisure
DH-MIN	Committee of Experts on Issues relating to the Protection of National Minorities
DGEMPL	Directorate General for Employment and Social Affairs
DGJLS	Directorate General for Justice, Freedom and Security

DR	Decisions and Reports of the European Commission of Human Rights
EBLUL	European Bureau of Lesser Used Languages
EBRD	European Bank for Reconstruction and Development
EC	European Community
ECHR	European Convention on Human Rights
ECJ	European Court of Justice
ECR	European Court Report
ECRI	European Commission against Racism and Intolerance
ECRML	European Charter on Regional or Minority Languages
ECtHR	European Court of Human Rights
EEC	European Economic Community
EES	European Employment Strategy
EHRLR	*European Human Rights Law Review*
EHRR	European Human Rights Report
EIDHR	European Initiative for Democracy and Human Rights
EIDHR	European Instrument for Democracy and Human Rights
EJIL	*European Journal of International Law*
ELR	*European Law Review*
EMO	Ethnic Minority Outreach (programme)
ENP	European Neighbourhood Policy
ENPI	European Neighbourhood and Partnership Instrument
EP	European Parliament
EPC	European Political Cooperation
ERDF	European Regional Development Fund
ESDP	European Security and Defence Policy
ETS	European Treaty Series
EU	European Union
EUFOR	European Union Force
EUI	European University Institute
EUMC	European Monitoring Centre on Racism and Xenophobia
FCNM	European Framework Convention for the Protection of National Minorities
FRA	Fundamental Rights Agency
FRY	Federal Republic of Yugoslavia
FYROM	former Republic of Yugoslavia Macedonia
GSP	Generalised System of Preferences
GSP+	Special Incentive Arrangement for Sustainable Development and Good Governance
HALDE	Haute Autorité de Lutte contre les Discriminations et pour l'Egalité, Independent High Authority for Equality and Against Discrimination (High Authority for the Fight against Discrimination and for Equality)
HCNM	High Commissioner for National Minorities
HDM	Human Dimension Mechanism

HRC	Human Rights Council
HRLJ	*Human Rights Law Journal*
HRLR	*Human Rights Law Review*
HRQ	*Human Rights Quarterly*
ICC	International Criminal Court
ICCPR	International Covenant on Civil and Political Rights
ICESCR	International Covenant on Economic, Social and Cultural Rights
ICJ	International Court of Justice
ICLQ	*International and Comparative Law Quarterly*
IJHR	*International Journal of Human Rights*
ILM	International Legal Materials
ILO	International Labour Organization
ILR	International Law Reports
IPA	Instrument for Pre-Accession Assistance
JEMIE	Journal on Ethnopolitics and Minority Issues in Europe
JHA	Justice and Home Affairs
LGTU	London Gypsy and Traveller Unit
MAF	Multi Annual Framework
MEP	Member of the European Parliament
NATO	North Atlantic Treaty Organization
NGO	non-governmental organisation
NHRI	National Human Rights Institution
NIHRC	Northern Ireland Human Rights Commission
NQHR	*Netherlands Quarterly of Human Rights*
ODIHR	Office for Democratic Institutions and Human Rights
OJ C	Official Journal, C-Series (information)
OJ L	Official Journal, L-Series (legislation)
OMC	Open Method of Coordination
OSCE	Organization on Security and Cooperation in Europe
PC	Permanent Council (of OSCE)
PCIJ	Permanent Court of International Justice
PHARE	Poland and Hungary Aid for Reconstruction and the Economy
RSC	Robert Schuman Centre
RT	*Riigi Teataja* (Estonian state Gazette)
SAA	Stabilisation and Association Agreement
SAP	Stabilisation and Association Process
SEA	Single European Act
SEED	Scottish Executive Education Department
SFRY	Socialist Federal Republic of Yugoslavia
STEP	Scottish Traveller Education Programme
TEC	EC Treaty
TEC	Treaty on European Community

TEU	Treaty on European Union
TFEU	Treaty on the Functioning of the European Union
ToA	Treaty of Amsterdam 1997
UKMIL	UK Material on International Law
UN	United Nations
UNCHR	UN Commission on Human Rights
UNDP	United Nations Development Programme
UNESCO	United Nations Educational, Scientific and Cultural Organization
UNGA	United Nations General Assembly
UNTS	United Nations Treaty Series

1 Overview

1.1 Introduction

When Europe lay destroyed after the Second World War, there was a shared interest in recreating the continent to achieve economic recovery and political and social stability. This enterprising idea led to the establishment of the European Community (EC), with human rights carrying little focus from its inception in 1957 and throughout the Cold War. Furthermore, the end of the Cold War has ushered in a restructuring of the institutions of the EC, which then became the European Union (EU), culminating into its enlargement to include former communist states in Central and Eastern Europe,[1] under the aegis of economic integration, democracy and human rights.

Against this background, the aim of this book is to examine the development and expansion of human rights and in particular minority rights in the European Union, which started as an economic cooperation project and became an organisation of European states with an international political agenda. There is no dearth of literature on human rights and the EU,[2] however, there has been no systematic treatment of this issue that combines aspects of human rights, minority rights and foreign policy in the EU, including the enlargement of the EU and the influence of international law in this area. The book does not analyse EU human rights law in great detail but rather reviews its historical development in the context of the Treaties (from Rome to Lisbon) and critically assesses the EU's policy on minority rights as part of its human rights policy/policy on enlargement, including a comparative study of four new EU Member States in Eastern Europe and three old Member States. Furthermore, the level of protection for minorities within the framework of international human rights law will be considered, and in particular the extent to which international law standards can have any impact on the EU's policy on minority rights.

The book is justified on account of the growing use of human rights in the development of the institutional structures and the legal order of the EU, and in connection with the increased application of human rights not only in the foreign policy of the EU, but also with regards to its internal development.[3] In addition, the protection of minorities has become a very topical issue in Europe since the end of the Cold War, and has played an important role in the EU's policy on enlargement. In this context, the role of other international organisations and their contribution to a minority protection regime will be assessed.

In modern society, the respect for human rights together with freedom and democracy form core values of every societal organisation or polity, as manifested in various international treaties and conventions concluded under the auspices of the United Nations (UN) or the Council of Europe (CoE). The EU, however, proclaimed in 1957 economic prosperity and the exercise of economic freedoms as its main objective.[4] Nevertheless, the founding fathers of the European Economic Community (EEC) cannot deny that peace and the protection of human rights on the European continent, after the horrors of two World Wars, were higher goals to be achieved *through* economic recovery. Also, the jurisprudence of the European Court of Justice (ECJ) reveals how the exercise of economic freedoms has influenced human rights awareness in the EU.

In the Western part of Europe, the adoption of the European Convention for the Protection of Human Rights and Fundamental Freedoms in 1950 (ECHR)[5] preceded the economic agenda, which was greatly achieved through what was then the EEC, founded in 1957.[6] Since then, the EC developed over the years into a very complex organisation that has undergone a dynamic process of integration and has assumed ever more competencies with the result of creating the EU in 1992 under the Treaty of Maastricht (Treaty on European Union, TEU).[7] The EC became one of the three pillars of the EU, the other two being the Common Foreign and Security Policy (CFSP) and Justice and Home Affairs (JHA). The Treaty of Maastricht also introduced for the first time a provision on human rights into the EC Treaty. Seven years later, with the Treaty of Amsterdam[8] a new Article 13 was inserted into the EC Treaty (TEC), enabling the Council to 'take appropriate action to combat discrimination based on sex, racial or ethnic origin, religion or belief, disability, age or sexual orientation' whereas before discrimination was simply prohibited on the basis of nationality of the Member States. On the basis of Article 13, TEC, Council Directive 2000/43/EC of 29 June 2000 (the Anti-Discrimination Directive) was issued, requiring the Member States to implement the principle of equal treatment between persons irrespective of racial or ethnic origin.

Before the Maastricht Treaty entered into force, human rights made early significant inroads in the sphere of economic dispute settlement mechanisms arising from the market-oriented EC. In this regard, human rights could be invoked when the ECJ was confronted with violations of fundamental rights as early as in the 1960s as a standard of conduct used to determine whether fundamental rights had been observed by the institutions or the Member States when their actions fell within the scope of Community law.[9] However, the relevant cases mainly concerned economic human rights such as the freedom to trade or the right of property, and the ECJ usually accorded higher importance to the Community interest than to the individual complainant. The ECJ would refer to the ECHR and other international treaties on human rights as 'sources of inspiration' for its decisions but did not consider them as binding and the much discussed accession of the EC to the ECHR was rejected by the ECJ in its opinion 2/94[10] and has only recently, with the Treaty of Lisbon, been revived.

With the international recognition of human rights, reference is increasingly being made to human rights and democracy in international relations. The book demonstrates that at the same time the EU's human rights policy has duly expanded in scope and the operators in this area have accordingly increased. Recent developments, such as giving the EU's Charter on Fundamental Rights[11] the same value as the founding Treaties (according to the new Article 6 Treaty of Lisbon),[12] the creation of the EU Fundamental Rights Agency, and the planned accession of the EU to the ECHR (according to Article 6(2) Treaty of Lisbon), underline the EU's attempt to give itself a more ethically oriented image, while being an organisation with mainly economic interests. Furthermore, the EU has attempted to mainstream human rights into its foreign and external trade policy, be it by political declarations or a system of trade preferences, human rights dialogues or other specific programmes of cooperation for third countries.

With regards to minority rights, the main issues revolve, on the one hand around states' opposition to minority entitlements as they might see their sovereignty or territorial integrity endangered and, on the other hand, the need to ensure that persons belonging to minority groups are able to maintain their identity and to enjoy their rights. As there is no internationally agreed definition of the term 'minority', one has to distinguish between ethnic minorities stemming from immigration and so-called traditional or national minorities. Under the League of Nations, the system for the protection of minorities in Europe accorded rights to minorities as a consequence of the war; these minorities are typically seen as 'national minorities' and can mostly be found in Eastern Europe. Whether traditional minority rights concepts are sufficiently dynamic to respond adequately to modern challenges, in view of the increasing flows of immigrants and refugees into Europe, cannot be discussed in the context of this book. The question why immigrants, who have lived in the EU for many generations and who possess the nationality of an EU Member State (in particular in the old Western Member States) are not being recognised as a 'national minority', compared to the 'old minorities' in Eastern Europe, whose status stems from the First and Second World Wars, is also an issue that needs to be addressed by policy and law makers.

Today, minority questions arising from immigration have more prominence, which makes cultural pluralism a central concern for the EU. The reference to ethnic discrimination, inscribed in Article 13, TEC (Article 19 TFEU – Treaty on the Functioning of the European Union, since the Treaty of Lisbon came into force on 1 December 2009) after the Amsterdam reform, is an explicit reflection on this convergence and means that ethnic minority questions will remain very topical throughout the EU. Apart from economic advancement, the protection of various forms of cultural pluralism, and the integration of immigrants and national minorities might become a central concern of the EU.

There has been much criticism that minority rights are not part of the EU's *acquis*, as there is no legal basis in the treaties and no discernable EU minority policy, except in the context of enlargement; however, it is submitted that minority rights are a sub-category of human rights and, therefore, since the protection of human rights is an established principle in EU law and part of the *acquis*, as manifested in Articles 6 and 2 TEU, the protection of minorities is covered by this concept.

Provisions and instruments within the framework of international human rights law provide sources for the analysis of the role and status of minority rights. Since no clear provisions on minority rights can be found in EU legislation, the book draws from these sources as a reference point for EU policies. However, the framework for the international protection of human rights provides few legally binding provisions relating to minority rights and the current implementation mechanisms leave much uncertainty regarding Member States' obligations. The relevant instruments and provisions of the international framework for the protection of human rights/minority rights will be introduced below but analysed in more detail, and with appropriate references to case law, in chapter 4 of the book.

1.2 The framework for the protection of minority rights in international law

Neither the United Nations Charter[13] nor the 1948 Universal Declaration on Human Rights[14] includes a reference to minorities. The only legally binding text of a universal nature which refers specifically to minorities – albeit without defining them – is Article 27 of the International Covenant on Civil and Political Rights (ICCPR) of 1966,[15] which provides:

> In those States in which ethnic, religious or linguistic minorities exist, persons belonging to such minorities shall not be denied the right, in community with the other members of their group, to enjoy their own culture, to profess and practice their own religion, or to use their own language.

Article 27 ICCPR is the only provision in the Covenant that is negatively phrased ('shall not be denied … rights') and it leaves Member States the option to declare that no minorities exist on their territory. In addition, it is uncertain whether states have any positive obligations beyond non-interference with the rights of persons belonging to minorities to enjoy their culture, profess and practise their religion, and use their language. The wording of Article 27 ICCPR appears not to indicate any duties for states to provide special rights for members of minority groups, but rather forbids states to deprive minorities of the status that they already possess. Also, the jurisprudence under the First Optional Protocol to the ICCPR with regard to Article 27 ICCPR remains limited.[16]

1.2.1 The concept of non-discrimination

Other sources of the system of international human rights law provide that, at a minimum, states are prohibited from discriminating against minorities (see e.g. Article 26 ICCPR, Article 2(2) International Covenant on Economic Social and Cultural Rights (ICESCR),[17] Article 2 International Convention on the Elimination of All Forms of Racial Discrimination (CERD),[18] and Article 2 Convention on the Protection of the Rights of the Child (CRC)).[19] According to these provisions, states are required to ensure that all persons enjoy the rights and freedoms guaranteed by law without distinction of any kind (which would always include ethnic origin, language, culture or religion). Such non-discrimination clauses are found in all major human rights instruments, both universal and regional in scope.

However, the concept of non-discrimination is not sufficient for the protection of minorities, as positive measures from states are required to accord members of a minority group particular rights, as opposed to purely equal treatment. Thus, it is not sufficient to recognise non-discrimination and equality only as a matter of law, but equality must also be ensured in fact through the enactment of certain measures (see chapter 4, section 4.3). In this context CERD embraces the concept of positive duties for states (mainly put into place through 'affirmative action'). However, according to Article 1(4) CERD, measures must be discontinued after the desired objectives (of racial and ethnic equality) have been achieved. This concept of 'affirmative action' is not appropriate for national minorities, as permanent regulations are required to put minorities in a position that allows them, apart from being factually equal with the majority population, to practise their own culture, language and religion, and to participate effectively in public affairs in the state of their residence.

1.2.2 Council of Europe instruments

Further legally binding provisions for the protection of minorities can be found in the ECHR[20] and the European Framework Convention for the Protection of National Minorities (FCNM),[21] both CoE instruments. The CoE was initially set up to protect human rights through the legal and institutional structure of the ECHR. After 1989 the CoE also became a human rights monitor for Europe's post-communist democracies that applied for membership of the EU. The accession of 21 countries of Central and Eastern Europe (the most recent being Serbia and Montenegro in April 2003) increased the CoE's membership to 45 countries.

Before the FCNM entered into force in 1998, the possibilities for minority protection within the structure of the CoE were quite limited; only Article 14 ECHR provided some protection, containing a non-discrimination provision on the basis of 'association with a national minority'. However, cases invoking this provision at the European Court of Human Rights (ECtHR) were hardly ever decided in favour of the minority claimant. Nevertheless, in some cases, other provisions of the ECHR (e.g. Articles 9, 10 or 11) were found to have been violated in the context of minority-related claims (see chapter 4, section 4.5).

The FCNM, the first legally binding document on the protection of minorities, defines minority rights in terms of obligations for the State Parties and requires them according to Article 4(2) and (3) FCNM:

> to undertake to adopt, where necessary, adequate measures in order to promote, in all areas of economic, social, political and cultural life, full and effective equality between persons belonging to a national minority and those belonging to the majority. In this respect, they shall take due account of the specific conditions of the persons belonging to national minorities ... The measures adopted in accordance with paragraph 2 shall not be considered to be an act of discrimination.

And Article 5 provides:

> The Parties undertake to promote the conditions necessary for persons belonging to national minorities to maintain and develop their culture, and to preserve the essential elements of their identity, namely their religion, language, traditions and cultural heritage. Without prejudice to measures taken in pursuance of their general integration policy, the Parties shall refrain from policies or practices aimed at assimilation of persons belonging to national minorities against their will and shall protect these persons from any action aimed at such assimilation.

The endorsement of special measures by the FCNM for the protection of minorities is commendable, but its efficiency is diminished by the frequent use of 'escape clauses' such as *where necessary* or *where appropriate*. In addition, the FCNM provides for a monitoring/reporting mechanism and no individual or inter-state complaints procedure. The Advisory Committee, which was set up for the purpose of monitoring compliance, is required to examine state reports, prepare an opinion on the measures taken by the State Party and forward it to the Committee of Ministers. The Advisory Committee's opinion is made public, together with the recommendations and conclusions of the Committee of Ministers, while the ECtHR is not involved.

1.2.3 Non-binding instruments

Since non-binding instruments are usually more specific than legally binding ones, at least in international law, the book also addresses the 1992 UN Declaration on the Rights of Persons Belonging to National or Ethnic, Religious or Linguistic Minorities,[22] and texts adopted within the Conference on Security and Cooperation in Europe/Organization for Security and Cooperation in Europe (CSCE/OSCE) framework.

1.2.3.1 The UN Declaration on the Rights of Persons Belonging to National or Ethnic, Religious and Linguistic Minorities

The UN Declaration on the Rights of Persons Belonging to National or Ethnic, Religious and Linguistic Minorities was meant to provide clarification of Article 27 ICCPR, but should also be viewed in its own right as it has been described as the new minimum standard regarding minority rights.[23] The Declaration commits states to taking measures to ensure that persons belonging to minorities may exercise fully and effectively all their human rights. Under Article 1, the Declaration requires states to adopt measures to protect the identity of minorities within their territory, however, due to its non-binding nature, states have no obligation to apply the rights contained in the Declaration. Although it is laudable that the Declaration acknowledges that state obligations go beyond mere non-interference, Article 1 mainly functions as a programmatic provision, giving a rather broad sense of direction without indicating any concrete requirements. This can be said about all provisions of the Declaration, which are cautiously formulated and concede a wide margin of appreciation to the State Parties (for further analysis, see chapter 4, section 4.8.1).

1.2.3.2 The Organization for Security and Cooperation in Europe

Apart from the UN, the Organization for Security and Cooperation in Europe (OSCE), formerly the Conference on Security and Cooperation in Europe (CSCE), consistently dealt with the issue of minority protection, contributing significantly to the creation of soft law in this area. Having evolved from a process of regular conferences and follow-up meetings into an organisation with permanent structures in 1994, among them the High Commissioner for National Minorities in Europe (HCNM), the OSCE is now a regional security organisation with 55 participating states from Europe, Central Asia and North America. It is mainly active in early warning, conflict prevention, crisis management and post-conflict rehabilitation. The mandate of the OSCE includes a wide range of security-related issues including preventive diplomacy, confidence- and security-building measures, democratisation, election monitoring and human rights.

In the framework of the CSCE/OSCE, the basic norms concerning minorities are soft law documents, with no legally binding force, but politically persuading force, such as the Document of the Copenhagen Meeting of 1990,[24] the Charter of Paris for a New Europe of 1990[25] or the Helsinki II Concluding Document of 1992,[26] establishing the post of the High Commissioner for Minorities.

The Copenhagen Document is generally considered as the high point of standard setting in this area. It provides for specific measures to be taken by states for the protection of minorities with regards to language rights, education, religious and cultural rights, financial assistance in exercising these rights, and in particular the establishment of local or autonomous administrations. Being a non-legally binding instrument though, it leaves states a broad margin of discretion regarding the adoption.

The High Commissioner on National Minorities is an instrument of early warning and conflict prevention. He/she cannot act as an Ombudsman for minorities or investigate individual complaints of violations of OSCE commitments. However, he has commissioned the development of standards related to the main fields of minority protection such as, *inter alia*, The Hague Recommendations on Educational Rights for Minorities of 1996, the Oslo Recommendations

Regarding Linguistic Rights (1998) and the Lund Recommendations on the Effective Participation of National Minorities in Public Life (1999).[27] These Recommendations fill the international framework for the protection of minority rights with more contents and give states concrete guidance on how to implement these rights. The Commissioner's conflict prevention functions will not be addressed in detail as the focus of the book lies in the analysis of the EU's human rights and minority policy with regard to old and new Member States.

1.3 Methodology

Following this introduction, chapter 2 assesses the EU's internal development of its human rights policy. The chapter considers the EU's history and analyses how human rights policy within the EU developed over the years in its legislation, policy and institutional developments. The influence of the ECJ and its interplay with the jurisdiction of the ECtHR is being analysed in the context of the Lisbon Treaty. As the EU's accession to the ECHR is imminent, the relationship between the two courts, the ECJ in Luxembourg and the ECtHR in Strasbourg, has become even more significant. Chapter 2 also touches on the CFSP, which was introduced by the Maastricht Treaty as an instrument for promoting human rights externally as well as first pillar external relations and human rights activity in this field.

The analysis traces back the historical development of the EU and its institutions through the Treaties of Rome and Paris of 1957 (the EC Treaty), the Single European Act of 1986, the Treaty of Maastricht of 1992, which created the EU with its CFSP, the Treaty of Amsterdam of 1997, the Treaty of Nice of 2000, including the EU Charter on Fundamental Rights of 2000; it also takes a brief look at the Constitutional Convention of 2003 and gives a more detailed analysis of human rights aspects under the Treaty of Lisbon, which came into force on 1 December 2009.

Having established the EU's *internal* human rights approach, chapter 3 discusses the CFSP as a new means for regulating the conduct of the EU's *external* human rights policy and takes a closer look at the EU's cooperation with other international organisations in the context of human rights and minority rights. Given the transformation of Europe after the break-up of the Soviet Union, the recognition of the new Eastern European states and their application for EU membership, also begs the question why, as a part of its foreign policy, the EU has decided to enlarge to the East despite the various costs and risks involved. Against the background of the Yugoslav War, the EU required the applicant countries, as part of the political criteria for accession (the so-called 'Copenhagen Criteria') to provide for the protection of minorities while this was never a criterion during the preceding accession rounds, revealing an incoherence between the EU's internal and external level in dealing with human rights and minority rights. Despite the EU's attempts since 1992 to give itself a more ethical orientation, it seems that human rights in foreign policy were often overruled by either economic or other political interests, i.e. realist considerations. Although the end of the Cold War has led to human rights assuming a stronger position in international law and has also influenced the EU's foreign policy, at the end of the day, the EU is not a human rights organisation but remains a regional organisation with the main purpose of fostering economic prosperity in the region.

Chapter 4 examines the current standard of minority protection applicable in Europe under relevant international instruments and in particular under instruments applicable at EU level. The chapter discusses the definition of the term 'minority', which has not been agreed on in international law, especially in relation to the 'nationality requirement'. While many scholars argue about the question of whether minority rights should be granted 'collectively' or whether rights can only apply individually, it is generally recognised that 'special minority rights' are human rights that go beyond mere non-discrimination principles,[28] as already mentioned above. These two strands of human rights discourse, non-discrimination and positive minority rights, have developed separately. Non-discrimination has to be seen as an approach that strives for achieving equality, while minority rights aim at guaranteeing rights for different treatment. In this context the chapter develops what type of rights would constitute specific minority rights, which is important for the case studies in chapter 5.

The ECHR, FCNM and various OSCE and UN instruments relating to minorities provide a substantial source for the legal analysis of the current level of protection for minorities in Europe and in the EU. Since none of the standards developed in the international framework has found its way into EU law, other than indirectly, existing EU law (Articles 2 and 6 TEU, Articles 13 and 151 TEC, now Articles 19 and 167 TFEU), the EU Charter of Fundamental Rights, initiatives by the European Parliament and EU programmes and certain policies developed by the European Commission that apply to minorities, including the enlargement strategy, are discussed in detail. Since the new Eastern European Member States bring with them internal minority issues, which impinge directly on the EU's external and internal policy, the EU is required to adopt a coherent approach to minority protection in order to guarantee a harmonious post-enlargement environment for minorities.

To illustrate the actual situation of minorities in the new Member States, chapter 5 gives an overview of how four Eastern European, at the time 'first-wave' (Estonia and Slovenia) and 'second-wave' (Lithuania, and Slovakia) applicant countries, have dealt with the protection of their particular minorities so far and compares them with the level of protection for minorities in Germany, France and the UK. Methodologically, the situation of minorities in these countries is assessed against eight criteria, which have been identified in chapter 4 as essential conditions for an adequate protection of minority rights. The chapter demonstrates how these Eastern European countries have provided for more extensive minority legislation than some Western EU Member States, such as France or Greece.[29] However, whether the de facto situation of minorities in these countries is ideal, or whether it might lead to disharmony in a post-enlargement environment despite appropriate provisions in their national legal system, will also depend on the EU's internal policy on minorities.

Resolving minority issues is a prerequisite for the successful enlargement to Central Eastern Europe and cannot be ignored by the EU. The EU itself does not have a coherent internal policy on minorities for the post-enlargement period, so that consideration of the protection of minorities has only been part of its external foreign policy. As the new Eastern European Member States all have recognisable minorities, the current lack of a common minority policy within the framework of the EU might lead to a disharmonious situation throughout the EU after enlargement, which may become a setback for the integration process. In case the EU continues to apply its human rights and minority rights policy in an inconsistent manner, it will fail to achieve its aim of gaining more international credibility and influence. It is therefore inevitable to have a common policy on minorities that would also enhance the EU's credibility as an international institution with an ethical agenda and further its influence in the international community.

The period under consideration of the book ends in December 2009.

2 A background to the establishment of human rights in the law and policies of the European Union

2.1 Introduction

The principal theme of this chapter is the historical analysis of the relevant institutional structures that play a direct role in the establishment of human rights within the European Union (EU), and their development from the Treaty of Rome to the Treaty of Lisbon. Apart from the various institutional developments, relevant legislation in the area of human rights will be addressed. The first section gives a basic description of the EU's institutional framework, followed by a chronological assessment of the respective instruments that established this framework, i.e. the Treaties of Rome 1957,[1] the Treaty of Maastricht 1992,[2] the Treaty of Amsterdam 1997 (ToA),[3] the Treaty of Nice 2000,[4] the Constitutional Treaty 2004[5] and the Treaty of Lisbon 2007,[6] and considers how far these Treaties reflect the development of the EU's human rights policy. The following chapters will draw on this assessment of institutions and legal sources, in particular chapter 4 reflects on their suitability for the protection of minority rights in the EU; incidental references to minority rights can already be found in this chapter, whenever appropriate in the context of an institutional development.

Starting out as an organisation with mainly economic objectives, the development of human rights policy in the EU from the early 1960s until today eventually led to a codification of 'EU human rights' with the EU's Charter on Fundamental Rights, adopted in 2000, which has become legally binding with the entering into force of the Treaty of Lisbon on 1 December 2009. The implications of this Charter and its relationship with the European Convention for the Protection of Human Rights and Fundamental Freedoms (ECHR)[7] will be examined, but not the individual human rights that are provided by the Charter. In addition, the role of the European Court of Justice (ECJ), which has been instrumental in developing EU human rights policy since the 1960s will be assessed in the context of the Lisbon Treaty, together with the EU's accession to the ECHR and the relationship with the Strasbourg European Court of Human Rights (ECtHR).[8]

2.2 The EU's institutional framework

The structure of the EU contains many complexities that are almost incomprehensible to the average citizen. One particularity is the fact that the European Community (EC) existed alongside the EU, even with its own foreign policy, albeit trade policy that also includes human rights policy. This complicated institutional structure with supranational and intergovernmental elements contributed to a lack of a coherent human rights policy, despite the EU's declarations to promote human rights and democracy, particularly through its foreign policy. The Constitutional Convention tried in 2004 to simplify this structure by uniting the three pillars, repealing the existing treaties and replacing them with a single document called the 'Constitution', but this project failed due to negative referenda in France and the Netherlands. However, under the Treaty of Lisbon the Treaty on the European Union (TEU) will retain its existing name, while the EC Treaty (TEC) will be called Treaty on the Functioning of the European Union (TFEU), with the EU having a single legal personality.[9] The word 'Community' will be replaced by the word 'Union' throughout and it is stated that the Union replaces and succeeds the Community. The amendments introduced by the Treaty of Lisbon resulted in a new consolidated version of the TEU which includes both the TEU and the TFEU, and, as a consequence, the numbering of the Treaty provisions have changed from those in the existing EU and EC Treaties. Hence, the two different treaties as well as the pillared structure have been largely but not entirely retained.

The following sections will assess the creation process of the EU from its foundation as the European Economic Community (EEC) to the EU of today against the background of its human rights policy, from the initial silence of the original treaties to the recognition of human rights as a general principle of EU law.

2.2.1 The Treaties of Rome and Paris

The origins of the EU date from the formation of the European Coal and Steel Community in 1951 (Treaty of Paris),[10] the European Atomic Energy Community and the EEC in 1957 (Treaty of Rome),[11] all of which merged in 1967 to become the EC.[12] The EC focused on the economic objectives of establishing a Common Market among the Member States,[13] progressively approximating the economic policies of Member States and promoting throughout the EC a 'harmonious development of economic activities, the raising of the standard of living and closer relations between the states belonging to it'.[14]

The treaties in question were not suited to the inclusion of fundamental rights, particularly since the ECHR of the Council of Europe (CoE), signed in 1950, already provided an advanced model for the protection of human rights in Europe. Fundamental human rights in the context of the EU are to be distinguished from 'fundamental economic freedoms' such as the four freedoms of free movement of goods, services, people and capital, which were essential to achieve the objectives of the Common Market.

2.2.2 Basic overview of the institutional framework

The Treaty of Rome (as amended by the Single European Act of 1986,[15] the Maastricht Treaty of 1992,[16] the Treaty of Amsterdam of 1997,[17] the Treaty of Nice of 2000[18] and finally reformed by the Treaty of Lisbon)[19] sets out the EC's constitution and framework, containing a complex institutional structure which may be summarised as set out in the following sections.

2.2.2.1 The Council of the European Union

The Council of the European Union (also called Council of Ministers) was established in 1957 under the Treaty of Rome – now Article 16 TEU[20]– and is the EU's main decision-making institution, consisting of ministers of the Member States, authorised to commit the government of their Member State. The office of Presidency is held in turn by each Member State in the Council for a term of six months. The Council not only ensures the coordination of the general policies of the Member States but also enjoys a law-making capacity, approving legislative initiatives emanating from the Commission before they become law.

In 1987 the Council created a special working group for human rights within its Political Committee, called COHOM. The working group meets at least twice a year and its main tasks are the discussion and submission of recommendations to the Political Committee on general guidelines for common reactions to actual or predictable violations of human rights.[21] COHOM also coordinates the Member States' position on human rights in international fora, such as the UN, and reports annually to the Political Committee on actions taken in the area of human rights by the Member States. In 2003 the Committee agreed to extend the mandate of the Human Rights Working Group to include first-pillar issues so as to have within purview all human rights aspects of the external relations of the EU. The EU guidelines on human rights are policy documents adopted by the Council. They cover issues of particular importance to EU Member States, including the death penalty (1998, updated 2008), torture and other cruel, inhuman or degrading treatment or punishment (2001, updated 2008), human rights dialogues (2001), children and armed conflict (2003, updated 2008); human rights defenders (2004) and rights of the child (2007). COHOM advocates a systematic inclusion of human rights issue in the agenda of experts' meetings on thematic issues (terrorism, for instance) and first- and third-pillar decisions, and at summits between the EU and third countries. In May 2008 the Council issued the first handbook entitled *Mainstreaming Human Rights and Gender into European Security and Defence Policy* (ESDP), which is mainly destined for those who cooperate with, plan, train, carry out, evaluate and report on EU crisis management.

2.2.2.2 The European Council

The European Council has to be distinguished from the Council of the EU; the former is a political organ which was established under the Maastricht Treaty on the European Union and comprises the heads of state or government of the EU Member States, together with the President of the Commission (see below). The European Council defines political guidelines and the priorities thereof, it has no legislative functions as the Council of Ministers does (see Article 15 TEU). The Treaty of Lisbon creates the function of President of the European Council elected for two and a half years (Article 15 (5)).

2.2.2.3 The European Commission

The European Commission fulfils an executive and civil service function and is the source of all legislative proposals; it has a role as a guardian of the treaties, as defined in Article 17 TEU. The Commission manages many EC policies, but its key function in relation to the decision-making process is that of initiator of legislation such as regulations, Directives or decisions.[22] The Commission is organised into Directorates-General, their main areas of regulatory activities lie in agriculture, competition, economic and financial affairs, education and culture, employment and social affairs, energy and transport, enterprise, environment, fisheries, health and consumer protection, information society, internal market, justice and home affairs, regional policy, research, taxation and customs. The Treaty of Lisbon introduces a direct link between the election of the Commission President and the results of the European elections (Article 17(7) TEU) and provides for new arrangements for a smaller Commission (Article 17(5) TEU).

The Commission's Directorate-General on external relations primarily deals with human rights in third countries while the Directorate-General on justice, freedom and security deals with internal human rights issues and is the main generator of the EU's human rights legislation.

2.2.2.4 The European Parliament (EP)

The EP consists of representatives of the Member States, elected by direct universal suffrage.[23] It has an advisory and supervisory role as well as various legislative and budgetary powers.[24] Furthermore, the EP is answerable to petitions and complaints from any citizens of the EU, which are either dealt with by the Ombudsman or the relevant Member of the European Parliament (MEP). Petitions have to be 'on a matter which comes within the Community's fields of activity and which affects him, her or it directly'.[25] Petitions to the EP can be exercised in association with other people and can therefore be very important for minority groups that wish to voice their concerns at European level. In addition, according to Article 228 TFEU (ex-Article 195 TEC) the Ombudsman deals with any complaint from any person residing in the EU, even if not directly concerned regarding 'instances of maladministration in the activities of the Community institutions'. As minorities can in particular be vulnerable to maladministration, the Ombudsman is an institution that could prove to be very helpful.[26]

The EP has been at the forefront of proclaiming itself on human rights issues in the EU. However, its legislative powers only gained relevance with the coming into force of the Treaty of Amsterdam in 1999, which extended the co-decision procedure; before, the EP was confined to issuing non-binding declarations and resolutions, and giving advisory opinions. The work of the EP is organised in different committees and subcommittees. The Subcommittee on Human Rights within the Foreign Affairs Committee is the main institution for discussions on human rights in the EP. It takes parliamentary initiatives with regards to human rights and provides a permanent forum on the human rights situation and the development of democracy in non-EU countries. Regarding human rights issues within the EU, the Subcommittee liaises with the Committee on Civil Liberties, Justice and Home Affairs (LIBE). The Subcommittee cooperates with other international institutions such as the UN Special Rapporteurs and representatives of the United Nations Development Programme (UNDP), the CoE, government representatives, human rights defenders and non-governmental organisations (NGOs). By drafting guidelines for the Inter-parliamentary Delegations with third countries, the Subcommittee contributes to the mainstreaming of human rights issues into all aspects of the external relations of the EU.[27] Under the German EU Presidency in 2007 the Network of Human Rights Parliamentary Committees of the European Union was established in Berlin, and a first meeting with a special focus on the fight against torture was hosted by the Subcommittee on Human Rights in 2008.

The Committee on Political Affairs, Security and Human Rights has established the practice of a standing point on human rights on every agenda, prepared by a small working group which includes the Chair of the Subcommittee on Human Rights. Another important element of the EP's activities consists of passing resolutions on particular human rights violations in specific countries and, in particular, on individual cases of concern, which are dealt with in the monthly plenary debates on urgent subjects. Aside from the resolutions mentioned before, regular démarches are conducted by the President of Parliament, the Chair of the Subcommittee and the Chairs of the Parliamentary Delegations, which usually serve to urge Council, Commission and the governments involved to take action.[28]

2.2.2.5 The European Court of Justice (ECJ)

The ECJ is the supreme judicial authority on EC law issues, ensuring compliance by the Member States and institutions with the treaties. Under the Treaty of Lisbon, the ECJ can also review the legality of acts of all EU bodies and agencies that produce legal effects relative to third parties,[29] paying tribute to the many new agencies and EU bodies that have been created in the recent years and which have powers over sensitive matters, e.g. in justice and home affairs. The ECJ is made up of one judge per Member State, assisted by Advocates-General who are appointed for six years by agreement among the Member States.[30] The EU institutions and the Member States as well as individuals can bring matters pertaining to EC law before the ECJ.[31] Since 1989 there has been a Court of First Instance (CFI) attached to the ECJ, with jurisdiction to hear direct actions including cases brought by individuals.[32] However, with the Treaty of Lisbon, the CFI will be renamed 'General Court', and judicial panels, which will be attached to the General Court, will be renamed 'specialised courts' (as prescribed in Article 19(1) TEU).

The EC developed a comprehensive human rights approach, in particular through the jurisdiction of the ECJ and later through treaty amendments. ECJ case law had already shaped the EU's human rights policy in the 1960s before any of the treaties made specific reference to human rights. Before the Treaty of Amsterdam entered into force, it was mainly the ECJ's long-standing case law which was the centre piece and an important driving force for the development of the EU's human rights policy. It was the ECJ's jurisprudence that made it possible for human rights to enter into the legal framework of the EU, with consecutive treaties concluded by the Member States. The ECJ's role in the protection of human rights will be discussed in more detail below (under section 2.8) in the context of the Lisbon Treaty, together with the EU's accession to the ECHR and the ECJ's relationship with the ECtHR.

2.2.3 Fundamental human rights under the TEC

At the time of the Treaty of Rome, human rights were not of evident concern to the EC. The original constituent treaties of the EC only contained such 'human rights' that were important for the functioning of the Common Market, and did not provide for Member States to question human rights compliance within the Community. Some fundamental economic freedoms, which remain fundamental principles of the TEC, can be considered as fundamental (economic) human rights that were inscribed in the TEC under the Treaty of Rome together with two non-discrimination provisions:

1. The freedom of movement for workers, now Article 45 TFEU (ex Article 39 TEC) which was recognised by the ECJ as a human right in the 1980s;[33]
2. The freedom of establishment of nationals of one Member State in the territory of another Member State, Article 49 TFEU (ex Article 43 TEC);
3. The freedom to provide services within the EC, Article 56 TFEU (ex Article 49 TEC);
4. The recognition of the principle of equal pay for equal work, Article 157 TFEU (ex Article 141 TEC);
5. The general principle of prohibiting discrimination on the grounds of nationality, Article 18 TFEU (ex Article 12 TEC).

These basic principles continue to be core principles or fundamental economic freedoms of the TEC while the non-discrimination principle has become more elaborated with the subsequent treaties. The general concept of the protection of human rights in terms of civil and political rights was introduced with the Treaty of Maastricht in1992 and became justiciable with the Treaty of Amsterdam in 1999. Given the strong emphasis on economic matters and the fact that the competence of the EC authorities was initially rather limited, the lack of human rights provisions was not conceived as a problem. Although the EC was, after all, a large bureaucracy engaged in an enormous amount of regulatory legislation affecting all areas of people's lives, there was no clause, which could limit the exercise of institutional power that might relate to human rights concerns under the TEC.

At the time, the ECJ's jurisprudence was a source of inspiration for treaty provisions such as the Preamble to the Single European Act of 1986 (SEA), which was the first major revision of the original Treaty of Rome, to coincide with an important new political impetus to European integration, namely the creation of the Single Market.

2.3 The Single European Act

The main objective of the SEA was to achieve an internal market among the Member States, characterised by the free movement of goods, services, people and capital by the end of 1992. The third preambular paragraph of the SEA provides that Member States 'are determined to work together to promote democracy on the basis of the fundamental rights recognised in the constitutions and laws of the Member States, the European Convention for the Protection of Human Rights and Fundamental Freedoms and the European Social Charter, notably freedom, equality and social justice'. These declarations were primarily symbolic, although in legal terms they did add weight to the ECJ's development of unwritten EC law, and could be drawn on when 'harder' sources of EC law were being interpreted. In addition, the object and purpose of a treaty can always be found in its preamble.

Already in 1979 the idea that the EC as such should accede to the ECHR had begun to circulate, as it would at least partly satisfy the demand for an EC catalogue of fundamental rights. In the 1979 Memorandum entitled 'Accession of the Communities to the European Convention for the Protection of Human rights and Fundamental Freedoms'[34] the Commission analysed this option and concluded that such accession would be the most efficient way of strengthening human rights protection within the EC and proposed accession as soon as possible. In 1990 the Commission repeated this request by requesting from the Council a mandate to start the negotiations process with the CoE.[35] Even then, the Commission had anticipated problems regarding Member States' responsibility for non-conformity with the ECHR when implementing EC law domestically,[36] which in fact did happen in the case of *M & Co v. Federal Republic of Germany*[37] and happened again not much later in the cases of *Matthews*[38] or *Bosphorus*,[39] which were decided by the ECtHR.

As a consequence of the Commission's strong recommendations for accession to the ECHR, the Council sought the ECJ's opinion as to whether accession to the ECHR would be compatible with the treaties. In its opinion 2/94 on the Accession by the Communities to the European Convention for the Protection of Human Rights and Fundamental Freedoms[40] the ECJ held that, as EC law stood at the time, the EC was not competent to accede to the ECHR. In paragraph 27 of the opinion the ECJ ruled that no treaty provision conferred on the EC institutions any general power to enact rules on human rights or to conclude international conventions in this field. The opinion, however, concluded that Article 235 TEC (now Article 308)[41] could be a basis for adopting measures regarding the protection of human rights, so long as an amendment of the treaties were not required. But the ECJ also concluded that the Community's accession to the ECHR would bring with it fundamental institutional and constitutional changes, which would actually require a treaty amendment and could therefore not merely be seen as a piece of EC legislation under Article 235 TEC. As a result, the accession to the ECHR would go beyond the scope of the EC's competence. In 2009, with the prospect of the coming into force of the Treaty of Lisbon, the accession to the ECHR has become a reality, at the same time as the EU's acquiring legal personality.

Nonetheless, as over the years the ECJ developed a jurisprudence that recognised fundamental rights as part of the EC's legal framework, this development has been given increasingly formal recognition within the amended EC treaties, which will be shown in the following sections on the Treaty of Maastricht, the Treaty of Amsterdam and the Treaty of Nice.

2.4 The Treaty of Maastricht

References to the ECHR in the preamble of the SEA, the ECJ's case law on human rights, and the Joint Declaration of 1977 by the EP, the Council and the Commission on the protection of fundamental rights[42] signal developments that were further pursued when Member States signed the Treaty on European Union in Maastricht on 2 February 1992, which came into force in November 1993. The TEU was first and foremost a structural device founding the EU on three pillars:

1. The EC (first pillar);
2. The two flanking pillars of the provisions on Common Foreign and Security Policy (CFSP) (second pillar);
3. Cooperation in the spheres of Justice and Home Affairs (JHA) (third pillar).

The three pillars came under one 'roof' with the establishment of the EU, called the 'Union' in terms of Article A of the Common Provisions of the TEU. The objective of consistency in a single institutional framework was to be ensured by the Commission, the Council and in particular the European Council. The European Council would bring together the heads of state or government and the President of the Commission, to provide the necessary impetus for the development of the Union and to define general political guidelines for the EU. The European Council would in particular take charge of defining the principles and guidelines for the CFSP.

The Maastricht Treaty codified for the first time fundamental rights as an integral part of the EU by introducing Article F(2) TEU:

> The Union shall respect fundamental rights as guaranteed by the European Convention for the Protection of Human Rights signed in Rome on 4 November 1950 and as they result from constitutional traditions common to the Member States, as general principles of Community law.

This Article was a restatement of what the ECJ had already established since the late 1960s in its case law. However, the reference to human rights and the ECHR was now contained in a treaty article and not merely in a paragraph of a preamble, as under the SEA. It is debatable whether the wording of Article F(2) TEU, providing that fundamental rights must be respected 'as they are guaranteed by the ECHR', suggests that the material provisions of the ECHR have been introduced into the EC legal order. From the last part of the sentence of Article F(2) it appears that the provisions of the ECHR apply as general principles of law, whereas before the Treaty of Maastricht, the ECJ had only used the ECHR as an interpretative 'source of inspiration'.

It has to be noted, though, that these human rights principles only apply in the context of the first pillar, as Article F(2) TEU seems to affirm by recognising said fundamental rights 'as general principles of *Community* law'. This concept had already been stressed in the *Internationale Handelsgesellschaft*, case,[43] where the ECJ held that 'the protection of such rights, while inspired by the constitutional traditions common to Member States, must be ensured within the framework of the structure and objectives of the Community'. In *Hauer*,[44] the Court also declared that 'the question of a possible infringement of fundamental rights by a measure of the Community institutions can only be judged in the light of Community law itself. The introduction of special assessment criteria stemming from the legislation of the constitutional law of a particular Member State would, by damaging the substantive unity and efficacy of Community law, lead inevitably to the destruction of the unity of the Common Market and the jeopardizing of the cohesion of the Community'.

On the one hand, Article F(2) TEU added little to the principles already adopted and applied by the ECJ in its case law in practical terms, on the other hand, it declared human rights to be 'general principles of Community law', giving human rights at least in theory a place in EC law.

However, by virtue of its Final Provisions, and more specifically Article L, all the articles contained in the section 'Common Provisions' had been excluded from the jurisdiction of the ECJ by the TEU, including Article F TEU. Therefore, the powers of the ECJ did not extend to Article F. Under the Maastricht Treaty, the ECJ was consequently not competent to decide on any compliance with Article F TEU. The ECJ itself drew attention to the fact that legal problems may arise because of the denial of judicial protection to individuals affected by the EU's activities, especially in the JHA context.[45] Until the entry into force of the Treaty of Amsterdam, any complaint of an infringement of the ECHR would have to be brought before the courts of the Member States directly involved. Contrariwise, Article L did not detract from the ECJ's human rights case law or deny the justiciability of human rights in EC law. The ECJ continued to apply the principles of its former jurisprudence and case law and even slipped a few references to Article F(2) TEU into its judgments, despite its inability to interpret the clause outright.[46]

Apart from the reference to human rights in the Common Provisions, the Treaty of Maastricht also contained human rights provisions in all three pillars, as outlined below.

2.4.1 Human rights under the first pillar, external relations

In the framework of the newly established EU of 1992, the TEU added to the ECJ's developing of the EC's human rights approach in a number of its provisions. Under the Title 'Development Co-operation' Article 130u(2) TEC was amended, stating that:

> Community Policy in the area of development co-operation shall contribute to the general objective of developing and consolidating democracy and the rule of law, and of the respecting human rights and fundamental freedoms.

Article 130u(2) TEC therefore promoted respect for human rights and fundamental freedoms to official policy objective. The ECJ confirmed in the case *Portugal v. Council*[47] that 'the objectives laid down in Article 130u reflect a complex vision of development, the product of interaction between its economic, social and political aspects, which are taken into account by the most recent cooperation agreements' and found that the EC was entitled to introduce human rights initiatives in development policy practice. The relevance of human rights for the external policies of the EC under the first pillar was explicitly recognised and found its practical application through so-called 'human rights clauses' in agreements with third countries.[48] In order to give development aid a more political content, human rights were linked to unilateral trade preferences and comprehensive programmes on technical (financial) assistance for democracy and human rights building activities, as under the Lomé Treaty (now the Cotonou Agreement, see below), which dealt with trade benefits for African, Caribbean and Pacific countries (ACP countries).[49]

The Lomé agreements started in the 1970s with Lomé I of 1976, Lomé II of 1981 and Lomé III of 1985, none of which provided for human rights compliance in the agreements.[50] It was only Lomé IV of 1989, coinciding with the fall of the Iron Curtain, which brought significant change and included a specific human rights clause in the agreement. It has to be noted though, that, as these human rights clauses made no reference to the ECHR, it can be concluded that the applicable standard of human rights protection had to be drawn from the widely ratified international human rights instruments such as, e.g. the ICCPR.[51]

Lomé IV,[52] concluded in 1989 by 69 countries, emphasised human rights by stipulating in Article 5(2)(2) 'every individual shall have the right, in his own country or in a host country, to respect for his dignity and protection by the law'. This was the closest the drafters of the Convention could get to a human rights clause in 1989.[53] At this time the Commission also issued a communication that explicitly referred to the connection between the protection of human rights and the development and democratic process in developing countries.[54]

However, Lomé IV did not contain an explicit suspension clause for cases of violation, neither did it clarify whether any such violation would amount to an essential breach of a treaty obligation under Article 60(3)(b) Vienna Convention on the Law of Treaties, i.e. breaching the treaty by violating 'a provision essential to the accomplishment of the object or purpose of the treaty'.[55] As a consequence, negotiations relative to the revision of the Lomé Treaty, commenced in May 1994, showed broad consensus on the acceptance of a non-compliance clause. Article 5(1) Lomé IV (1995)[56] stipulates in sub-paragraph 3:

> Respect for human rights, democratic principles and the rule of law, which underpins relations between the ACP States and the Community and all provisions of the Convention, and governs the domestic and international policies of the Contracting Parties, shall constitute an essential element of the Convention;

and Article 366a Lomé IV (1995) provides:

> If one Party considers that another Party has failed to fulfil an obligation in respect of one of the essential elements referred to in Article 5, it shall invite the Party concerned, unless there is special urgency, to hold consultations with a view to assessing the situation in detail and, if necessary, remedying it.

The Lomé Conventions illustrate the EC's attempt to develop a stronger commitment to human rights in its external relations with non-Member States, although the above-mentioned provisions are weak, as non-compliance or violation of an essential element will not lead automatically to a suspension of the treaty, but will first initiate a consultation procedure. However, these human rights clauses represent more than just programmatic principles, as the following list of suspension measures against ACP countries under the Lomé Treaty illustrates:

Equatorial Guinea	1992 suspension following the abandonment of the democratic process, 1996 consultations, resumption of development cooperation.
Burma/Myanmar	since 1997 EU sanctions on account of forced labour.

Ivory Coast	consultation after military coup and popular uprising of 1999, no interruption of development cooperation.
Gambia	1994 military coup, suspension of development cooperation, 1997 and especially 2000 normalisation.
Guinea-Bissau	1999 suspended.
Comoros	1999 suspended.
Liberia since 1989	de facto suspension, 1997 confirmed.
Malawi	at first resistance with the abolition of the single{hy}party state 1991/92, which was then overcome; resumption of development cooperation
Niger	1999 after military coup, consultations, normalisation.
Nigeria	1993 first sanctions, 1995 more severe sanctions after execution of Ken Saro-Wiwa, 1999 lifted.
Congo, Dem. Rep.	since 1992 assistance limited to emergency aid and rehabilitations; 1997 resumption of development cooperation made dependent on democracy and human rights. New development cooperation sought.
Congo, Republic	1997 suspension of development cooperation on grounds of security, 2000 National Indicative Programme concluded; full resumption made dependent on political progress.
Rwanda	1994 development cooperation suspended, 1999 normalised.
Sierra Leone	1992 suspended.
Somalia	suspended since early 1990s, support for rehabilitation measures.
Sudan	suspended since early 1990s.[57]

It has to be noted that in the above-mentioned examples suspension usually occurred due to the breakdown of governments, not necessarily due to individual human rights violations. In the event of serious and persistent breaches of human rights, the human rights clause would enable one party to the agreement to take restrictive measures against the offending party in proportion to the gravity of the breaches.

The Lomé Convention was eventually replaced by the Cotonou Agreement,[58] which came into force in April 2003. The Cotonou Agreement reflects the changes, which have occurred internationally, whereby issues of the rule of law, democracy and governance are now accepted as inseparable from economic development and trade, and 'sovereignty' is no longer acceptable as a criterion for non-interference in the case of serious violations of internationally accepted norms of behaviour. The Cotonou Agreement sets out in Article 9 that human rights and democratic principles are an 'essential element' of the Agreement. Article 96 of the Cotonou Agreement (based on Article 366a Lomé) regulates the procedure in cases where a contracting state – in spite of regular political consultations – fails to comply with its undertaking to respect human rights, fundamental freedoms, democratic principles and respect for the law (the essential elements according to Article 9(2)). The contracting state must then inform the other signatories thereof, in order to permit a comprehensive examination of the situation and introduce consultations with the aim of remedying the deficiencies. In the case where the consultations do not reach an acceptable solution for all the parties, or in a situation of special urgency, the EC may take 'suitable measures', which can be rescinded as soon as the grounds for them are removed.[59] Accordingly, suspension of the agreement is the most extreme measure that has to be preceded by consultations.[60] Article 8 provides the basis for this political dialogue. According to Article 8(6) of the Cotonou Agreement the dialogue with regards to human rights should be flexible and 'formal or informal according to need, and conducted within and outside the institutional framework, in the appropriate format and at the appropriate level including regional, sub-regional or national level'. This procedure has been applied in actions against Haiti, Ivory Coast, Zimbabwe and Fiji.[61] Similar 'essential element' clauses were included into association agreements with Central Eastern European countries (see chapter 3). The Cotonou Agreement was amended in 2005 in relation to the International Criminal Court (ICC).[62]

Looking at these provisions and the measures that have been taken, it can be concluded that the EU at the time lacked a systematic and transparent procedure for human rights violations. Clear criteria for the measures that have been taken are hardly discernable. Sanctions are mostly applied for reasons of undemocratic changes of government and not everyday human rights violations which have so far not led to the introduction of consultation procedures by the EC.[63] It is therefore questionable whether economic interests take priority here; it appears that sanctions are imposed for realist considerations, as undemocratic changes often hinder Western investments, and not for human rights violations of the average citizen in the countries concerned. Already the Lomé Conventions were called 'neo-colonial in character because, *inter alia*, as they sought to further European political and economic goals and not to establish a new justice in relations with the South'.[64] In 2008 the EP continued to deplore the fact that the human rights and democracy clause was not being implemented in a concrete fashion, due to the lack of a mechanism that would allow it to be enforced. The EP reiterated its call for human rights clauses to be implemented through a more transparent procedure of consultation between the parties.[65]

Apart from the Cotonou Agreement, the EU provides additional tariff preferences for vulnerable countries which have ratified and effectively implemented a number of international conventions on core human and labour rights, the environment and good governance under the Special Incentive Arrangement for Sustainable Development and Good Governance (known as GSP+), which is part of the EU's Generalised System of Preferences (GSP).[66] The 15 GSP beneficiary countries that received GSP+ benefits were Bolivia, Colombia, Costa Rica, Ecuador, El Salvador, Georgia, Guatemala, Honduras, Moldova, Mongolia, Nicaragua, Panama, Peru, Sri Lanka and Venezuela. GSP+ benefits for Moldova were removed in January 2008 when the EC implemented further reaching autonomous trade preferences specifically for that country. On 15 October 2007, the EC concluded an Interim Agreement on Trade and Trade-Related Matters with the Republic of Montenegro which also contained a human rights clause.[67]

2.4.1.1 The European Instrument for Democracy and Human Rights (EIDHR)

In addition to the trade agreements with ACP countries, the EIDHR (2000–6),[68] was introduced by Regulation 975/1999 to support human rights, democratisation and conflict prevention activities to be carried out primarily in partnership with NGOs and international organisations, including the United Nations (UN), the Organization on Security and Cooperation in Europe (OSCE) and the CoE, for different projects, in support of a wide range of policy objectives of the EU. Starting with a budget of €5 million in 1999, by 2007–8, EIDHR resources for human rights and democracy projects amounted to over €108 million, making it possible to fund a wide range of projects in more than 80 countries. The EIDHR can finance projects without the consent of a third-country government or other public authorities, which makes it a politically independent and effective instrument. The European *Instrument* for Democracy and Human Rights, which in 2007 succeeded the previous EIDHR[69] (then called European Initiative for Democracy and Human Rights) includes the possibility to support actions on the rights of persons belonging to minorities. Under its objective 'Strengthening the role of civil society in promoting human rights and democratic reform, in facilitating the peaceful conciliation of group interests and in consolidating political participation and representation', there is scope for specific actions in the field of minorities, to be implemented at country, transnational or regional levels. Several new projects involving the rights of persons belonging to minorities were contracted during 2007 under the EIDHR country-specific calls, for example in Bangladesh, Bosnia and Herzegovina, Burundi, former Yugoslav Republic of Macedonia (FYROM), Georgia, Nigeria, Pakistan, Rwanda, Russia and Serbia.

The EIDHR has been the subject of a number of EP reports and evaluations. These have generally acknowledged the positive contribution made by the EC towards the protection of human rights and the development of democratic processes in third countries, including human rights dialogues and projects in the new democracies in Eastern Europe, such as PHARE.[70] However, the EP has also commented that the impact of EC assistance through both the EIDHR and the main assistance programmes is reduced because of a lack of focus on priorities, as well as the limited sustainability of action. The EP reports suggested that its impact could be considerably enhanced through the development of a more strategic vision of how to use the instruments available to the EC in support of human rights and democracy objectives. In short, the management of the programme, its efficiency and again the lack of a consistent policy have been criticised. In addition, the reports by the EP comment extensively on the technical and financial management of human rights projects within the Commission. The Lenz Report, for example, reproaches the Commission on the basis that its communications on projects implemented by NGOs omit a good many details, including those on success rates, their continuance when the programmes expire (the continuity aspect) and the administrative share in grant support. The Commission itself commented on the difficulty of procedures for selecting projects and allocating support: 'The ensuing delays in funding are frequently counter-productive, in terms not only of their intentions but also of the important role the EU plays as a source of funding'.[71]

In response to the EP's criticism on a lacking strategy and focus on priorities for the EIDHR, the Commission drafted in 2002 its EIDHR Programming Document 2002–4,[72] proposing that the EIDHR should support a limited number of thematic priorities aimed at addressing specific medium to long-term goals. The four thematic priorities which have been identified are:

1. support to strengthen democratisation, good governance and the rule of law;
2. activities in support of the abolition of the death penalty;
3. support for the fight against torture and impunity and for international tribunals and criminal courts; and
4. combating racism and xenophobia and discrimination against minorities and indigenous peoples.

In addition, the Commission suggested the identification of a limited number of 'focus' countries on which the Commission should concentrate EIDHR support; 29 focus countries have been identified after extensive consultation with geographical desks of the Commission services and Commission delegations in third countries.[73]

New financial regulations now allow for more flexible and innovative ways of financing, which means that the new EIDHR includes the possibility under certain circumstances to finance not only registered organisations, but also non-legal entities. It furthermore provides the possibility of 're-granting', meaning that in order to enhance human rights in situations where they are most at risk, civil society organisations in charge of the project implementation can award small grants to other local organisations, non-legal entities or individual human rights defenders.

The fight against racism, xenophobia and discrimination against minorities and indigenous people is a priority for funding under the EIDHR. Through EIDHR funds, the EU supports the UN High Commissioner for Human Rights in the implementation of existing international standards on equality and non-discrimination, particularly the Durban Declaration and Programme of Action and the International Convention on the Elimination of Racial Discrimination. Project activities include awareness-raising campaigns and seminars, the provision of advice through technical cooperation projects with governments, and research and analysis. As already mentioned, the main partners of EIDHR are the OSCE, the CoE, UNDP, United Nations Educational, Scientific and Cultural Organization (UNESCO), the World Bank, the International Labour Organization (ILO) and other international organisations, as well as human rights institutions and civil society organisations.

2.4.2 Human rights under the second pillar, CFSP

The CFSP was first introduced by the Treaty of Maastricht and was further amended by the Treaty of Amsterdam, the Treaty of Nice, and finally consolidated by the Treaty of Lisbon. The distinction between CFSP and external relations policy under the first pillar was not always entirely clear; in general, external relations policy, dealt with under the TEC, mainly focused on external trade relations, whereas the CFSP is rather concerned with political relations. However, there were overlaps between the CFSP and EC external relations and both directorates worked closely together.

As regards human rights under the second pillar, then Article J.1(2) TEU provided that one of the objectives of the CFSP should be to:

> develop and consolidate democracy and the rule of law and respect for human rights and fundamental freedoms.

It has to be noted that CFSP is based on intergovernmental cooperation and not on legislative action like the first pillar. For example, at the multilateral level, the EU is active in the UN Human Rights Council (HRC) and in the United Nations General Assembly (UNGA). Under the CFSP, Member States have a trio of instruments at their disposal, such as General Guidelines and Common Strategies,[74] Joint Action[75] and Common Positions[76] to be adopted by the Council (these are now all united in one single provision under Article 25 TEU Treaty of Lisbon).

General Guidelines are practically the statements in the Conclusions of the Presidency at the various European Council meetings; Joint Actions have covered various matters under the Maastricht Treaty, e.g. assistance in the supervision of free and democratic elections in South Africa,[77] support for the Middle East Peace Process,[78] on the Great Lakes Region[79] or on anti-personnel landmines.[80]

Common Positions under Article J.5 TEU were initially only adopted in connection with politically motivated restrictions on trade,[81] but their scope has since broadened considerably to embrace the EU's objectives and priorities on matters as diverse as problems in Rwanda,[82] Ukraine,[83] East Timor[84] and Myanmar.[85] Even an arms embargo could be imposed through a Common Position on the basis of Article J.5 TEU,[86] which shows that the Member States take the view that arms do not fall under EC law by virtue of Article 223 TEC (now Article 296(1)(b) TEC, renumbered 346(1)(b) TFEU), which provides: 'any Member State may take such measures as it considers necessary for the protection of the essential interests of its security which are connected with the production of or trade in arms, munitions and war material; such measures shall not adversely affect the conditions of competition in the Common Market regarding products which are not intended for military purposes' but can be part of CFSP.

Although the TEU represented the Member States' response to the international situation arising at the end of the Cold War, the introduction of human rights at the centre of the new CFSP made little difference to the number of statements and démarches concerning human rights made by the Member States in their coordination of foreign policy in the past.[87] The principle of a CFSP was formalised by the time war had broken out in the former Yugoslavia, and the EU tried unsuccessfully to broker a diplomatic deal to end the fighting. It was evident that the EU did not act very decisively and handled this situation without much political or diplomatic clout. As minority claims lay at the heart of the Yugoslav conflict, the EU was unable to offer much assistance in solving the conflict, due to its lack of expertise and experience. Without a European intervention capacity, EU countries could only intervene as part of the UN peacekeeping force and subsequently, under US leadership, as part of a NATO force – as they did in Bosnia-Herzegovina, Kosovo and the former Yugoslav Republic of Macedonia.

In view of the disastrous human rights policy of the EU towards the former Yugoslavia and the dispute between its Member States over the EU resolution on human rights abuses in China during the 1997 session of the UN Commission on Human Rights (UNCHR), the EU has been criticised for being torn between its moral ambitions and its economic interests, and the CFSP was seen as an insufficiently adequate framework for the promotion and protection of human rights.[88] Already then it was clear that the intergovernmental approach has hindered decision-making procedures in the EU with regards to foreign affairs. It has to be stressed though, that the Maastricht Treaty created with the provisions on CFSP a *framework* within which the Member States would be enabled to create a common foreign policy but did not create a common policy for the EU as such as it still operates at intergovernmental level.

2.4.3 Human rights under the third pillar, JHA

The cooperation in JHA under Article K TEU was meant to serve the purpose of further integration through common policy, particularly regarding the free movement of persons. Article K.2(1) required that the matters of common interest referred to in Article K.1:

> shall be dealt with in compliance with the European Convention on Human Rights and the Convention relating to the Status of Refugees of 28 July 1951 and having regard to the protection afforded by Member States to persons persecuted on political grounds.

The matters of common interest referred to were: asylum policy in Article K.1(1), rules and controls on the crossing by persons of the external borders of the Member States in Article K.1(2), certain aspects of immigration policy and policy regarding nationals of third countries in Article K.1(3), combating drug addiction in Article K.1(4), combating fraud on an international scale in Article K.1(5), judicial cooperation in civil matters in Article K.1(6), judicial cooperation in criminal matters in Article K.1(7), customs cooperation in Article K.1(8) and police cooperation for certain purposes and the establishment of Europol in Article K.1(9).

Issues related to JHA and human rights will not be discussed any further, as these provisions mainly touch on the human rights of either EU citizens or immigrants and refugees (third-country nationals), which shall not be the focus here. Immigration and asylum law applies to minorities who do not possess EU citizenship. These minorities fall into a different category of law (immigration and asylum) than the national minorities who are part of the EU's foreign policy with regard to the Eastern European applicant countries. The distinction between minorities as in 'immigrants' or 'new minorities' and national minorities is controversial in international law and will be discussed in detail in chapter 4, on the definition of the term 'minority'.

The value of Articles K (justice and home affairs), F (respect for fundamental rights as a general principle of EC law) and J (the CFSP) of the Maastricht Treaty was, however, greatly diminished by Article L, which provided that the ECJ had no jurisdiction over the TEU, as already discussed (section 2.4, above). The almost total exclusion of the ECJ inevitably formed a handicap for the solidity and continuity of policies in the second and third pillars. However, recourse to judicial supervision still lay with the Member States and thereby could lead to different interpretations and approaches in the different judicial systems, which eventually could defeat the purpose of further integration. The Report of the Expert Group on Fundamental Rights (within the Commission) of 1999 criticised: 'if the European Union's commitment to human rights, is to be taken seriously, both the Member States and the European Union's institutions must act under the same premises in all the three pillars'.[89] This problem was recognised by the Member States and has consequently been acknowledged in the amendment of the TEU by ToA.

2.5 The Treaty of Amsterdam

The Treaty of Amsterdam (ToA) was signed on 2 October 1997 and entered into force on 1 May 1999. It represented a further step towards a more decisive recognition of human rights by the EU; even though the EU failed to provide for a catalogue of human rights in the treaties, the ToA contained the following more specific provisions on fundamental rights:

1 Article 6 (ex-Article F) of the EU Treaty was amended in its first paragraph so as to reaffirm that the Union is founded 'on the principles of liberty, respect for human rights and fundamental freedoms, democracy and the rule of law'.
2 A procedure was laid down in Article 7 for dealing with cases where a Member State has committed a breach of these principles provided for in Article 6.
3 More effective action was to be taken to combat discrimination, not only based on nationality but also based on sex, racial or ethnic origin, religion or belief, disability, age or sexual orientation (Article 13).
4 New provisions on equal treatment for men and women were inserted in the TEC.

5 Article 6 was rendered justiciable, so that the ECJ would have jurisdiction not only under the TEC, but under any provision of the other two pillars over which it has been given jurisdiction. This amendment strengthened what the ECJ in practice had been doing for many years, at least with regard to the jurisdiction it had claimed to review the actions of the institutions for compliance with human rights principles.

2.5.1 The principles of Articles 6 and 7 ToA

The human rights provision Article F(2) was renumbered Article 6(2), but remained otherwise unchanged. The new Article 6(1) provided that:

> The Union is founded on the principles of liberty, democracy, respect for human rights and fundamental freedoms, and the rule of law, principles which are common to the Member States.

This clearly specifies that human rights principles not only apply to the EC, but also to the EU, although Article 6(2) still referred to 'Community law'. The principles laid down in Article 6 have also been made a condition for EU membership applications under Article 49 ToA, which shows how Member States and the political institutions wish to present the role and the image of the EC, by asserting the role of fundamental human rights within the EU. How this concept has been put into practice with regard to the applicant countries for the enlargement in 2004–7 will be further discussed in chapter 3.

Furthermore, Article 6 TEU has become justiciable by virtue of the new Article 46 TEU (ex-Article L TEU) empowering the ECJ to examine the compatibility of 'action of institutions' with fundamental rights, in the normal exercise of its powers under the TEC and the TEU.

Another new instrument, which was supposed to show the EU's growing commitment to human rights principles was the introduction of a procedure for enforcing these principles according to Article 7 TEU:

> On the proposal from the Commission or one third of the Member States, the Council may determine the existence of a breach of Article 6 by a Member State. The breach must be 'serious and persistent'.

The EP has to give its assent by a majority of its members and a two-thirds majority of the votes cast. The government of the Member State in question is first invited to submit its observations. The Council's decision establishing a breach will be considered unanimously even where a Member State abstains. Once a serious breach has been established, the Council may suspend some of the Member State's rights under the treaty. However, the country remains bound by its obligations. The suspension of rights might, for instance, involve withdrawing the Member State's voting rights in the Council.

Despite the potentially grave consequences of a determination that there is a serious and persistent breach of Article 6 TEU by a Member State, the ECJ has no role in this enforcement mechanism. Since this procedure does not relate directly to the application of EC law as such, it has to be distinguished from the judicial procedures, which operate in the event of human rights violations in the application of EC law by the institutions or the Member States. It appears striking, however, that the process of enforcement is purely a political one involving solely the political institutions of the EU to the exclusion of the ECJ. Anthony Arnull commented on the new Article 7: 'the heaviness of the procedure by these provisions and the potentially damaging consequences of invoking them make them weapons of last resort. They will do little to reinforce the protection afforded to individuals in concrete cases.'[90] According to Article 309 TEC voting rights shall also be suspended with regard to the TEC, where a decision has been taken to suspend voting rights of the representative of the government of a Member State in accordance with Article 7(3) TEU.

So-called 'preventive sanctions' were imposed when the Austrian FPÖ (Freedom Party of Austria) came to power in 2000. However, voting rights were not suspended but 14 bilateral sanctions imposed, which were announced by the former Portuguese Presidency and thereby appeared as a 'Union' measure. The sanctions introduced were of little impact, however, and after a few solemn statements by the Austrian government, sanctions were lifted and Austria was welcomed back into the EC. This episode led to an ad hoc monitoring procedure and the commissioning of a report by a three-person committee appointed by the President of the ECtHR.[91] The committee recommended an amendment to Article 7, which was undertaken in due course under the Treaty of Nice (see 2.6.3, below).

2.5.2 Discrimination

Due to an increase in asylum seekers and immigration into the EU, racism and discrimination have become a very topical issue in the EU that warranted new legislation and various political declarations. For example the year 1997 was declared as the year of anti-racism, and was the major theme of consideration in the Council's Annual Report on Human Rights since 1999. The ToA introduced further important non-discrimination provisions, contained in Articles 12 and 13 TEC, now Articles 18 and 19 TFEU.

Article 12 of the TEC provided that any discrimination on the grounds of nationality is prohibited, and Article 141 TEC (now Article 157 TFEU) laid down the principle of non-discrimination between men and women as far as equal pay is concerned. Whereas the latter pursues a double aim, which is both economic and social, the former is not necessarily a human rights provision; it merely intends to ensure the proper functioning of the Common Market. The ToA however, restates the principle of non-discrimination in stronger terms; Article 13 (now Article 19 TFEU) which complements Article 12 (now Article 18

TFEU), enables the Council to 'take appropriate action to combat discrimination based on sex, racial or ethnic origin, religion or belief, disability, age or sexual orientation'.

Up to then, discrimination on grounds of sex and nationality was expressly prohibited by EC law (see ex-Articles 6, 6a TEC). In the 1996 case *P v. Sand Cornwall County Council*,[92] concerning the dismissal of a transsexual employee for a reason arising from his/her gender reassignment, it appeared that a more general prohibition in discrimination, extending beyond sex and nationality to embrace transsexuality and other grounds were already part of 'the great value of equality'. The ECJ ruled that 'the fact of tolerating the dismissal of a person because he or she is a transsexual or because he or she has undergone a gender reassignment operation would be tantamount, as regards such a person, to a failure to respect the dignity and freedom to which he or she is entitled, and which the Court has a duty to safeguard'.[93] Similarly, in *K. B. v. NHS*[94] the ECJ ruled in favour of a woman to obtain a survivor's pension as the widow of her post-operative transsexual partner, as being a violation of Article 141 TEC on equal pay for men and women.

However, in *Grant v. South West Trains*[95] the ECJ retreated from the broader implications of its earlier judgment in *P v. Sand Cornwall County Council*, and ruled in the context of an employee who had been refused travel benefits for her same-sex partner, that EC law did not currently cover discrimination on the grounds of sexual orientation. This restrictive approach towards same-sex discrimination (as opposed to the more liberal approach towards transsexuals) was confirmed in *D v. Council*[96] regarding unequal benefits of an EU employee who had his same-sex partnership formally recognised under Swedish law. The ECJ took a deferential judicial stance by referring to the non-equivalence of traditional and same-sex marriages. In making reference to the new provision of the ToA concerning sexual orientation which was not yet in force, the ECJ stressed that it was not for it to extend EC law beyond the scope provided for in the treaty, since the new provision is not in itself a prohibition on discrimination on grounds of race, disability, sexual orientation, etc., but instead enables the EC to adopt measures to combat such discrimination within the scope of the policies and powers otherwise granted in the treaty. It is not a directly effective provision on which individuals can rely, but rather creates the possibility for the Commission to submit proposals to combat discrimination on certain grounds.[97] As a consequence, the Council adopted on 29 June 2000 the Anti-Discrimination Directive[98] on the basis of Article 13, implementing the principle of equal treatment between persons irrespective of racial or ethnic origin.

The Directive has a wide scope, including employment, training, social protection including social security and healthcare, social advantages, education, and access to goods and services, including housing. Member States must designate a body for the promotion of equal treatment irrespective of racial or ethnic origin, which will, among other things, provide assistance to victims of discrimination in pursuing their complaints. However, by 2007, the Commission was not satisfied with the implementation of the Directive in a number of Member States and sent reasoned opinions to 14 Member States.[99] Four infringement procedures were successfully brought against four Member States.

Since the right to non-discrimination is one of the most essential elements of human rights law, Article 13 provides a foundation on which a comprehensive EU human rights policy can be build.[100] However, in relation to minorities the principle of non-discrimination acquires a totally different meaning. As introduced in chapter 1, minority rights require states to take special measures to afford minorities de facto and not only de jure equality. Non-discrimination is an approach that strives for more equality and sameness between different individuals and groups of peoples. Minority rights for their part seem to represent a clearly different approach in which the guaranteeing of the rights to difference and to different treatment take the highest ranking. This aspect will be further pursued in chapter 4, section 4.3.3 with regard to specific minority rights.

2.5.3 The European Monitoring Centre on Racism and Xenophobia (EUMC)

At the European Council in Florence in 1996 the establishment of another protection mechanism, the European Monitoring Centre on Racism and Xenophobia (EUMC) was decided, which has now been replaced by the Fundamental Rights Agency (FRA) – see below. The EUMC started its work in 1998 and its aim was to provide a process of scrutiny within the EU with regards to racism and xenophobia. Its main task was the comparative collection of data and analyses relating to racism and xenophobia, as well as the diffusion of knowledge concerning good practices. The EUMC has published reports on anti-discrimination legislation in the Member States, on the situation of Islamic communities in five European cities, on racism in the media and hostility towards Islam after 11 September 2001. The European Racism and Xenophobia Information Network (RAXEN) was also set up with contact points in 15 countries, establishing a website, a documentation centre and organising conferences on specific topics related to racism.

As the EUMC could only acquire data but could not undertake investigations on its own, it was dependent on information that was public or that it was given by Member States, which severely diminished its powers. Another problem for the EUMC was the enforcement or practical effect of its work. According to Council Regulation 1035/97, which created the EUMC, its main purpose was to 'provide the Community and its Member States … with objective, reliable and comparable date at European level on the phenomena of racism, xenophobia and anti-Semitism in order to help them when they take measures or formulate courses of action within their respective spheres of competence' (Article 2). However, there was no mechanism that would force the EC institutions or the Member States to pay any regard to the findings of the EUMC or to take its recommendations into consideration; neither was there any possibility for the EUMC to raise issues under Articles 6 or 7 TEU in case a Member State or EU institution did not act on its recommendations. The EP criticised this lack of enforcement mechanisms and requested that the EUMC should be entitled to draw attention to breaches of Article 6 TEU and advise accordingly on action under Article 7 TEU,[101] however, neither Council nor Commission responded to this request. Whether these pitfalls have been addressed with the creation of the FRA will be addressed below.

2.5.4 Police and judicial cooperation – an area of freedom, security and justice

The ToA incorporated a large part of the third pillar, which under the Maastricht Treaty had covered JHA, into the body of the TEC, the first pillar. Matters which have arisen under JHA (third pillar) called for greater accountability and legal controls because they touched on fundamental human interests and rights such as immigration, asylum, border controls, constraints on movement etc. The overall aim of the third pillar is now declared to be the creation of 'an area of freedom, security and justice' by developing 'common action' in three areas: police cooperation, judicial cooperation in criminal matters, and the prevention and combating of racism and xenophobia. Particular targets are terrorism, drug and arms trafficking, trafficking in persons and offences against children, corruption and fraud through closer cooperation between customs, judicial and other relevant Member State authorities and the approximation of certain criminal laws in the Member States.

The formal justiciability of these provisions has been changed with the new Article 46 TEU, providing that the ECJ can interpret the provisions of Title VI (Provisions on Police and Judicial Cooperation in Criminal Matters). The Court's jurisdiction can now also apply to the protection of fundamental rights in the areas of visa, asylum and immigration, which have been transferred from the third pillar to the first pillar, including special rules on the ECJ's jurisdiction; for example only national courts of final appeal are able to make preliminary references on the interpretation and validity of this part of EC law,[102] probably in order to avoid a flood of cases from lower courts on asylum issues.

However, there was no longer a human rights reference specific to the third pillar, with Article K.2(1) deleted and not replaced.[103] While the pre-Amsterdam Article K.2 TEU, as noted above, restricted the sources of third-pillar human rights law to the ECHR, the Geneva Convention and national rules on the politically persecuted, the lack of a post-Amsterdam replacement for this clause means that Article 6(2) TEU is the only written source of third-pillar human rights rules. The place of Article 6(2) TEU in the common provisions of the TEU indicates a clear intent to extend human rights principles to all aspects of EU cooperation, i.e. all pillars, despite the reference to EC law. The new Article 46(d) TEU confirms this interpretation by providing for the application of the powers of the ECJ to the following provisions of the treaty:

> Article 6(2) with regard to action of the institutions, insofar as the Court has jurisdiction under the Treaties establishing the European Communities and under this Treaty.

As the amendments to the Treaty were intended to authorise the Court's jurisdiction over human rights principles in the first and third pillars, it can be concluded that the reference to 'Community law' in Article 6(2) is vestigial, and the Article should be read as referring to 'Union law'.[104]

2.5.5 The CFSP under the ToA

A number of modifications were made to the second pillar by the ToA regarding some institutional and structural changes, such as e.g. the establishment of the post of a High Representative of CFSP, according to Article 18(3) TEU. As far as human rights are concerned, the terms of the Maastricht Treaty have not been changed. Article 11(1) TEU (now Article 24) provides for the key objectives of the CFSP and human rights appear under the last indent (same wording as former Article J.1(2)):

> to develop and consolidate democracy and the rule of law, and respect for human rights and fundamental freedoms.

In the framework of the CFSP, in particular in the Council's Human Rights Working Group (COHOM), which is composed of human rights experts from Member States and the Commission, as well as in the regional working groups, the EU maintains a systematic coordination on human rights issues.

In addition, the EU seeks to address human rights issues through the instruments already explained above (Common Strategies, Common Positions, Joint Actions) aiming to enhance the overall coherence of the EU's international action. A few examples will illustrate how the CFSP was used for developing human rights policy in foreign relations since the entry into force of the ToA.

The EU had defined a Common Position on human rights, democracy, the rule of law and good governance in Africa in May 1998,[105] which it reviewed every six months. In this Common Position, the EU set out principles and a framework for its action and the action of Member States. The EU, working with both governments and civil society on the basis of partnership and cooperation, considered to increase its support for African countries in which positive changes are engaged towards respect for human rights and democratic principles. Where changes are negative, it would consider the appropriate responses that could help reverse those developments. For example, in 1998 the EU repealed some of the sanctions it had imposed against Nigeria in 1995 following the human rights violations perpetrated by the military regime. Through a Joint Action the EU notably supported the democratic process in Nigeria by providing technical assistance for the preparation of the February 1999 elections and sending a contingent of 100 EU observers within the framework of the international monitoring mission coordinated by the UN.[106] It lifted the remaining restrictive measures in May 1999 in view of the fact that the conditions it had laid down had been met, with the establishment of a democratically elected civilian government and concluded a Common Position to strengthen the mutually beneficial relations between the EU and Nigeria in all areas of common interest.[107]

In view of the further deteriorating human rights situation in Burma/Myanmar, the EU reinforced its Common Position of 1996[108] by agreeing on additional restrictive measures against the authorities of that country and prolonging the validity of the common position in 2001 and 2002. This Common Position has been extended and reinforced as a regulation[109] with additional measures, in particular a ban on visa.[110]

As already mentioned above with regard to the CFSP under the Maastricht Treaty, the EU practised this conditionality policy almost exclusively with regard to Third World countries and negative measures were only taken with regard to small African countries and Myanmar, which are countries of less economical importance to the EU. For example Algeria, despite the employment of questionable methods in combating terrorism during the 1980s and reported human rights violations, continues to receive support through the EU. Between 1991 and 1994 the Ethiopian dictatorship received EU financial support. And the repressive regime of Sali Berisha in Albania was supported from 1990 onwards. Even Yugoslavia was able to count on a financial aid package in the spring of 1997. These examples speak for incoherent foreign policy choices by the EU with regard to human rights and third countries.

Further instruments of CFSP for the promotion of human rights are démarches/declarations and political dialogue. Démarches are usually carried out, sometimes in confidential manner, in 'troika' format (i.e. the Commission President, the President of the European Council and the High Representative on CFSP), or by the Presidency, while declarations, calling on a government or other parties to respect human rights, are made by the Presidency on behalf of the EU and are always public. Troika consultation take mainly place with 'important' countries such the US, Canada, Japan, New Zealand and candidate countries. Human rights consultations with the candidate countries – Croatia, FYROM and Turkey take place biannually.

In 2008 the EU continued to carry out démarches in third countries to encourage the ratification of the Rome Statute and the Agreement on Privileges and Immunities, and to discourage states where possible from signing bilateral non-surrender agreements regarding the ICC.[111] In relation to the Darfur situation, the EU has also increased pressure on Sudan in various Council Conclusions,[112] and a declaration by the Presidency on behalf of the EU,[113] and deployed EUFOR in 2008 on the basis of Council Decision 2008/101/CFSP. In August 2009 the Council issued a declaration on the occasion of the 60th anniversary of the adoption of the four Geneva Conventions of 1949[114] and the 150th anniversary of the battle of Solferino.[115]

Political dialogue meetings cover a wide range of issues; human rights-specific dialogues are conducted with about 30 countries, but initially started with China in 1996. During these exchanges, human rights topics are discussed at governmental level and with NGOs, as well as with representatives of civil society.

The 2001 Guidelines on dialogues lay down the framework for these human rights dialogues with third countries. They have been supplemented by a 2004 communication from the Political and Security Committee on their implementation. This coherent working framework does not prevent the specific features of each dialogue being adapted to local circumstances in a flexible and pragmatic way. Whatever format is adopted, the aim of all these dialogues is to raise the issue of human rights with a view to examining, with the third countries concerned, ways of improving the situation on the ground.

The China dialogue resumed in 1997, raising concerns about the severe crackdown on dissidents in December 1998, the situation in Tibet, the lack of due process, the excessive use of the death penalty and cases of individuals detained in China.[116] However, Common Positions with human rights conditionality as they were formulated for African countries were never initiated with regard to China, especially since China refused to accept human rights clauses in trade agreements. Two further rounds of the EU–China dialogue on human rights were held during 2008: the 24th round took place in Beijing on 17 October 2007 and the 25th in Brdo, Slovenia, on 15 May 2008. After a year's interruption, the practice of holding a human rights legal seminar back to back with the dialogue was resumed in May 2008.

The dialogue with Iran was interrupted for a long time but recommenced in December 2002. No significant progress has been accomplished with regard to the death penalty and other inhuman and degrading treatments, the status of ethnic and religious minorities, the unfair trials, the repression of human rights defenders, lawyers and journalists and women rights and the freedom of expression in general. The EU's dialogue with Iran was linked since its inception in 2002 to negotiations for an EC–Iran Trade and Cooperation Agreement, confirming the observations already made above that the EU's economic interests are often important motives for dialogue and negotiations (which is also true for China, since trade with China flourishes without any serious requirements on human rights criteria). The dialogue with Iran (the last meeting took place in January 2004, further meetings have not been scheduled so far) has not yielded any tangible benefits but allowed Tehran, despite the 'nuclear crisis' in 2006, to maintain 'good relations' with EU countries, however, it has not led to a decrease of repression in Iran. The human rights dialogue with Iran has been frozen since Iran cancelled the fifth round in December 2006.

Between 2002 and 2008 structured human rights dialogues increased dramatically at Working Party on Human Rights (COHOM) troika level with the African Union, Kazakhstan, Kyrgyzstan, Tajikistan, Turkmenistan, Uzbekistan, Georgia and Belarus.[117]

2.5.6 Justiciability of CFSP

The jurisdiction of the ECJ did not apply to the second pillar as Member States are eager to maintain the intergovernmental nature of the CFSP. According to Article 46 of the TEU, the Court does not have jurisdiction with regard to CFSP acts. Article 47 of the TEU, however, states that no provision of that treaty shall affect the provisions of the TEC. Under Article 46 of the TEU, the provisions of the TEC concerning the powers of the Court and the exercise of those powers apply to Article 47 of the TEU. The Court is therefore competent to ensure that acts concluding CFSP agreements do not encroach on the powers conferred by the TEC on the EC. This was emphasised by the Court in 1998 in the *Airtransport Visa Case.*[118] Where an action in the CFSP field provides for economic sanctions against a third country, implementation measures at EC level are necessary; they are taken on the basis of Articles 60 and 301 TEC (now Article 75 TFEU).[119] The Court exercises its judicial control with regard to all such implementing acts in accordance with the TEC.

2.6 The Treaty of Nice

The Treaty of Nice resolved institutional issues that had not been settled at Amsterdam and that had to be concluded before the enlargement round in 2004. The Treaty of Nice itself restricts itself to setting out the principles and methods for changing the system as the EU grows; these principles and methods are enlisted in the protocol on enlargement and attached declarations.[120] New important treaty provisions introduced a new system of decision making in the Council by qualified majority. While the number of votes has been increased for all Member States, the increase is higher for the most populated Member States.[121] The treaty also increased the number of Articles subject to qualified majority voting rather than unanimity, and amended provisions on closer cooperation (enhanced cooperation), which can be considered to make the legislation process more flexible and efficient.[122] Apart from these structural improvements, the Treaty of Nice introduced the EU's very own Charter on Fundamental Rights.

2.6.1 The Charter of Fundamental Rights under the Treaty of Nice

The Intergovernmental Conference in Nice decided not to include a reference to the Charter of Fundamental Rights in the treaties. However, it did adopt a declaration on the future of the EU with a wide-ranging, detailed discussion of a number of topics, including the status of the Charter.[123]

As mentioned, the internal human rights policy in the EU mainly developed through the jurisprudence of the ECJ, thus protection was accorded on a case-by-case basis and inevitably became very complex and fragmented, necessitating a more systematic approach, also necessitated by the increase in rules that affected individuals in more than just the economic context (see in particular pillar three). In December 2000 at the meeting in Nice the heads of governments of the EU proclaimed the Charter of Fundamental Rights of the European Union. Apart from the classic civil and political rights, the Charter contains also a multitude of economic and social rights.[124]

After the EU's crisis of legitimacy and credibility in 1999, culminating in the collective resignation of the Commission due to allegations of corruption and incompetence of individual commissioners and a very low participation of the public in the elections to the EP, the Cologne European Council proclaimed in June 1999: 'there appears to be a need, at the present stage of the EU's development, to establish a Charter of Fundamental Rights in order to make their overriding importance and relevance more visible to the Union's citizens'.[125]

Why Member States only decided in 1999 to commit finally to the elaboration of a human rights charter can be seen in two different reasons: on the one hand, the EU sought an enhancement of its legitimacy and identity with a view to the expected East enlargement, on the other hand, it had to overcome its credibility crisis after the events of 1999.

The citizens of the EU will now get in addition to their nationally and internationally protected human rights,[126] protection of human rights at EU level. Is there too much protection against the background of a confusing quantity of conventional rights, fundamental, human and civil rights with more or less the same contents? Or as Weiler calls it a 'rights saturation rather than rights deprivation'.[127]

Does it make sense to have a human rights charter within the framework of the EU? Since all Member States have ratified the ECHR and the ECJ has generally upheld ECHR rights, it has been argued that there is no pressing need for the adoption of another human rights instrument, considering that there is no obvious human rights deficit in the legal orders of the Member States, which the ECJ would have to remedy. In addition, creating a separate competing system of human rights could undermine the authority of the CoE and might have a dividing effect on human rights protection in Europe as coherence between two such systems cannot be guaranteed.[128] Member States, however, overcame this criticism and agreed eventually on according the Charter legally binding value with the Treaty of Lisbon.

The meaning of human rights, as the protection of the citizen against the authority of the state, guaranteeing the dignity, liberty and equality of the citizens is the aim of every human rights charter and one of the main objectives of every state. The EU, however, is not a state in the classic sense and without a state there would be no addressee of human rights claims.

Without any doubt, the EC has established an autonomous legal system, which accords rights and imposes obligations like any other state legislator. Consequently it is not relevant that the EU does not qualify as a state, as long as it acts as an authority that intervenes in citizens' rights, EU citizens need to have protection of their fundamental rights against any EC intervention. With the proclamation of the Charter and its incorporation into the treaties, the EU does not create or accord any new rights; these rights rather exist already as preceding superior rights which the European legislator always had to respect. Therefore the objective of the Charter of Fundamental Rights of the European Community is to confine EC legislation to the boundaries of respect for those fundamental human rights. This principle had been developed by the ECJ since

1966 by interpreting the fundamental human rights of the EC in its jurisdiction. However, the ECJ developed its principles on the protection of human rights in a piecemeal fashion. Due to the lack of a an EU codified catalogue of human rights, protection was only accorded *ex post facto*, on the basis of complaints by individuals to the Court, without the possibility for EU citizens to anticipate which fundamental rights they are entitled to claim. In addition, this jurisprudence is only known to legal experts and not accessible for the average citizen. A legal framework, however, is supposed to be transparent and accessible for those who have to live by it, i.e. the citizens. This gap will be filled by an enforceable EU human rights charter. Apart from the aspect of transparency, the Charter also has to define its concrete rights, in order to provide legal certainty and to express clearly the EU's commitment not only to economic freedoms but also to civil liberties of its citizens.

This commitment has become particularly important with regard to the changing structure and expansion of competences of the EU, including enlargement. The adoption of the Charter of Fundamental Rights changed the mercantile orientation of the EC to a more ethical orientation of protection and welfare of the individual, accentuating the legitimacy of the EC. In addition, the EU's enlargement process included countries with a shorter experience of democracy, necessitating a strengthening of human rights guarantees in the EU's legal order, which the ToA did not provide.

The much lamented lack of democracy of the EU mainly refers to the legislative activities of the EU (Commission and Council are not directly elected), but it also has to be taken into account that guaranteed 'visible' fundamental rights (as they would become visible if they were part of the treaties) can control the political processes and make the democratic structure of the EC more accessible and more tangible to the public. Thereby the individual citizens' perception of the EU, which currently appears to most people as an entity that does not concern them, could be strengthened. Also, the Comité des Sages stated in 1999 'fundamental rights must be visible … It could be argued that most fundamental rights can be found in national constitutions and international treaties, and that an explicit enumeration of these rights by the European Union would therefore add very little. This, however, does not justify a system of citations that conceals the fundamental rights and makes them thus incomprehensible to the individuals.'[129]

The fact that the EU drafted its own Charter also shows that the original function of human rights has changed: human rights are not only rights that protect the citizen against the authority of the state, they also represent a whole value concept and socio-political norms to which the EC is committed and which are basic principles for every act of legislation.

The Charter distinguishes between rights, freedoms and principles and contains in its Title VII general provisions on the interpretation and application of the Charter, limitations to recognised rights and the relationship with other sources of human rights protection. The distinction between freedoms, rights and principles can also be found in the preamble of the Charter (recital 7). Article 51 of the

Charter, which defines the scope of the Charter,[130] clarifies that the Charter will not create new competencies for the EC organs, but will rather oblige those organs to act within the boundaries of the Charter, i.e. every EC act has to comply with the protection of fundamental rights as prescribed in the Charter ('respect the rights, observe the principles and promote the application of the rights). Article 51 also makes clear that the drafting of the Charter was more a consolidation process of already protected rights, scattered around in different sources, rather than the creation of new rights and did not turn the EU into a human rights organisation. As regards Member States, Article 51(1) suggests that the Charter only applies when Member States are implementing EC law and is not applicable to Member States' activities outside the scope of EC law.

According to Article 52(1) of the Charter: 'Any limitation on the exercise of the rights and freedoms recognised by this Charter must be provided for by law and respect the essence of those rights and freedoms. Subject to the principle of proportionality, limitations may be made only if they are necessary and genuinely meet objectives of general interest recognised by the Union or the need to protect the rights and freedoms of others.' Limitations can therefore also be seen in the economic objectives of the EU, which was often the case when the ECJ had to pronounce itself on fundamental rights of the individual citizen being breached by EC law (see 2.8.3.1, below).

Hence, limitations would only apply to the exercise of rights and freedoms but not to principles. This is only logical as rights and freedoms give rise to direct action by the EU or the Member States, while principles have to be implemented by the legislative or executive and can only be relevant for the interpretation of their acts. Also, Article II-112(5) of the EU Constitution[131] confirmed this by clarifying that 'the provisions of the Charter which contain principles may be implemented by legislative and executive acts taken by institutions, bodies, offices and agencies of the Union, and by acts of Member States when they are implementing Union law, in the exercise of their respective powers. They shall be judicially cognizable only in the interpretation of such acts and in the ruling of their legality.'

Many of the provisions of the Charter have already been recognised as legally binding by the ECJ in its jurisdiction as a matter of general principles of EC law, on the basis of Article 6(2) TEU.[132] However, the Charter is far more extensive in its scope and contains '*ratione materie* more fundamental rights the Court of Justice has so far effectively guaranteed but less than the Court *could* guarantee on the basis of Article 6(2) TEU'.[133] In particular, the Charter contains, apart from the classic civil and political rights, important economic and social rights such as the right to social benefits and healthcare under its 'Title IV Solidarity', as well as innovative rights such as the 'prohibition on making the human body and its parts as such a source of financial gain' under Article 3, reflecting recent societal developments.

The fact that fundamental rights already enjoy protection on the basis of Article 6(2) TEU, which only allows human rights protection to develop on a case-by-case basis, does not, however, diminish the value of the Charter; as the

ECJ will only be able to protect human rights *ex post facto* on the basis of Article 6 (2) TEU and depending on the particularities of the case at hand. Where the Charter and the ECJ's case law protect the same right, Article 53 becomes relevant, stating that the protection afforded by the Charter may not fall below the protection guaranteed by other provisions of EC law, as the case law has a broader scope of application regarding a wider category of national measures.

The commitment of the whole EC to the Charter also requires a common concurring interpretation and application of the fundamental rights agreed on in every Member State, from the British common law to the *liberté, fraternité, égalité* of the French Revolution. As there is an undeniable link between fundamental rights and legitimacy, the adoption of the Charter is also an instrument to bring the EU closer to its citizens and to overcome its legitimacy crisis.

On the basis of these old consenting elements of European culture, influenced by the pluralism of modern ethics, the Charter reveals an impressive consensus on the fundamental values of the European peoples by providing for civil, political, economic and social rights. Considering that the EU is in a process of dynamic development, one might even argue that it is on the verge of a confederation or a federal state. Though the sovereign nation state remains the basic element of the EU, Member States divested themselves of sovereign rights and individual powers, in order to achieve sovereignty and more power on a higher level. This is an irreversible process, which carries on.

In *Parliament v. Council*,[134] which concerned the EP's application (according to Article 230 TEC) to annul parts of Directive 2003/867 EC on the right to family reunification, the ECJ for the first time had to deal directly with the EU Charter, namely whether the Directive's provisions comply with the right to family life and the right to non-discrimination, before the Charter had come into force.[135] The Court held:

> The Charter was solemnly proclaimed by the EP, the Council and the Commission in Nice on 7 December 2000. While the Charter is not a legally binding instrument, the Community legislature did, however, acknowledge its importance by stating, in the second recital in the preamble to the directive, that the directive observes the principles recognised not only by Article 8 of the ECHR but also in the Charter. Furthermore, the principal aim of the Charter, as is apparent from its preamble, is to reaffirm rights as they result, in particular, from the constitutional traditions and international obligations common to the Member States, the Treaty on European Union, the Community Treaties, the [ECHR], the Social Charters adopted by the Community and by the Council of Europe and the case-law of the Court … and of the European Court of Human Rights.[136]

Thereby the ECJ rejected the EP's application as the Directive would give Member States a margin of appreciation in the implementation of the Directive, which allows for derogations from the Directive under certain conditions. However, the ECJ noted that even though the Charter was not legally binding, it recognised its legal effect as standard setting for EU legislation.[137] This approach was confirmed in *Reynolds Tobacco*[138] in relation to the right to an effective remedy (Article 47 Charter) stating that 'although this document does not have legally binding force, it does show the importance of the rights it sets out in the community legal order'. References to the Charter have also been made by Advocates-General[139] and the CFI for example in the *max.mobil* case,[140] where the CFI relied on Article 41(1) of the Charter, which provides for a duty to good administration, or in *Jégo-Quéré*,[141] the CFI referred to Article 47(1) of the Charter regarding the right to an effective remedy.

In 2005 the Commission adopted the Communication 'Compliance with the Charter of Fundamental Rights in Commission legislative proposals methodology for systematic and rigorous monitoring',[142] ensuring that the Charter rights are respected in every Commission legislative proposal, together with an impact assessment[143] and an explanatory memorandum, which will enhance the effectiveness of the internal scrutiny of fundamental rights in draft proposals.[144] Since 2001, all legislative proposals must include a section in the explanatory memorandum pointing out how fundamental rights are taken into account. These initiatives indicate efforts to implement Article 51(1) of the Charter, which stipulates: 'the provisions of this Charter are addressed to the institutions and bodies of the Union … they shall therefore respect the rights, observe the principles and promote the application thereof in accordance with their respective powers.' The Commission's Communication clearly points out that all legislative proposals should be reviewed against the Charter, a task that is now in the hands of the FRA (see below) and which will ensure that fundamental rights are taken into account already at the drafting stage.

With the Treaty of Lisbon the Charter will finally become enforceable, nine years after its proclamation in Nice. It will be interesting to observe, how the 'new rights' introduced by the Charter will be interpreted in the EU.

2.6.2 The EU Network of Independent Experts on Fundamental Rights

The EU Network of Independent Experts on Fundamental Rights was contracted by the European Commission between 2002 and 2006 as a private network that delivered annual and thematic reports on human rights issues within the EU on the basis of the EU's Charter on Fundamental Rights. It was set up by the European Commission's Directorate-General on Justice, Freedom and Security, at the EP's request. Since 2002, it has monitored the situation of fundamental rights in the Member States and in the EU, on the basis of the Charter of Fundamental Rights. The network delivered four annual reports (on the Member States as well as on the EU), each accompanied by a thematic report (in 2002 'The balance between freedom and security in the response by the EU and its Member States to the terrorist threats'; in 2003 'On the exercise by the Union or the Community of their external competences in the fields of justice and asylum or immigration'; in 2004 'The protection of minorities in the European Union'; in 2005

'Implementing the rights of the child in the European Union').[145] Moreover the network has delivered 15 legal opinions on specific topics, and a Synthesis Report with conclusions and recommendations for the EU and its Member States.[146]

2.6.3 Article 7 under the Treaty of Nice

Due to the controversial FPÖ affair, Article 7 TEU was amended to include the possibility to act before a breach occurred:

> The Council, acting by a majority of four-fifths of its members, after receiving the assent of the European Parliament and having heard the Member State concerned, may decide that there is a *clear risk of a serious breach* by a Member State of the fundamental rights or freedoms on which the Union is based. The Council may send appropriate recommendations to that State. The initiative for such decisions can come from one-third of the Member States, the Commission or the European Parliament.

The Treaty of Nice has supplemented the original procedure with a preventive instrument. Compared to the original Article 7 TEU, now, action can already be taken when there is a 'clear risk' of a serious breach, not only on proposal by the Commission or the Member States but also by the EP. The new Article 7 lowers the threshold from the 'determination of the existence of a breach of Article 6 by a Member State' to a 'clear risk of a serious breach'. Instead of suspension of rights, 'appropriate recommendations' will be addressed to the state concerned, which, on the one hand, offers a wider scope for taking measures, on the other hand, it could water down the original provision by eliminating the sanction of suspending voting rights. The procedure laid down by Article 7 TEU aims to remedy the breach through a political approach, it is not designed to remedy individual breaches. It appears that the risk or breach identified must go beyond specific situations and concern a more systematic problem. However, there is no systematic or continuing monitoring or reporting process related to Article 7 TEU, therefore it is unclear what amounts to a serious breach by a Member State. The newly established FRA might step in and undertake human rights monitoring in the Member States which is essential if the Article 7 procedure were ever to be used effectively (see below for the FRA's mandate).[147]

2.6.4 Further developments in CFSP under the Treaty of Nice

The European Neighbourhood Policy (ENP) was developed in 2004, with the desire for a zone of peaceful countries on its borders, and the objective of avoiding the emergence of new dividing lines between the enlarged EU and its neighbours by promoting, e.g. legislation protecting human rights and fundamental freedoms, enforcement of international human rights conventions, fight against racial hatred and xenophobia, human rights training and enforcement of international conventions on core labour rights.[148] In 2008 12 ENP action plans

(Armenia, Azerbaijan, Georgia, Egypt, Israel, Jordan, Lebanon, Moldova, Morocco, the Palestinian Authority, Tunisia and Ukraine) were implemented. The implementation of these action plans is jointly monitored through subcommittees. The EU provides substantial technical and financial support for ENP implementation through its external assistance programmes, in particular the European Neighbourhood and Partnership Instrument (ENPI), often in cooperation with the Council of Europe. The EU also supported the launch of the Universal Periodic Review, an innovative HRC mechanism for carrying out reviews of the human rights situation in every country at four-year intervals, which several Member States agreed to undergo. The ENP is, together with the human rights dialogues, an important instrument of the EU to promote human rights and the rule of law in its external relations.

In 2005 the EU succeeded in implementing human rights dialogues with Russia after the pattern of human rights dialogues with China (since 1996) and Iran (since 2002). The first focus of the Russian human rights dialogue was the situation in Chechnya, as well as measures taken by the Russian authorities in response to recurrent human rights abuses, such as disappearances. The EU encouraged Russia to strengthen cooperation with international human rights mechanisms, and sought assurances on the protection of human rights activists. The human rights situation in Russia was also discussed in general, in particular the state of media freedoms and the situation of minorities in Russia (such as the Finno-Ugric indigenous people). As a result of these consultations the EU unfortunately renounced support for a country resolution on Chechnya at the 61st UNCHR with the 'aim of taking forward co-operation' although it did so the previous years.[149]

2.6.5 The High Representative's Personal Representative for Human Rights

Under the Treaty of Nice a new high-profile post for the CFSP was created especially for the promotion of human rights in the EU's foreign policy. According to Article 18 TEU (now Article 33 under the Treaty of Lisbon) the Council may, on a proposal from the High Representative of the EU for Foreign Affairs and Security Policy, appoint a special representative with a mandate in relation to particular policy issues, who shall carry out his mandate under the authority of the High Representative. The first EU High Representative's Personal Representative on Human Rights was appointed on 17 January 2005. The Personal Representative's field of work focused on the implementation of human rights guidelines, EU policy in the international institutions like the UN, the CoE and the OSCE, the human rights dialogues, mainstreaming, relations with the EP, visibility of EU human rights policy and outreach activities. The High Representative's Personal Representative for Human Rights enhanced the EU's visibility at the 61st session of the UNCHR and lobbied effectively for EU positions, enhancing the visibility of the EU's action on respect for human rights worldwide. The current Representative for Human Rights, who has held this post since January 2007, while heading the Council Secretariat's Human Rights Unit, addressed the question of human rights with the Africa Working Party in April 2008 and the Political and Security Committee and the Asia/Oceania Working Party in June. She also advocated that human rights be more fully taken into account in political dialogues and by EU Special Representatives. This mainstreaming of human rights in the EU external policy remains, however, one of the principal challenges for the Member States, the Council and the Commission.

To avoid the danger that this position only gains a representative rather than a operative function, the EP demanded for extra staff with a human rights background attached specifically to his office, to work on human rights issues only.[150] With an annual EIDHR budget of EUR 140 million and more than 30 specific human rights dialogues with third countries, the creation of the post of the High Representative's Personal Representative for Human Rights can be seen as the peak of institutional developments in the EU that bring the EU to the forefront of human rights activity.

2.6.6 Enhanced cooperation

The Treaty of Nice introduced the concept of enhanced cooperation in its Article 27. Where the objectives of the EU and the EC cannot be achieved by the Member States as a whole, those Member States in a position to do so (at least eight Member States) may establish between them 'enhanced' cooperation. Since CFSP initiatives have often been held back by the diverse interests of the Member States, CFSP might provide a fertile ground for the use of enhanced cooperation for some Member States. In the CFSP field, this cooperation may relate solely to the implementation of a Joint Action or a Common Position but not to arms initiatives or to security and defence initiatives contributing to the acquisition of crisis management.[151] The provisions of the Treaty of Nice on enhanced cooperation represent a development in the formalisation of differentiated integration and are a courageous step forward to make CFSP more flexible and effective.[152] An important agreement where the concept of enhanced cooperation found practical expression was the implementation of the Schengen area, which enabled a group of Member States to curtail progressively border checks and to establish freedom of movement for persons.

2.6.7 Human rights impact assessment

The concept of impact assessment is not new; it has been particularly prominent in the context of environmental assessment of development plans or projects, required within Member States by EC law.[153] The International Association for Impact Assessment states that 'impact assessment, simply defined, is the process of identifying the future consequences of a current or proposed action'.[154] Impact assessments may also be used to examine and scrutinise *proposed legislation and policy* rather than specific land use or development plans or projects.[155]

In March 2001, the Commission decided to check all of its proposals against the provisions of the Charter, and continued to develop this practice in April 2005 by integrating fundamental rights in every impact assessment.[156] Of further relevance for human rights impact assessments are assessments of social impacts provided for in the guidelines of 15 June 2005.[157] These guidelines prescribe that every impact assessment has to check nine subgroups of potential social impacts of a legislative proposal, including one subgroup of potential effects under the heading 'Social inclusion and protection of particular groups' and another on 'Equality of treatment and opportunities, non-discrimination',[158] which can potentially be very relevant for aspects of minority protection.

However, the effectiveness of these human rights impact assessments has been questioned as impact assessments concerned with social impacts were found to be 'particularly difficult to identify, time and resource intensive to apply, and/or difficult to reach agreement on, since quantitative/monetary methodologies and indicators were not always available'.[159] In addition, the evaluation report states that 46 per cent of the Commission officials agreed that appropriate tools were not in place to assess the social impacts of the proposals.[160] The evaluation report recommended 'improved guidance to services, including a study on assessing social impacts' which was followed up with DG JLS and DG EMPL both launching studies on how to improve the assessment of social impacts.[161] In this context, Toggenburg remarked that the examination of fundamental rights required special knowledge – a fact which legitimises calls for an active role of the FRA in human rights impact assessments.[162] Hence, it is commendable that the Commission endeavours to include fundamental rights in its impact assessments of EU legislation, which shows that human rights mainstreaming is being taken seriously. However, the relevant processes and methodologies applied need further testing and fine-tuning and possibly the involvement of more specialist actors, such as the FRA.[163]

2.7 The Constitutional Convention and Draft Constitution

Due to the enlargement of the EU, Europe's leaders launched, in 2002, a 'Constitutional Convention' chaired by Valéry Giscard d'Estaing, with delegates from all current and future Member States to rethink the design of an enlarged EU, and in particular to simplify the EU's complicated treaty structure. In June 2003 a 'final draft' was released by the Convention, it was signed in Rome on 29 December 2004[164] but was never ratified since France and the Netherlands rejected the Constitution in a referendum in June 2005.

The Constitution suggested a variety of changes in the setup of the EU, e.g. two presidencies, one representing the Member States and one the EU itself; the creation of the new position of a foreign minister, and a more effective common foreign policy, although decisions in this area would still require unanimity vote. In addition, some aspects of criminal law would become EC law. With regard to human rights the draft Constitution for Europe of 18 July 2003 provided in Article 7 that 'the Union shall recognise the rights, freedoms and principles set out in the Charter of Fundamental Rights which constitutes Part II of this Constitution'; and in paragraph 2 that 'the Union shall seek accession to the European Convention for the Protection of Human Rights and Fundamental Freedoms'; both aspects have been followed up under the Reform Treaty.

One remarkable development that took place at the Inter-Governmental Conference under the Italian Presidency (note, not at the drafting stage) in December 2003 was the insertion of minority rights into Article I-2 ('The Union's Values'), brought about by an initiative of Hungary. Article I-2 of the draft Constitution stipulated:

> The Union is founded on the values of respect for human dignity, liberty, democracy, equality and the rule of law and respect for human rights, *including the rights of persons belonging to minorities.* These values are common to the Member States in a society in which pluralism, non-discrimination, tolerance, justice, solidarity and equality between women and men prevail. [emphasis added]

The same provision on the EU's values can now be found in Article 2 of the new Treaty of Lisbon. As mentioned, the Constitution was rejected by referendum in France and the Netherlands, and as a consequence the 'Reform Treaty' followed to pick up the constitutional project, which was renamed the Treaty of Lisbon.

2.8 The Treaty of Lisbon

In June 2007 the European Council found agreement on a revised version of the EU Constitution, which gave birth to the Reform Treaty, eventually named the Lisbon Treaty, according to its place of signature in December 2007. With the last Member State approving the Treaty in November 2009, it came into force on 1 December 2009. The Treaty of Lisbon largely repackaged the innovations contained in the EU Constitution, on the basis of which the Treaty of Lisbon was agreed. The Member States, however, failed to address why the Constitutional Treaty was rejected during the reform process, as a consequence, the ratification of the Lisbon Treaty took longer than anticipated, due to a negative referendum in Ireland and protracted negotiations in the Czech Republic; nonetheless there was much political will behind a successful conclusion of these treaty negotiations, thus Member States that endangered the process of ratification were under significant collective political pressure to alter their position.[165]

As regards human rights, the Lisbon Treaty provides for the EU's accession to the ECHR and renders the EU Charter on Fundamental Rights legally enforceable by according it the same value as the treaties; both issues will be the focus of this section, taking into consideration the perspectives of the ECJ and the ECtHR.

2.8.1 The status of the EU Charter on Fundamental Human Rights and the relationships with the ECJ and the ECtHR/ECHR

As already discussed (2.6.1, above), the EU Charter on Fundamental Rights unites a number of fundamental human rights norms that were previously dispersed in different sources. Article 51(1) of the Charter clarifies that it will not create new competencies for the EC organs, but will rather oblige those organs to act within the boundaries of the Charter, i.e. every EC act has to comply with the protection of fundamental rights as prescribed in the Charter. In other words, the Charter is not applicable to Member States' activities outside the scope of EC law.

The Charter contains provisions that are borrowed from the ECHR, which means, according to Article 52 of the Charter, that the exact level of protection of that right has been determined by the ECtHR, that being the minimum level recognised by Article 52(3) of the Charter which stipulates: 'In so far as this Charter contains rights which correspond to rights guaranteed by the Convention for the Protection of Human Rights and Fundamental Freedoms, the meaning and scope of those rights shall be the same as those laid down by the said Convention. This provision shall not prevent Union law providing more extensive protection'.

With regards to the precise meaning to be given to the wording of the provisions, as well as the right balance to be struck when fundamental rights are conflicting, the ECtHR and the ECJ might find themselves at odds when interpreting the rights embodied in both the Charter and the ECHR (once the EU has joined the ECHR), especially if they have to decide on issues that have not previously been decided on. As there have been differences in interpretation by the ECJ and the ECtHR of certain human rights in the past (see below), the preamble of the Charter 'reaffirms ... the rights ... as they result from the case law of the ECtHR'. Thus, as a member to the ECHR, the EU has to give effect to its provisions, as Article 1 ECHR states that 'The High Contracting Parties shall secure to everyone within their jurisdiction the rights and freedoms defined in Section I of this Convention'. This includes the case law of the ECtHR, as a member to the ECHR the ECJ would be prevented from giving a different interpretation to ECHR rights in the first place. However, as the Charter goes above and beyond the level of protection of the ECHR, in particular with regards to economic and social rights for which the Charter provides in Chapter IV, and which do not have corresponding provisions in the ECHR, enough scope remains for the ECJ to develop its own jurisdiction in this area. In this context, Article 52(3) of the Charter can also be seen as an attempt to tackle the past experience with divergence in interpretation of the ECHR by the two courts.

When the Charter was first adopted, the CoE showed concern that a legally binding Charter would affect the harmonious and consistent interpretation of fundamental rights by the ECtHR and the ECJ, as preliminary references regarding human rights to the ECJ would increase and with it the risk that the ECJ's interpretation of certain rights might differ from the ECtHR's interpretation. At the same time, the CoE promoted the idea of the EU's accession to the ECHR, which would avoid such risk of conflicting case law.[166] Not only the fact that the provisions of the ECHR differ considerably from the ones in the Charter, but also, the aspect of limitation clauses, attached to every right, are used differently in the ECHR and the Charter, poses problems that can only be overcome by accession.[167]

In addition, the CoE promoted the idea to give the ECtHR the task of providing the EU institutions with an authoritative interpretation of those ECHR rights which are also contained in the Charter, so as to guarantee perfect harmony in the interpretation of the two instruments. Also, a system of references to the ECtHR was suggested to prevent any divergences between the two European courts.[168] However, this idea did not find much support as it would prolong the already lengthy proceedings before the courts. With imminent accession of the EU to the ECHR, it remains uncertain how strictly the ECJ will apply the ECtHR's case law and its standards of interpretation.

2.8.2 Article 6(1) Lisbon Treaty and the interpretation of the EU Charter on Fundamental Rights

Article 6(1) TEU Lisbon Treaty[169] recognises the general provisions of Title VII of the Charter and not the ECtHR or the ECHR as providing authority in the interpretation of Charter rights. However, as discussed above according to Article 52(3) of the Charter, in so far as the Charter contains rights which correspond to rights guaranteed by the ECHR, the meaning and scope of those rights shall be the same as those laid down by the ECHR; trying to avoid discrepancies between the ECJ and the ECtHR, the authority of the ECHR is still relevant for the interpretation of the EU Charter on Fundamental Rights and provides the minimum standard of interpretation for EU fundamental rights.

In addition, Article 6(3) stipulates 'fundamental rights, as guaranteed by the European Convention for the Protection of Human Rights and Fundamental Freedoms and as they result from the constitutional traditions common to the Member States, shall constitute general principles of the Union's law'. This wording suggests that ECHR rights, qualified as 'general principles' by Article 6(3) TEU, rank lower than the Charter rights which are specifically given the same value as the treaties, i.e. the EU Charter would prevail over the ECHR in case of conflict. However, this provision can only be seen as pointing out the ECHR and constitutional traditions of Member States as the basis of interpretation for Charter rights, otherwise, it would be irreconcilable with Article 52(3) of the Charter and the EU's membership to the ECHR if the EU, as a member to the ECHR designates its own human rights provisions as higher ranking than the ECHR rights.

Despite the clear wording of Article 6(1) TEU, Protocol 7 of the Treaty of Lisbon[170] emphasises *again* that the Charter does not extend the field of application of EU law beyond the powers of the EU or establish any new power or task for the EU, an aspect that appeared to be of crucial importance to the Member States. Furthermore, the United Kingdom and Poland negotiated a protocol, stating that 'neither in the UK nor in Poland may any national court declare domestic law incompatible with the Charter'.[171]

The protocol further states in Article 1(2) that nothing in Title IV of the Charter (solidarity rights), creates justiciable rights applicable to Poland or the United Kingdom except in so far as Poland or the United Kingdom has provided for such rights in its national law, which basically means that both countries want to avoid the imposition of new solidarity rights by the Charter. In addition, Article 2 of the protocol provides that insofar as a provision of the Charter refers to national laws and practices, it shall only apply to Poland or the United Kingdom 'to the extent that the rights or principles that it contains are recognised in the law or practices of Poland or of the United Kingdom'.

It is deplorable that in 2005 the United Kingdom had signed the EU Constitutional Treaty, which included the Charter, and did so without any such reservations of the kind found in the protocol attached to the Treaty of Lisbon. Nothing has changed in the area of solidarity rights in the EU in those two years between the failure of the Constitutional Treaty and the Lisbon Treaty. The 'official view', however, is that the government engaged in some rethinking of the possible impact of the Charter on UK business, in particular relating to the solidarity rights contained in Title IV. It is, however, difficult to avoid the conclusion that the inclusion of the protocol was motivated more by the government's desire to show that the Treaty of Lisbon differed in certain respects from the EU Constitution, and that therefore a referendum on the former was not necessary.[172] Presumably, the avoidance of a referendum in the UK and Poland was the reason why the other Member States did not challenge the protocol, as the common goal was to advance the reform process.

The Commission has provided no clear guidance on how the UK and Polish exemptions will operate, as the protocol would undermine the fundamental principle of EU law supremacy and the obligation to apply EU law uniformly to all Member States. The German Presidency at the time appeared willing to give in to the Polish and UK requests for the sake of saving the reform process, and put any difficulties or discrepancies that might appear later, on hold. For the Intergovernmental Conference in 2007 the Commission stated in its Opinion on the Draft Mandate simply that 'The Charter of Fundamental Rights will offer Europeans guarantees with the same legal status as the treaties themselves, bringing together civil, political, economic and social rights ... Its provisions will also apply in full to acts of implementation of Union law, even if not in all Member States'.[173] Because of the limits imposed by the protocol, citizens in the UK and Poland will have to rely on the *acquis communautaire* if they cannot rely directly on the Charter for their human rights/solidarity rights protection.

2.8.3 The ECJ–ECtHR relationship under the Treaty of Lisbon and EU accession to the ECHR

With the coming into force of the EU Charter on Fundamental Rights, the question could be raised whether it would still be necessary for the EU to accede to the ECHR. On the one hand, the EU's accession to the ECHR can be seen as complementary, just like Member States have their own constitutions and bill of rights and at the same time have submitted themselves to external control by international organisations such as the CoE. As all EU Member States have ratified the ECHR and are subjected to the control of the ECtHR, it would make sense for the EU to be subjected to the same system of control in order to ensure consistency in the protection of human rights in Europe and eliminating the risk of differing interpretation of human rights by the two courts. In addition, the ECJ's primary function does certainly not lie in its human rights jurisdiction, but it is rather the ECtHR that has been entrusted with pronouncing itself on the protection of human rights in Europe.

With accession to the ECHR the EU will be able to make a stronger defence of its commitment to human rights, as the EU has often been accused of double standards and its focus on the advancement of economic goals instead of genuinely protecting human rights as 'fundamental values upon which the Union is based'.[174] Apart from ensuring coherence and harmony between the two institutions, accession will also strengthen the principle of legal certainty in Europe and within the EU in particular, as the EU institutions will be subject to the same review of conformity with the ECHR of their acts and decisions as are its Member States.[175] So far there has been, on occasion, some indirect review of EU/EC acts by the ECtHR, which left Member States in the unsatisfactory situation of being liable for breaches of the ECHR when implementing EU law, such as in the case of *Bosphoros*. In addition, individuals can bring complaints against the EU institutions directly before the ECtHR, and would not have to go through the procedure according to Articles 230ff TEC (now Article 263 TFEU),[176] which is not always open to the citizen.

As fundamental rights have acquired a more prominent role in today's world, the protection of human rights is a benchmark for the accountability and legitimacy of every polity. Hence, it is also important for the EU from a political point of view to ensure a uniform standard of human rights protection throughout Europe. Since the case law of the ECtHR and the ECJ showed divergences in the past in their human rights jurisdiction, it is important to recount how human rights violations in the context of the EU have been treated in the past by the two courts, the ECJ in Luxembourg and the ECtHR in Strasbourg.

2.8.3.1 The ECJ's human rights jurisdiction in the past

Despite the fact that there were no human rights provisions in the original EC treaties, the ECJ started referring to human rights in its decisions already in the 1960s. It was the Court's jurisprudence that made it possible for human rights to enter into the legal framework of the EU. As the powers of the EC gradually expanded, the lack of human rights provisions in its treaty framework was perceived as an absence of legitimacy.[177] Mainly German applicants challenged various EC decisions before the ECJ, alleging that they were incompatible with fundamental rights protected under the German constitution. The Court, at the time, simply stated that it was not competent to review EC decisions in the light of national constitutional law.[178] This approach changed when the Court started to apply the concept of *direct effect*,[179] which conceded that individuals could rely on EC law and that nationals of a Member State under certain conditions can lay claim to individual rights which the national courts must protect.[180]

Partly under the influence of discussions in German legal circles about the relationship between EC law and national constitutional law, the ECJ began in the late 1960s to affirm in its judgments the respect shown for fundamental rights by the EC institutions and the Member States whenever they took action within the areas covered by EC law.

The *Internationale Handelsgesellschaft v. Einfuhr-und Vorratstelle für Getreide und Futtermittel* case[181] was one of the first human rights cases to come before the Court in 1970.[182] The issue was whether an EC regulation, which established a deposit system for exporters, was consistent with certain principles of the German Constitution. While the national court considered the EC measure being contrary to the principles of its national constitutional law,[183] the ECJ held that the validity of EC measures could only be judged in the light of EC law and could not be overridden by national law. However, the ECJ conceded that human rights, which are protected in national constitutions, had an interpretative role for EC decisions. In its view, 'fundamental rights form an integral part of the general principles of law, the observance of which the Court ensures. In safeguarding these rights, the Court is bound to draw inspiration from the constitutional traditions common to the Member States and it cannot therefore uphold measures which are incompatible with fundamental rights recognised and protected by the constitutions of those States.' The case of *Staatsanwalt Freiburg v. Keller*,[184] however, indicates the ECJ's reluctance to declare an EC measure invalid because it would conflict with a right contained in the constitution of a Member State. Keller claimed that Council Regulation 355/79 laying down general rules for the description and presentation of wines and grape must limit German wine producers in their choice of describing their wines which is incompatible with the freedom to pursue their trade as guaranteed by Article 12 of the German Constitution.[185] The Court found that 'the validity of measures adopted by the institutions of the Community can be judged only in the light of Community law. A claim that fundamental rights laid down in the constitution of a Member State have been infringed cannot in itself affect the validity of a Community measure or its effects within the State.'[186] In case Member States provide for a higher level of protection, it is questionable how far EU law can interfere with basic constitutional norms of the Member States.[187]

In practice, many Member States apply higher standards of protection than those required by EC law, which constitutes a challenge to the concept of supremacy of EC law. In *Internationale Handelsgesellschaft* and the later case of *Re Wünsche Handelsgesellschaft*[188] the German Constitutional Court found the EC measure in question was incompatible with its Constitution, and held that as long as the EC had not removed the possible conflict of norms between EC law and national constitutional law, the German Court would ensure that national constitutional law took precedence and preserved its final authority to intervene if real problems regarding the protection of fundamental rights arose.[189]

In the *Nold case*,[190] the Court not only stated that fundamental rights form an integral part of the general principles of law and that it draws inspiration from constitutional traditions common to Member States, but also emphasised that 'measures which are incompatible with fundamental rights *recognised by international treaties* for the protection of human rights on which the Member States have collaborated or of which they are signatories, can supply guidelines, which should be followed within the framework of Community law' [emphasis added]. That concept was later recognised by the joint declaration of the EP, the Council and the Commission of 5 April 1977,[191] which, after recalling the case law of the ECJ, referred to the ECHR of 1950. The ECJ referred to the ECHR for the first time in the *Rutili case*,[192] in order to support the finding that restrictions on the right to free movement on grounds of public policy cannot be justified unless they are limited to what is necessary in order to protect the objectives in view.

From then onwards the Court took on occasion international treaties as guidelines for its decisions and explicitly referred to provisions of the ECHR; one of the first cases was the *Hauer* case[193] where the Court recognised the right to property, which is protected by the First Protocol to the ECHR.[194] The applicant had applied to the Land Rheinland Pfalz for authorisation to undertake a new planting of vines on her land. She was refused authorisation on grounds that the land was unsuitable for wine growing and on her objection to this refusal, she was told that in the meantime a Council Regulation has been passed prohibiting the new planting of vines in that administrative unit where her land was situated. She appealed the decision of the administration at the competent German court claiming that the Council Regulation was incompatible with the right to property and the right to pursue freely trade and professional activities, which are protected as basic human rights under the German Constitution. The ECJ referred to the extra-Community instruments, under which states have undertaken international obligations in order to ensure better protection for those rights and held that 'without any question of their being incorporated as such in the Community order, be used to establish principles which are common to the States themselves'. The Court, on the one hand, acknowledged the rights of ownership and the right freely to choose trade and profession as part of EC law, but denied, on the other hand, that they had been impermissibly infringed in this case. The ECJ concluded that, although the challenged Regulation restricted the right to property, as protected by the ECHR, that restriction was not disproportionate to the aim of the Community measure and that it did not infringe the substance of the right.

Despite the fact that the ECJ started referring more and more to human rights in its decisions, it rarely struck down an EC decision on the basis of human rights considerations and it became obvious that the ECJ favoured market rights over human rights. In the case of *Wachauf*,[195] the ECJ made it clear that economic considerations impact considerably on the enforcement of human rights in the Community context by stating that:

> fundamental rights recognised by the Court are not absolute, however, must be considered in relation to their social function. Consequently, restrictions

> may be imposed on the exercise of these rights, in particular in the context of a common organisation of the market, provided that these restrictions in fact correspond to objectives of general interest pursued by the Community and do not constitute, with regard to the aim pursued, a disproportionate and intolerable interference impairing the very substance of those rights.

The ECJ also made clear in its decisions that it is beyond its jurisdiction to decide on the application of human rights in Member States outside the ambit of EC law. The standard of human rights protection provided by the Court only applied to EC law and to national measures that implement it, or which come within the EU's legal framework in some other way. The ECJ found in *Kremzow*[196] 'where national legislation ... does not fall within the field of application of Community law, the Court cannot give the interpretative guidance necessary for the national court to determine whether that national legislation is in conformity with the fundamental rights ... deriving in particular from the ECHR.' This approach was also necessary to ensure that there was no possibility of overlapping jurisdiction with the ECtHR.

These early cases, *Internationale Handelsgesellschaft*, *Nold* and *Hauer* illustrate, however, the fundamentally different approaches of the ECJ and the ECtHR. The ECJ applied a stricter interpretation of human rights than the ECtHR, as its proclaimed aim was to uphold the Community interest.[197] The object and purpose of the ECHR, on the other hand, was to uphold 'the protection and promotion of individual human rights'.[198] While the ECJ weighed the EC interest against the interest of the individual and used constitutions of the Member States or relevant international treaties as guidelines for its decisions, the ECtHR follows a completely different approach; namely, it emphasises the individual's interest, allowing Member States a certain margin of appreciation. This concept became clear in further decisions of the ECJ where the protection of fundamental rights, i.e. the right in itself, was taken from the ECHR but its interpretation was seen in the light of the Community interest. For example:

1 In *Prais*,[199] the applicant relied specifically on Article 9 of the ECHR (freedom of religion)[200] as a ground of annulment of a decision of the Council. The impugned decision had fixed a date of an open competition for a post for which the applicant had applied to take place on a Jewish fast-day, during which she could neither travel nor write. Although the Court did not annul the Council's decision, its reasoning implied that the Council should take steps and amend its practice accordingly, to respect the requirements of a candidate's religion so long as it was given sufficient notice of these requirements by the candidate.[201]

2 In *Oyowe and Traore*,[202] the ECJ ruled in favour of human rights and required the Commission to change its employment practice in relation to journalists from African Caribbean Pacific (ACP) countries, in such a way as to respect their freedom of expression protected under Article 10 ECHR.[203] The Commission had refused to appoint these journalists, who were working for

the Community's European Cooperation Agency, as officials on the ground that their role of representing perspectives of the ACP States would be incompatible with their duty of allegiance. The Court took the view that the Commission was imposing the duty of allegiance in a way that would infringe the fundamental right to freedom of expression of employees as protected under Article 10 ECHR.

3 In 2002 in the *Schmidberger* case,[204] the ECJ ruled again in favour of fundamental human rights protection, rather than in favour of the Community interest of free movement of goods. In this case, the Austrian courts and the ECJ had to consider a demonstration of an environmental group on the Brenner motorway, which caused the motorway to be closed for traffic for almost 30 hours with the authorisation of the Austrian authorities. Schmidberger, an international transport company brought an action for financial losses resulting from the motorway closure and a violation of the freedom of movement of goods. The Austrian authorities argued that the freedom of expression and freedom of assembly (Articles 10, 11 ECHR) justified the closure. The ECJ held that the free movement of goods *may* in certain circumstances be subject to restrictions for reasons spelled out in the treaty or for overriding requirements relating to public interest. Applying the proportionality test, the ECJ found that allowing the demonstration was proportionate regarding the pursued aim.

4 Similarly, in the *Omega Spielhallen* case,[205] the ECJ weighed the protection of human dignity (Article 2 ECHR) against the freedom to provide services, and had to define public policy as a human dignity issue. Inspired by the *Schmidberger* case, the ECJ acknowledged that fundamental rights are able to restrict the EU's economic freedoms as long as they are recognised as general principles of EC law, and did not find a breach of the proportionality principle.

5 Finally in the cases of *Kadi* and *Yussuf*,[206] the ECJ, in an unprecedented move, held that it had jurisdiction and was even obligated to review the lawfulness of all EC measures even if such measures give effect to UN Security Council resolutions dealing with the international terrorism sanctions regime. In conclusion the ECJ found that the freezing of assets imposed on the claimants' accounts infringed their fundamental rights under EC law and found that the regulation violated their rights of the defence and their right to property. This decision is remarkable as international obligations under the UN Charter, were effectively subordinated to EC law by the ECJ.

These last decisions can be seen as indications that the ECJ, since the proclamation of the EU Charter on Fundamental Rights, is moving away from its strict approach and is starting to give human rights a more prominent place in the Community order. However, these cases were also taken to criticise the ECJ's approach in the past, for having considered human rights simply as general principles of law and not as the ultimate limits on the powers of all constitutional organs.[207] For the ECJ it was always the four economic freedoms (free movement of goods, persons, services and capital) that formed the basis of the Community legal order and against which all other considerations, including human rights, had to be reviewed. In the *Omega Spielhallen* case, Advocate-General Stix-Hackl addressed this issue of whether there is a general priority between fundamental rights and economic freedoms and questioned whether 'fundamental and human rights can be afforded a certain precedence over 'general' primary legislation', concluding that 'fundamental rights are to be considered as part of its primary legislation and rank in hierarchy at the same level as other primary legislation, particularly fundamental freedoms'.[208]

2.8.3.2 Discrepancy with the ECtHR's jurisdiction

The ECJ's endeavour to lay foundations for the development of fundamental rights in EC law has not been unproblematic, as some decisions of the ECtHR were in contrast with decisions of the ECJ in their interpretation of certain rights provided for in the ECHR. Cases like *Funke*,[209] *Niemitz*[210] and *Hoechst*[211] illustrate that the fact that the ECJ drew on recognised and shared sources for the rights in question, did not mean that there would be agreement with the ECtHR on the scope and practical application of any given right in a specific context:

1 In *Hoechst*, the applicant company brought an action for the annulment of various Commission decisions which had ordered an investigation into its affairs, in the context of suspected anti-competitive practices, and which had subsequently imposed penalty payments on it for refusing to permit the carrying out of this investigation. The applicant argued that the decisions had violated procedural rights and the right to inviolability of the home as protected under Article 8 ECHR. The ECJ recognised the right to inviolability of the home as a principle common to the laws of the Member States and a right protected under the EC legal order, but only in regard to the private dwellings of natural persons and not with respect to undertakings.
2 The ECtHR, by the same token, stressed in *Niemitz* that Article 8 ECHR[212] did indeed extend to business premises. The case concerned the search of a lawyer's office pursuant to a warrant drawn in very broad terms in the absence of an independent observer and impinging on professional secrecy. The ECtHR held that 'to interpret the words "private life" and "home" including certain professional or business activities would be consonant with the essential object and purpose of Article 8, namely to protect the individual against arbitrary interference by the public authorities.'[213]
3 In 2002, however, the ECJ revisited its jurisdiction of *Hoechst* and found in *Roquette Frères*,[214] that referring to the development of the case law of the ECtHR relating to the right to privacy of commercial enterprises, businesses can in fact benefit from the protection of Article 8 ECHR.
4 In relation to the right to a fair trial protected under Article 6(1) ECHR and the issue of self-incrimination, the ECJ ruled in the case of *Orkem*[215] in the

context of a European anti-trust investigation that 'as far as Article 6 ECHR is concerned, although it may be relied upon by an undertaking subject to an investigation relating to competition law, it must be observed that neither the wording of that article nor the decisions of the ECtHR indicate that it upholds the right not to give evidence against oneself.'

5 The ECtHR meanwhile held in the case of *Funke*[216] that Article 6 did indeed protect 'the right to remain silent and not to contribute to incriminating oneself'. On that note, Advocate-General Darmon pointed out in *Orkem* that it would be undesirable that the interpretation of the same provision can result in two different outcomes by the two courts.[217] Similarly in *Danzer*[218] the applicants tried to extend the right against self-incrimination to business secrets, but were unsuccessful as the CFI found the measures in question to be proportionate and justified as the right against self-incrimination would not apply to the requirement on companies under an EC Company Law Directive.

6 Another example where the ECJ departed from the jurisdiction of the ECtHR is the *Emesa Sugar* case.[219] Here, the ECJ rejected a party's application to submit written observations on the opinion of the Advocate General, on the basis of Article 6 ECHR (right to a fair trial). The ECtHR, by way of contrast, had ruled in *Vermeulen v. Belgium*[220] that Article 6 ECHR 'means in principle the opportunity for the parties to a criminal or civil trial to have knowledge of and comment on evidence adduced or observations filed, even by an independent member of the national legal service, with a view to influencing the court's decision,' which clearly would be applicable to an Advocate-General's opinion. Other cases that showed differences in interpretation on the same issue were e.g. the ECtHR case of *Open Door Counselling*[221] and the opinion of Advocate-General in *Grogan*[222] on the right to freedom of information and abortion; or the ECJ's decision in *ERT*[223] and the Strasburg decision in *Lentia v. Austria.*[224]

Admittedly, there are not many cases that illustrate this conflict in interpretation of ECHR rights by the two courts. However, the fact that both courts took fundamentally different approaches – one mainly protects the internal market whereas the other protects the human rights of the individual – which led to different results in determining the scope of a right, is a situation of legal uncertainty that should be avoided, as pointed out by Advocate-General Darmon in *Orkem*. Further, these cases not only show that different courts come to different interpretations of the same provisions, given the different contexts in which they exercise jurisdiction, but also that the ECJ did not feel that it was bound by other international human rights treaties such as the ECHR; in its own words, it only used them as 'inspirations' or 'guidelines'; and as the new Article 6(3) TEU states that the ECHR shall be part of the 'general principles of the Union's law'.

It remains to be seen whether this provision is strong enough to prevent the ECJ from contradicting ECHR rights and their interpretation given by the ECtHR. This difference in approach leading to contradictory decisions has been widely criticised, questioning the credibility of the ECJ and CFI.[225] O'Leary anticipated a 'real danger' in the ECJ's free interpretation of the ECHR that is incoherent with the ECtHR's interpretation.[226] However, *Roquette Frères* showed that the ECJ has become more willing to follow the case law of the ECtHR, and in this case it departed from its own precedent. As the EU's accession to the ECHR is imminent this might be a sign of avoiding tension between the two courts. Despite the potential problems arising from conflicting rules and different approaches, it should be noted that the ECJ has mostly followed the case law of the ECtHR and their relationship can be seen as cooperative rather than confrontational. As mentioned above, since the declaration of the EU Charter on Fundamental Rights in 2000, the ECJ has shown a tendency towards heeding the ECtHR's interpretations, while at the same time broadening and deepening its own human rights jurisdiction.[227] With the increasing amount of litigation involving fundamental rights (also due to the EU Charter on Fundamental Rights), more and more references to the ECHR might however create the risk of more and more differences in interpretation. Since the ECtHR is already facing a huge backlog of cases, the prospect of EU-law-based claims, which will increase applications in the ECtHR substantially, might require the ECtHR to restructure its system dramatically.[228] At the same time the ECtHR has deferred to the ECJ's human rights standards when required to indirectly review a EC measure with its ECHR compliance, as will be discussed below.

2.8.3.3 How the ECtHR dealt with cases of alleged violation of the ECHR rights by EU law or EU institutions

In the past, the ECtHR, took a very restrained approach in relation to violations of ECHR rights by the EU. In the decision *Pafitis and Others v. Greece*,[229] the ECtHR was asked to determine whether judicial proceedings before the Athens Regional Court went beyond the reasonable time limit referred to in Article 6(1) ECHR, or constituted a violation of the right to a fair trial. Apart from various factors such as the complexity of the case, the conduct of parties and judicial authorities, also the proceedings before the ECJ prolonged the trial. The ECtHR responded that it could not take into consideration the period during which the matter was referred to the ECJ when assessing the length of the proceedings as that 'would be detrimental to the system established by Article 177 TEC'.[230]

In the case of *Matthews v. UK*,[231] however, the ECtHR found that the EC Council Decision amending the EC Act on Direct Elections of 1976, requiring the UK to exclude Gibraltar citizens from voting rights in the EP elections contravened Article 3 Protocol 1 of the ECHR on the right to vote in elections for the legislature.[232] The ECtHR observed that Acts of the EC as such cannot be challenged before the ECtHR because the EC is not a Contracting Party. However, the alleged violation flows from an annex to the 1976 Act on Direct Elections, freely entered into by the UK.

The ECtHR distinguished between primary and secondary legislation of the EC and the fact whether the Act can be challenged before the ECJ or not. The

1976 Act on Direct Elections cannot be challenged before the ECJ as it is not a 'normal' EC Act but an international agreement within the EC order entered into freely by all the Member States, which cannot be reviewed by the ECJ. As long as the EC Act can be challenged within the EC legal order itself, offering 'equivalent protection' for the rights guaranteed by the ECHR, the ECtHR cannot intervene. In the absence of any such possibility of judicial review the EU Member States may be held responsible under the ECHR for any infringement of the provisions of the latter resulting from 'international instruments which, they freely entered into'.[233] The Court found that 'The United Kingdom, together with all other parties to the Maastricht Treaty, is responsible *ratione materiae* under Article 1 of the Convention and, in particular under Article 3 of Protocol No. 1, for the consequences of that Treaty.'[234]

With the *Matthews* decision, the ECtHR took the approach that EU Member States can very well be held responsible under the ECHR for infringements committed by giving effect to EC law in their national jurisdictions. To summarise the above: responsibility for Member States arises under Article 1 ECHR when 'primary legislation' (EC treaties) is concerned, while the concept of 'equivalent protection' applies to 'secondary legislation', which cannot be challenged under the ECHR as judicial review within the framework of the EU prevails. The ECtHR furthermore held '[T]he Convention does not exclude the transfer of competences to international organisations provided that Convention rights continue to be "secured". Member States' responsibility therefore continues even after such a transfer.'[235] The circumstances under which this responsibility continues have been at issue in subsequent decisions.

In the case of *Bosphorus Airlines v. Ireland*,[236] the ECtHR confirmed this principle with regard to acts of EC institutions. Here, the ECtHR was required to clarify when states could be held responsible for actions taken in compliance with international legal obligations deriving from the membership of an international organisation, such as the EU. In this case the ECJ upheld Ireland's impounding of an aeroplane that was leased by a Turkish company from the Yugoslav national airline according to Regulation 990/93 as part of the sanctions regime against Yugoslavia. The Turkish airline claimed before the ECtHR a breach of its right to property under Article 1 of Protocol 1 to the ECHR. The ECtHR held that, in such a case 'a rebuttable presumption' arises that such action is consistent with the ECHR, provided that the organisation in question offers human rights protection 'at least equivalent' to that provided for under the ECHR. This presumption may be rebutted where 'it is considered that the protection of the Convention was manifestly deficient';[237] i.e. the Member State's action will be considered justified and lawful, unless the breach of the ECHR is manifestly obvious. Because this was not the situation in the case at hand, and the organisation in question – here the EU – provided 'at least equivalent human rights protection', Ireland was found not to be in violation of any of its obligations under the ECHR.

By the same token, as regards national implementation of EU and other international obligations, i.e. where states have discretion as to the implementation of duties arising from the membership in such organisations, the states generally do remain responsible under the ECHR. In *M & Co v. Federal Republic of Germany*,[238] the European Commission of Human Rights stated:

> Under Article 1 of the Convention the Member States are responsible for all acts and omissions of their domestic organs allegedly violating the Convention regardless of whether the act or omission in question is a consequence of domestic law or regulations or of the necessity to comply with international obligations.

There are numerous examples of such scrutiny.[239] However, this judgment also clarified that no judicial review may be performed of national acts that are purely an *implementation of acts of EU institutions with no discretionary power for the Member States, as long as the EU provides for 'equivalent protection'* of fundamental rights. In this context it would be crucial if the Member State argues as a defence that it had no discretion in implementing EC law; then it would be for the ECtHR to decide whether there was discretion or not, i.e. it will have to rule on the interpretation of EU law. If the breach is a consequence of the implementation of a Directive, which has given the Member State a certain margin of appreciation when transposing the Directive into national law and the problem lies with the transposition and not the Directive itself, then the Member State would be held liable for the breach.

The equivalent protection doctrine has been criticised by Judge Ress, in his separate concurring opinion in the *Bosphorus* case, where he warned against the emergence of double standards through too readily made assumptions of 'equivalent protection'. In particular he noted that the ECtHR had 'not addressed the question of whether [the] limited access [to the ECJ under Article 230(4), EC][240] is really in accordance with Article 6(1) of the Convention and whether the provisions … must not be interpreted more extensively in light of Article 6(1)'. In addition, he expressed reservations about reaching a finding of 'equivalent protection' without examining the detail of the ECJ's case law, in particular, 'on the level and intensity of property rights'.[241]

It also has to be considered that often individuals were excluded from challenging decisions under Article 230(4) TEC (now Article 263 TFEU), in particular with regards to third pillar/JHA decisions, and an application under the preliminary reference procedure according to Article 234 TEC might fail when the national court refuses to make such a reference. In fact, if the ECtHR according to the equivalent protection doctrine would always refer to the generally available protection via Article 230ff TEC (263ff TFEU), any claim against the EU under Article 6 ECHR would become meaningless. The fact that there are means of reviewing EU decisions within the EU system does not necessarily mean that there is always equivalent protection for the claimant, as evidenced by discrepancies in interpretation of human rights by the two courts, in particular regarding the right to a fair trial (Article 6 ECHR). More challenges of procedural issues under EU law and their compliance with Article 6 ECHR can therefore be anticipated.

Looking at the case law regarding indirect review of EU law by Strasbourg, Member States found themselves punished by one international organisation for an action they have taken in order to comply with their obligations imposed by another international organisation.[242] With the EU acceding to the ECHR, such situations can be avoided if the Member State concerned can defer liability to the EU directly in case the implementation of EU law would entail an infringement of the ECHR. A distinction between primary or secondary law would no longer be necessary, and the equivalent protection doctrine will become superfluous as the ECtHR will have to review EU law as well as acts of EU institutions irrespective of these concepts once the EU has acceded to the ECHR.

However, with the EU's accession to the ECHR, the equivalent protection approach might still be taken into consideration in the context of the margin of appreciation doctrine, which allows the ECtHR to accommodate different national approaches. The margin of appreciation doctrine has been used extensively by the ECtHR, and has been defined as 'the outer limits of schemes of protection which are acceptable under the Convention',[243] i.e. the ECtHR will not interfere with actions which are within the margin of appreciation of the Member State.[244] In the case where national law is the subject matter of a complaint to the ECtHR, it is assumed that the Contracting States are in a better position than the judges to decide on the nature and scope of a law. The same approach can quite easily be applied to the EU; however, being in a better position than the ECtHR to assess matters that are specific to EU law will require substantial expertise in EU law. According to Article 27(2) ECHR, the judge who is a national of any State Party concerned automatically sits in the Grand Chamber in order to ensure acquaintance with the legal system and the background to the case.[245] Whether the 'EU judge' who will sit as a member of the Grand Chamber, in cases where the EU is a concerned party, can accomplish such task fully, or whether the ECtHR would concede the EU as a member to the ECHR a wide margin of appreciation remains to be seen. Much will depend on how strict the ECtHR is prepared to be in reviewing whether the presumption of equivalent protection of human rights in EU law has been rebutted. In light of *Bosphorus*, a high degree of deference to the ECJ has to be expected.[246] The concept of 'manifest deficiency' as established in *Bosphorus* is a very high threshold which suggests that the ECtHR is reluctant to intervene in EU law. Hence, there have been mixed signs by the ECtHR, making it hard to predict how far the ECtHR will take the margin of appreciation in EU cases.

Another aspect to consider in this context is the protocol relating to Article 6 (2), which is attached to the Treaty of Lisbon[247] stating that 'the agreement relating to accession to the ECHR must make provision for preserving the specific characteristics of the European Union and EU law'. Presumably this not only concerns technicalities related to accession but also alludes to the consideration of the ECJ's past jurisdiction on human rights in the context of EC law. The aspect of preserving the specific features of EU law is repeated in a declaration appended to the Treaty of Lisbon, which also emphasises the existence of regular dialogue between the ECJ and the ECtHR, stating that such dialogue could be reinforced when the EU accedes to the ECHR.[248]

The requirement of regular dialogue between the ECJ and ECtHR according to Declaration No. 2 might entail the ECJ having to consult the ECtHR every time the violation of an ECHR right is essential for an ECJ decision. This is of particular importance in cases where the issue at hand has not been subject to any relevant precedent yet. This possibility of dialogue between the ECtHR and the ECJ has to be effected without establishing any hierarchical order between the two courts, and might represent an option towards a harmonic and coherent jurisprudence of the two courts. With the declaration and protocol relating to Article 6(2) TEU of the Lisbon Treaty, stressing that 'specific features of EU law have to be preserved' the EU expresses the expectation that human rights will have to be interpreted in the EU context by the ECtHR, as the ECJ did in the past. A clash of different interests is foreseeable: the ECtHR would want to apply closer scrutiny to the EU's human rights standards and the EU would want its specific features to be taken into account, i.e. maintaining its economic objectives. It has to be remembered though that the ECtHR can only establish violations of the ECHR and cannot rule on the general validity or interpretation of the laws of the Contracting Parties. As the ECJ still remains the only court competent to judge on the interpretation of EC law, while the ECtHR can only decide on violations of the ECHR, the concern about the EU's loss of autonomy is not entirely justified.[249]

What still needs to be addressed though is the question of which protocols of the ECHR the EU should accede to and whether it should make reservations to the ECHR or the protocols as well as the modalities of participation by the EU in the decision-making structures of the ECHR, e.g., the representation of the EU in the Committee of Ministers, status and participation in the ECtHR of an EU judge, and the standing of the EU in proceedings before the ECtHR. It does not look like the already complex system will become any less complex with the EU's accession to the ECHR.

2.8.4 CFSP and JHA under the Treaty of Lisbon

The rules regarding foreign and security policy, which are set out in Article 2(4) TFEU did not undergo significant change. More detailed rules concerning the CFSP are set out in Title V TEU, Article 24 TEU providing that the CFSP is subject to specific rules and procedures defined and implemented by the European Council and the Council acting unanimously, except where the treaties provide otherwise; and that the adoption of legislative acts is excluded.[250]

The ECJ continues to be largely prevented from reviewing CFSP but does have jurisdiction in relation to Article 40 TEU, which ensures that exercise of CFSP powers does not impinge on the general competences of the EU, and vice versa; the ECJ also has jurisdiction under Article 275 TFEU to review the legality of decisions imposing restrictive measures on natural or legal persons adopted by the Council under Chapter 2 of Title V TEU.

The provisions on JHA have been largely incorporated into the TFEU, JHA is moved from the TEU and merged with the provisions of what was Title IV TEC, dealing with immigration, asylum and civil law, now form a new Title V TFEU called 'Area of Freedom, Security and Justice'. The old Article 35 TEU, which limited the ECJ's jurisdiction under the third pillar, is repealed by the Treaty of Lisbon with the exception of Article 276 TFEU (preliminary ruling procedure), which continues to exclude the ECJ from reviewing the validity or proportionality of operations carried out by the police or other law-enforcement services of a Member State. Clearly this is an area that Member States want to be able to control and therefore any interference of the ECJ is precluded.

Finally, an important change, which is not specifically related to human rights, is the creation of the new post of High Representative of the EU for Foreign Affairs and Security Policy and External Action Service who will coordinate and promote the CFSP of the EU (Article 18 TEU). The High Representative will be appointed by the European Council and approved by the President of the Commission. The holder of this position will not only carry out tasks which are currently carried out by the High Representative on CFSP, but he/she will also be Vice President of the Commission and as a member of the Commission be responsible for external relations and the European neighbourhood policy. By merging these two functions, the EU's foreign policy will become more consistent as its external action as a whole will be managed by one office holder and thereby do without the division of foreign policy under the first pillar, conducted by the Commission, and under the second pillar, conducted at intergovernmental level.

2.8.5 The FRA

The idea of an EU Human Rights Agency arose already in the 1990s but it was only in 2003 that representatives of the Member States announced their intent to establish such an agency. The FRA has been officially operational since March 2007 but is still in a transitional period as of 2009. Its role and functions are set out in the Founding Regulation168/2007.[251] FRA took over the monitoring tasks of the network of independent fundamental rights experts (see above) while at the same time it is supposed to be the 'National' Human Rights Institution (NHRI) of the EU.[252] As FRA cannot deliver legally binding decisions, neither do individual violations of human rights fall within its ambit of responsibility, it is, legally speaking, a rather weak institution.

In the initial Commission proposal on the function of the FRA, the FRA was entirely excluded from commenting on proposals or opinions delivered in the context of the legislative process of the EU.[253] However, Article 4(2) of the Founding Regulation now provides for a certain limited role in commenting on concrete legislative developments at EU level. The Commission proposal also included that the FRA would be empowered to pursue activities in the area of police and judicial cooperation in criminal matters, but such an extension of the FRA's competences did not find consensus in the Council.

According to Article 2 of the Founding Regulation the FRA's objective is to provide assistance and expertise in the field of fundamental rights to bodies of the EC as well as to Member States. However, with regard to Member States, the Agency can only act when the Member States are 'implementing Community law'. The preamble of the Founding Regulation at paragraph 4 indicates that the FRA is also involved in *actively promoting* fundamental rights stipulating that developing 'effective' institutions for the protection 'and promotion' of human rights is a common value of European societies. Hence, the FRA should not only monitor the implementation and enforcement of existing EU legislation, but should also identify areas where improvements are necessary.[254]

The Founding Regulation identifies in its Article 4(1)(a)–(g) eight tasks that the Agency is set to fulfil, which can be subsumed under three major functions, such as data collection in the field of human rights, the production of expert opinions for the EU and the Member States, and the establishment of a communication strategy. When it comes to the formulation of expert opinions on human rights issues in the context of the legislation process in the EU, the FRA can only act on request by the EU institution concerned. This dependency is a crucial limitation of the FRA's function, but it is hoped that institutional practice might show that there is a margin of appreciation for the FRA in deciding whether to comment on certain legislative processes on its own initiative.[255]

The role of the FRA is also detailed in its so-called Multi Annual Framework (MAF), which is adopted by the Council, acting on a proposal from the Commission and after consulting the EP. The EP, however, when expressing its opinion on the draft MAF, argued for the inclusion of a flexibility clause that would enable the FRA to undertake tasks in thematic areas that are not covered by the MAF, 'where there are exceptional and compelling circumstances'.[256] This clause was not taken up by the Council but the first MAF offers considerable room of manoeuvre for the FRA since it defines the thematic areas in very broad terms. Apart from the permanent thematic area ('racism, xenophobia and related intolerance') it also includes the fight against discrimination based on the elements listed in Article 13 TEC (now Article 19 TFEU), interestingly including also discrimination of 'persons belonging to minorities'.

The mandate of the FRA is clearly much broader than that of the EUMC; however, the same problems which the EUMC faced with regards to enforcement still remain. In the context of the legislation process FRA can only give expert opinions when being asked to do so by the relevant institution; the same is true with regards to monitoring human rights compliance in Member States. Hence, it remains to be seen how influential the FRA will become in mainstreaming and monitoring human rights within the EU and how much it will be able to accomplish on its own initiative.

As regards the relationship with the CoE, on 18 June 2008, the EC and the CoE signed an agreement establishing a comprehensive cooperation framework concerning the Fundamental Rights Agency and the CoE. The agreement includes provisions on the organisation of regular meetings, exchange of information and coordination of activities. It provides for the appointment by the CoE of two independent persons to sit on the Management and Executive Boards of the FRA as member and deputy member and, sets out the CoE's voting rights in these organs. This development has to be welcomed, in particular with regard to the imminent accession of the EU to the ECHR.[257]

2.9 Conclusion

This chapter has shown how human rights over the years have acquired a central position in European law and policies. The EU developed from an economic project in the 1950s with a limited mandate to a very complex supranational institution that has become involved in a variety of issues. In response to global developments, its constitutionalisation process has placed human rights at the centre of European integration as the end of the Cold War led to the inclusion of more than purely economic issues into the mandate of the EU. JHA as well as a CFSP were two major novelties in EU law that also led to significant institutional changes. The role of human rights, which already found their way into EC law through the jurisprudence of the ECJ in the 1960s is now proclaimed to be an established part of the *modus operandi* of the EU. However, human rights scrutiny in the EU is not just judicial scrutiny; different actors – Council, Commission, the EP and the ECJ – have influenced human rights issues at EU level, which led to multi-layered and multifaceted governance, combining legislative, executive and judicial powers in the area of human rights, including policy making, mainstreaming or monitoring. A wide range of instruments such as guidelines on priority thematic issues (death penalty, torture, human rights defenders, child soldiers, rights of the child, etc.), public declarations, démarches on individual cases of human rights violations, dialogues or consultations with third countries, Common Positions and EC instruments for financing civil society projects (such as EIDHR) are all tools available to the EU for promoting human rights.

Its mainstreaming strategy is illustrated by the practice of systematically taking human rights into account internally through impact assessments, and by integrating clauses on human rights and core labour standards into EC negotiations and EU agreements in its external operations (e.g. the Cotonou Agreement, ENP and as GSP+). The EU's economic resources and its considerable market capacity help to ensure that developing countries feel pressured to abide by the human rights standards and give the EU more leverage than other human rights organisations. Even though many of these external developments in the EU's role in human rights protection were motivated by economic considerations, they nevertheless brought the EU's human rights profile to the world's attention. The increase in external human rights presence is also illustrated in the enlargement context and the Copenhagen criteria for accession, which will be discussed in the following chapter.

Finally, the ECJ's more recent decisions, such as *Schmidberger* or *Omega Spielhallen* show that the ECJ has changed its original approach of favouring economic freedoms over human rights, and acknowledged that economic freedoms are conditioned by human rights.[258] In light of the overall developments at EU level, such as the creation of the Charter on Fundamental Rights, the FRA, the CFSP Representative for Human Rights and the increased reference to human rights in the EU's external relations, this change of direction by the ECJ is not surprising. In addition, the ECJ accords more importance to the ECHR and 'is in a mood of convergence' with the case law of the Strasbourg Court.[259]

3 The Common Foreign and Security Policy as an instrument of human rights policy

3.1 Introduction

The foreign policy of the European Union (EU) is a process of integrating policies and actions of Member States towards the outside world. It is based on the need to protect and defend the common interests of the Member States abroad and to respond adequately to global demands by coordinating their common bodies. The fact that most foreign policy theories or concepts are based on state sovereignty by individual states means that common foreign policy of a group of states is so unorthodox in international relations that it defies traditional political science theory. For this reason, some have dismissed the EU as ineffective in harmonising common policies and as irrelevant to the foreign policy of the individual European states and to international relations.[1]

Foreign policy is that area of EU intergovernmental activity which is concerned with relationships between the Member States and other actors, particularly other states or 'third countries', in the international system. Foreign policy can also entail the use of economic instruments, but its aims are explicitly political or security related.[2]

Human rights became integrated in the TEU at the same time as the Common Foreign and Security Policy (CFSP) with the Treaty of Maastricht and were further consolidated with the Treaties of Amsterdam, Nice and Lisbon. While the end of the Cold War ushered the EU's expansion in competencies, other regional organisations such as the Council of Europe (CoE) and the Conference/Organization of Security and Cooperation in Europe (CSCE/OSCE) underwent similar important changes, leading to an overlap of tasks and responsibilities with the EU, which necessitates an analysis of their cooperation.

The chapter begins with a synopsis of the development of the EU's foreign policy from the 1970s up to the Treaty of Amsterdam (ToA) in 1999 and then examines why the EU gives expression to its concern over human rights (and sometimes minority rights) in third countries and how it interacts in cooperation with other international organisations within the framework of the CFSP.

3.2 The progression of CFSP in the EU

Foreign policy is an area of great symbolic value for the Member States of the EU, with each nation trying very hard to maintain an outward appearance of sovereign control over foreign policy. The rapprochement of EU Member States in this area has always been an extremely complicated exercise. Starting from 1970, it was dealt with in the framework of European Political Cooperation (EPC), which was based on traditional diplomatic mechanisms operating outside the European Community (EC) institutions.

During the 1970s and 1980s, however, Member States multiplied their common diplomatic declarations, but without producing any notable concrete results. The influence of the EC in the important conflicts of that period – armament negotiations with the Soviet Union, the Middle East peace process, American military action in Central America or the survival of the apartheid regime in South Africa – was extremely weak.

The more ambitious CFSP of the 1992 Treaty of Maastricht, which replaced the old EPC, had increased expectations of a strengthened performance in foreign policy. What had previously been a relatively modest attempt to coordinate the foreign policies of the Member States within the EPC was supposed to develop into a *common* foreign policy for the new EU in the 1990s.

Under the Maastricht Treaty CSFP became the so-called 'second pillar' of the general framework of the EU. The pillared structure designated the CFSP as an intergovernmental sphere of activity as a compromise between contrasting ambitions of the Member States, which means that CFSP remains outside EC policy with its particular mechanisms and decision-making processes.

Its provisions envisaged a reinforcement and expansion of political cooperation; however, the decision-making mechanisms remained essentially unchanged: the European Council was invested with the power of defining guidelines for the CFSP, thus ensuring an intergovernmental approach to foreign policy making which satisfied those Member States that were determined to preserve national influence over foreign policy.

The end of the Cold War provided a unique opportunity to push the EU's political cooperation forward, via its new CFSP and also through coordination in international organisations. However, the major obstacle to the formation of a common policy and a solution to the conflict in the former Yugoslavia was precisely the heterogeneity of perceptions and responses of the Member States to the crisis. It was ironic that the crisis initially appeared to offer an opportunity for the EU to demonstrate its new-found unity but it soon became apparent that this conflict was beyond the means of the Union since the Member States had different interests in the region. During the subsequent crisis in Rwanda in 1994 and in 1996 in the Great Lakes Region the EU adopted a similarly passive policy.

While the period of opportunity to forge an ambitious foreign and defence identity existed prior to Maastricht, the subsequent period did not necessarily reinforce the political will of the Member States to make the system work, and the ToA of 1997 became more an exercise in institutional fine-tuning rather than substantive reform. Despite declarations to the contrary, still, there is no consistency between the fact that albeit being an economic power today, the EU continues to be weak in political terms; its role is too often confined to financing decisions taken by others. The situation in Afghanistan after 9/11 offered another opportunity for the EU to prove its unity and the functioning of its CFSP as a peace power but it did not fully use its potential; while during the 2003 intervention in Iraq the EU was deeply divided.[3]

3.3 Why human rights in CFSP?

Before the Treaty of Lisbon, the EU had not declared that it is conducting foreign policy with an ethical dimension, but it repeatedly stressed respect for human rights as an important objective of its relations with third countries in the context of development aid.[4] Since 1995, agreements with third countries are to contain a 'human rights clause', which allows for measures to be taken if human rights and democratic principles are violated by the parties to the agreement.[5] The offer of trade and association agreements, technical and development assistance, political dialogue and other instruments is now made conditional on respect for human rights and democratic principles. The 'universality' of these conditions suggests that these are not just EU-specific values, but reflect widely accepted principles, indeed the EU justifies this stance by explicit reference to universal instruments, in particular the United Nations Declaration on Human Rights (UNDHR).[6]

Today human rights are considered to be at the heart of Western society, respect for human dignity is written into the founding documents of nearly every nation and human rights have become an object of international legal standards. In particular the post-Cold War environment was conducive to the expression of so-called 'milieu goals' such as the promotion of human rights or the protection of the environment whereby the protection of human rights has become a socio-political norm of the second half of the twentieth century, i.e. it is more or less expected of every public authority that they include the promotion of human rights in their agendas. As foreign policy needs conviction, consistency and public support, an international actor who wants to be a credible international actor cannot do so without being committed to human rights.

Realists would claim that the consideration of human rights is used for masking other interests. Carr argued that so-called universal principles are really the 'unconscious reflections of national policy based on a particular interpretation of national interests at a particular time'.[7] As aid budgets decrease, violations of human rights – however defined – could provide an excuse to cut off aid to strategically or commercially unimportant states. Or, considerations of human rights and democratic principles could merely mask the objective of forcing states to undertake economic and good governance reforms, which would benefit Western investors.[8] However, the use of CFSP in the human rights field has duly expanded over the years as Member States, despite often being divided on foreign policy issues, have recognised its advantages.

One of the reasons why Member States engaged CFSP can be seen in the benefit of the 'politics of scale'. The notion of 'politics of scale' refers to the advantages of collective over unilateral action in the conduct of civilian foreign policy. It enables members to conduct joint foreign policy actions at lower costs and risks than when they act on their own.[9] The use of CFSP instruments compared to national foreign policy instruments has a considerably greater impact if undertaken by a group of 27 states instead of one Member State acting on its own. This is especially apparent in the context of the United Nations (UN), where the EU acts as a group. As a result, considerable attention is paid to the interventions made by the Presidency on behalf of the EU, and most countries are concerned about the way in which they will be mentioned in the EU's declaration on the worldwide human rights situation. Significant lobbying takes place to ensure inclusion or exclusion of country references in the EU statements.

Similarly, sanctions will have a greater impact if they are undertaken by the EU rather than on a national level. Furthermore, the EU has more foreign policy instruments at its disposal than an individual Member State, especially the conduct of a regular political dialogue/human rights dialogues with third countries could not be done with the same frequency and with the same effect at the national level, particularly not by the smaller states, since Member States found it increasingly difficult to maintain viable diplomatic and military capacities in an era of post-Cold War budget cuts.[10] In addition, states sometimes prefer to hide behind the façade of CFSP in order to prevent criticism or countermeasures from abroad.[11] In other words, the political costs are lower if concerted action can be taken by several states at once.

Contrariwise, a clear disadvantage of CFSP as a framework for the protection and promotion of human rights is that most Member States' positions are watered down in order to find a consensus on the lowest common denominator. As a consequence, no action will be undertaken if one or more Member States oppose it due to its particular economic or political interests. In this context the EU has been criticised for the almost automatic priority given to economic interests over respect for human rights in international trade, as pointed out by the European Parliament (EP) against the background of enlargement:

> Community policy has focused largely on the economic liberalisation of Eastern European countries and the lion's share of resources have also been devoted to this. Little regard has been given to the social rights of individuals within these states. The culture of Communism, which ensured theoretic equality and employment for all, was overnight replaced by the competitiveness of an open economy. The Community must take into consideration the social rights of citizens when formulating policy. It is no good to wave the banner of human rights when primary concerns are economic and trade possibilities.[12]

The in chapter 2 discussed human rights clauses, which have been included in every post-1995 agreement with third countries, have been applied variably. Cooperation agreements with 'important countries' such as Canada, China, the countries of the Association of South East Asian States (ASEAN) which have been concluded pre-1995 were not renegotiated to include the human rights clause. In fact, in 1997 when the EU and Australia halted negotiations on a framework cooperation agreement because Australia refused to agree to the human rights clause, a less formal joint declaration was signed instead. The same scenario repeated itself in negotiations with New Zealand. Also, human rights violations in countries such as Russia,[13] the USA, China or Pakistan[14] are treated much more benevolently.[15] This is a common dilemma: political (strategic) and economic considerations outweigh human rights considerations. This inconsistency in the EU's human rights policy questions the credibility of the EU's efforts to become a genuine defender of human rights in foreign policy, which the EU tried to forge since Maastricht, and makes the EU rather look like a realist actor. Human rights policy has repeatedly been determined by the reaction of the impugned state and human rights considerations have affected different states – important or unimportant – differently.[16] It should also be kept in mind that some human rights démarches – mainly those regarding the USA – remain secret. Consequently, it is very difficult to assess to what extent the EU's human rights policy is really unbalanced.

In the Communication from the Commission entitled 'The European Union's Role in Promoting Human Rights and Democratisation in Third Countries'[17] the Commission required the EU to:

> promote coherent and consistent policies in support of human rights and democratization. This applies both to coherence between European Community policies, and between those policies and other EU action, especially the Common Foreign and Security Policy. It also relates to the promotion of consistent and complementary action by the EU and Member States, in particular in the promotion and mainstreaming of human rights through development and other official assistance ... To promote human rights and democratisation objectives in external relations, the EU draws on a wide-range of instruments ... These tools should be used in a coherent manner, to achieve synergy and consistency and to ensure maximum effective use of resources to promote sustainable development and respect for human rights and democratisation world-wide.[18]

In its Action Points in Annex 2 of the same Communication, the Commission required to 'promote greater consistency and coherence between the European Community, other European Union and Member State activities, to work for a transparent approach to human rights and democratisation, which is coherent and consistent between countries and regions and avoids double standards and makes use of all available instruments'. The previous chapter described the numerous initiatives undertaken by different players at EU level not to let these declarations remain meaningless, but the reproach of double standards still exists.

Another criticism concerns the lack of comprehensiveness of the EU's human rights policy, since no clear criteria have been established to determine when action under CFSP should be taken and what instruments should be used for human rights purposes. No provision in the Treaty defines situations in which specific CFSP measures can or even 'must' be used. Since CFSP is exercised by the Council and not by the Commission, and cannot be reviewed by the ECJ, guidelines on human rights issues and the good practice of CFSP instruments in this area are necessary. It has to be conceded that every situation involves different political considerations and requires individual treatment, but it has been suggested that a 'human rights catalogue' or 'a code of conduct for the EU's promotion of human rights in its foreign policy' would be desirable. A catalogue could provide guidelines for the formulation of the EU's foreign policies and enhance the consistency when including human rights in the development of these policies. It could even be argued that a catalogue of human rights would have more 'added value' when applied in the framework of the CFSP instead of only applying to the Community's internal order.[19] Despite the fact that CFSP has a legal basis in the TEU, it remains a political instrument of the EU, hence, the question when and if joint action in the framework of CFSP is taken, is a political decision; the creation of a 'human rights catalogue' for CFSP therefore appears unrealistic. Also, it has to be remembered that the TEU's provisions on CFSP established a *framework* within which the Member States would be able to create a CFSP but did not create a common policy for the EU as such.

As the effectiveness of CFSP mainly depends on the Member States' political will, rather than on the CFSP framework and other legal provisions, CFSP cannot always live up to its declarations of promoting human rights and the universal principles laid down in the UN Charter, but can be seen as driven by realism in its policy choices. Despite the fact that all Member States recognise that an effective EU will always exert more power and influence than any one of them could individually, there is little appreciation of how irreconcilable the maintenance of national authority in foreign policy is with a *common* foreign policy. It is certainly not easy to define interests common to all 27 Member States in this particular policy area, but a relatively new approach to improve the EU's efficiency in CFSP, which has gained momentum in the recent years, is the cooperation with other international institutions (discussed at section 3.7, below).

3.4 The legal basis for human rights under the treaties

Before assessing the EU's current human rights policy in foreign relations and the reasons behind it, the legal basis for human rights in CFSP will briefly be outlined.

During the greatest part of EPC the protection of human rights was based on non-binding documents, under the Single European Act (SEA) of 1987 it was given a weak legal basis in its preamble:

> Aware of the responsibilities incumbent upon Europe to speak increasingly with one voice ... in particular to display the principles of democracy and compliance with the law and human rights to which they are attached.

Since the commitments made by the Member States regarding human rights under the SEA solely appeared in the preamble, they were more political than legal in nature.

Under the Treaty of Maastricht of 1992 the legal basis for the promotion and protection of human rights in the framework of CFSP was contained in Article J.1 (2) (renumbered Article 11(1) TEU), which defines the principles and objectives of CFSP:

> The Union shall define and implement a common foreign and security policy covering all areas of foreign and security policy, the objectives of which shall be:
>
> a. to safeguard the common values, fundamental interests, independence and integrity of the Union in conformity with the principles of the United Nations Charter;
> b. to strengthen the security of the Union in all ways;
> c. to preserve peace and strengthen international security, *in accordance with the principles of the United Nations Charter, as well as the principles of the Helsinki Final Act and the objectives of the Paris Charter, including those on external borders;*
> d. to promote international co-operation;
> e. to develop and consolidate democracy and the rule of law, and respect for human rights and fundamental freedoms. [emphasis added]

In addition, Article 6 TEU which is also applicable to CFSP, declares that the EU is founded on the principles of liberty, democracy, respect for human rights and fundamental freedoms, and the rule of law.

However, under the Treaty of Lisbon, the former Article 11 TEU has not been retained. Under the Treaty of Lisbon, Article 21 on the general provisions on the EU's external action declares:

> The Union's action on the international scene shall be guided by the principles which have inspired its own creation, development and enlargement, and which it seeks to advance in the wider world: democracy, the rule of law, the universality and indivisibility of human rights and fundamental freedoms, respect for human dignity, the principles of equality and solidarity, and respect for the principles of the United Nations Charter and international law. The Union shall seek to develop relations and build partnerships with third countries, and international, regional or global organisations which share the principles referred to in the first subparagraph. It shall promote multilateral solutions to common problems, in particular in the framework of the United Nations.

This provision constitutes a very far-reaching commitment to a number of human rights-related principles such as 'universality and indivisibility of human rights and fundamental freedoms, respect for human dignity, the principles of equality' etc. Furthermore, it is pointed out that these principles have inspired its own development and enlargement which the Union now seeks to promote worldwide. None of the preceding treaties has ever been so clear on this change in the Union's objectives, from the advancement of economic development within Europe to the worldwide promotion of human rights. At earlier times this high rhetoric on human rights has been sharply criticised as not being based on genuine concern to take human rights seriously but rather on the desire to extend the scope and impact of EC law which lacks legitimacy.[20] However, today there is hardly any doubt that in recent years the significance of human rights in the EU has increased considerably; not only because Member States and EU institutions renewed calls for more accountability, transparency and legitimacy, but also the fact that respect for human rights is nowadays seen as an indispensable 'yardstick in assessing a polity's democratic credentials'.[21]

3.5 The recognition of Eastern European countries and the first appearance of minority rights in CFSP

In 1991 the EC convened a Peace Conference on Yugoslavia following the eruption of civil war in the Socialist Federal Republic of Yugoslavia (SFRY). An Arbitration Commission, the so-called Badinter Commission,[22] was set up by the Conference as a body to which the 'relevant authorities will submit their differences'. The Commission had to consider questions concerning the extinction of the SFRY and succession to its rights and obligations of newly formed states. Minority issues were the key to human rights abuses in the Yugoslav war, triggered by Slovene and Croatian independence movements in 1991. Post-1945 Yugoslavia had six republics (Serbia, Croatia, Slovenia, Bosnia-Herzegovina, Macedonia, Montenegro) in a federal relationship, plus two autonomous regions within Serbia, each of them intended to safeguard minority rights, for Albanians in Kosovo and Hungarians in Vojvodina. This situation provided a fertile breeding ground for conflict among the different ethnic groups after the breakdown of the communist regime, which had held these different groups together by dictatorial rule.

The EC adopted the 'EC – Guidelines on the Recognition of New States in Eastern Europe and in the Soviet Union'.[23] With a view to elaborating an approach regarding relations with the new states in Eastern Europe and in the Soviet Union, these guidelines start from reaffirming the principles of the Helsinki Act of 1975 and the Charter of Paris of 1990, in particular the principle of self-determination.

Specific requirements laid down in the EC Guidelines for recognition and the establishment of diplomatic relations are:

> The Community and its Member States confirm their attachment to the principles of the Helsinki Final Act and the Charter of Paris, in particular the principle of self-determination. They affirm their readiness to recognise, subject to the normal standards of international practice and the political

realities in each case, those new States which, following the historic changes in the region, have constituted themselves on a democratic basis, have accepted the appropriate international obligations and have committed themselves in good faith to a peaceful process and to negotiations. Therefore they adopt a Common Position on the process of recognition of these new states, which requires:

a. Respect for the provisions of the Charter of the United Nations and the commitments subscribed to in the Final Act of Helsinki and in the Charter of Paris, especially with regard to the rule of law, democracy and human rights,
b. Guarantees for the rights of ethnic and national groups and minorities in accordance with the commitments subscribed to in the framework of the CSCE,
c. Respect for the inviolability of all frontiers which can only be changed by peaceful means and by common agreement,
d. Acceptance of all relevant commitments with regard to disarmament and nuclear non-proliferation as well as to security and regional stability,
e. Commitment to settle by agreement, including where appropriate by recourse to arbitration, all questions concerning state succession and regional disputes.

Apart from the 'classic' criteria for friendly relationships between states, such as the inviolability of frontiers and the commitment to refrain from using force, the EC stressed the importance of human rights, the rule of law and democratic principles, *including the protection of minorities*. In its Opinion No. 1[24] the Commission emphasised that the – now peremptory – norms of international law require states to ensure respect for the rights of minorities. In its Opinion No. 2[25] the Commission spelled out that 'where there are one or more groups within a state constituting one or more ethnic, religious or language communities, they have the right to recognition of their identity'. The inclusion of the protection of minorities reflected the 'lessons learned' from the Yugoslav war, and in addition the striving for peace on the European continent. However, the humanitarian concern, to put an end to ethnic cleansing and to protect persecuted minorities, was also accompanied by a more self-interested concern, namely the fear of the Western European countries that escalating ethnic violence would lead to large-scale refugee movements into Western Europe, which indeed took place in the case of Bosnia and Kosovo.[26]

The Badinter Commission changed international law on the recognition of states, the four formal criteria for the recognition of statehood 'permanent population, defined territory, government and a capacity to enter into relations with other states' were not considered sufficient by the Badinter Commission for the former Yugoslavia. The EC Member States declared in the Guidelines that recognition of new states be 'subject to the normal standards of international practice and the political realities in each case'. Recognition of states has thus become more of an optional and discretionary political act. The protection of minorities had never been an aspect in the state practice of the recognition of states, but several decades of relatively consistent state practice in the decolonisation period had been overtaken by the events in Eastern Europe.[27]

Applying the guidelines of the Badinter Commission, the EC and its Member States recognised 11 of the 15 republics of the former USSR as states; the three Baltic States of Estonia, Latvia and Lithuania were recognised before the Guidelines were adopted. At the Luxembourg Council of 1991 the European Council exposed its position on the close relationship between social and political transition, democratic stability and minority rights when it stated:

> The protection of minorities is ensured in the first place by the effective establishment of democracy. The European Council recalls the fundamental nature of the principle of non-discrimination. It stresses the need to protect human rights *whether or not the persons concerned belong to minorities*. The European Council reiterates the importance of cultural identity as well as rights enjoyed by members of minorities which such persons should be able to exercise in common with other members of their group. Respect of this principle will favour political, social and economic development.[28][emphasis added]

Also, at the Council meeting in May 1992, a declaration on the relationship between the EC and CSCE Member States was proclaimed, stating that 'respect for democratic principles, as set out in the Helsinki Final Act of 1975 and the Paris Charter for a new Europe … constitute an *essential element* of agreements between the EC and its CSCE Partners'.[29] Both documents, the Helsinki Final Act and the Paris Charter contain references to the protection of minorities.

In continuation of this policy the EU approached the human rights issue at the Council meeting in Copenhagen in 1993,[30] after the Eastern European countries had applied for EU membership. The Member States created a framework for EU enlargement by spelling out the principle of conditionality based on three crucial requirements for accession, which are referred to as the 'Copenhagen Criteria'.

According to these Criteria, membership requires that the candidate country:

a. Has achieved stability of institutions guaranteeing democracy, the rule of law, human rights, and *respect for and protection of minorities*,
b. The existence of a functioning market economy as well as the capacity to cope with competitive pressures and market forces within the Union, and
c. Has the ability to take on the obligations of membership (*acquis communautaire*), including adherence to the aims of political, economic and monetary Union. [emphasis added]

Human rights, democracy, the rule of law and the protection of minorities were put at the top of the selection criteria in accordance with the growing importance of these issues in international law. In 1993 it was relatively new for the EU to address minority rights directly, drawing inspiration from texts agreed on in the framework of the UN, the CSCE and the CoE and to use them as a condition for accession. This was a surprising step since so far the EU has shown little commitment on this issue within its own borders (assessed in more detail in the next chapter).

With regard to the applicant states in the western Balkans (third-wave applicants), the EU revised its conditionality policy. The so-called second-generation conditionality (or SAP – stabilisation and association process) was proclaimed in the 'Council Conclusions on the Application of Conditionality with a view to developing a Coherent EU – Strategy for the Relations with the Countries in the Region'[31] which applies to current applicant states and those aspiring to applicant status, i.e. Bosnia and Herzegovina, Croatia, the Federal Republic of Yugoslavia (FRY), the former Yugoslav Republic of Macedonia (FYROM), Turkey and Albania. Unlike the Copenhagen Criteria, a graduated approach is being applied, which requires the fulfilment of a schedule for the application of conditions to different levels of relations and cooperation, i.e. different conditions are applied to different countries. In the annex to the Conclusions, the fulfilment of a number of criteria is expected equally from all countries (elements for the examination of compliance with), which includes among other issues, the 'respect for and protection of minorities'. Under this sub-heading the following specifications are spelled out:

- the right to establish and maintain their own educational, cultural and religious institutions, organisations or associations;
- adequate opportunities for these minorities to use their own language before courts and public authorities; and
- adequate protection of refugees and displaced persons returning to areas where they represent an ethnic minority.

Considering that the Copenhagen Criteria gave no further explanation as to what the protection of minorities entails and what standards will be applied in assessing compliance, the SAP conditionality is a huge improvement as it spells out clearly a number of specific minority rights albeit at a very basic level and without referring to other international standards of minority protection.

The monitoring procedure of applicant countries by the European Commission required a regular analysis of the state of legislation in candidate countries, against the background of the Copenhagen Criteria. In the annual Regular Reports and in the Accession Partnerships minority rights were evaluated in the framework of individual human rights, focusing on the social integration of minorities (especially the Roma) and on the implementation of anti-discrimination legislation and policies in candidate states.[32] Under the EU's foreign policy strategy, and in light of the crisis in Yugoslavia, fostering the improvement of minority protection in Central Eastern European countries (CEECs) became one of the more substantial elements in the EU's external policy on 'conflict prevention' from the early 1990s onwards.[33]

3.6 CFSP and the enlargement process

Enlargement of the EU is, in itself, a form of EU foreign policy. It puts the EU in a position to shape large parts of applicant states' domestic and foreign policies. Despite the fact that it was only officially put on the EU's agenda at the Copenhagen Council summit in 1993, the issue of enlargement became predominant in the EU's policies towards CEECs immediately after the end of the Cold War. Although the Eastern European applicant countries were third countries when they applied for membership and thus the object of foreign policy, the EU's enlargement policy was entrusted to EC bodies (the Commission), while foreign policy was otherwise conducted at intergovernmental level, i.e. in the framework of the CFSP. The EU's policy towards Eastern Europe has overcome the Member States' differences that normally exist in foreign policy and has unanimously decided on the enlargement to Eastern Europe, finalised by the Irish referendum on the Nice Treaty, so that the end result of this policy turned the former 'objects' of EU foreign policy into EU Member States.

The EU's enlargement to the East posed challenges to the CSFP, on the one hand, raising questions about the CFSP's ability to function effectively and, on the other hand, by redefining the EU's borders, new issues and new tasks will fall into the scope of the CFSP, such as, e.g. minority issues. A pure rationality approach[34] is inappropriate for explaining EU enlargement to the emerging democracies in the East, which might be explained with arguments other than material gain. In particular the sense of community, the EU's foundation myth of a shared past, the maintenance of peace and being a community of values are arguments that have to be taken into account. Enlargement is designed to foster security and democracy among its members based on shared principles and values. Karen Smith suggests that Eastern Europe is a special case where the production of a common policy with supranational elements was feasible due to Eastern Europe's geographic proximity, the sense of shared history between Eastern and Western Europe and a belief that the EU has a particular responsibility towards Central and Eastern Europe.[35]

3.6.1 Why enlarge to the East?

What are the reasons that caused the Western European Member States to share their wealth with the economically underdeveloped Eastern European States? There seems to be general agreement that the increased trade with the applicant states that will result from enlargement will be beneficial to the EU economy and strengthen its competitiveness in the long run. However, most studies of enlargement have come to the conclusion that the economic cost of enlargement will outweigh the gains in the short to medium term.[36] Substantial investment is required from the EU in order to prepare the applicant countries for accession and some of the old Member States had to accept cuts in their subsidies from the EU.

Economic cost has been used as an argument for delaying the enlargement process but not for abandoning the idea of enlargement. Most feared is the influx of people from the poorer Eastern into the richer Western countries, particularly in countries that have borders with the Eastern states, such as Germany, Italy and Austria. Furthermore, given the setbacks in terms of security in the Balkans, these could easily spill over into the new Member States and thereby become a problem of the EU.

Realist assumptions of egotism, as well as rationality are unable to explain the EU's policy on enlargement. According to Habermas' theory of communicative action, actors are rational when they are able to justify and explain their actions and not only when they seek to maximise their own interests. These reasons could be material gain, but they could also be formulated with reference to an actor's sense of identity or understanding of the 'good life'.[37] This is a different notion of rationality than the one put forward by realist concepts. This sense of identity can be found in Europe's history that is shared between the 'East' and the 'West'.

Furthermore, it has to be considered how the EU defines its self-interest and what beliefs and values it takes into account. Arnold Wolfers argues that states sometimes pursue policies of 'self-abnegation'. For Wolfers self-abnegation is the goal of those who place a higher value on such ends as international solidarity, lawfulness, rectitude, or peace than they place even on national security and self-preservation'.[38] With the EU's endeavours to include principles that go beyond economic integration in its foreign policy as well as in its internal policies it does not necessarily show 'self-abnegation' but certainly its commitment to achieve higher values such as peace and international solidarity, which effectively is the whole idea behind the new EU.

Keohane's concept of empathetic interdependence offers another explanation for the EU's behaviour: actors may be interested in the welfare of others for their own sake, even if this has no effect on their own material well-being or security. The parties involved are assumed to have similar values. Benefits have to be regarded as beneficial to both sides (the EU and the applicant countries), otherwise supposed empathy could become a rationale for domination, as in the ideology of 'the white man's burden', which justified much nineteenth-century imperialism.[39] The reference to particular values of a community, however, has become an important factor in the enlargement policy and its justification. According to Article 49 TEU, membership is open to all European states with a democratic system of governance and the respect for human rights, which is repeated in the Copenhagen Criteria. These values are seen as constitutive of European identity but at the same time rely on universally valid principles. Finally, the conditions can be interpreted as utility enhancing: the more the applicants do for themselves in terms of implementing political and market economic reforms, the less burden they cause the EU.[40]

The enlargement process is influenced by clear political objectives, which can be broadly described as reshaping the political order in Europe. The larger overall value of enlargement lies in the promotion of the EU's strength and influence in international relations. With a larger and more diverse membership, the EU tries to promote its own interests and mission in the world, increasingly independent of US sponsorship, and ridding itself of the notion to be simply an economic project and a 'rich man's club'. Despite the CFSP's failures, in particular in the Balkans, it has contributed to the increasing recognition of the EU as an international actor in its own right.[41] In addition, the enlargement procedure, or even CFSP in general, represents a common effort to reconcile shared experiences of the World Wars, promoting peace and thereby boosting its legitimacy in the eyes of other international actors and its citizens.

The concept of reconciliation in the European context has been analysed by two schools, one focusing on forgiveness rooted in religious thought, the other equating reconciliation with rapprochement and post-conflict negotiation of differences from a more interest-based approach, which shall not be analysed here.[42] Reconciliation points to the dual nature of the EU – as a set of states pursuing material interests while simultaneously committed to the construction of new institutions that mark a break with a destructive past.[43] The historical development of the EU has generated an appreciation of both the pragmatic and moral dimensions of reconciliation as a proven source of security and prosperity and a break with age-old animosities.[44] The concept of economic cooperation for the sake of peace in post-war Europe was one of the founding ideas of the European Coal and Steel Community (ECSC) designed to make war between Germany and France impossible, at the same time it was a contribution to push the economic recovery forward. The peace in Europe for more than 50 years has brought economic prosperity on a continent that was torn by wars for centuries.

Thus, the EU's motivation for enlargement is not only the promotion and strengthening of its own position in the international sphere but also peace and reconciliation in Europe can count for valid objectives of the enlargement process. Apart from a strong interest in addressing the causes of the conflicts in the former Yugoslavia and the Balkans, namely minority claims, another reason linked to the Copenhagen Criteria, was the sense in the West that the ability to protect minorities would be a test of their overall political democratic maturity and readiness to become a Member of the EU as meeting international norms for the protection of minorities is seen as a proof that a country has left behind its 'tribal nationalisms' and is able to join a 'modern and liberal' Europe.[45] However, the EU's enlargement policy included a conditionality approach towards Eastern Europe, which has given rise to much criticism,[46] in particular with regard to the requirement of minority protection, as this requirement was not part of the *acquis* and which was not equally applied to the old Member States (those that joined before 2004).

Having introduced aspects of the EU's enlargement policy and the role of human rights in CFSP, the following section will look at other international organisations and how far they acted as partners with regards to their human rights and minority rights expertise for the EU's activities in these areas.

3.7 CFSP – cooperation with other international institutions

International cooperation is explicitly mentioned in Article 11 TEU (now in Article 21 TEU) as a CFSP objective. After the end of the Cold War the development of cooperation between the EU and other international organisations such as the UN, the North Atlantic Treaty Organization (NATO), the Council of Europe (CoE), and the Conference/Organisation on Security and Cooperation in Europe (CSCE/OSCE) was considered to be necessary but in practice policy coordination between different organisations, with different histories, priorities, and memberships was, and still is, problematic.[47] Not only the EU but also the above-mentioned international organisations have expanded their membership as well as their competences, leading to overlaps in responsibilities. In view of the common goals to maintain peace and stability in Europe, promoting human rights and democracy, cooperation with other international organisations can be an effective tool for the EU and help to increase its influence beyond its borders.

This section looks at cooperation with the CoE and the OSCE as both are regional organisations in Europe, but with mandates that differed considerably from that of the EU when they were first founded; however, due to the opening up of the East and ever more 'interpenetration of tasks', they represent key partners with regards to their human rights and minority rights expertise for the EU's activities in these areas. Apart from cooperation during the enlargement process, the ENP[48] and post-conflict reconstruction in South Eastern Europe have led to close cooperation with the OSCE and the CoE.

The legal basis for the EU's cooperation with other international organisations can be found Article 302 TEC (now Article 220 TFEU under the Treaty of Lisbon) which provides:

1. The Union shall establish all appropriate forms of cooperation with the organs of the United Nations and its specialised agencies, the Council of Europe, the Organisation for Security and Cooperation in Europe and the Organisation for Economic Cooperation and Development. The Union shall also maintain such relations as are appropriate with other international organisations.
2. The High Representative of the Union for Foreign Affairs and Security Policy and the Commission shall be instructed to implement this Article.

It is interesting to note that this provision, dealing with the EU's relations with international organisations is to be found in the TEC/TFEU and not in the TEU, when at the same time it is the High Representative of CFSP who is responsible for its implementation, alongside the Commission. This might be partly due to the fact that pre-Lisbon the EU was unable to enter into legal agreements in the context of CFSP as it lacked legal personality, which has now been remedied by Article 47 TEU, which confers legal personality on the EU. With the creation of the new post of High Representative of the EU for Foreign Affairs and Security Policy and External Action Service under the Treaty of Lisbon, this division of first-pillar competences of the Commission and second-pillar competences at intergovernmental level will be abolished and thereby provide for a more consistent and coherent approach to aspects of CFSP.

3.7.1 Cooperation between the EU and CoE

With regard to the CoE, which has greater expertise in the field of human rights than the EU, closer cooperation between both organisations has developed since the 1980s to include democratic institution building, legal affairs, education, cultural heritage, local government and the protection of national minorities. This broad area of cooperation was the object of exchanges of letters.[49] In the first exchange of letters between the Secretary General of the CoE, the President of the Commission of the European Economic Community and the President of the European Atomic Energy Community the modalities of the relationship between the three institutions were defined.

In 1989 it was decided to set up quadripartite meetings for political dialogue between the EC and the CoE that took place twice yearly between the EU Presidency and the Commission and, the CoE Chairmanship and Secretary General.[50] These meetings became increasingly necessary since, apart from enabling both parties to exchange views on matters of common interest and to identify new areas of cooperation, the meetings also provided an opportunity for both parties to evaluate the advantages of their cooperation as well as avoiding duplication or overlap in their work. The last quadpartite meeting of November 2008 was concerned with the recent conflict in Georgia, and underlined the importance of commitments that Georgia and Russia have undertaken under international law, including their commitments in the CoE, *inter alia*, to respect human rights and the territorial integrity and sovereignty of states. The EU and CoE agreed to consider ways to enhance their cooperation in order to further consolidate the principles and standards of human rights, democracy and the rule of law in the south Caucasus.[51]

In April 2001 another joint declaration was signed by the European Commission and the CoE which, among other things, stated that both organisations henceforth would endeavour to intensify their dialogue with a view to identifying those countries and objectives where joint action will add value to their respective activities. The Declaration also emphasises that respect for human rights and protection of minorities form an important part of the cooperation.[52]

The CoE Summit of May 2005 produced the 'Warsaw Declaration' which deals in its appended Action Plan – Part IV with the cooperation between the CoE, the OSCE and the EU, stressing that the CoE and EU's achievements and future standard setting work should be taken into account in each other's activities and furthermore, to strengthen cooperation with the EU in the field of human rights and other areas of common interest.[53]

On the basis of the appended Guidelines to the Warsaw Declaration and in view of the success of the joint programmes between the CoE and the EU, a Memorandum of Understanding[54] was signed between the EU and the CoE in May 2007, providing thus a new framework for enhanced cooperation and political dialogue between the two organisations. The Memorandum of Understanding provides for the participation of a number of senior CoE officials, including the Commissioner for Human Rights and the Deputy Secretary

General of the CoE, in meetings of Working Groups of the Council of the EU. This high level involvement of CoE officials in the work of the EU Council, can only provide general guidance on human rights policies from the CoE's perspective, however, it is an effective means for avoiding overlap in the work of both organisations. At the (lower) working level it is the joint EU–CoE programmes, where a close relationship between the two organisations exists. The Memorandum of Understanding reaffirmed that the two partners are to reinforce ongoing cooperation in the framework of joint programmes.

3.7.1.1 Joint programmes

The end of the Cold War represented a defining moment in the EU–CoE relationship as the joint-programme format was first initiated in 1989. In the beginning it was intended to facilitate cooperation with countries which had joined the CoE after the fall of the Iron Curtain. Under the auspices of the CoE's Venice Commission, the programmes were designed to strengthen democracy and constitutional development in Central and Eastern Europe. Of course, the EU had a great interest in the development of these countries in view of their (then) future accession, and many countries that were the object of a joined programme developed increasingly close links with the EU, eventually resulting in their membership.

After the accession of ten Eastern European countries to the EU between 2004 and 2007, joint programmes are still the most visible and important instrument of cooperation between the two partners; in 2007–8 there were 39 active joint programmes between the European Commission and the CoE with 11 per cent of these joint programmes addressing human rights issues and a further 51 per cent addressing rule-of-law issues. The European Commission and the CoE provide joint funding for the programme, and the CoE is responsible for its implementation. In most cases funding is shared equally but on some occasions the European Commission has contributed proportionally more resources. A large number of joint programmes have been concluded with the EC's European Initiative for Democracy and Human Rights (EIDHR, see chapter 2, section 2.4.1.1). For geographical assistance programmes, the CoE has benefited from funding under the Instrument for Pre-Accession Assistance (IPA) and the European Neighbourhood Policy Instrument (ENPI, see chapter 2, section 2.6.4). Remarkably, with a total financial envelope of €50,771312 the European Commission's financial contribution represented some 80 per cent of total financing.[55] Apart from country-specific programmes[56] there are also a number of regional and multi lateral thematic joint programmes regarding, for instance, national minorities/ Roma, and in particular on the implementation of the European Charter for Regional and Minority languages.[57]

3.7.1.2 Cooperation with other specialised bodies of the CoE

Part IV as well as Guideline 7 of the Action Plan of the Warsaw Declaration provides for strengthened cooperation between the EU and specialised

CoE bodies, such as the Venice Commission, the Committee for the Prevention of Torture, the European Commission against Racism and Intolerance, and Representatives of the European Commission participate regularly in plenary sessions of the Venice Commission, which aims at providing legal advice on the development and functioning of democratic institutions and constitutional law, especially in Eastern Europe.[58] Clearly, the EU has an interest in promoting democracy in Central Eastern Europe in view of its enlargement process and therefore benefits considerably from the Venice Commission's expertise, and discussions are in progress concerning a formalisation of this cooperation. In the context of closer cooperation between other CoE specialised bodies and the EU, the participation of EU officials/bodies in the deliberations of the advisory board of the FCNM could be envisaged, in order to provide the EU with the necessary expertise on minority rights, which is currently still lacking.

3.7.1.3 The CoE–FRA relationship

The CoE had reservations when the Fundamental Rights Agency (FRA) was newly established as it was concerned that its position as the benchmark for human rights in Europe would be challenged by the FRA; the CoE therefore requested that the FRA's mandate remains limited to human rights issues in the context of EC law to avoid controversy with the human rights activities of the CoE.

Due to the CoE's concerns, an agreement was signed between the Commission and the CoE on 18 June 2008,[59] in relation to the cooperation with the FRA. The Agreement includes provisions on the organisation of regular meetings, exchange of information and coordination of activities. In addition, the Agreement provides for the appointment by the CoE of two independent persons to sit on the FRA's management and executive boards as member and deputy member and sets out the CoE's voting rights in these organs (paragraph 17 of the Agreement). Allowing CoE officials to be part of the FRA's management and executive board are far-reaching provisions that reveal not only an ever-closer relationship between both organisations but also the CoE's recognition of the EU's growing importance in human rights matters in Europe. With regard to using CoE sources and reports as a benchmark or reference for its work, the Agreement provides in paragraph 8 that 'The Agency shall take due account of the judgments and decisions of the European Court of Human Rights concerning the areas of activity of the Agency and, *where relevant*, of findings, reports and activities in the human rights field of the CoE's human rights monitoring and intergovernmental committees, as well as those of the CoE's Commissioner for Human Rights.' The CoE's Commissioner for Human Rights is not further mentioned in the Agreement despite potentially being an important partner for the FRA, who could be involved, in a non-consultative capacity, in the work of FRA's managing bodies.

3.7.1.4 Coordination of legislative initiatives in the human rights field

The CoE involves the EU whenever new conventions are being prepared by inviting representatives of the European Commission to meetings where conventions are being drafted that might affect the EU. This practice of legal cooperation has been emphasised under Guideline 5 of the appendix to the Warsaw Declaration which points out that 'Legal cooperation between the CoE and the EU should continue and be further developed as useful and appropriate ... the EU shall strive to transpose those aspects of CoE Conventions within its competence into European Union Law', which does not only encourage cooperation but also the 'transposition' of CoE conventions into EU law. In the recent past the EU has acted quite contrarily to this provision when it refused to apply the higher standard provided by the CoE Convention on Action against Trafficking in Human Beings[60] to the EU law on trafficking persons and insisted on including a 'disconnection clause' (see Article 40(3) of the Convention) with regard to relations between EU Member States.[61]

At the same time, the CoE is not represented when the EC bodies are preparing EC legislation, or when political and/or legal measures are being planned at EU level.[62] There is, however, no reason why the EU should be deprived of the CoE's legal and human rights expertise, when it is preparing Directives or other political and/or legal measures in the relevant areas, in particular the CoE's experts on, e.g. preventing torture, combating racism, protecting national minorities and human trafficking should participate in a strengthened cooperation. Furthermore, reports, conclusions or recommendations submitted by the Commissioner for Human Rights or other monitoring bodies of the CoE, are already consulted by EU institutions when appropriate; it would thus seem sensible that EU bodies should give formal effect to this practice, according to paragraph 8 of the Agreement on Cooperation, by making it a working rule that the decisions, reports, conclusions, recommendations and opinions of these monitoring bodies will be systematically taken as reference sources for human rights legislation of the EU, in order to ensure coherence and consistency among the two organisations and in the Member States.

3.7.2 Cooperation with the OSCE

Unlike the EU, the OSCE had a political role from the outset and human rights were originally part of the Helsinki Process as an important element to promote peace and security in Europe. The OSCE of today is an intergovernmental organisation, which is consensus based, with non-legally binding decision-making procedures, aiming primarily to prevent disputes between and within its participating states. The idea of a pan-European security conference was originally raised by the Soviet Union in the 1950s, seeking to secure confirmation of the status quo and recognition of its role as a protagonist in Europe's security. With the launching of the 'Helsinki Process' in 1973, 35 participating states from the whole of Europe (except Albania) plus the USA and Canada engaged in a multilateral East–West negotiation process, the end result was the Final Act of the CSCE signed on 1 August 1975. The new Eastern European EU Member States were involved in this process from the beginning, either as part of the Soviet Union or as 'independent' communist states, such as Poland and Hungary, which were admitted to the CSCE in June 1973. Despite major differences between the two organisations, their agendas started to overlap in the post-Cold War era and both responded to the changes of 1989/1990 with the restructuring of their institutional framework, and with the EU adopting conflict prevention as a key objective in its external relations policy, which before was an activity exclusively exercised by the OSCE.[63]

The EC has been involved in the Helsinki Process from its beginning as well as in subsequent CSCE follow-up meetings until 1989. At the end of the Cold War the call for greater international cooperation was accompanied by a number of European armed intra-state conflicts. In the aftermath of messy, difficult and costly organisational interventions, conflict prevention, with its focus on root causes, early warning and crisis management, gained greater currency as a strategy to prevent the outbreak of intractable conflict. As the media and public called for organisational intervention in former Yugoslavia and elsewhere, the relationship between the two organisations, with increasingly overlapping memberships and objectives, emerged as an important factor in pan-European security and the practice of conflict prevention.[64] The EU Member States now make up close to half of the OSCE participating states and contribute more than two-thirds of the OSCE budget.

Since the Treaty of Maastricht, cooperation with the OSCE has considerably intensified and has taken place in all three of its dimensions, namely the politico-military, the economic and environmental and the human dimension. The 'Pact on Stability in Europe' launched by the EU at the CoE Meeting on 21 and 22 June 1993 in Copenhagen as a main thrust of the CFSP formed the basis for a joint action adopting decisions on the inaugural conference on the Stability Pact of the CSCE/OSCE.[65] The inaugural conference of the Stability Pact was held in Paris on 26–27 May 1994 and was attended by the EU Member States and the then candidate countries. This Pact was seen as a blueprint for inter-organisational cooperation for conflict prevention: the EU gained legitimacy for its objectives by combining bilateral political and financial agreements with the new democracies, with a multilateral political declaration involving Eastern and Western European States, Russia, the United States, EU institutions, the OSCE, the CoE and the UN. The Pact consists of a declaration and a list of good neighbourliness and cooperation agreements and includes bilateral treaties between Hungary, Poland, Romania, Bulgaria, Czech Republic, Slovenia, Slovakia, Russia and the three Baltic States. The respect for the rights of minorities represented an essential component of the Stability Pact. The Pact states clearly at paragraph 1.5 that:

> stability in Europe … will be achieved through the promotion of good-neighbourly relations, including questions related to frontiers and minorities … .[66]

Furthermore, it claims at paragraph 1.9:

> We hope that our continent, which has for so long been torn by war, will become an example of accepted diversity for the international community.

This is a very ambitious goal but the main political aim was to ensure that the future EU partners organise neighbourly relations to avoid the resurfacing of border and minority problems and at the same time preparing the associated CEECs for membership. Evidently, political and economic stability in the OSCE area is of great interest to the EU. For this reason, OSCE field missions have helped applicant countries to work towards democratic and rule-of-law standards as well as the protection of minorities (see chapter 4). In South East Europe OSCE missions work with the current applicant countries and with EU representatives on achieving the objectives of the EU Stabilisation and Association Agreements (SAAs) regarding civilian crisis management, democratisation, human rights and judicial reform.

There is no doubt that the active role and apparent commitment shown by the EU in this matter was a decisive factor in convincing some of the CEECs to start negotiations with their neighbours in preparation for the Stability Pact. The Pact included one important new instrument for minority protection, namely the bilateral treaty between Hungary and Slovakia.[67] The negotiations on a similar treaty between Hungary and Romania were not concluded until 1996.[68] This treaty won international acclaim as a major step forward in reconciliation between the two states.

The Stability Pact was deposited with the OSCE, which was entrusted with the monitoring of the implementation of the obligations contained in it, and hence can apply its machinery of conflict prevention as well as the Convention on Conciliation and Arbitration.[69] The EU lost interest in the Pact and now directs its efforts mainly at bringing about reforms in the domestic laws of the CEECs, it will remain involved, however, among other things, on a financial level.

In the context of civilian crisis management, cooperation between the EU and the OSCE has intensified, in particular with regards to police missions and election monitoring, mainly taking place in South East Europe. Close cooperation between the EU and OSCE missions took place in Kosovo and during the Macedonian conflict between Albanian and Macedonian communities in 2001.[70]

During the Kosovo Crisis in 1999 the EU adopted a Common Position concerning the Stability Pact for South Eastern Europe[71] to be developed and implemented in close association with the OSCE. This Common Position was only marginally concerned with minorities and rather focused on measures for long-term stabilisation, security, democratisation, economic development and good neighbourly relations in the area. The Stability Pact for South Eastern Europe was perhaps the most comprehensive Common Position, which involved the Commission and Member States working together with the OSCE and the CoE to press South Eastern European Countries to resolve border and minorities' issues. The Pact aimed at strengthening countries in South Eastern Europe in their efforts to foster peace, democracy, respect for human rights and economic prosperity, in order to achieve stability in the whole region. One of the objectives of the Pact is to 'bring about mature democratic political processes, based on free and fair elections, grounded in the rule of law and full respect for human rights and fundamental freedoms, including the rights of persons belonging to national minorities …'. A multitude of treaties and agreements resulted from this Common Position, regarding good neighbourly relations between the countries in the region. EU–OSCE cooperation in Kosovo contributed significantly to its stability, eventually leading to its independence in 2008, despite the Russian veto in the UN Security Council.

3.7.2.1 Institutionalisation of EU–OSCE cooperation

Since 1989 the President of the Commission and the EU Presidency have participated in OSCE Summits and, while the two organisations worked on an ad hoc basis during the 1990s, in 2002 a special working party within the CoE was established for relations with the CoE and OSCE. At the same the time, the Commission established a special unit within the DG for External Relations for relations with the OSCE and the CoE. The increase in cooperation between these two organisations was stressed by the High Commissioner for CFSP, Javier Solana, when addressing the Permanent Council (PC) of the OSCE in 2002:

> We recognize … the shared commitment of the EU and the OSCE to democracy, prosperity and stability in Europe as a whole, and beyond. International organisations like ours should not be working solely in parallel but in joint efforts towards the same goals … Cooperation is not an option, it is an imperative.[72]

It was also decided that briefings between the High Representative on CFSP and the Commissioner for External Relations to the OSCE's PC should be set up whenever considered necessary, in addition to regular meetings at staff level and informal meetings with relevant EU working groups and representatives of the OSCE Secretary General, Heads of Missions and Heads of OSCE Institutions.

At the 'Partners in Prevention Conference' in 2002[73] the two organisations agreed on a better practice in information sharing as officials of the OSCE's Conflict Prevention Centre requested greater cooperation from the EU's Situation Centre, which has been reluctant to create a more structured dialogue as it preferred to work on an ad hoc basis.[74] This was a common criticism as coordination for early-warning purposes requires more regular and structured dialogue between the two organisations, including other OSCE institutions, such as the High Commissioner on National Minorities (HCNM) and ODIHR.[75]

In 2003 the Council of the EU published the 'Draft Conclusions on EU–OSCE Cooperation in Conflict Prevention, Crisis Management, and Post-Conflict Rehabilitation'.[76] Despite this formalisation of relationships between the two organisations, there were not many visible results of this cooperation, which might not have been due to political deadlock in the OSCE alone, but also the fact that OSCE personnel consists mainly of frequently changing diplomats who work at intergovernmental level in the PC or in field missions, is not advantageous for longer term cooperation. In addition, successful cooperation would often depend on the individual diplomats and officials on site.[77]

However, the main problem of effective OSCE–EU cooperation lay with different priorities of the two organisations, especially during the enlargement process in the candidate countries. For example in Estonia and Latvia, the European Commission did not properly evaluate the problems related to minority issues, i.e. the Russian minorities in those countries, as it pursued the swift acceptance of Estonia and Latvia as EU Member States, and concentrated more on economic rather than political criteria for membership. This obviously had negative effects on the OSCE's long-term missions, which had been operating there since 1993 and which had tried to convince the host countries to grant appropriate citizenship rights to the Russian minorities. The host countries forced the OSCE missions to close down in 2001 with the justification of imminent EU accession, even though the work, in particular in Estonia, was unfinished. In the end, it was due to the HCNM's influence and persistence that these rights were finally granted, but it became very clear that the EU was not objective in its assessment of the minority rights problems and, the standards and objectives of the two organisations were not mutually reinforcing but openly conflicting with regards to human rights/minority rights standards.[78] At the time it was not sufficiently recognised that success in cooperation will depend on defining common goals and common interpretations of the causes of conflict, which was later stressed at the Partners in Prevention Conference in 2002.[79]

3.7.2.2 Cooperation with ODIHR and the HCNM

In the human dimension, the EU attaches particular importance to OSCE/ODIHR election observation and welcomed a number of OSCE/ODIHR election observation missions undertaken both in EU and non-EU States.[80] Representatives of ODIHR participated in CoE working group meetings on several occasions, and their participation provided a valuable opportunity for a regular exchange of views. Since 1998 the ODIHR has carried out joint programmes with the EU, which were partly funded by the EU's EIDHR (see chapter 2); Almost half the projects of ODIHR in Central Asia during 2002 have been funded by the EU,[81] and in 2003 the CoE declared that it would take account of the OSCE *acquis* with respect to human rights standards.[82]

The EU supported the crucial role that the HCNM played in the protection of rights of persons belonging to minorities, namely in the areas of frozen conflicts and in Kosovo, and shared the emphasis placed on the participating states' responsibility towards the Sinti and Roma populations.[83] In view of the EU's enlargement to the East, the Commission (DG on Enlargement) started to consult the OSCE's HCNM regularly on legal developments and minority issues in the applicant countries.[84] Since the conclusion of the accession round in 2004, the HCNM continues to advise the EU on minority issues, and stresses that the successful accession of CEECs does not mean that minorities in those countries no longer require attention. In 2008 the OSCE PC underscored the need for increased OSCE–EU complementarities, particularly in Kosovo and the unresolved conflicts in the OSCE area, and sought support from the EU for the stabilisation of Afghanistan.[85]

3.8 Conclusion

The role of fundamental rights in the external relations of the EU gained momentum with the introduction of CFSP under the Treaty of Maastricht. However, as illustrated in chapter 2, due to political (realist) considerations, the EU's human rights foreign policy often lacked consistency and coherence; in particular, its enlargement policy was criticised for applying a conditionality policy that was not applied equally to existing EU Member States.[86] Nevertheless, there have been significant improvements, in particular regarding the cooperation with other international organisations such as the CoE and OSCE. The Stability Pact and the Pact for South Eastern Europe are examples of beneficial cooperation between the EU and the OSCE. Due to its lack of resources and expertise regarding the protection of human rights in Eastern Europe, the EU was dependent on other international organisations in order to put its political objectives into practice. The cooperation experience in the Balkans should provide a firm basis for the development of further cooperation activities between the EU and the OSCE in other areas, as there is scope and need for more operational activities in Central Asia and the south Caucasus. In addition, the EU depends on OSCE support for the successful implementation of its ENP and other foreign policies in particular with regards to democratisation and human rights in Central Asia.

4 The EU and the protection of minority rights in Europe

4.1 Introduction

As the two preceding chapters have shown, with the end of the Cold War the European Union (EU) has embarked on developing a common foreign and security policy (CFSP) that promotes human rights and fundamental freedoms. With its powers under the CFSP the EU often reacted to human rights concerns in Third World countries with a conditionality policy that tied trade agreements to human rights, such as the Lomé and Cotonou Agreements. A similar kind of conditionality policy is pursued by the EU in the context of enlargement, the fulfilment of certain human rights standards – including the protection of minorities – now conditions membership to the EU.

Against the background of the disintegration of the Soviet Union and ethnic conflicts in the Balkans, EU accession in 2004 has become different from the previous rounds.[1] Minority issues are more salient with the accession of the new democracies in Central and Eastern Europe in 2004 and 2007 and, despite NATO intervention in Kosovo in 1999, minorities in the area still experience human rights abuses, as cases of violence against minorities in Serbia have shown.[2] Less extreme abuses concern mainly social discrimination that affects particularly the Roma, a minority present in the whole of Central Eastern Europe, as well as in Western Member States.[3] With the continuing enlargement of the European Union to the East, current candidates being Croatia, Turkey and the Former Yugoslav Republic of Macedonia (FYROM), and, Serbia, Kosovo, Montenegro applying for candidate status, the call for a framework for the protection of national minorities at EU level has become louder.[4]

Whether minority rights are part of human rights doctrine or an entirely different category of rights has been controversial. Traditionally, human rights are categorised into civil and political rights (first-generation rights) and economic, social and cultural rights (second-generation rights) as provided for in the International Covenant on Civil and Political Rights (ICCPR) and the International Covenant on Economic, Social and Cultural Rights (ICESCR). Minority rights encompass both categories and are not confined to purely cultural rights, as for example the effective participation in public life is a very important right for minority members. While the EU and other international organisations provide protection with general non-discrimination provisions, including the prohibition of discrimination on the basis of ethnicity, the current standard of minority protection does not provide for a framework with enforceable individual or group rights that could lead to achieving substantive equality for members of minority groups at EU level.

The dichotomy of reconciling diversity and integration leads to the question of whether the best way of protecting minorities can be achieved by a strong protection of individual rights backed up by the non-discrimination principle, or by according minorities their special (positive) rights.[5] While the equal treatment approach may be well suited for the integration of immigrants, this is not the case for minority groups who have a long-term relationship with a certain territory and find themselves sharing the same nation state with a different ethnic majority due to changing borders or forced population transfers.[6]

Jackson-Preece discusses the problems of diversity and integration as a 'dilemma' between the individual's freedom and equality, on the one hand, and the desire for social belonging to a particular community, on the other hand.[7] As 'freedom necessitates and indeed perpetuates a diversity of choices and so promotes a variety of values, beliefs and identities; belonging necessitates and indeed perpetuates social cohesion and so constrains choices to preserve common identity and its concomitant values and beliefs'.[8]

In the context of minority rights, however, equality has to presume an equal right to maintain one's distinct identity, as a right of defence against 'assimilation'. Minority rights aim to prevent conflict by encouraging an environment in which people belonging to a minority group can practise their religion, language and other aspects of culture; majorities, by way of contrast, are required to respect the minority's desire to preserve their culture and way of life to promote a peaceful multicultural society. While secession from the (majority) state is precluded, minorities that are supported by the state in which they reside in preserving their way of life are less likely to strive for secession or territorial autonomy. Hence, the minority rights approach does not consider the existence of minorities to be a prima facie threat to the political order but rather seeks positive action from governments to promote diversity by supporting minorities in exercising their specific culture and way of life.

As already mentioned in the previous chapter, the EU's enlargement policy reveals a double-standards approach as it requires minority protection in the new Eastern European Member States but does not make the same demands regarding the old Western Member States. This will lead to incoherence and different standards for minorities in an enlarged EU. Establishing minority rights in Europe in a consistent manner – that is, the right of minorities to achieve equality with the majority and thereby to practise their culture, religion and language and, to participate fully in the political and economic life of the state – is a necessary prerequisite for peace and stability in Europe.

As there is no clear legal basis for an EU wide harmonisation of minority policy, it appears that the EU will continue to deal indirectly with minority rights through its established policies of prohibition of discrimination/racism/social exclusion and possibly certain aspects of cultural policies. However, this chapter will attempt to show that not only international commitments undertaken by the EU Member States in the context of minority protection but also a number of internal developments in the EU, inspired by the enlargement process, do provide for a certain standard that could be seen as being part of the *acquis*.

Thus, this chapter examines the current situation of minority protection in Europe and reviews how far the existing system is appropriate for fostering minority rights in view of the enlarged EU. Since the EU does not have a common policy on minorities for its Member States yet, it can only draw from either existing international instruments or from ad hoc projects and programmes. The main part of the chapter analyses the tripartite system of minority protection under the different international instruments currently existing in Europe: treaty obligations, such as under the Treaty on European Union (TEU)/Treaty on European Community (TEC/TFEU), including the EU Charter on Fundamental Rights, the European Convention on Human Rights (ECHR), the International Covenant on Civil and Political Rights (ICCPR)[9] and the CoE's Framework Convention on the Protection of National Minorities (FCNM),[10] non-binding legal instruments (political declarations and commitments under the Organization on Security and Cooperation in Europe (OSCE) and the United Nations (UN) and the protection by the High Commissioner on National Minorities (HCNM) under the OSCE system.

4.2 The history of minority rights in Europe

The minority situation in Europe has always been linked to instability as opposed to other continents such as Australia or North America, where minorities have a history of suffering from discrimination but not of conflict caused by violent secessionist movements. With the outbreak of the First World War the problem of vindicating the rights and liberties of the various nationalities in Europe acquired international significance. The war began with overt acts of aggression by the Central Powers against two small nations, Belgium and Serbia.[11] The Treaty of Versailles imposed the creation of new states and through the shifting of borders these new states were populated by different national groups, some representing the majority of the state, others a minority.[12] Obviously, this taking apart of national groups led to instability after the First World War.

President Woodrow Wilson, who was active in pressing for international protection of 'racial and national minorities', declared at the Peace Conference on 31 May 1919: 'Nothing, I venture to say, is more likely to disturb the peace of the world than the treatment which might, in certain circumstances be meted out to the minorities ....'[13]

To safeguard against the disturbance of peace the League of Nations concluded peace treaties that included the protection of minorities: between the Allied Powers and Poland, Austria, the Serb-Croat-Slovene state, Czechoslovakia, Bulgaria, Romania, Hungary, Greece, Albania, Lithuania, Latvia, Estonia, Iraq, the Free City of Danzig, Upper Silesia, Turkey and in the territory of Memel.[14]

Apart from granting all inhabitants protection of their life and liberty, free exercise of any creed, religion or belief, the treaties distinguished between inhabitants and nationals. While nationals were accorded equality before the law and equal enjoyment of civil and political rights, there were additional provisions for minorities: *nationals belonging to racial, religious, or linguistic minorities* were to enjoy the same treatment in law and fact as other nationals; in particular, they had an equal right to establish schools and charitable, religious and social institutions at their own expense; they could use their own language, even before courts, and freely exercise their own religion. Furthermore, it was agreed to establish minority schools in areas with a considerable proportion of nationals whose mother tongue was not the official language of that country. Finally, the treaties provided that in areas with considerable minorities, they would be accorded an equitable share in the enjoyment and application of sums provided out of public funds under state, municipal or other budgets for educational, religious or charitable purposes. The Romanian Treaty also contained autonomy provisions for some minorities and further special provisions were made for a variety of minorities in other treaties.[15]

These treaties formed one of the cornerstones of the international peace structure after the First World War; in addition there was a petition system under the League System which allowed minorities to bring complaints before the League Council when their rights were violated. Furthermore, violations of the Treaty articles with regard to minorities could be regarded as a dispute of international character under Article 14 of the Covenant of the League of Nations, which provided for the competence of the Permanent Court of International Justice (PCIJ) to hear international disputes.

Between 1930 and 1932 there were 305 petitions to the PCIJ of which 153 were declared admissible, while in 1939 there were four petitions, three of which were rejected. This drop in petitions indicated that the system was no longer working properly. Not only the Member States which claimed that the system posed a threat to their internal stability, but also the minorities themselves, beneficiaries of the system, were very critical of the system and demanded greater autonomy and a liberalisation of the petition procedure. In addition, minority protection under the League of Nations was not an internationalised system that established internationally recognised standards, but rather consisted of a number of multilateral treaties for the protection of particular minorities while leaving others unprotected, which was also a reason why minority protection in the post-world war era remained largely ignored in international law. These treaties were mainly concluded in the interest of the territorial integrity of the new states rather than in the interest of aggrieved minorities.

However, the significance of this system of minority protection under the League of Nations, which is the basis of the system of minority protection in Europe today, cannot be denied. It was also clear that the minority protection system depended on the general state of international order and relations at the time, and inevitably when that order disintegrated due to external political reasons, the minority system collapsed with it. Not to mention that the use of minority protection by Nazi Germany to start the Second World War wholly undermined its credibility. In the period between the two World Wars, minorities had been used for subversion against the states of which they were citizens.[16] Minority sentiments were inflamed through propaganda emanating from kin states such as Germany, Austria, Hungary, and Bulgaria, all committed to a fundamental revision of the Versailles settlement. In particular Hitler abused the system of minority protection by inciting autonomy claims of the German minority against Czechoslovakia and eventually used the German minority as an excuse for his intervention there (Sudetenland) in 1938. Boundary changes, forced population transfers and the annihilation of substantial portions of the Jewish and Roma peoples during the Second World War significantly altered the percentages of minorities and majorities in many countries of post-war Europe.[17]

4.2.1 Security aspects with regard to minorities

The development of the League of Nations system in the aftermath of the First World War mainly reflected concerns about international security. As one contemporary commentator described it, 'if you have in Europe anything like forty million people seriously discontented and looking beyond the frontier of their own country for the remedy of grievances … [there is] a serious danger to the peace of the world.'[18]

The progress of disintegration of the communist regimes in Europe in 1990 has brought about a radical shift in geopolitical balance on the European continent. While the threat of large-scale conflict has been reduced, it has fostered the re-emergence of ethnic-based territorial claims. Not surprisingly, the end of the Cold War and the subsequent dissolution of the USSR and Yugoslavia have brought an abrupt revival of interests in minority rights. Conflicts in the Balkans, like the Yugoslavian war from 1991 to 1994,[19] the Kosovo war in 1999,[20] the conflict in Macedonia in 2001[21] and even the conflict between Russia and Georgia in 2008[22] have revealed the actual and potential threats inherent in the problems of minority protection.

Some European institutions that aimed at protecting minority rights also intended to protect international peace: The preamble of the FCNM justifies minority rights protection largely in terms of conflict prevention by stipulating in its preamble:

> Upheavals of European History have shown that the protection of national minorities is essential to stability, democratic security and peace in this continent.

Furthermore, the OSCE has justified minority protection primarily in terms of the danger of international conflagrations. The mandate of the HCNM, for example, focuses on 'early action' and 'early warning' with regard to 'tensions involving national minority issues … [that] have the potential to develop into a conflict within the OSCE area.[23]

Although minorities might not be on top of the political agenda of some states, in the context of international stability the European states have recognised the importance of promoting minority rights, hence the creation of the FCNM and the HCNM. The question of whether minorities represent an obstacle to democratisation or how far they represent a factor affecting regional and political instability or a security threat (the security track) will not be treated any further in this chapter.[24] It is rather the EU's policy and the legal rights of minorities (the legal rights track) and with regard to its Member States that is of interest here.

However, it has to be stressed that security concerns were always the trigger for establishing a system of minority protection, starting from the League of Nations after the First World War to the OSCE system and the CoE's FCNM after the end of the Cold War and the Yugoslav War. Also, the EU's Copenhagen Criteria for the enlargement of the EU included the need for the protection of minorities as a consequence of the human rights/minority rights abuses during the war in FYR. This war, which took place in the 'backyard of Europe', signified an important security risk for the EU, hence there was a strong interest in addressing the causes of this conflict, namely minority claims, especially with regard to the EU's enlargement to the East. In the early 1990s, many commentators feared that ethnic tensions would spiral out of control; for example civil war between the Estonian majority and Russian minority in Estonia, or the Slovak majority and Hungarian minority in Slovakia were predicted.[25] These security concerns also explain the new approach for the recognition of states that was taken by the Badinter Commission (see chapter 3). It has to be taken into account that the EU's interest in peace and security in Europe is a very realist interest, as an outbreak of conflict would always result in a loss of power and control for the EU. As a logical consequence of this interest, the EU has taken some significant innovative steps and has become more and more involved in conflict prevention and crisis management in the emerging post-Cold War European security architecture.[26]

The political criteria for accession to the EU by Eastern European states have already been considered in the preceding chapter in the context of the EU's foreign policy. The obvious aspiration of all Central and Eastern European Countries (CEECs) to *return to Europe* presented the EU with an opportunity to influence developments by including minority rights into a broad definition of political conditionality. As will be demonstrated in this chapter, by now, Western states have developed an international system of minority protection, not only on the basis of numerous political declarations but also with various institutions committed to minority protection. Before analysing these developments and the current practice of minority protection in Europe the term 'minority' and the special rights this term entails will be assessed.

4.3 What are minorities? A variety of definitions

This section will elaborate on what constitutes a recognisable minority protected by international law. There is no generally accepted definition of the term 'minority' or 'national minority' in international instruments dealing with minorities, due to the difficulty of classifying minorities in a homogenous manner, and also due to the reluctance of states to commit themselves to such a definition in order to avoid protection for the persons concerned. In political documents, the lack of a definition might be intentional; however, legal documents must indicate clearly who the entitled subject is. It is therefore essential to discuss the issue of defining the term 'minority' in order to be able to evaluate the significance of the relevant instruments dealing with minorities.

Under the League of Nations system, following an action on behalf of the Greek minority in Albania regarding a decision of the Albanian government to close all private schools the PCIJ stated in its advisory opinion *Minority Schools in Albania*:

> The idea underlying the treaties for the protection of minorities is to secure for certain elements incorporated in a State, the population of which differs from them in *race, language or religion*, the possibility of living peacefully alongside that population and cooperating amicably with it, while at the same time preserving the characteristics which distinguish them from the majority, and satisfying the ensuing special needs.[27]

This interpretation of the minority treaties defines minorities as those members of the population who differ from the majority in 'race, language or religion' and accords them special needs that have to be satisfied by the state. These three factors were reproduced in almost unchanged form by Article 27 ICCPR of 1966, which states:

> In those States in which ethnic, religious or linguistic minorities exist, persons belonging to such minorities shall not be denied the right, in community with the other members of their group to enjoy their own culture, to profess and practise their own religion, or to use their own language.

However, until today, many different definitions for the protection of 'minorities' under international law have been proposed by different working groups of international organisations and scholars but no official definition has been agreed on. In particular, the United Nation's Sub-Commission on the Prevention of Discrimination and Protection of Minorities,[28] which was instrumental in the drafting of Article 27 ICCPR, also worked on a definition of the term 'minority'.

The most widely accepted definition was drafted in 1979 by Professor Francesco Capotorti, the then Special Rapporteur of the UN, appointed by the Sub-Commission on Prevention of Discrimination and Protection of Minorities, stipulating that

> A minority is a group numerically inferior to the rest of the population of a State, in a non-dominant position, whose members – being nationals of the State – possess ethnic, religious or linguistic characteristics differing from

> those of the rest of the population of a State and show, if only implicitly, a sense of solidarity, directed towards preserving their culture, traditions, religion or language.[29]

The proposal adopts both objective and subjective criteria. The former includes size, non-dominant position and stable (ethnic, religious, linguistic) characteristics, including nationality, while the latter states the self-identification of the minority, the will to preserve the specific identity of the group. Capotorti suggested that one could deduce the subjective factor or the 'sense of solidarity' from the objective existence of a group possessing distinct ethnic, religious, or linguistic characteristics, i.e. the wish of the group to continue to exist as a group could be implicit.[30] As it would be difficult to evaluate such a subjective element, it has to be considered that a minority manifests its existence already in many physically tangible ways, such as language or physical features. Accordingly, there will be at least an implicit sense of solidarity if a group that has survived historically as a community with a distinct identity since it could hardly have done so unless it had positively so wished.[31]

Another definition attempt was made by the Sub-Commission in 1985 and a text prepared by Jules Deschênes was transmitted to the Commission on Human Rights with the following definition:

> A group of citizens of a state, constituting a numerical minority and in a non-dominant position in that state, endowed with ethnic, religious or linguistic characteristics which differ from those of the majority of the population, having a sense of solidarity with another, motivated, if only implicitly, by a collective will to survive and whose aim is to achieve equality with the majority in fact and law.[32]

However, this proposal was not acceptable to the UN Commission and since then no other officially instigated attempt to come up with a universally accepted definition has been made.

The *travaux préparatoires* of Article 27 ICCPR and the 1973 report of the Committee of Experts on Minority Rights of the Council of Europe indicate that in the UN's documents 'ethnic' includes national, while Council of Europe (CoE) documents subsume ethnic within 'national'.[33] The UN General Assembly's 1992 Declaration on the Rights of Persons Belonging to National *or* Ethnic, Religious and Linguistic Minorities[34] speaks of 'national' as a variety of a minority and not as a precondition. This choice of words was probably motivated by the desire to extend the protection accorded by the Declaration to as many persons as possible that can be 'ethnically defined'. Eide's commentary clearly states that 'there is hardly any national minority, however defined, that is not also an ethnic or linguistic minority'.[35]

The UN Human Rights Committee concluded in its General Comment on Article 27 ICCPR that individuals designed to be protected by Article 27 ICCPR need not be citizens of the State Party, nor even permanent residents. Thus migrant workers or even visitors in a State Party constituting such minorities are entitled not to be denied the exercise of their rights under Article 27.[36] Hence, the distinction between 'national' and 'ethnic' minorities in international law remains unclear.

In Europe, it was generally undisputed that international protection of minorities only applies to minorities that have the nationality of the state where they reside, but they do not need to be connected to a kin state, which is particularly relevant for the Roma minority. It has to be taken into account here that at UN level a definition of the term 'minority' would have to be applicable globally, whereas in Europe minority protection is rooted in the League of Nations System, which always referred to 'national' minorities. Apart from the historical argument, the reason for the nationality requirement also lies in the fact that other instruments already protect minorities such as immigrants,[37] stateless people or refugees (so-called 'new minorities'), they therefore fall into a different category of law.[38] The justification for the distinction between these two types of minority will not be further discussed in this context as it would require sociological and political arguments that lie outside the realm of this chapter.

The proposal for an additional protocol to the ECHR prepared by the Parliamentary Assembly of the CoE in 1993 ventured to formulate a definition for the purposes of the CoE.[39] According to this proposal, the expression 'national minority' refers to a group of persons in a state who:

1. reside on the territory of that state and are citizens thereof;
2. maintain longstanding, firm and lasting ties with that state;
3. display distinctive ethnic, cultural religious or linguistic characteristics;
4. are sufficiently representative, although smaller in number than the rest of the population of that state or of a region of that state; and
5. are motivated by a concern to preserve what constitutes their common identity, including their culture, their tradition, their religion or their language.

The most controversial issues of this definition relate to the size of the minority and their subjective feeling of solidarity. Unlike Capotorti's definition, this proposal does not contain any reference to the requirement of non-dominance but mentions a vaguely termed numerical factor (in 4). Presumably, it was not considered necessary in the European context as the minorities concerned were *per se* in a non-dominant position. Furthermore, the CoE's requirement of durable ties with the state of residence cannot be found in any UN documents. This condition would mainly apply to minorities that have lived for a long period of time in a certain country, maybe even before that country existed, i.e. in pre-war times. Thus, immigrants who deliberately moved to Europe would not qualify as a minority according to this definition of Recommendation 1201 (1993).

However, the Parliamentary Assembly has no legislative powers but can only make recommendations to the Committee of Ministers, which has to adopt the proposal with a two-thirds majority. The proposal was rejected due to the lack of political will by the Member States of the CoE at its Vienna Summit in October 1993,[40] which deprived the proposal of any binding effect on the Member States. However, it has to be noted that the European Parliament (EP) as well as the Network of Independent Experts on Fundamental Rights[41] advocate this definition of Recommendation 1201 (1993); it was particularly endorsed by the EP in its 'Resolution on the Protection of Minorities and Anti-Discrimination Policies in an Enlarged Europe' adopted on 8 June 2005.[42]

The CoE's FCNM does not contain any definition of minorities that it aims to protect. The drafters of the FCNM were unable to reach a consensus on a definition and therefore chose 'a pragmatic approach' in elaborating programme-type provisions for which it was asserted a definition would be less necessary.[43] Some states have made unilateral declarations concerning their understanding of whom the term 'national minority' applies to, restricting it to nationals of the state or in the case of Germany, protection under the FCNM only applies to the Danes, Friesians, Roma and Sorbs.[44] Questions as to the legal quality of such declarations, whether they are legally binding on the CoE's Advisory Committee or whether they might even constitute reservations have not been clarified.[45]

The Advisory Committee, established under the FCNM, notes in its Explanatory Report[46] that 'it should also be pointed out that the Framework Convention contains no definition of the notion of 'national minority'. It was decided to adopt a pragmatic approach, based on the recognition that at this stage, it is impossible to arrive at a definition capable of mustering general support of all CoE Member States. In the absence of a definition and in light of the Member States' declarations, it is up to the Member States to examine the scope of the application of the FCNM, i.e. States Parties are given a certain margin of appreciation, which in turn will be examined and evaluated by the Advisory Committee in its reports, in order to verify that no arbitrary or unjustified distinctions are made by the Member States.

The FCNM confines its applicability to 'national' minorities; however, this term can have different meanings in different European states. In France, for example, nationality will always refer to 'citizenship', whereas in Germany the concept of a national minority refers to a distinctive cultural or linguistic group that does not necessarily have to have citizenship but must be connected to another kin state; thus the term 'national minorities', subsumes in particular ethnic, linguistic or religious distinctions. However, a minority does not necessarily need to have a kin state in order to qualify as a national minority, as there are recognised minorities such as the Roma, the Tartars, Sorbs or Vlachs (Aromaniens) that lack a kin state,[47] thus 'national' can simply be a descriptive term for a minority.

The question of whether religious minorities are to be considered as forming part of a national minority has been answered by the FCNM's Advisory Committee in its opinion on Cyprus, regarding the situation of Maronites and other religious communities, where it clarified that religious minorities have to be considered as national minorities for the purposes of the FCNM.[48]

With regards to new minorities, the domestic situation varies in every country, which can also be seen in the different statements/declarations made by state parties to the FCNM. The Advisory Committee to the FCNM has held that some of the provisions of the FCNM such as Article 11(3) FCNM which explicitly refers to 'areas traditionally inhabited by persons belonging to a national minority can evidently only apply to 'old minorities', while Article 6 FCNM applies to 'all persons living on the territory' and would therefore also include 'new' minorities.[49] It is apparent that the Advisory Committee is taking an inclusive approach, trying to give as many people as possible protection under the FCNM, as it is possible to argue that also Articles 3, 5, 7 and 8 FCNM could be applicable to new minorities. This inclusive approach mirrors a trend that would make it possible to extend the applicability of the FCNM on an article-by-article basis to new minorities.[50]

With regard to a prospective enlarged EU, it is important to develop a clear understanding about the nature of the intended beneficiaries in order to recognise them under law and accord legal standing to those beneficiaries with regard to the relevant entitlements. While the criteria 'religious' and 'linguistic' are undisputed, it is debatable whether protection under the EU system should only apply to persons possessing the nationality of their state of residence and who maintain a certain territorial link over a period of time with that country. It could be argued that the nationality requirement could easily be manipulated by the state, by not according citizenship to minorities and thereby depriving them of minority protection. This was the case in Estonia with regard to the Russian minority after independence in 1990.[51] However, historically this requirement made sense, as minority protection under the League of Nations was accorded to minorities that were already resident in the state in question, before the borders were redrawn and people had to be resettled.

The requirement of durable links could also be used for excluding minorities from protection since there is no provision or case law concerning the length of time this link has to have existed and it is debatable from when onwards minorities stemming from immigration can qualify as a recognisable minority, if at all. This leads to a situation where ethnic minorities as for example the Turks in Germany, the Algerians in France or various groups of Asian origin in the UK, who have lived for generations as a minority in these countries do not qualify as a national minority despite their durable link with that country as they stem originally from immigration.

The difficulty of coming up with a general definition of the term 'minority' accounts for the evasion of the problem by the international community, which reflects how politically undesirable judicially enforceable rights for minorities are seen by states. How the lack of an internationally recognised definition of the term 'national minority' impacts on judicial decisions regarding minority issues by the European Court of Human Rights (ECtHR) can be seen below under section 4.5.

Finally, the HCNM has declared on numerous occasions 'I know a minority when I see one' reflecting on the overlap between the protection of ethnic, cultural, linguistic and religious minorities, on the one hand, and national minorities, on the other.[52] Hence, the terms used by states, such as 'national minorities', 'nationalities' or 'communities' are without adverse effect.

For the purposes of this chapter, i.e. the analysis of EU minority policy, the definition of Recommendation of 1201 (1993) is the most appropriate, as other normative concepts apply to 'new' minorities throughout the EU.

4.3.1 What type of rights are protected? Collective rights or individual rights?

Before discussing the contents of specific minority rights, the question whether minority rights should be granted 'collectively' or whether they can only be exercised as 'individual rights' will be assessed.

After the Second World War it was generally accepted that minority rights are part of general human rights doctrine. This was one of the major differences with the League of Nations system for the protection of minorities, where minority rights were not embedded in the concept of human rights. It was recognised that in order to develop their identity, minorities needed special protection and it became evident that positive measures would be necessary to guarantee linguistic, cultural and educational rights and the right to effective participation in the political, economic and social fields, which are the main principles of minority protection. Article 27 ICCPR is an acknowledgement of the need for such special protection of minorities, going beyond general non-discrimination, which is provided for in Article 26 ICCPR; otherwise this provision would have been unnecessary. However, the inclusion of minority rights (that require positive measures) into the concept of human rights can cause problems, as it would contradict the principle of equal treatment and non-discrimination. These concerns have been addressed by 'affirmative action', i.e. policies that take race, ethnicity, or gender into consideration in an attempt to promote de facto equality and to redress discrimination.[53]

The human rights approach, which is the most accepted perspective of minority protection[54] deals with the rights of minorities as part of universally recognised human rights, and has been recognised by international organisations by including minority rights in various international instruments such as the already–mentioned ICCPR, CERD, the ECHR, or the UN Declaration on the Rights of Persons Belonging to National or Ethnic, Religious and Linguistic Minorities. However, the corps of international human rights instruments focuses on the protection of the individual and distinguishes clearly between individual and collective rights granted directly to human beings. Under Article 27 ICCPR or Article 14 ECHR, minority protection is not group based, minority rights are formulated as individual rights, albeit individual rights to be exercised in community with others; only Article 1 ICCPR which provides for the right of self-determination is considered to be a group right as it applies to 'peoples',[55] but does not however apply to minorities as defined above, since national legislation usually gives rights to individuals and not to communities, groups or endangered populations.

add in the strategies

A cautious attempt to position minority rights as collective rights was undertaken by the Ad Hoc Committee for the Protection of National Minorities (CAHMIN), which was established in the CoE in 1993, composed of independent experts on minority rights. CAHMIN's first working paper on certain principles of the FCNM states in its Article 1: 'The international protection *of rights of national minorities*, as well as the rights of persons belonging to those minorities … is a fundamental component of the international protection of human rights, and as such falls within the scope of international cooperation' [emphasis added].[56]

By referring to 'rights of national minorities', CAHMIN uses a collective rights approach, which is, however, then followed by the individual rights approach 'as well as the rights of persons belonging to a minority'; but no further discussion of this approach followed from this first working paper. Another important aspect of this Article refers to the fact that minority protection no longer falls within the exclusive competence of states but warrants cooperation with international institutions.

In 2001 the CoE's Parliamentary Assembly made a very similar point in its Recommendation 1492 'the importance of effectively protecting the *rights of minorities* …' and considered 'that the adequate protection of *persons belonging to minorities* and *their communities* is an integral part of the protection of human rights' [emphasis added].[57] It can be inferred from this wording that collective rights and individual rights with regards to minorities are being used at the same time in one document, which leads to the conclusion that collective rights in this context are taken into consideration, which, however, does not mean that there is a fully fledged policy for the protection of collective rights. The authors of the FCNM stressed in their Explanatory Report to the FCNM that the implementation of the principles set out in the FCNM would be effected through national legislation, 'which does not imply the recognition of collective rights'.[58] Hence, the FCNM followed the individualistic approach like in any other international human rights instruments, where the individual is the rights holder and not a group. However, persons belonging to a minority group often claim the protection of their collective identity since part of their identity is to be a member of that group and the right to act as a group or to organise themselves as a group, to practise their culture as a group, etc. The FCNM has approached this potential conflict by allowing in its Article 3(2) persons belonging to national minorities to exercise their minority rights 'in community with others' which clearly gives the rights provided for in the FCNM a community/collective dimension.

When the ICCPR was drafted, the attitude towards group rights was more relaxed than it has since been; nevertheless it was felt that the construction of collective rights could create problems of legal character. It was claimed that a collective could not, technically speaking, be the subject of a legal right, the subject that carried a right had to be a person. That is why the UN adopted the concept of 'persons belonging to a minority', i.e. a member of a minority can exercise 'his minority rights' only as a member of that minority. Also Judge Tanaka in his dissenting opinion in the *South West Africa* case[59] stressed individual not group rights, following the concept of Article 27 ICCPR.

John Packer approached this problem in the context of the lack of a definition of minorities:

> It has been correctly observed that international law supposes the existence of minorities both in general and of specific types. However, while the existence of human beings and States are 'axiomatic' in international law, the existence of human groups is problematic. Conceptually, international law struggles with the definitions of actors beyond the 'State'; indeed the problem of defining actors has always troubled political theory in general and in international relations … [While] the catalogue and content of individual human rights has become relatively clear, the specificity of protection for groups, particularly minorities, has remained largely uncertain. Paramount among this uncertainty has been the very definition of 'the' or 'a minority' to whom any rights may accrue.[60]

However, there have been developments in the international community to expand the human rights system by giving specific consideration to the needs of minorities and groups qua collectivities.[61] Dinstein argues for example that 'collective human rights are afforded to human beings communally, that is to say, in conjunction with one another or as a group, a people or a minority. Nevertheless, collective human rights retain their character as direct human rights … [which] … shall be exercised jointly rather than severally.'[62]

De Witte argues that 'minority protection can also be described as group accommodation, especially when considering specific minority rights as those which involve the sharing of state power, either through recognition of autonomous legislative powers to institutions which represent minorities' interests (autonomy) or by organising the participation of ethnic minority groups in the decision-making process at the central state level itself; those are arguably the most advanced forms of minority protection.'[63]

Many studies suggest that societies with minority conflicts could be stabilised by institutional arrangements that accommodate diversity, i.e. through federalism or some other form of institutionalised power-sharing arrangement.[64] However, whether minorities are best served with federalism, autonomy, centralisation or assimilatory policies cannot be answered within the context of this chapter. Nevertheless, 'group-specific' cultural and linguistic rights or power-sharing mechanisms for minorities have been widely accepted in democratic states and in international instruments, although they often remain contested and controversial. For example under the Hungarian Constitution, Article 68(4) states that 'national and ethnic minorities shall have the right to form local and national bodies for self-government'. The Slovenian Constitution adopts a similar approach in Article 64 albeit only in relation to the Italian and Hungarian minorities. The Estonian Constitution accords the collective right to establish educational and cultural institutions in Article 50 but uses individual rights language when it comes to the right to 'receive responses from state agencies, local governments and their officials in minority language' in Article 51(2).[65]

Also, the position of indigenous populations or peoples have influenced the promotion of the concept of group rights. The 1989 International Labour Organization (ILO) Convention (No. 169)[66] on Indigenous and Tribal Peoples in Independent Countries stipulates in its preamble:

> Recognising the aspirations of these peoples to exercise control over their own institutions, ways of life and economic development and to maintain and develop their identities, languages and religions, within the framework of the States in which they live ... and in Article 1 (a) ... peoples in independent countries whose social, cultural and economic conditions distinguish them from other sections of the national community, and whose status is regulated wholly or partially by their own customs or traditions or by special laws or regulations.

Another important international instrument that explicitly recognises and promotes group rights is the International Convention on the Elimination of All Forms of Racial Discrimination (CERD) of 1969. Following below is a brief outline of CERD's influence in the recognition of group rights.

4.3.1.1 CERD

Article 2(2) CERD[67] stipulates an approach that promotes formerly suppressed groups:

> States Parties shall, when the circumstances so warrant, take, in the social, economic, cultural and other fields, special and concrete measures to ensure the adequate development and protection of *certain racial groups or individuals belonging to them*, for the purpose of guaranteeing them the full and equal enjoyment of human rights and fundamental freedoms. These measures shall in no case entail as a consequence the maintenance of unequal or separate rights for different racial groups after the objectives for which they were taken have been achieved. [emphasis added]

It is unusual for an international human rights law instrument to accord rights also to groups, as human rights law is traditionally based on the notion of the individual as the bearer of rights. Article 2(2) CERD was put into practice especially in the USA with 'affirmative action' programmes, i.e. positive discrimination of formerly discriminated groups, in particular the Afro-American community. Theodor Meron notes that 'Article 2(2) CERD does not concern individual rights but protects groups of persons or individuals qua members of the group. While CERD addresses "racial groups" rather than "minorities" this usage may encompass protection of ethnic minorities as defined for the purposes of Article 27.'[68] Hence, as long as there is no definition in international law that would exclude national minorities (as discussed at section 4.3, above) from protection under CERD, there is no impediment why it should not be used for the purposes of 'national minorities', even though it is not specifically designed to do so.

Concluding on the question of individual rights and group rights, it has to be noted, that the very nature of the term 'minority' inevitably involves the existence of a group since, giving special rights to a minority automatically has a group dimension. Even though most states construe their domestically guaranteed minority rights as individual rights, which can be exercised in community with others, there is no impediment under international law for states to accord collective or group rights to minorities. The granting of specific minority rights, such as the right to receive education in minority language, the right to publicly represent minority interests or the right to practise minority culture only make sense when these rights are exercised within a group. The discourse evolving around group rights is therefore somehow indistinct as minority rights can only be exercised when a minority group exists and even if these rights could only be challenged or enforced by individuals, any challenge would automatically affect the whole group. Hence, the granting of minority rights goes beyond the granting of individual human rights as it inevitably involves group aspects.

4.3.2 What are specific minority rights?

What type of rights are considered to be 'minority rights' that supplement the corps of human rights and promote de facto equality with the majority will now be assessed. Those rights are mainly provided for by the FCNM, the CSCE Copenhagen Document, the UN Declaration on the Rights of Persons Belonging to National or Ethnic, Religious and Linguistic Minorities and the ECHR.

Certain individual human rights, which are provided for in most human rights instruments are of special significance to minorities, which can be civil and political rights (such as the freedom of religion, the freedom of media or the freedom of association) or economic and social rights (such as the right to education in one's mother tongue). In the relevant international instruments for minority rights, these individual human rights have been further elaborated thus:

1 Fundamentally important rights that cannot be found in non-minority-specific international human rights instruments are the right to *self-identification and the prohibition of forced assimilation*, as provided for in Articles 3(1) and 5(2) FCNM and paragraph 32 of the CSCE Copenhagen Final Document (the Copenhagen Document). Despite its fundamental importance, no recognised standards seem to have developed regarding the right to freely identify oneself as a person belonging to a national minority. It can, however, be concluded from the wording of the above provision that persons belonging to a national minority should be encouraged to identify themselves as such but cannot be forced to do so.
2 Also *the obligation to protect and promote the distinct identity of national minorities, including by positive measures*, as provided for in Articles 4(2) and 5(1) FCNM

and paragraphs 32 and 33 of the Copenhagen Document is evidently a very minority-specific provision that imposes duties on states. This provision can be seen as the counterpart of the prohibition of forced assimilation, worded in positive terms. In this context, the Advisory Committee to the FCNM has stressed that these measures in support of national minorities should be 'identified and implemented in close contact with the persons concerned'.[69] In a number of specific cases, the Committee found a breach of this provision under the FCNM, for example in the Sami Land rights issue,[70] the lack of stopping rights for Travellers in the UK and Ireland,[71] and the forced dissolution of Horno, a Sorbian municipality in Germany, which led to displacement of the population.[72]

3 The *right of non-discrimination and effective equality* has already been discussed (chapter 1 section 1.2.1, and chapter 2 section 2.5.2). Although states are generally in agreement as to the concept of non-discrimination and the protection of the identity of their minorities, they are far from reaching a consensus on the scope of the rights to be granted. The only common ground for the Member States consists in the rights recognised by various international instruments adopted within the UN, the OSCE and the CoE (i.e. the ICCPR, CERD, the UN Declaration on the Rights of Persons Belonging to National or Ethnic, Religious and Linguistic Minorities, the CSCE Copenhagen Document, the ECHR and the FCNM, as introduced in chapter 1). All documents recognise that minorities should enjoy the same rights as the majority of the population and equal protection before the law, as it is provided for in general non-discrimination clauses.[73] The right not to be discriminated against is closely associated with minority rights, but they are not the same rights. Persons belonging to minorities often feel discriminated against but legally speaking non-discrimination rights and minority rights are two separate concepts. The entitlements in general non-discrimination clauses are available to everyone. They may be invoked by women, or by persons identified with particular political causes, or illegitimate persons and others. They are not reserved to ethnic, religious or linguistic minorities.[74] While non-discrimination may appear to be sufficient to resolve many of the problems associated with minorities, the very nature of minority protection implies that special measures have to be taken in favour of persons belonging to a minority group.

In this context, Article 4 FCNM states that:

(1) The Parties undertake to guarantee to persons belonging to national minorities the right of equality before the law and of equal protection of the law. In this respect, any discrimination based on belonging to a national minority shall be prohibited.

(2) The Parties undertake to adopt, where necessary, adequate measures in order to promote, in all areas of economic, social, political and cultural life, full and effective equality between persons belonging to a national minority and those belonging to the majority. In this respect, they shall

take due account of the specific conditions of the persons belonging to national minorities.

(3) The measures adopted in accordance with paragraph 2 shall not be considered to be an act of discrimination.

While subsection (1) provides for a general non-discrimination clause which can be found in every human rights instrument, subsection 2 requires states to undertake positive measures to promote de facto equality for minorities, which is specific to the FCNM, and subsection 3 clarifies that such positive measures shall not be considered to be discriminatory, evidently to those persons who are not entitled to benefit from the measures. The Advisory Committee has not only commented on legislation protecting national minorities from discrimination but also whether effective remedies against discrimination are in place.[75] In addition, the discrimination of the Roma minority has been pointed out over and over again by the Committee regarding almost every State Party to the FCNM; in particular attention should be paid to the situation of Roma women.[76]

4 As almost every national minority in Europe is characterised by its mother tongue which differs from the official language of the state of its residence, the right of persons belonging to linguistic minorities *to use their mother tongue in private and in public* is guaranteed by all of the above-mentioned international instruments (see in particular Articles 10–11 FCNM and paragraph 32 of the Copenhagen Document).

Difficulties arose with regard to the use of minority language in official relations. Some states claim that the acceptance of several languages might threaten national cohesion. Although the Copenhagen Document and the FCNM accepted the principle of the use of minority language in relation with administrative authorities, the state obligation is worded in rather vague terms and leaves a large margin of appreciation; Article 10(2) FCNM provides:

> In areas inhabited by persons belonging to national minorities traditionally or in substantial numbers, if those persons so request and where such a request corresponds to a real need, the Parties shall endeavour to ensure, as far as possible, the conditions which would make it possible to use the minority language in relations between those persons and the administrative authorities.

The right to submit documents in a minority language to public authorities or to have bilingual street signs in areas where minorities form a local majority are strengthened by provisions in the Oslo Recommendations regarding the Linguistic Rights of National Minorities (1998).[77] In this context the Advisory Committee has welcomed legislation in Austria, Romania and Slovakia that allows for the use of minority language in areas where the minority population represents at least 10 per cent in Austria and 20 per cent in Romania and Slovakia of the overall population. At the same time, the Committee held that a similar quota of 50 per cent was too high.[78] With regards to the Advisory Committee's opinions on the use of minority language in relations with administrative authorities and on topographical signs, a certain trend can be observed: the use of minority language *should* be allowed in areas where minorities represent 10–20 per cent of the overall population, however, with a minority population of 30–40 per cent it is still within the margin of appreciation of the State Party to allow the use of minority language, while the requirement of 50 per cent minority population is considered to be outside the State's Party margin of appreciation.[79]

5 The obligation on states to promote possibilities for minority members to receive *education or training in their mother tongue* is provided for in Article 4.3 of the UN Declaration, in paragraph 32.2 of the Copenhagen Document and in Articles 12–14 FCNM.

The right to education and the right to use minority language are particularly important rights, especially for linguistic minorities, as it is essential for the survival of a minority group to pass on the minority language, hence educational rights are of utmost relevance. The function of language in contacts and in school interaction strongly influences the overall status of a national minority. The teaching of cultural values, history and patterns of language use achieves much greater societal support if it is transmitted in schools, and not only in the families. It is therefore evident that education in ethnically mixed areas does not concern the minority population alone but is also beneficial for the whole society for mutual understanding and a harmonious coexistence. The Hague Recommendations regarding the Education Rights of National Minorities (1996)[80] reflect this approach.

The Advisory Committee had to give particular attention to the situation of the Roma as Roma children show an abnormally high degree of absence in schools and, it seems to be common practice in some countries that Roma children are placed in special schools for children with learning difficulties or even for mentally disabled children in order to segregate them from children belonging to the majority group. The Advisory Committee also criticised the shortage of textbooks and teachers for minority languages.[81] In opinions on Austria, Estonia and Switzerland, the Committee went even so far as to consider a bilingual education the most appropriate way of guaranteeing the right to education in minority language.[82]

The right to use the mother tongue in criminal proceedings is only contained in Article 10(3) FCNM and in Article 6(3)(a) ECHR as part of the right to a fair trial. The right to be addressed in a minority language during criminal proceedings would only apply, however, if the accused speaks but the minority language.

6 The *right to have access to – and visibility in – public media* and to establish minority print and audio-visual media are of fundamental importance to

minorities, particularly in the modern age where society is greatly influenced by media. Print and audio-visual media are also essential for learning and keeping minority language alive and for understanding minority culture. These rights are provided for in Article 10 ECHR, paragraph 32 of the Copenhagen Document, as well as Article 9 FCNM. While there have been a few decisions on media rights by the ECtHR that concerned minorities (see section 4.5, below), the Advisory Committee of the FCNM has commented mainly on the lack of access of minorities to public radio and television broadcasting programmes as well as insufficient funding for certain minorities and their private radio and television programmes, but it has not developed any standards of good practice in this regard yet. In relation to print media the criticism has been mostly positive.[83] Also, the Guidelines on the Use of Minority Language in the Broadcast Media, developed under the auspices of the HCNM are concerned with state policies regarding the establishment of independent bodies that regulate broadcast media to take into account the promotion of the use of minority language in the broadcast media.[84]

7 The freedom to freely *practise one's religion* is recognised in Article 9 ECHR, Article 2.1 UN Declaration on the Rights of Persons Belonging to National or Ethnic, Religious and Linguistic Minorities and in Article 8 FCNM;

Article 32 paragraph 3 of the Copenhagen Document indicates in more detail that:

> persons belonging to minorities have the right to profess and practise their religion, including the acquisition, possession and use of religious materials, and to conduct religious educational activities in their mother tongue.

Whilst the Advisory Committee to the FCNM found that a state church system is not in breach of Article 8 FCNM and that there is no state obligation to fund different religious groups, it held nevertheless that where such funding exists, it must be distributed in conformity with Article 4 FCNM, i.e. without discrimination.[85] In addition, in its opinion on the UK it was held that blasphemy laws must not be restricted to just one religion.[86]

8 The right to *preserve one's culture* is provided for in Article 1 of the UN Declaration on the Rights of Persons Belonging to National or Ethnic, Religious and Linguistic Minorities, Article 5 FCNM, paragraph 32 of the Copenhagen Document and in Article 27 ICCPR. The term 'culture' might include religion, language, art, literature but can also include a particular lifestyle, which has been found to be part of the private life, as protected by Article 8 ECHR (see for more details and case law on this Article in section 4.5, below). 'Culture constitutes the platform for the intended continuation of group-culture and from this it follows that words such as "culture", "existence", "identity" and even "dignity" are very much intertwined.'[87] The

right to 'enjoy one's culture' encompasses the right to funding for minority schools, media, the use of minority language and the right to practise freely one's religion, all of which have already been discussed above.

In relation to the 'right to culture' Kymlicka points out that apart from Article 27 ICCPR, other documents (FCNM and OSCE documents) included the right to minority culture against the background of violent conflict in post-communist Europe. In this context the right to culture does not contribute to any solution of those conflicts as the minorities involved in violent conflict are usually large, territorially concentrated groups who require more far-reaching rights than mere cultural rights.[88] However, the right to enjoy one's culture is an indispensable right for minorities, in particular in countries where conflict potential does not exist, as for example in Hungary, Slovenia, Estonia, Slovakia and the Czech Republic, despite their large minority groups.

9 The right to *participate in public affairs* is recognised by paragraph 35 of the Copenhagen Document and by the UN Declaration in Article 2.3. The Copenhagen Document states that 'the participating states will respect the right of persons belonging to national minorities to effective participation in public affairs, notably participation in affairs relating to the protection and promotion of the identity of such minorities.' And the UN Declaration even provides in Article 2.1 for a 'right to participate effectively in decisions on the national and, where appropriate, regional level concerning the minority to which they belong or regions in which they live, in a manner not incompatible with national legislation'. The FCNM indicates in Article 15 that 'the Parties shall create the conditions necessary for the effective participation of persons belonging to national minorities in cultural, social and economic life and in public affairs, in particular those affecting them'.

It is of particular relevance to minorities to be able to participate in shaping a society that takes into consideration its various different cultures. The importance of equitable representation of minorities in Parliament, and the creation or development of bodies and institutions whose aim is to promote dialogue and minority participation in the decision making and implementation of those policies is supported by the OSCE's 1999 Lund Recommendations on the Effective Participation of National Minorities in Public Affairs[89] and the 2001 Warsaw Guidelines to Assist National Minority Participation in the Electoral Process.[90] The underlying ratio of effective participation lies in the understanding that only members of minority groups who feel supported and represented in their state of residence, will identify with that state and integrate better, which in turn will improve minority–majority relations.

The freedom of association for minorities is connected to the right of participation in public affairs and provided for in Article 2.4 of the UN Declaration, Article 11 of the ECHR, Article 7 FCNM, and the Copenhagen Document adds to this the right to participate in non-governmental organisations (NGOs) in paragraph 32.6. This also includes that minorities must enjoy the right to freedom of association with a view to promoting or strengthening their 'common features' which needs to be supported through the right to maintain contacts with other members of the minority, especially when they are scattered throughout the territory of one or more states.[91] The freedom of association and assembly with regards to minorities has been the subject of a number of decisions by the ECtHR (see 4.5, below), mostly in favour of the minority concerned. In general, the ECtHR's approach regarding activities of political organisations aimed at the promotion of national minorities has been that such activities do not per se represent a threat to national security unless there are indications that these groups are using non-democratic means, which coincides with the Advisory Committee's approach.[92]

10 The right of participation in public affairs also touches upon the right to *internal self-determination (autonomy)* where matters lie exclusively or primarily in the interests of national minorities. The above discussed right to effective participation is a milder and less extreme form of the right to self-administration or autonomy. Self-government or regional autonomy have always been much contested concepts with regard to minority rights due to fears of secession. It has to be noted though, that ethnic violence in post-communist Europe has mainly occurred where minority groups were of such size that they were capable of organising and sustaining their own self-administration, leading to a battle with the state over control of public institutions, which is not the case for the new Eastern European EU Member States or candidate countries.

Under the League of Nations system,[93] regional autonomy was granted to groups such as the Vlachs in Greece, the Szeklers in Romania and the Ruthenians in Czechoslovakia. Electoral safeguards were provided for minorities in Albania and Iraq, and several treaties guaranteed that where a minority constituted a 'considerable proportion' of the population, states had to provide an 'equitable share' of public funds.[94]

As there are deep disagreements about the rights to territorial autonomy or self-government, modern standards are generally weaker, Article 15 FCNM simply provides that 'the Parties shall create the conditions necessary for the effective participation of persons belonging to national minorities in cultural, social and economic life and in public affairs, in particular those affecting them, which does in no way point to a right of autonomy or self-administration.

As to the definition of autonomy Bernhardt concludes: 'The essential element of autonomy is the granting of certain rights to a specific part of the state population, in view of its characteristics which differ from the majority population … They are interested in excluding state and majority interference as far as their specific background, tradition and way of life are concerned.'[95] Eide asserts that self-determination is 'almost synonymous with local autonomy'; however, there is no international standard 'with regard to the degree to which a people is entitled to internal autonomy'.[96]

In international law the most common form of 'autonomy' is territorial autonomy, therefore the *Encyclopedia of Public International Law* does not talk of 'autonomy' but only defines 'autonomous territories',[97] which can be created by constitution or international treaties, such as the Aaland Islands, south Tyrol, Greenland and the Faro Islands, whereby the former two were created by international treaty and the latter two by Danish legislation. Generally, it can be stated that territorial autonomy involves the granting of separate powers of internal administration, to whatever degree, to regions possessing some ethnic or cultural distinctiveness, without those areas being detached from the state.[98] In this context, one must differentiate between minorities with a strong community feeling and minorities with less strong ties; it also has to be considered whether they live concentrated in one area or scattered in the country concerned. While the former might have a strong common will to organise themselves, the latter might be satisfied with individual rights that will help them preserve their identity and will not evoke autonomy claims.

Although autonomy arrangements exist in many areas, it is not recognised as a principle of international law since state practice differs considerably in defining the scope and the practical application of autonomy.[99] In addition, many states have reservations as they see autonomy as a first step to self-determination and secession. Broms states that 'autonomous territories are also as a rule interested in becoming independent'.[100] However, internal self-determination or autonomy does not necessarily become a principle of secession, but can become a principle of inclusion for minorities through the right to participate, to establish their own institutions, to be represented in the decision-making process, as practised for example in Italy, Spain, Belgium or Finland. Therefore, internal self-determination might lead to more stability rather than less, and its importance for minorities living concentrated in one area of their country of residence cannot be underestimated. Furthermore, internal self-determination can guarantee a more effective protection of the minority's identity by way of institutionalising the relations with the majority.

However, since autonomy is being interpreted differently in state practice, as e. g. in Palestine, Bosnia-Herzegovina, Tibet or Galicia, it cannot be seen as a principle of international law. Bernhardt notes for example 'organisational as well as substantive rules for autonomous entities or groups do not follow a given and uniform pattern; the particular form will depend on the specific group, on the preparedness of the majority to grant autonomous rights and on the influence of other states and the international community in general.'[101] As every country's situation differs with regards to their minorities and, as pointed out by Bernhardt, with regards to a variety of social, political and economic aspects, autonomy claims do not necessarily make sense for every country and their minorities.

In documents that are only politically but not legally binding, European states have indicted a greater willingness to address calls for autonomy. Most notably Article 35 of the Copenhagen Document provides for the creation of 'local or autonomous administrations corresponding to the specific historical and territorial circumstances of such minorities as one of the possible means for minority protection'. This provision does not recognise a 'right' to autonomy but recommends it as a 'possible means' for protecting minorities. Also, the above discussed CoE's Recommendation 1201 states in Article 11:[102] 'in regions where they are a majority, the persons belonging to a national minority shall have the right to have at their disposal appropriate local or autonomous authorities or to have a special status, matching this specific historical and territorial situation and in accordance with the domestic legislation of the state' and thereby recognises autonomy as a possible right under certain circumstances.

The fact that autonomy has so far only been mentioned in non-binding international instruments (the Copenhagen Document and Recommendation 1201) confirms that it cannot be regarded as being part of the recognised corps of minority rights; in addition, the Venice Commission ruled that national minorities do not have a right to autonomy.[103] Nevertheless autonomy appears to be a suitable instrument to defuse potential tensions as it does not affect national borders. A more modern approach to (internal) self-determination/autonomy is therefore required from the international community and from the decision makers concerned in Europe, in order to bring about the urgently needed clarifications with regard to this right. However, since such prospects are unrealistic, the concept of minority rights in Europe has rather relied on less controversial ideas, of particular importance being the right to exercise one's culture and the right to effective participation in public affairs. Yet, in Western Europe the concept of territorial autonomy has been implemented in many countries where sizeable minorities exist, such as on the Aaland Islands in Finland for the Swedish–speaking minority, South Tyrol in Italy, federal autonomy has been accorded to Catalonia and the Basque Country in Spain, Flanders in Belgium and, Scotland and Wales in the UK since the 1990s. These different systems of internal autonomy have quickly become well established in the political structure of these countries, and have proved to be a successful model for accommodating minorities. In addition, it should be mentioned that self-determination has been recognised for indigenous people in the UN Declaration on the Rights of Indigenous Peoples 2007.[104] Parallels can easily be drawn between national minorities in Eastern Europe and national minorities in Western Europe as well as indigenous peoples. However, the fear of secession, particularly dominant in the Eastern post-communist countries where violent national movements have destabilised the whole area in the early 1990s, discouraged any autonomy claims. Almost two decades later, with the consolidation of frontiers and a successful peace process, the concerns today relate to the minorities' loyalty to their 'kin state' as minorities could serve as a 'fifth column' for their kin state, such as ethnic Russians in Estonia or Hungarians in Slovakia. However, similar concerns existed in the West (in particular with regard to the German minority in Belgium) and have proved to be exaggerated and unfounded.[105] Nevertheless, claims for territorial autonomy in Eastern European countries have met strong resistance from the states concerned with the consequence that international organisations take a more pragmatic approach and focus on less controversial minority rights, such as the above discussed cultural rights, as well as effective participation in public life.

The analysis will now turn to the EU's practice in the area of minority protection.

4.4 Minority policy in the EU

The EU approached the minority rights issue at the Council meeting in Copenhagen in 1993, after the Eastern European countries had applied for EU membership. At that meeting the Member States created a framework for EU enlargement by spelling out the principle of conditionality based on three crucial requirements for accession, which included 'human rights and the respect for and protection of minorities';[106] against this background there has been much discussion as to whether minority rights are also part of the *acquis*.

EU Member States themselves have by no means been immune to ethnic minority tensions, minority nations exist throughout Western Europe. Naming only the largest ones, Spain contains 'three historic nations': Catalonia, the Basque country and Galicia; in the UK, there are four: England, Northern Ireland, Scotland and Wales; in France, the Corsicans and Bretons continue to resist French assimilation; in Belgium the Constitution of 1970 recognises two sub-state nations, the Flemish and the Walloon communities, and the Italian Constitution from 1948 gives special status to Trentino-Alto Adige, Sardinia and Sicily.[107] Special Protocols to the Act of Accession of Austria, Sweden and Finland were adopted to preserve, against the impact of EU law, the special status of the Aaland Islands (within Finland) and the special rights of the Sami in Sweden and Finland.[108] And, it is not only the Central Eastern European countries who bring minority problems into the EU: Cyprus joined the EU in 2004 with an unresolved minority conflict regarding the Turkish minority in Northern Cyprus.[109]

Different approaches have been taken by the Member States according to their specific circumstances; some countries such as France, Greece (and Turkey) deny that minorities exist on their territory, while other countries apply the term differently. For example, in the UK the term 'minorities' generally refers to post-war immigrants (mainly from former colonies) but not to the historic national groups such as Scots, Irish and Welsh. However, in other Western countries and the new Eastern European Member States, it is normally referred to historic minorities, such as the Slovenes in Austria, the Sorbs and Friesians in Germany.

Minority rights have rarely featured on the EU's internal agenda. Even in violent minority conflicts, such as Northern Ireland, the Basque country and Corsica, the EU regarded the situation rather as a national and not a Community problem. Nevertheless, the inclusion of minority rights as an item of political conditionality in its external relations and with the applicant countries has been a new and controversial departure in external policy. At the same time, it has exposed the EU to the charge of 'double standards' for imposing requirements under the Copenhagen Criteria that it has not applied to its old Member States.

So far no general policy with regard to minority protection within the borders of the EU has been adopted, neither has the EU adopted any legally binding instrument devoted especially to minorities, as there is no explicit competence in the area of minority protection, i.e. minority rights were not seen as part of the EU's *acquis* as all the other criteria for accession. Initiatives in this area were rather confined to non-discrimination legislation, resolutions by the EP and some cultural/educational programmes sponsored by the Commission. However, academics and Members of the EP have considered 'constitutional resources' that can be used for the protection of minorities,[110] hence it is questionable whether minority rights are part of the *acquis* or not. Those relevant TEU and TEC/TFEU provisions are assessed below but first the role of minority rights in the EU's enlargement process will be discussed.

4.4.1 Enlargement policy with regard to CEECs

The EU's concern about human rights and the protection of minorities in Eastern and Central Europe has been reflected in – apart from the Copenhagen Criteria – a number of the EC's Association Agreements or SAAs that require the recognition of minorities, signed with at the time potential new Member States. This awareness was certainly due to the role that national diversity had played the collapse of the Soviet Union and in FYR in 1991. Considering that the harmonious development of the EU is linked to the political balance of the whole of Europe, the Member States decided to link the recognition of CEECs to various conditions, among them the 'inviolability of all frontiers' and 'the guarantees for the rights of ethnic and national groups and minorities as already discussed in chapter 3.[111]

The EU provided pre-accession assistance for the candidate countries to prepare for membership by granting them financial and technical support. The main instrument for this technical support was the PHARE programme (PHARE originally stood for 'Poland and Hungary Aid for Reconstruction and the Economy'), which ran out in 2000.[112] The PHARE programme provided support to the countries of Central and Eastern Europe since 1989, helping them through a period of massive economic restructuring and political change and has now been reoriented to address the accession priorities set by the EU for the CEECs in 1997. Projects to facilitate the resolution of disputes relating to minority nations in Eastern Europe were funded by the PHARE programme for Democracy, organising bilateral meetings between state and minority nation representatives in an effort to reduce the tensions within Eastern Europe. Minority policy cannot be seen as a priority of the PHARE programme, however, as it did not even have a separate budget line for assistance in the policy area of minority protection, and the heading 'civil society and democratisation' accounted for only 1 per cent of the total PHARE budget distributed to the CEECs.[113] However, one PHARE project in Slovakia aimed at the continuing improvement of the educational standard of the Roma population and the improvement of the living conditions of socially disadvantaged Roma.

In 2000 aid to the region was streamlined through a new programme called CARDS (Community Assistance for Reconstruction, Development and

Stabilisation).[114] The programmes' wider objective was to support the participation of the countries of the western Balkans (Albania, Bosnia and Herzegovina, Croatia, Serbia and Montenegro, including Kosovo, under UN Security Council Resolution 1244/99 of 10 June 1999, and FYROM) in the Stabilisation and Association Process (SAP). The CARDS Regulation on financial assistance In the SAP – Framework stipulates that minority rights are an 'essential element' for the application of the Regulation and a precondition for the eligibility for EC assistance. If these principles are not respected, the Council can revoke any financial assistance.[115] The CARDS programme worked on the basis of a Regional Strategy Paper and was complemented by a so-called Multi-annual Indicative Programme. Its priority areas have been identified as: institution building, justice and home affairs, cross-border cooperation, private sector development and, finally, infrastructure development. The EU summit in Zagreb in November 2000 gave the official stamp to this new policy and at the same time, initialled the SAA with the Republic of Macedonia.

The new Instrument on Pre-Accession Assistance (IPA)[116] which since 2007 replaces the former PHARE and CARDS instruments provides EU funding to promote, *inter alia*, non-discrimination and equal opportunities in countries that are preparing for EU membership, including the promotion and protection of the rights of persons belonging to ethnic and religious minorities; under IPA, for example a regional project on Roma is being sponsored with €1 million.

The EU's association policy evolved from the Europe Agreements (1) signed by Hungary, Poland, the Czech Republic, the Slovak Republic, Romania, Bulgaria, Slovenia and the three Baltic states, through the declarations of the European Council in Copenhagen (June 1993) and Essen (1994),[117] the White Paper on Enlargement (1995)[118] and the Accession Partnerships (2), finally leading to SAAs (3) adopted by the European Commission with the candidate countries, which are currently Croatia, Turkey and FYROM.[119] All these agreements refer to minority rights, or refer back to the Copenhagen Criteria.

1. The Europe Agreements refer only in their preambles explicitly to minority rights. In the operative (and legally binding) part of the agreements, only the agreements with Romania, Bulgaria, the Czech and the Slovak Republics mention human rights as principles that 'inspire the domestic and external policies of the Parties and constitute essential elements of the [respective] association' (Article 6).[120] In the Agreements concluded with the Baltic states explicit reference to minorities is only to be found regarding cooperation between the parties in the area of education, stating that 'the cooperation should focus in particular on the following areas … promoting language training in Lithuania, in particular for resident persons belonging to minorities.'[121]
2. More comprehensive information as to what the EU requires from candidate states to fulfil the 'minority' accession condition can be found in the Accession Partnerships. The conditionality established in the Accession Partnerships goes beyond the legal requirements of the Europe Agreements

by referring back to the Copenhagen Criteria. Article 4 of the Partnership Regulation establishes that, where an element that is essential for continuing to grant pre-accession assistance is lacking, in particular when the commitments contained in the Europe Agreement are not respected 'and/or progress towards fulfilment of the Copenhagen Criteria is insufficient, the Council … may take appropriate steps with regard to any pre-accession assistance granted to an applicant State',[122] i.e. minority protection is a mandatory aspect of the agreement. The Accession Partnerships mention the FCNM as the normative benchmark of the pre-accession minority policy against which the Commission may assess whether the candidates meet the 'minority' accession condition. For example, the 2006 and 2008 Accession Partnership with FYROM requires it to 'Fully comply with the European Convention on Human Rights, the recommendations made by the Committee for the Prevention of Torture as well as the Framework Convention for the Protection of National Minorities'.[123] Considering that the earlier Accession Partnerships (regarding the countries that joined in 2004 and 2007) did not refer to the FCNM but only to the ECHR,[124] it is quite remarkable that by now compliance with the FCNM is considered to be equally important as compliance with the ECHR in terms of the candidates' obligations for the accession process.[125]

3 Under the SAAs, Article 3 provides that human rights and the respect and protection of minorities 'are central to the Stabilisation and Association Process' but minority rights are not listed as 'essential elements' in the sense of Article 2 of the agreements.[126] However, it appears that the CoE cannot suspend the agreement for the violation of minority rights as they are not essential elements. As already discussed in chapter 3, the SAP with reference to the western Balkan states (who are current and potential applicants), operates with a more fine-tuned conditionality approach. This so-called SAP conditionality was established by the Council in its 'Conclusions on the Application of Conditionality' stipulating that financial assistance requires 'respect for human and minority rights' and the offer of 'real opportunities to displaced persons'. Moreover, negotiations for contractual relations are only possible where the country at hand shows 'a credible commitment' to 'generally recognized standards of human and minority rights'. These standards are further defined as enshrining three elements, namely the '[r]ight to establish and maintain … own educational, cultural and religious institutions, organisations or associations', '[a]dequate opportunities for … minorities to use their own language before courts and public authorities' and '[a]dequate protection of refugees and displaced persons returning to areas where they represent an ethnic minority'. These conditions are very clearly defined minority rights as part of a comprehensive conditionality clause embodied in an EC law measure.

As regards the continuing assessment of the applicant countries (also called 'screening' by the Commission) the Council meeting in Luxembourg in 1997 invited the Commission to draw up Regular Reports[127] on the progress made towards accession by each of the candidate countries, in light of the Copenhagen Criteria. In November 1998, the European Commission issued the first of these Regular Reports for each candidate country. These reports were updated for the first time in October 1999. In November 2000, the updated Regular Reports underlined the need to improve the situation of the Roma population in Bulgaria, the Czech Republic, Hungary, Romania and Slovakia. The 2002–3 Regular Reports continued to criticise the policy on Roma in Bulgaria and the Czech Republic but noted progress in this area in Romania and Slovakia.

The Enlargement Strategy Paper,[128] which reviewed progress on enlargement, indicated in 2002:

> In all countries with considerable Roma communities, progress has been made with the implementation of national action plans to improve the difficult situation the members of these communities are facing. Continued efforts are required to ensure that the various action plans continue to be implemented in a sustained manner, in close co-operation with Roma representatives. Adoption and due implementation of comprehensive anti-discrimination legislation, in line with the Community anti-discrimination *acquis*, would be an important step forward where such legislation is still missing. Further positive developments can be noted with regard to the protection of minorities. In Estonia and Latvia, continued progress was made in the integration of non-citizens. In several countries, the legal and institutional framework for the protection of minorities was further reinforced. In Bulgaria, Slovakia and Romania members of minority communities continued to play an important role in national political life.

It is interesting to note here that the Commission stressed the implementation of anti-discrimination legislation in order to promote the protection of minorities, rather than requiring entitlements for the minorities concerned. In addition, the Regular Reports only focus on two minority groups, the Roma and the Russians (in the Baltic states), which suggests that the Commission was mainly concerned about uncontrollable migration of Roma to the richer Western Member States and Russian political sensibilities rather than the interests of disadvantaged members of a minority group. However, the situation of the Roma or the Russian-speaking minorities never led to any serious questioning of the candidate's status as a democratic, rule-of-law respecting country in the enlargement process.

The Enlargement Strategy Paper of 2007/2008[129] is more pronounced and detailed on issues of human rights and minorities stating e.g. regarding Croatia that:

> Serbs face particular difficulties in the area of employment. The Roma minority still faces difficult living conditions and discrimination, especially in the areas of education, social protection, health care, housing and employment. Legal provisions and programmes need to be implemented with more

> determination, especially in the area of employment. A comprehensive strategy and action plan on all forms of discrimination has not yet been adopted … .

Regarding Serbia, it states 'In Serbia the overall conditions for respect of human rights and the protection of minorities have improved … The new constitution contains several provisions on human and minority rights, but a track record of judicial enforcement needs to be developed, including constitutional appeal.' Regarding Montenegro, the Paper found:

> In May 2007 Montenegro acceded to the Framework Convention for the Protection of National Minorities as well as to the European Charter on Regional and Minority Languages. The complex issue of the definition of the minorities and the minority protection is only partly covered by the 2006 Law on the Rights of National Minorities. The constitution provides a solid legal basis for the protection of minority rights. The conditions of refugees and displaced persons, including Roma, give cause for serious concern. In particular the Roma population continues to face very difficult living conditions and discrimination, especially in the areas of education, social protection, health care, housing and employment.

Surprisingly, the issue of the definition of minorities is being commented on, as well as aspects of implementation and specific areas of discrimination. Hence, it can be observed that the assessment of the human rights/minority rights situation for these third-wave applicants or potential applicants is far more detailed and critical than in the previous accession rounds of 2004 and 2007. Whether this is due to the fact that the EU is less inclined to complete the accession of these countries as swiftly as with the previous applicants, or whether it is due to the heavy criticism it has been faced with regarding its superficial screening in the earlier Regular Reports,[130] cannot be answered here. Nonetheless, one can conclude that in the context of enlargement, the momentum of minority protection has not faded away after the 'big-bang enlargement' of May 2004 but has rather been fine-tuned and further developed in the context of South Eastern Europe.[131]

4.4.1.1 Criticism of the EU's policy with regard to CEECs

The above-discussed EU initiatives aim at preparing the CEECs for membership and therefore discontinue with their accession. While the Copenhagen Criteria pronounce strong conditionality for compliance, they are poorly elaborated in substance, and there are no indications as to how compliance is evaluated.[132] Compared with other areas of the *acquis,* the EU's mechanisms for enforcing and monitoring compliance with minority protection in the candidate countries are hardly developed. While market-related achievements could be easily linked to certain chapters of the *acquis*, expertise with regard to minority rights in the Commission is insufficient and tends to rely on external bodies such as the CoE, the OSCE, in particular the HCNM and NGOs (which can sometimes give a biased view) to perform monitoring functions.[133] In addition, minority rights have no basis in EU law and are implemented differently in the old Member States, and can therefore not easily be translated into the *acquis*.

The early Accession and European Partnerships for preparing the EU's enlargement to Eastern Europe showed a lack of officially recognised benchmarks that can determine whether conditions have been met by the applicants, however, this changed with the third-wave applicants. In those Agreements, the Commission consistently urged candidate states to ratify and comply with the FCNM while old Member States such as France, Greece, and Luxembourg have either not signed or ratified the FCNM, and Latvia, a second-wave applicant, was able to join the EU in 2004 without ratifying the FCNM. Contested international standards (in particular with regard to the definition of minorities), the diverse approaches of Member States, and the lack of influence of the Commission and the ECJ in this area in the old Member States, weakened the EU's commitment to the protection of minorities, as provided for in the Copenhagen Criteria, and were seen as particularly problematic for the implementation of a coherent minority policy within an enlarged EU during the enlargement procedures with first- and second-wave applicants.[134]

For first- and second-wave applicants, the existence of legal provisions on minority rights was seen by the Commission as a sufficiently positive development, while their efficient implementation, or the coherence between the needs of minorities affected and the law were scarcely analysed in the Regular Reports. The Regular Reports dedicated approximately one page to minority rights (out of maybe 3–4 pages in total dedicated to human rights), characterised by a lack of any detailed analysis of the individual minority situation of the country concerned. It appeared that the Commission simply regarded the formal existence of a law as sufficient for compliance, without assessing the actual implementation of the law under the particular circumstances of every country. The Regular Reports provided generic statements such as: 'minorities are well integrated into Hungarian society' or 'Hungary has a well-developed institutional framework protecting the interests of its minorities'.[135] The Reports of first- and second-wave applicants did not assess the structure and operation of such institutions or minority policies in the applicant countries in any systematic manner, neither did they provide any substantiated evidence for the 'successful integration of minorities' in the applicant countries. They referred to 'international standards' or 'European standards' but never specified what these standards were, neither did they describe any implementation strategies or practical application of these standards in the relevant applicant countries.[136]

However, the Commission's assessment has improved in this regard in relation to the western Balkan States under the SAP conditionality. Regular Reports have since 2001 occasionally referred to the evaluation and recommendations of the FCNM Advisory Committee and to the resolutions of the Committee of Ministers of the CoE, as well as to OSCE documents.[137]

An indication of seeing minority rights as part of the *acquis* and not only as an accession criterion can be found in the Commission's Comprehensive Monitoring Report of the European Commission on the state of preparedness for EU membership of the Czech Republic, Estonia, Cyprus, Latvia, Lithuania, Hungary, Malta, Poland, Slovenia and Slovakia for the 2004 accession round.[138] Under the chapter on 'Social Policy and Employment', the Commission made various comments on discrimination in employment and on social exclusion suffered by minorities, for instance the Roma community in the Czech Republic, thereby suggesting that respect for and protection of minorities is not only a political criterion for the accession process, but it is also part of EU employment and social policies with which the candidates will have to comply as a membership obligation.[139]

From the above, an incremental entry of minority protection in the 'obligations of membership' can be observed; also, the FCNM has progressively become a normative basis of the Commission's assessment of the applicant countries' preparedness for accession. In addition, the Commission borrowed assessments and conclusions of the FCNM monitoring organs, to substantiate its own reports. The fact that minority rights are an important issue for the enlargement process, has led to a number of internal initiatives in the EU that have promoted awareness and sometimes even led to concrete measures regarding minority protection, which will be discussed below. In this context, minority policy is being treated as part of human rights policy; given that human rights are part of the EU *acquis*, minority rights can also be viewed as belonging to the *acquis*.

What other developments took place in the area of minority rights in Europe and whether the current standard is sufficient in an enlarged EU, taking into account the above-discussed issues will now be assessed.

4.4.2 EP initiatives

The EP has been the main Community organ to recognise the importance of giving attention to minority protection within the EU. With the Treaty of Amsterdam (ToA) the EP has become an increasingly self-confident institutional player, which has adopted several resolutions[140] identifying the area of human rights as a means for fostering its institutional and value-oriented profile. Already at its meeting of 20 December 1989, when the Iron Curtain started to fall, the EP Committee on Legal Affairs and Citizen's Rights, on an initiative by Graf von Stauffenberg, decided to draw up a report calling on the governments of the Member States 'by means of the insertion of an appropriate title in the TEU at the next Intergovernmental Conference on the amendment of the Treaties to be concluded by 1996, to give recognition, binding guarantees and lasting protection to the rights of ethnic groups and their members as defined in the following *Charter of rights of ethnic groups* … '[141]

Considering the traditional reluctance of Member States to grant collective rights, this proposal gave an unusually large scope to the collective aspect of minority rights. However, the initiative failed due to the lack of political support in the Council. In 1994 the EP then adopted a narrower approach: 'The Resolution on Linguistic and Cultural Minorities in the European Community'[142] which emphasised the necessity for Member States to recognise their linguistic minorities, declaring that 'all peoples have the right to respect for their language and culture and must therefore have the necessary legal means to protect and promote them'. Other provisions were devoted to specific measures aimed at the protection and development of minorities' languages and cultures. The Resolution supported and was built on the substantive provisions of the European Charter for Regional or Minority Languages of 1992, adopted within the CoE,[143] calling on the Member States and local and regional authorities to encourage and support specialised associations, and to create trans-frontier linguistic institutions.

By simply focusing on linguistic issues the EP considerably limited the scope of its original initiative. Interestingly, this resolution underlined the new cultural dimension of the EU by quoting the then new Article 128 TEC (Article 151 TEC, now Article 167 TFEU) noting that the minority languages and cultures are also an 'integral part of the Union's culture and European heritage' and that therefore the EC should provide minorities with 'legal protection and appropriate financial resources'.[144] According to the Resolution, the EC should especially encourage action by Member States in cases where the protection is inadequate or non-existent. Member States are called on to recognise their linguistic minorities and create the basic conditions for the preservation and development of minority languages. National legal acts should 'at least cover the use and encouragement of such languages and cultures in the spheres of education, justice and public administration, the media, toponomics and other sectors of public and cultural life'.[145] Finally, the Resolution calls on the Commission and the Council to accommodate minority languages in all its educational and cultural programmes and to propose a multiannual action programme for minority languages.

Another initiative was taken in 2003, when the EP's Committee on Culture presented a 'Resolution with Recommendations to the Commission on European regional and lesser used languages – the languages of minorities in the EU – in the context of enlargement and cultural diversity' based on the report tabled by Michl Ebner.[146] In its annex the Resolution contains recommendations such as the establishment of a European Agency for linguistic diversity and language learning and regular monitoring on the basis of Article 6 TEU which should pay particular attention to the protection of human rights in general, and the protection of minorities in particular, not only in relation to external policy, but also within the Member States. In addition, the Resolution calls for further cooperation between the EU institutions and the CoE bodies in the area of minority protection. Moreover, the Ebner Resolution suggests the extension of Article 13 TEC to discrimination on the grounds of language and, the extension of qualified majority voting to cultural matters (regarding Article 151 TEC/167 TFEU, see below).[147]

In light of the continuing enlargement to the East, the EP in 2005 issued the 'European Parliament Resolution on the protection of minorities and anti-discrimination policies in an enlarged Europe' (the Moares Resolution)[148] which declares under subheading A: 'bearing in mind that there is a difference between the protection of minorities and anti-discrimination policies; noting that equal treatment is a basic right, not a privilege, of all citizens, and tolerance should be a general attitude in life, not a favour granted to some and not to others; considering, therefore, that all forms of discrimination must be fought with equal intensity; recalling that national minorities contribute to the richness of Europe ....'

It is interesting to note here, that the EP clearly recognises the difference between mere non-discrimination and the protection of minorities, the latter requiring positive measures for placing minorities in a *more equal position.* This was not the case three years earlier, as it is clear from the EU's Annual Report on Human Rights of 2003 that minority protection is simply viewed as a special form of the general non-discrimination principle, stating that 'The protection of persons belonging to minorities is covered by the non-discrimination clause in Article 13 of the Treaty establishing the European Community.'[149]

The Moares Resolution is the most far-reaching and encompassing resolution on minority rights the EP has issued so far. It takes up the criticism the EU has been faced with pointing out 'the inconsistency of policy toward minorities – while protection of minorities is a part of the Copenhagen Criteria, there is no standard for minority rights in EC policy nor is there an understanding of who can be considered a member of a minority'; and proposes that a future EU definition of minorities should be based on the CoE Recommendation 1201(1993).[150] Furthermore, it is interesting to note that the EP admits that there exists 'no single solution' for improving the situation of minorities in all Member States. However 'some common and minimum objectives for public authorities in the EU should be developed'.[151] In this context the EP underlines that 'effective participation in decision-making based on the principles of subsidiarity and self-governance is one of the best ways of handling the problems of traditional minority communities.'[152] And, finally recommends a number of TEC provisions that could be used to implement a coherent general strategy on the problems facing minorities in the EU, by continuing to enforce existing anti-discrimination legislation and considering possible further action based on Articles 13, 18, 49, 65, 95 and 151 TEC.[153]

Like in many other resolutions, the Moares Resolution also underlines the special relevance of the Roma, a community that became with enlargement one of the largest minorities in the EU and that is in need of 'special protection', as it is not only the largest but also the most disadvantaged minority group in Europe.[154] However, in its capacity as a resolution, there is no legally binding effect attached to this document, it rather remains a political declaration. Apart from issuing numerous resolutions on minority issues, the EP also established an Intergroup dealing specifically with minority rights.[155] Aspects of the Moares Resolution, such as the promotion of minority rights on the basis of Articles 13 and 151 (now Articles 19 and 167 TFEU) are the main issues to be addressed by the Intergroup. In recognition of these efforts, on 2 April 2009, a Roma delegation handed an award of the Roma Community in Europe to the EP.

4.4.3 Minority protection under the TEU and TEC/TFEU provisions

As already mentioned above, minority rights are not anchored in any long-standing EC law tradition. The ToA did not introduce a concept of minority rights into the founding treaties despite their requirement under the Copenhagen Criteria. However, there are Articles in the TEU/TEC/TFEU that assume some kind of indirect protection for minorities and can serve as a basis for developing a more solid minority policy at EU level.

4.4.3.1 Article 6 TEU

The principles enumerated in the old Article 6(1) TEU were widely regarded as a confirmation of the Copenhagen Criteria, but they are not identical. Article 6(1) TEU defines the principles 'common to Member States' as 'liberty, democracy, respect for human rights and fundamental freedoms, and the rule of law'. While under the old Article 49 TEU only a European state 'which respects the principles set out in Article 6(1) may apply to become a member of the Union', the new Article 49 TEU under the Lisbon Treaty now refers to the principles set out in Article 2 TEU, which differs from Article 6(1) in so far as it includes the protection of minorities as one of the fundamental values on which the EU is founded. As the Copenhagen Criteria for accession to the EU laid special emphasis on the protection of minorities, the EU was heavily criticised that this criterion was not explicitly included in Article 6(1) under the ToA or Nice, neither could it be found elsewhere in the constituent Treaties. However, this situation has now been remedied with the new Article 2 TEU and the relevant reference in Article 49 TEU respectively.

The new Article 6(3) TEU (Lisbon Treaty) provides that 'the Union shall respect fundamental rights, as guaranteed by the European Convention for the Protection of Human Rights and Fundamental Freedoms signed in Rome on 4 November 1950 and as they result from the constitutional traditions common to the Member States, as general principles of Community Law'. In addition, as the EU is required to accede to the ECHR under Article 6(2) TEU Treaty of Lisbon, all actions of the institutions have to be compatible with the provisions of the ECHR and the jurisdiction of the ECtHR, which has become the key reference for the protection of human rights within the EU's legal order. By committing itself to the ECHR in the context of its internal legal order, the EU requires its institutions to respect fundamental rights at a level that is being upheld in the wider Europe represented in the CoE, to which all Member States must – of necessity – belong. Hence, the protection of minorities under the ECHR via Article 6(3) TEU will be analysed in the next section 4.5.

4.4.3.2 Article 13 TEC/19 TFEU

Article 13 of the TEC (renumbered Article 19 TFEU under the Treaty of Lisbon) enables the Council 'to take appropriate action to combat discrimination' based on – among others – racial or ethnic origin. This provision is not in itself a prohibition of discrimination on grounds of race or ethnic origin but rather creates the possibility for the EC to adopt measures to combat discrimination within the scope of the policies and powers granted in the Treaty, i.e. it has no direct effect for Member States and does not condemn discrimination explicitly. The fact that Article 13 TEC uses the term 'appropriate action to combat' allows the Council and Commission to use a wide range of different instruments to achieve this objective of 'combating discrimination', such as special outreach programmes or action plans, since it is not limited to legislation.

The non-discrimination principle, as enshrined in Article 13 TEC/19 TFEU is a necessary prerequisite for achieving equality for minorities. However, differential treatment is often necessary to achieve de facto as opposed to de jure equality. The concept of non-discrimination, as provided for in all human rights instruments, does not sufficiently take into consideration the fact that persons belonging to minorities, compared to the majorities, are subject to different conditions in the enjoyment of their human rights. The purely formal equal treatment is therefore inadequate to achieve real equality; as the ECtHR stated in its *Belgian Linguistics* case that 'Discrimination exists … when different situations are treated in the same way or similar situations are handled in a different way.'[156] In addition, it has already been noted above that Article 4 FCNM points out in paragraph 2 that 'The Parties *undertake to adopt … adequate measures* in order to promote … full and effective equality between persons belonging to a national minority and those belonging to the majority …' and in paragraph 3: 'The measures adopted in accordance with paragraph 2 shall not be considered to be an act of discrimination' [emphasis added]. It is therefore necessary that human rights systems are supplemented with a system of positive protection for minorities in order to balance out the disadvantages members of minorities experience in society.

Unlike the original non-discrimination provision in Article 12 (renumbered Article 18 TFEU), which prohibits discrimination on the grounds of nationality for EU citizens, Article 13 prohibits discrimination on the basis of personal attributes that apply to everybody, including third–country nationals. 'National minorities' (as defined above under 4.3) would be protected under the attributes of race or ethnicity. By acknowledging these characteristics, Article 13 TEC helps to mainstream issues regarding racism and discrimination in the EC order but does not benefit national minorities directly. Procedurally, Article 13 TEC requires the Council to act unanimously on a proposal by the Commission and after obtaining the consent of the EP, i.e. it is not subject to qualified majority voting. The requirement of unanimity in the Council on a sensitive issue such as discrimination is a restriction of the effectiveness of Article 13 TEC/19 TFEU.

Much less clear is whether Article 13 EC could form the basis for legislation that requires positive measures or even group rights. In 2003, the Commission stated in its Annual Human Rights Report that minority rights were protected by the non-discrimination principle;[157] however, by now one can identify various tendencies which might indicate that the EU is slowly moving away from this formal idea of equality and increasingly applying (or at least arguing for) a more substantive reading of equality – a fact which could legitimise calls for affirmative actions taken at EU level.[158]

Legislation that has emerged to date, based on Article 13 TEC, focused largely on discrimination in the field of employment.[159] In addition, on the basis of Article 13 TEC the Council adopted the 'Anti-Discrimination Directive' 2000/43/EC implementing the principle of equal treatment between persons irrespective of racial or ethnic origin. The Directive's scope of application encompasses *all* persons according to Article 3 and is not limited to EU nationals. The Directive applies to a broad range of situations, covering for example discrimination in the area of employment, social protection, healthcare, education, housing etc. which makes it a powerful instrument as it has a much wider scope of application than e.g. the FCNM. Even though the Directive was adopted summarily in reaction to the election of the right-wing Freedom Party in Austria and does not mention national minorities, it nevertheless provides a solid framework for more protection from discrimination EU wide, which can also benefit minorities.

In particular, Article 5 of Directive 2000/43/EC is of interest here as it specifically provides for the possibility of undertaking positive measures:

> With a view to ensuring full equality in practice, the principle of equal treatment shall not prevent any Member State from maintaining or adopting specific measures to prevent or compensate for disadvantages linked to racial or ethnic origin.

This provision is similar to Article 2 of the Directive on Equal Treatment[160] and is also mirrored in Article 141 TEC with regard to equality for men and women in the workplace.[161]

The concept of requiring positive measures to prevent discrimination or remedy discrimination of the past is also known, in particular in the US, as 'affirmative action'.[162] In two decisions, in the *Kalanke* case of 1995[163] and the *Marschall* case of 1997[164] the ECJ decided on the admissibility of positive measures or 'affirmative action' in the context of EC law. Both cases concerned the equal treatment of men and women for working access and the legality of provisions in national law that promote women when equally qualified as they are underrepresented in the working place. While the ECJ rejected the admissibility of such affirmative action in the *Kalanke* case, it decided in *Marschall* that 'according to the Court, in the working world a male candidate will tend to be promoted even if a female candidate is equally qualified for the post in question. Certain deep-rooted prejudices and stereotypes as to the role and capacities of women in working life still persist'. The ECJ concluded that 'priority given to equally qualified women – which is designed to restore the balance – is not contrary to Community law provided that an objective assessment of each individual candidate … is assured and that, accordingly, promotion of a male candidate is not excluded from the outset.' The reasoning in *Kalanke* – the ECJ struck down a rule that provided that priority must be given to women as long as they were underrepresented, among equally qualified candidates for promotion – emphasised that Article 2(4) of the Equality Directive was an exception to the principle of equal treatment and therefore should be interpreted strictly. In a similar case of 2000,[165] the ECJ took again a very restrictive approach in the interpretation of Article 141(4) TEC and required, similar to *Marschall*, that 'an objective assessment which takes account of the specific personal situations of all candidates' is required.

Hence, on the basis of this jurisdiction, the interpretation of Article 5 of the Directive might require 'an individual objective assessment' before positive action for the promotion of minority rights in violation of the principle of equal treatment could be endorsed.[166] However, Article 5 of the Directive is very careful in its wording and uses the negative term of 'the principle of equal treatment *shall not prevent* any Member State from maintaining or adopting specific measures …' [emphasis added]. If compared to the FCNM, which expresses minority rights in terms of obligations incumbent on Member States, by requiring – for example – in Article 7 'The Parties *undertake to grant* all persons belonging to a national minority the right to manifest their religion or belief [emphasis added]', the Directive appears more reluctant to confer positive rights.

The provision in Article 13 of the Directive, which requires Member States to establish an independent body for the promotion of equal treatment, might assist members of minorities individually with individual complaints, but it is not suited to serve a minority as a group in achieving more equality through positive measures. However, it is interesting to note that the preamble of Council Directive 2000/43/EC, states in paragraph 9 that the Directive is based on the assumption that discrimination on the basis of racial or ethnic origin may undermine the achievement of the objectives of the TEC. Nevertheless, it has to be remembered that the Directive only sets the minimum standard Member States have to comply with, and leaves it up to the Member States to fill this with adequate laws.

4.4.3.3 Article 151 TEC (167 TFEU)

Article 151(4) TEC (renumbered Article 167 TFEU under the Treaty of Lisbon) requests the Community to take cultural aspects into account in its action under other provisions of the Treaty, 'in particular in order to respect and to promote the diversity of its cultures'. Article 151(1) provides the following: 'The Community shall contribute to the flowering of the cultures of the Member-States, while respecting their national and regional diversity'.

While Article 151 TEC is not explicitly aimed at ethnic minorities, it does represent certain recognition of the value of cultural diversity in the EU's basic constitutional document. However, the term 'respecting national and regional diversity' and 'contributing to the flowering of cultures' is first a rather vague concept and second 'respect' is far from the promotion of minority rights. However, Article 151 TEC recognises that Member States are not culturally homogenous and that regional diversity, in fact, exists. It also defies the widespread allegation that the EU aims at creating a homogenous super-state with the homogeneous EU citizen. The wording seems to suggest though that rather the different cultures of the different Member States should be promoted and not necessarily different cultures *within one* Member State.

Article 151 TEC makes a generic statement that the EU promotes European culture 'while respecting national and regional diversity and at the same time bringing the common cultural heritage to the fore'. It also has to be noted that the CoE, according to Article 151(5) can only adopt recommendations, rather than decisions, however, this has never been done; hence the impact of Article 151 on institutional developments and policy initiatives has been vestigial, since the contribution to regional cultural diversity by the Council of Ministers, the European Commission and the EP has been poorly coordinated and very unsystematic.

As a result, Article 151 TEC has not been used as a basis for developing a more minority-oriented cultural policy but it has been used for certain initiatives of various Commission Directorate-Generals to develop programmes intended to protect cultural diversity on the basis of Articles 149 TEC[167] and 151 TEC which opened a range of possibilities regarding the culture and education of minorities:[168]

1 The Culture 2007 Programme[169] aims to promote a wider knowledge of European literature and history among European citizens by translating literary, theatrical and references works into lesser used European languages and financially supports works written in those lesser used languages.
2 The European Bureau for Lesser Used Languages (EBLUL) seeks to promote Europe's regional autochthonous languages and the linguistic rights of their speakers.[170]
3 The Life Long Learning Programme[171] is – among other issues of education dedicated to the promotion of the intercultural dimension of learning and improvement of the quality of education for the children of migrant workers, children of Roma and children of occupational Travellers. Under the umbrella of this programme, the European Commission has taken measures to encourage and develop the participation of young Roma and to empower them to become actively involved in European youth initiatives.

The above-mentioned programmes promote education and culture in Europe generally, and are not specifically addressed to minorities; however, they do serve in parts the interests of members of the Roma minority (see Life Long Learning Programme), or linguistic minorities. They neither address religious rights, minority schools, funding of minority culture or self-administration issues, nor problems that might stem from secessionist movements, which currently exist, e.g. in Northern Ireland, the Basque Country or Corsica. The overall aim of these programmes is to promote European culture, which mainly refers to the different cultures of the different Member States but not to their minorities.

Nevertheless, one Community initiative for a support programme dealing with minority questions in a comprehensive manner has been taken as a result of the situation of violence: in the context of the peace process in Northern Ireland, a special Commission Task Force was created, in particular 'to consider ways to develop and refocus the policies of the EU to help those people who have been most affected by the conflict to live together in mutual respect and economic prosperity'.[172] However, it should be emphasised that this ad hoc project was launched on the express invitation of the UK and Ireland, and can therefore not be seen as an attempt by the EU to engage into solving minorities' problems of its Member States at Community level.

4.4.3.4 The Treaty of Lisbon and Articles 21 and 22 of the EU Charter

Article 2 of the TEU, Treaty of Lisbon, recognises for the first time the rights of minorities in a founding document by stating:

> The Union is founded on the values of respect for human dignity, liberty, democracy, equality and the rule of law and respect for human rights, *including the rights of persons belonging to minorities*. These values are common to the Member States in a society in which pluralism, non-discrimination, tolerance, justice, solidarity and equality between women and men prevail. [emphasis added]

This is a groundbreaking statement in a treaty document of the EU, which can provide a legal basis for minority rights legislation in the EU. Not only does it put minority rights on the same level as human rights but it will also strengthen the position of minority issues in the EU. As a basic provision that proclaims the principles and values that represent the moral underpinnings of the EU and their Member States, it carries considerable weight and brings minority rights closer to the *acquis*.

The wording of Article 2, speaking of *rights of persons belonging to minorities*, i.e. individual rights necessary for people who belong to minority groups, coincides with the standard of minority protection developed by international law, as for example under Article 27 ICCPR (see 4.3, above). Others might identify in the wording 'the attempt to overcome the tension between, on the one hand, an individualistic notion of rights and a rather formal perception of equality as is so far predominant in EU law and, on the other hand, the realisation that justice and the protection of group identities are hardly possible if any group dimension to rights and any more substantive perception of equality are ignored'.[173] Even though the new provision does provide for minority rights as individual rights, it nonetheless alludes to the fact that minority members are inevitably part of a group and thereby calls for awareness towards minority *groups*.

The same wording did already appear in Article I-2 of the draft Constitution, which was rejected by referendum in France and the Netherlands. It is particularly crucial that the French people rejected the Constitution, considering that the

French government which categorically opposed minority rights in the past was willing to sign the draft Constitution, including Article I-2 and now the Treaty of Lisbon with Article 2.

With regards to the EU Charter of Fundamental Rights, Article 6(1) TEU, Treaty of Lisbon awards the Charter the same status as the EU Treaties:

> The Union recognises the rights, freedoms and principles set out in the Charter of Fundamental Rights of the European Union of 7 December 2000, as adapted at Strasbourg, on 12 December 2007, which shall have the same legal value as the Treaties.

As such, the Charter will have to be interpreted by the ECJ, including Articles 21, 22 of the Charter, which will inevitably require a definition of the term national minorities, since Article 21(1) of the Charter provides that:

> Any discrimination based on any ground such as sex, race, colour, ethnic or social origin, genetic features, language, religion or belief, political or any other opinion, *membership of a national minority*, property, birth, disability, age or sexual orientation shall be prohibited. [emphasis added]

Article 21 of the Charter of Fundamental Rights adds 'belonging to a national minority' to the list of criteria on the basis of which discrimination is forbidden and is therefore the first instance of including 'national minority' into the internal *acquis*, as opposed to its previous use exclusively in external relations/ enlargement. Article 21(1) of the Charter does not specifically focus on minorities but also acknowledges other aspects as grounds for non-discrimination; at the same time it does not go any further than Article 13 TEC, except that Article 21(1) prohibits discrimination directly while Article 13 TEC has no direct effect, see above.

Furthermore, Article 22 of the Charter reiterates the commitment already made in Article 151 TEC that 'the Union shall respect cultural, religious and linguistic diversity'. According to the *travaux préparatoires* this provision was regarded as the constitutional space to be used for protecting minority interests during the drafting of the Charter.[174] However, like Article 151 TEC, Article 22 is not specifically designed to protect minorities; despite the vagueness of this provision, the cultural dimension provides, in contrast to the non-discrimination principle, an appreciation of cultural diversity as a much less institutionalised principle, which is only backed by generic formulations in the Treaties (as e.g. Article 151 TEC) but not by secondary EC legislation or ECJ rulings. Nonetheless, its reinforcement in the Charter and placement directly after the non-discrimination Article, which now includes national minorities, makes the link between the two principles visible and thus provides an additional argumentative basis for promoting minority rights and considering them as part of the *acquis*.

Provisions of the EU Charter are subject to Article 52(2), which limits the exercise of Charter rights to the conditions and limits set by the

Treaties, i.e. rights not based in these Treaties are not subject to its limitations; therefore, it was argued in the past that Article 52(2) of the Charter would not apply to Article 21(1) with regards to discrimination on the basis of membership of a national minority, as this has no foundation in the TEC or TEU.[175] However, with the entering into force of the Treaty of Lisbon, the rights of minorities are part of the fundamental principles on which the EU is founded, according to the new Article 2 TEU. Hence, restrictions of the Treaties will also apply to minority rights as provided for under Article 21 of the Charter.[176] By the same token, the wording of Article 21(1) which prohibits '*any* discrimination on any ground such as …' suggests that *any* discrimination can also include indirect discrimination or a de facto discrimination, which is particularly relevant for minorities. On this basis, even if not clearly spelled out, positive measures to remove de facto discrimination for minorities, could be claimed. Thereby the EU Charter on Fundamental Rights opens up opportunities to promote further reaching minority rights more convincingly on the basis of Articles 21 and 22 together with Article 2 TEU of the Treaty of Lisbon, giving the EU a basis for more minority-specific legislation, which until now never went beyond mere non-discrimination provisions. The Lisbon version of Article 13 TEC (Article 19 TFEU) does not explicitly empower the EU to combat discrimination based on membership of a national minority, leading to incoherence between Article 13 TEC and Article 21 of the EU Charter on Fundamental Rights.

In this context, it should also be mentioned that under Article 10 TFEU of the Treaty of Lisbon the EU 'shall aim to combat discrimination based on sex, racial or ethnic origin, religion or belief, disability, age or sexual orientation' when defining and implementing any of its policies and activities. Thus, in addition to the obligation to avoid discrimination under Article 13 TEC (now Article 19 TFEU) it has to mainstream actively and promote anti-discrimination in its legislation or as an executive organ. However, since this new mainstreaming obligation builds on the enabling provision Article 19 TFEU and not the prohibitive provision Article 21 in the Charter, it can be argued that Article 10 TFEU will not cover discrimination on the basis of membership of a national minority.

4.4.3.5 The jurisdiction of the ECJ with regard to minorities

So far the ECJ has pronounced itself in three cases on aspects of minority rights:

1 The ECJ decided in the *Groener* case of 1989[177] that the requirement of bilinguality is reasonable in order to protect a minority language. Anita Groener was a Dutch national acting as a teacher at a college in Dublin. In order to work as a teacher on a permanent basis in Ireland, she had to show an adequate knowledge of the Irish language. Since she failed the relevant Irish language examination, she argued, with some plausibility, that the requirement of Irish did not serve any practical purpose in her case (she would never be required actually to use Irish in her job) and, instead, was a measure resulting in the exclusion of foreigners and therefore a form of

indirect discrimination prohibited by Article 3 of EC Regulation 1612/68 of 15 October 1968.[178] The ECJ held:

> The EEC Treaty does not prohibit the adoption of a policy for the protection and promotion of a language of a Member State which is both the national language and the first official language … The importance of education for the implementation of such a policy must be recognised. Teachers have an essential role to play, not only through the teaching which they provide but also by their participation in the daily life of the school and the privileged relationship which they have with their pupils. In those circumstances, it is not unreasonable to require them to have some knowledge of the first national language.

Yet, the ECJ did not grant full discretion to the Member States in the definition of their linguistic policies. The ECJ rather confirmed its doctrine that any national policy standing in the way of one of the common market freedoms is to be carefully scrutinised, even if it involves a policy area (such as language policy) in which a role for the EC is not expressly recognised by the Treaty. The ECJ reserved itself the power to decide in future cases whether national language regulations have a disproportionate impact on the rights of EC nationals.[179]

2 In *Mutsch*,[180] the ECJ made clear that other aspects of language law could also be affected by the EC rights of free movement. Mr Mutsch, a Luxembourg national who was living and working in Belgium was prosecuted in Belgium and insisted that the trial should not be held in French, the normal language used by the competent criminal court, but in German. Indeed, those Belgian nationals belonging to the German-speaking minority in the East of Belgium (the area where Mr Mutsch happened to live) have the right to require that trials against them be conducted in German rather than French. However, Mr Mutsch was denied that benefit because, under Belgian law, the right to use German was reserved to Belgian nationals only. Mr Mutsch's argument that this was discrimination on grounds of his nationality, and therefore contrary to EC law (Regulation 1612/68), was upheld by the ECJ. The use of language in judicial proceedings has no direct connection with conditions of employment, but the ECJ held that equal treatment should not only be recognised for EU migrants in relation to the work itself but also in respect of all so-called 'social advantages', even if they were unrelated to the contract of employment. The ECJ held that the possibility, for a migrant worker, to use his own language in proceedings before the courts was such a social advantage and that it could meaningfully contribute to the integration of the migrant in the host country, and therefore facilitate the exercise of the free movement of persons.

3 Similarly, the ECJ decided in *Bickel/Franz*[181] that there was no undermining effect when the right in question – that a trial against a German speaker is

> to be held in German language on request – was also granted to other German-speaking EU nationals, who were not members of the German minority in Italy, and therefore ruled against the Italian government, which had argued that the measures were designed to protect the German minority and for that reason only to be applied to German-speaking Italian citizens. However, the ECJ also held in *Bickel/Franz* that 'the right for a linguistic minority to use their language in judicial and administrative procedures as a measure for the protection of such a minority may constitute a legitimate aim, which therefore does not in itself run contrary to the non-discrimination principle'.[182]

These decisions mainly concerned the prohibition of discrimination on the basis of nationality in the context of the free movement of persons and labour. All three cases have in common the extension of the scope of minority rights (here in particular the protection of minority language) to non-members of the minority group in question. From this – so far limited – case law it can be concluded that the ECJ uses the non-discrimination principle as a point of reference for recognising minority rights in Member States where relevant provisions for the protection of minorities exist, in order to extend this protection to non-members. This jurisdiction also suggests that minority protection cannot be excluded in ECJ rulings, however, the ECJ is still far from establishing minority protection as a general principle of EC law in its precedents. At the judicial level, the ECJ has recognised that the protection of minorities is a legitimate aim which could justify derogations to the fundamental freedoms underpinning the EU legal order, provided such derogations are proportionate to that aim. The ECJ thus accepts to balance minority and Community interests, and tolerates, in specific circumstances, Member States' measures of minority protection that fall foul of EC law. Beyond this judicial tolerance, the ECJ could develop more pro-active minority rights jurisprudence, through the prism of the general principles of EC law.

4.4.3.6 Protection by the Fundamental Rights Agency (FRA)

As already discussed in chapter 2, the FRA's objective is to provide assistance and expertise in the field of fundamental rights to bodies of the Community as well as to Member States, which mainly concerns data collection, the production of expert opinions, and the establishment of a communication strategy, including an institutionalised dialogue with civil society. Even though these tasks of the FRA are all additionally relevant and beneficial for minorities, FRA's activities will always depend on its Multiannual Framework (MAF). Even though the creation of the FRA was criticised as an unnecessary bureaucratic duplication of numerous treaties and institutions already in place, the FRA's focus on 'diversity management' is an important task regarding the challenge of integrating immigrant populations. Considering that No. 10 of FRA's Founding Regulation states that the FRA should continue to cover not only the phenomena of racism and xenophobia but also 'the protection of rights of persons belonging to minorities … as essential elements for the protection of fundamental rights'.[183] In addition, according to Article 4(1)(d) of the Founding Regulation the EP, Council and Commission (as well as FRA's management) can ask for opinions on specific thematic topics, i.e. minorities can be put on the agenda if one of the relevant institutions so wishes. It was not only proposed by the EP that a separate sector of the FRA should deal with the question of national minorities, but the EP also requested that the FRA should specifically address Roma and minority issues.[184] Also, the already mentioned Moares Resolutions criticised that minority issues in the EU have not been high enough on the agenda of the EU and that the FRA 'must play a key role' in this area,[185] hence, more initiatives by the EP in relation to FRA can be expected.

The first annual working programme of the FRA of 2008 shows that it is already active in the areas of discrimination and Roma rights, and will launch a new project on the situation of Roma and Travellers in the EU. The FRA's research activities include a project on the housing situation of Roma and Travellers in the EU. Furthermore, in 2009 the FRA was holding a joint expert seminar in Strasbourg in cooperation with the OSCE and the CoE's Commissioner for Human Rights to discuss human rights violations of Roma in the context of freedom of movement and migration. This was followed by an international high-level conference on freedom of movement and migration of Roma in November in Vienna.[186]

The FRA can only become active when authorised by EU institutions or by its MAF, which is ultimately decided on by the Council, acting on a proposal from the Commission and after consulting the EP. However, its broad mandate regarding discrimination and racism leaves opportunities for initiatives regarding minority rights, which it has already taken up in the area of Roma rights, a minority that requires special attention regarding social inclusion and positive rights. In this context, FRA has huge potential to push the debate on minority rights forward and to provide the currently lacking expertise on minority rights to Commission, Council and Member States. As already discussed in chapter 3, under Article 9 of the 2007 Regulation,[187] an agreement was concluded in February 2008[188] between FRA and the CoE with the aim of setting up a cooperation framework between the two 'in order to avoid duplication and ensure complementarity and added value'. Acknowledging that 'the Council of Europe has acquired extensive experience and expertise in intergovernmental cooperation and assistance activities in the field of human rights, having also established several human rights monitoring and control mechanisms', it notably stipulates that 'regular contacts' between the FRA and the CoE shall be established at the 'appropriate level', and foresees the appointment by the CoE of an independent person to sit on the FRA's management and executive boards. Methods of cooperation envisaged by the agreement include mandatory 'regular consultations', as well as 'exchange of information and data'. Indeed, the FRA 'shall take due account … where relevant, of findings, reports and activities in the human rights field of the Council of Europe's human rights monitoring and intergovernmental committees', defined as including the Advisory Committee of the FCNM for the purpose of the agreement (see chapter 3, section 3.7.1.3).

This agreement, which institutionalises cooperation between the FRA and the FCNM bodies, and also codifies the transfer of standards between both institutions not only provides a solid basis to improve standards for minority rights in the EU, but also enhances the impact of the FCNM within the EU. In combination with the recommendations of the Network of Independent Experts on Minority Rights[189] and the provisions of the Charter as interpreted in the light of the broader *acquis* of EU law, FRA is well equipped to develop the EU's very own minority policy.

4.4.4 Miscellaneous

The project 'Human and Minority Rights in the Life Cycle of Ethnic Conflicts', which was drawn up under the auspices of the European Academy of Bozen (EURAC),[190] examined in detail aspects of minority protection in the EU outside the area of hard law. Apart from human rights impact assessments (as already discussed in chapter 2) which are clearly relevant for minority policies, other instruments such as the application of the so-called Open Method of Coordination (OMC) in areas like employment, social inclusion and integration, and the provision of new financial stimuli, which allow for the development of the minority momentum within the EU framework, without adding any new EU competences, will be looked at briefly.

The OMC is regarded as a method to spread best practices among the Member States and thereby achieve greater convergence towards the main EU goals in areas where the EU does not have fully fledged legislative competence. Hence, OMC seems an ideal mechanism for areas such as minority protection, where the Member States do not want to give away their primary competence but where they, at the same time, recognise a need to exchange ideas, know-how and best practices.[191] OMC reporting takes account of minorities and their needs as exemplified by the implementation of the European Employment Strategy (EES),[192] which requires every Member State to describe how the Employment Guidelines[193] are put into practice at the national level. From 1999 onwards, these guidelines have expressly referred to 'ethnic minorities and other groups and individuals who may be disadvantaged',[194] 'ethnic minorities and migrant workers',[195] 'immigrants, and ethnic minorities'.[196] However, the Joint Employment Report of 1999,[197] which addressed the policy performance of the Member States, criticised a lack of comparable data describing the scale or nature of the needs of disabled people and ethnic minorities as a serious handicap for assessing policies addressed to these groups. Moreover, the Employment Reports complain about the fact that the term 'ethnic minorities' has been interpreted in the various National Action Plans in a different way which leads to a lack of comparability between them.[198] Again, the lack of an internationally agreed definition of the term minority represents a problem for the multilateral policy-shaping process in view of the divergent approaches to minority protection in the different Member States.

Furthermore, it is clear from the reports mentioned that the minority issue is, in this context, not addressed as a cultural rights issue or a question of political participation but as an issue of inclusion in the employment market; and traditional (national) minorities seem to play only a very limited role in the EES,[199] as for instance the Joint Employment Report of 2007/2008 makes no reference to minorities but refers to *migrants*.[200] However, the High Level Advisory Group of Experts on the Social Integration of Ethnic Minorities and Their Full Access to the Labour Market (established according to the mentioned Framework Strategy)[201] had the mandate to address among others 'the different situations and needs of minority groups, including recent migrants, established ethnic minorities, national minorities, the Roma and stateless persons' and is therefore also relevant for the employment situation of traditional minorities.[202]

The Social Inclusion Process as part of the OMC, established in 2000 by EU leaders, has provided a framework for national strategy development as well as for policy coordination between the Member States on issues relating to poverty and social exclusion.[203] Member States are required to submit national action plans on social inclusion, which are jointly evaluated by the Commission and the Member States. In the context of the new Member States, a certain emphasis was placed on Russian minorities and Roma.[204] The social inclusion of Roma is a recurring theme in this process, however, other 'traditional' minorities have not been addressed so far, as the focus is again on immigrants or 'new minorities'.

The report of the Sixth Framework Programme project 'Human and Minority Rights in the Life Cycle of Ethnic Conflicts' concludes that the EU has in the recent past advocated a more substantial reading of equality as Member States are encouraged 'to make use of the possibility to promote positive action'; however, this minority engagement of the EU primarily addresses the issue of economic inclusion and social integration and does not address special minority rights as such. Second, national minorities play, in comparison to new or migrant minorities, only a minor role. It is also suggested that the OMC regarding minorities should not just look at one policy area only (e.g. unemployment) but rather take a transversal look at the general situation of minorities within the different Member States in order to allow for a broad picture on how minority issues are tackled in the different national systems. 'Such an exercise could lead to cross-fertilization between the Member States systems without calling for any sort of harmonisation at the European level.'[205] Nevertheless, the fact that minorities are being taken into consideration in the context of employment and social inclusion policies reinforces the notion of considering minority rights as part of the *acquis*.

Finally, it should be mentioned that the EU provides financial stimuli through differently themed 'European Years' that focus on certain disadvantaged groups. For example 2007 was the 'European Year of Equal Opportunities for All'[206] and 2008 was the 'European Year for Intercultural Dialogue'.[207] Taken together with the Commission's Framework Strategy entitled 'Non-Discrimination and Equal Opportunities for All' of 2005[208] the term 'equal opportunities' now seems to advocate a new understanding of equality – namely one which includes de facto equality – within the EU context.[209] The Commission stipulates in its Framework Strategy on Non-Discrimination that:

> it is clear that the implementation and enforcement of anti-discrimination legislation on an individual level is not enough to tackle the multifaceted and deep-rooted patterns of inequality experienced by some groups. There is a need to go beyond antidiscrimination policies designed to prevent unequal treatment of individuals. The EU should reinforce its efforts to promote equal opportunities for all, in order to tackle the structural barriers faced by migrants, ethnic minorities, the disabled, older and younger workers and other vulnerable groups.[210]

It also states that 'positive measures may be necessary to compensate for long-standing inequalities suffered by groups of people who, historically, have not had access to equal opportunities'.[211]

These initiatives show that minorities are increasingly being taken into account in a number of policies. As it is difficult for legislation alone to tackle the complex and deep-rooted patterns of inequality experienced by some groups, it is important that the Commission's strategy papers are implemented by Member States and made part of the OMC, as, legally speaking, there is no duty arising from EU law to promote actively minorities or to make use of proper positive action, unless Article 2 TEU of the Lisbon Treaty, read together with the new mainstreaming provision in Article 10 TFEU can be raised to effect such a duty.

As mentioned above, the OMC, strategy papers and political declarations appear to give a different reading of the principle of equality than legislation, in particular Article 13 TFEC/19 TFEU, namely one that considers de facto as opposed to de jure equality. As already Article 5 of the Anti-Discrimination Directive 2000/43/EC provides for a valid legislative foundation for affirmative action, Article 13/19 could be used more courageously by the relevant EU institutions *and* the Member States for the benefit of minorities.

In the absence of a fully fledged minority rights framework at EU level, it will now be analysed how far other legal instruments can provide for minority protection in the EU. Despite the gradual recognition of minority rights into the *acquis*, the EU Treaty provisions appear still insufficient for a comprehensive minority protection system. Thus, the application of provisions of the ECHR via Article 6(2) TEU to EU institutions and their decisions can provide additional protection. This will become even more significant with the entry into force of the Lisbon Treaty, which provides for the EU's accession to the ECHR.

4.5 Protection through the ECHR and ECtHR

According to Article 6(3) TEU 'Fundamental rights, as guaranteed by the European Convention for the Protection of Human Rights and Fundamental Freedoms ... shall constitute general principles of the Union's law'. The relationship between the ECtHR and the ECJ and the relevance of its case law has already been discussed (in chapter 2, section 2.7.1); thus, the EU can be found in violation of ECHR rights, in particular once the EU joins the ECHR, as provided for in Article 6(2) TEU (Lisbon). This section will discuss the relevant ECHR provisions for minority protection and the ECtHR's jurisdiction regarding minority rights, which might constitute 'general principles of Union law'.

The ECHR contains no minority rights provision. Applicants seeking to preserve the rights of their minority group have to rely on Article 14 ECHR, which is purely a non-discrimination provision, and according to which 'the enjoyment of the rights and freedoms set forth in this Convention shall be secured without discrimination on any ground' such as– among others – *association with a national minority*.[212] However, the rights usually sought by minority groups relate to the preservation of cultural traditions, way of life or the use of language, either in education or in public life, and it is questionable whether this can be secured by Article 14 ECHR, as it remains a non-discrimination provision that does not oblige states to prevent discrimination by requiring positive action.

Despite the lack of an express guarantee of minority rights in the ECHR, the Strasbourg organs, in particular the European Commission of Human Rights,[213] did, on occasion, protect minority rights under the ECHR. The ECtHR decided first on a violation of Article 14 in connection with minorities in the *Belgian Linguistics* case.[214]

In most cases involving some element of minority rights, the ECtHR ignored the issue pertinent to minority status but decided on the basis of other 'substantive' provisions of the ECHR, as will be demonstrated below. This approach of not examining a violation of Article 14 when another article has already been found violated was justified by the ECtHR in *Airey v. Ireland*:

> if the Court does not find a separate breach of one of those Articles that have been invoked both on its own and together with Article 14, it must also examine the case under the latter Article. On the other hand, such an examination is not generally required when the Court finds a violation of the former Article taken alone. The position is otherwise if a clear inequality of treatment in the enjoyment of the right in question is a fundamental aspect of the case.[215]

This was the case in a number of decisions on racially abusive behaviour by the authorities towards Roma; for example in *Nachova*,[216] the ECtHR found violations of Articles 2 and 14 ECHR, regarding the racially motivated killing of Roma by Bulgarian police officers. In a similar case, *Bekos and Koutropoulos v. Greece*,[217] the ECtHR found a violation of Articles 3 and 14 ECHR. In a case against Romania,[218] which concerned violent attacks against Roma, exercised mainly by ordinary citizens and the involvement of local police officers, which resulted in the destruction of 18 Roma homes and the death of three Roma, the ECtHR found a violation of Article 3, since the authorities had failed to bring to an end the breaches of the applicants' rights and had not indicted any of the police officers involved in the attacks. The applicants had also been forced to endure harmful living conditions over lengthy periods. Such treatment was considered as diminishing their human dignity and arousing feelings of humiliation and debasement. The ECtHR further noted that the discriminatory remarks made by the domestic courts based on the applicants' Roma origin could be characterised as degrading treatment within the meaning of Article 3 ECHR. The ECtHR also found a violation of Article 14 ECHR in conjunction with Articles 6 and 8 in that the domestic courts, on the strength of remarks directly related to the applicants' ethnicity, reduced the awards in damages made to them for the destruction of their houses.

In the comparable cases of *Ognyanova and Choban v. Bulgaria*[219] and *Osman v. Bulgaria*,[220] the ECtHR, however, decided only on a violation of Article 2 in the former case, and Article 3 in the latter, without finding a violation of Article 14 ECHR.

The ECtHR focused mainly on racial discrimination and the failure of the State Party to investigate possible racist motives in these Roma cases, and not on minority-specific rights.

However, in a groundbreaking decision on discriminatory practice in education in *Ostrava*[221] the Grand Chamber of the ECtHR, by a vote of 13:4, ruled that segregating Roma students into special schools is a form of unlawful discrimination in breach of Article 14 ECHR taken together with Article 2 of Protocol No. 1 (securing the right to education). The ECtHR awarded €4,000 to each of the applicants in respect of non-pecuniary damage and €10,000 jointly in respect of costs and expenses. The ruling came in *D.H. and Others v. the Czech Republic*, a case launched in 1999 by 18 Roma children who sought legal redress for the practice – widespread in Central and Eastern Europe – of shunting Roma students, regardless of their intellectual abilities, into 'special' schools for children with learning disabilities.

It was only until the mid-1980s that specific minority rights were addressed in the context of the ECHR; in *G and E v. Norway*,[222] the Commission recognised the protection of a particular minority's lifestyle, here the Sami of northern Norway, under Article 8 ECHR. Also, in *Buckley v. United Kingdom*, the Commission endorsed that 'the traditional lifestyle of a minority may attract the guarantees of Article 8'.[223] The applicant was a Roma by birth who acquired land where she resided with her family in three caravans. The application for the planning permission in respect of the three caravans was refused by the local council on the basis that adequate provisions had been made for Roma elsewhere and that the planned use of the land would detract from the rural and open quality of the landscape. The Commission found that the applicant and her family were prevented from living in caravans on their own land and from following their traditional lifestyle, which constituted a violation of Article 8 ECHR. The ECtHR, however, reversed the decision, focusing on the applicant's right to a home, not to a particular way of life.[224]

In the similar case of *Chapman v. UK*,[225] the ECtHR found that:

> to accord to a Roma who has unlawfully stationed a caravan site at a particular place different treatment from that accorded to non-Roma who have

> established a caravan site at that place or from that accorded to any individual who has established a house in that particular place would raise substantial problems under Article 14 of the Convention. It is important to recall that Article 8 does not recognise a right to be provided with a home. Nor does any of the jurisprudence of the Court acknowledge such a right. While it is clearly desirable that every human being has a place where he or she can live in dignity and which he or she can call home, there are unfortunately in the Contracting States many persons who have no home. Whether the State provides funds to enable everyone to have a home is a matter for political not judicial decision. In sum, the issue to be determined by the ECtHR in the present case is not the acceptability or not of a general situation, however deplorable, in the UK in the light of the UK's undertakings in international law, but the narrower one of whether the particular circumstances of the case disclose a violation of the applicant's – Mrs Chapman's – right to respect for her home under Article 8 of the Convention.

In both cases, regarding the traditional lifestyle of Travellers in the UK, the ECtHR focused on whether the measures regarding the lack of adequate camping sites for Travellers constituted an unlawful interference with the right to private life protected under Article 8 and whether these measures could be considered to remain within the margin of appreciation. Deciding for the latter, the ECtHR did not have to discuss whether Travellers had to be recognised as a national minority in the UK.

Although these cases took the Strasbourg organs beyond mere non-discrimination principles, as established under Article 14, the general trend has been to deny minorities protection under the ECHR. In addition, the lack of specific minority rights articles weakens the importance of the case law for minorities. Given that the ECHR is designed to protect individual rights, the protection accorded to minorities as groups through Article 14 would only ever be incidental, although individual representatives of the group would be able to bring an application to uphold the rights of members of the group under Article 34 ECHR.

The question whether Article 14 ECHR can be read to include positive measures for the protection of minorities has never been clearly answered. According to Article 14 ECHR, the enjoyment of the rights and freedoms in the ECHR 'shall be secured' without discrimination implies that the State Party *may* have positive obligations, i.e. a duty to ensure effective enjoyment of the non-discrimination protection. However, as the ECtHR has never clearly indicated that Article 14 gives scope to assert positive minority-related rights, this provision is too weak to serve as a basis for developing a consistent policy on minorities within the EU.

Apart from Article 14 ECHR, certain individual human rights are of particular importance to minorities, such as the freedom of religion (Article 9), the freedom of expression (Article 10) and the freedom of association (Article 11). The jurisprudence of the ECtHR suggests that the ECHR can protect minorities with regard to these rights, although the ECHR is not designed to do so:[226]

The freedom of association was found to have been violated in *United Communist Party of Turkey & Others v. Turkey*.[227] The Turkish Constitutional Court had dissolved the United Communist Party of Turkey on the grounds that its objectives – ending the discrimination of Kurds and their recognition in the Constitution – would encourage separatism and the division of the Turkish nation. The ECtHR, however, found that dissolving the party because it sought to discuss in public the situation of a part of the state's population was disproportionate in the circumstances. The question of whether the Kurds would qualify as a national minority was not addressed, as the ECtHR focused on the margin of appreciation and whether the measures in question were proportionate.

Similarly, in *Sidiropoulos & Five Others v. Greece*,[228] the Greek authorities refused registration of an association whose members claimed to be of Macedonian origin and its aims were, *inter alia*, the cultural development, preservation and protection of the natural and cultural environment of the region. While the Greek authorities held that the real aim of the association was to promote the idea that a Macedonian minority existed in Greece and to undermine Greece's territorial integrity, the ECtHR found that territorial integrity und public order were not threatened by the association and that the refusal to register was disproportionate to the pursued objectives. The ECtHR even quoted the CSCE Copenhagen document: 'supposing that the founders of the association assert a minority consciousness, the Document of the Copenhagen Meeting on the Human Dimension of the CSCE of 29 June 1990 … allow them to form associations to protect their cultural and spiritual heritage'.[229]

Also, in *Ouranio Toxo*,[230] the ECtHR found a violation of Article 11 ECHR by Greece, regarding the vandalising of an office occupied by Ouranio Toxo, a lawfully established political party defending the interests of the Macedonian minority in Greece. In *Ilinden*,[231] the ECtHR found in favour of the minority applicant by deciding that Bulgaria's prohibition of meetings by the Ilinden Association (an organisation for people associated with Macedonian heritage in Bulgaria) was in breach of Article 11, as it was not 'necessary in a democratic society'. However, in a recent Spanish case, the ECtHR concluded that there was no violation of the ECHR in *Herri Batasuna*[232] and *Batasuna v. Spain*,[233] which concerned the dissolution of the political parties Herri Batasuna and Batasuna, on the grounds that they had links to the Basque separatist organisation ETA and had failed to dissociate themselves from its terrorist activities.

In *Gorzelik and Others v. Poland*,[234] the applicants (who all described themselves as 'Silesians'), together with 190 other persons, decided to form an association called 'Union of People of Silesian Nationality' and sought registration under Polish laws on association. The Polish government rejected the application and asserted that the registration would have enabled the Silesians – who were not a 'nation' but only one of several ethnically distinct groups of Poles – to claim several privileges granted by Polish law to genuine national minorities. The applicants claimed a violation of Article 11 ECHR, however, the ECtHR held that there was no violation of Article 11 as in the particular circumstances of the present case, it was reasonable on the part of the authorities to act as they did in order to protect the electoral system of the state, a system which is an indispensable element of the proper functioning of a 'democratic society' within the meaning of Article 11.

The main issue in this case was the irreconcilability of the 'Silesian minority's' self-identification as a national minority and the state's recognition of such a minority, i.e. a problem of definition as to who qualifies as a minority. The ECtHR, however, reluctant to address the definition issue dealt with the case in the context of its control of Poland's margin of appreciation when applying the provisions of the ECHR. It proclaimed that in view of the very different factual situations of national minorities in Europe, there was no uniform pan-European definition of the term 'national minority' and therefore concluded that it was both inevitable and consistent with the adjudicative role vested in the national courts to be left with the task of interpreting the notion of 'national minority' as distinguished from an 'ethnic minority' within the meaning of the constitution.[235]

Furthermore, the ECtHR observed 'that it is not its task to express an opinion on whether or not the Silesians are a 'national minority', let alone to formulate a definition of that concept. Indeed, the formulation of such a definition would have presented a most difficult task, given that no international treaty – not even the CoE's FCNM – defines the notion of 'national minority'.[236] Thus, the ECtHR concluded that Poland acted within its margin of appreciation and that the refusal to register that association was proportionate 'in order to protect the existing democratic institutions and election procedures in Poland'. As there is no recognised definition of the term 'national minority' in international law, states are free to apply any definition provided for in their domestic legislation. In this context, the ECtHR acted in accordance with the FCNM's Advisory Committee, which has considered that in the absence of a definition, States Parties must examine the personal scope of application to be given to the FCNM and, the position of every government as to the definition of the term 'national minority' must be reflected in declarations made on ratification or statements in a state report on the applicability of the FCNM (see section 4.6, below).

The freedom of expression was found violated in *Informationsverein Lentia & Others v. Austria*,[237] where the ECtHR found the monopoly of the Austrian state broadcasting organisation, which refused to grant a broadcasting licence to a private radio station for the Slovene minority, in violation of Article 10 ECHR. In its reasoning the ECtHR did not even mention that the main target audience was the Slovene minority, but required that pluralism should be taken into account in any regulation regarding the freedom of expression, however, it did not require that minority culture should enjoy sufficient coverage in the media.

In another Kurdish case, *Incal v. Turkey*,[238] the applicant had prepared leaflets criticising measures taken by the local authorities of Izmir, denouncing the hostility created against the Kurdish population. The authorities seized the leaflets because they allegedly contravened the law and propagated separatism. The ECtHR rejected Turkey's claim that the leaflets could be linked to the problem of terrorism in Turkey and found the seizure to be disproportionate and in violation of Article 10 ECHR.

This case law illustrates that the ECtHR has occasionally decided in favour of minority rights without using Article 14 ECHR and without referring explicitly to the minority as such. Although the ECtHR decided on the basis of the individual human right in question (e.g. Articles 8, 10, 11 ECHR), it provided effective minority protection in the above-mentioned cases in relation to issues of considerable relevance for national minorities. Apart from the fact that the ECtHR has been quite reluctant to make use of this potential (as demonstrated in *Buckley* and *Chapman*), it has limited powers to ensure compliance; while it may award compensation to the claimant, it has no power to change the law within the respondent state concerned. Although the decisions of the ECtHR are binding on the parties,[239] they are of declaratory nature and do not have the effect of quashing national legislation that has been found to breach the ECHR. In addition, the ECtHR has rejected requests from applicants to require particular measures, as indicated in *Marckx v. Belgium*, that 'the judgement leaves to the state the choice of the means utilised in its domestic system for performance of its obligations under Article 53'.[240]

Nevertheless, as evidenced by the case law of the ECtHR, there is great potential for the ECtHR to play a more important role in setting standards on minority issues. However, a major shift towards a system of positive obligation took place when the CoE pioneered the FCNM in 1995.

4.6 The European Framework Convention for the Protection of National Minorities (FCNM) of 1995

In the early 1990s there were political initiatives in the CoE to draft an Additional Protocol to the ECHR on the rights of national minorities, which would include the ECtHR as the competent judicial instance to enforce these rights. However, as these initiatives failed, it was decided at the 1993 Vienna Summit of CoE Heads of State and Governments to draft the FCNM, which resulted in an entirely different instrument as originally planned. The FCNM, which entered into force in 1998, adopts a minimum legal standard of minority protection in order to enable the participating states to take additional measures which would suit the special characteristics of their minorities (therefore only a framework convention). The enforcement mechanism of the FCNM consists of a reporting system whereby Member States have to submit a report giving full information on legislative and other measures taken to give effect to the principles of the Convention. These reports are evaluated by the Committee of Ministers, assisted by an Advisory Committee.[241] Within the Advisory Committee country-specific working groups are set up, which provide an opinion based on the state report or other sources, such as visits to the country concerned or information from the UN Human Rights Committee. These opinions have to be adopted by the Advisory Committee's plenary before they are transmitted to the Committee of Ministers and the governments concerned.[242] Despite the fact that the FCNM only provides a minimum standard, it appears that this minimum standard has become already the ceiling of what 'could be' achieved as evidenced by the States Parties' reports.

In the absence of a definition of the term 'national minority', the Advisory Committee requires states to determine themselves as to who qualifies as a national minority under the FCNM, to be reflected in declarations made on ratification or statements in a state report. States Parties have a certain margin of appreciation with regard to these declarations in view of the specific circumstances in their country, but the margin of appreciation has to be exercised in accordance with general principles of international law and the fundamental principals of Article 3 FCNM,[243] i.e. the States Parties must not make any arbitrary or unjustified distinctions as to who qualifies as a national minority. In a number of cases the Advisory Committee concluded in its country-specific opinions that such arbitrary distinctions have been made, as in the cases of Egyptians in Albania, Roma in Denmark, Silesians in Poland, Poles in Austria/Vienna, Csangos in Romania, Germans in Slovenia, with regards to the population of Ceuta and Melilla and their status as recognised minorities by Spain, the inhabitants of Gotland and Scania and their status as recognised minorities by Sweden, Bosniacs and Egyptians in Macedonia, Rusyians in the Ukraine and the Cornish in the UK. In some cases the Advisory Committee even invited States Parties to discuss the issues with representatives of the relevant minority group involved.[244]

As to the FCNM's contents, the provisions of the Framework Convention (which shall not be discussed here)[245] take up individual human rights as provided for in the ECHR, such as Articles 8, 9 or 10 supplemented by minority-specific requirements, reaffirming the principles relating to the promotion of the identity of national minorities with due respect for the rule of law, territorial integrity and the sovereignty of states. But the provisions adopted being no more than minimum legal standards show various shortcomings. The rights are strongly qualified, cautiously formulated, define obligations on states as 'programme-type provisions' and leave Member States partly uncertain about the minimum standards they are expected to guarantee:

1 The Convention expresses minority rights in terms of obligations incumbent on states by requiring '*The Parties undertake to promote, undertake to recognise, shall encourage, undertake to adopt, undertake to guarantee or shall not hinder* ...' [emphasis added]. Thus, persons belonging to national minorities do not have the positive right to freedom of religion (Article 7), but it up to the states to '*undertake to grant all persons belonging to a national minority the right to manifest their religion of belief*'. Hence, these rights cannot be asserted against the states in their internal legal system, neither can they be adjudicated under the Convention, as the ECtHR is not competent regarding the FCNM, neither is any other court. Thus, the Convention establishes the active role of states in the protection of minorities, encouraging them to take appropriate steps rather than giving minorities judicially enforceable rights.
2 The Convention contains a rather weak monitoring mechanism consisting of state reports to the Committee of Ministers aided by an Advisory

Committee of experts (the Advisory Committee). The supervision to which the State Parties are subjected remains very limited, as the monitoring arrangements are designed to encourage them to honour their obligations, rather than to sanction those that fail to do so. No sanction is envisaged for states that do not follow up their obligations under the FCNM, neither is there a system for individual petitions.

3 There is no definition of the term national minority, neither are minorities identified by their ethnic, religious or linguistic characteristics. The term 'national' can have different meanings (as already discussed in section 4.3). With the absence of a definition, it is left to the states which groups to recognise as a 'national minority' and to whom rights shall be accorded. The Advisory Committee, however, takes a flexible approach and on an article-by-article basis it has considered that some provisions of the FCNM can only apply to national minorities as defined in Recommendation 1201, such as Article 11(3) which refers to 'areas traditionally inhabited', while other articles can also apply to 'new' minorities, as for example Article 6 FCNM which refers to 'all persons living on the territory'.[246] Since it is up to the states to determine which groups will be protected under the Convention, there is great diversity regarding its application. In particular, the UK has chosen to apply the FCNM to its new minorities, such as immigrants from Asia and Africa.[247]

4 The FCNM sets out minority rights in rather vague and imprecise terms, giving states a great margin of appreciation. For example, Article 11(3) FCNM provides that:

> In areas traditionally inhabited by substantial numbers of persons belonging to a national minority, the Parties shall endeavour, in the framework of their legal system, including, where appropriate, agreements with other States, and taking into account their specific conditions, to display traditional local names, street names and other topographical indications intended for the public also in the minority language when there is a sufficient demand for such indications.

This provision avoids any reference or definition of 'sufficient demand' or 'appropriate' or of what constitutes a 'substantial number'. However, it has to be acknowledged that the display of topographical indications in minority language requires substantial administrative resources and can, understandably, only be put into practice when the region is dominated by a minority of that country, as e.g. in Brittany (France) or the Basque country (Spain).

5 According to Article 19, the rights might be subject to restrictions, envisaging the possibility of states to limit, restrict or derogate from these rights. The article does not mention, however, situations in which such exceptions may come into play but simply refers to the limitations that are provided for in other international legal instruments, without specifying whether

such limitations refer to security concerns, public interest or whether the lack of sufficient resources might also qualify as such a limitation. Again, the scope for interpretation is wide and leaves states a great margin of appreciation.

The above-discussed pitfalls of the FCNM show a lack of political will to confront minority rights throughout the CoE, since a great number of states were unwilling to confer judicially enforceable rights under any minority instrument on members of national minorities. The weaknesses of the FCNM have, for example, been recognised by the Slovak Republic, which sought to limit the obligations it owes to its Hungarian minority under a bilateral treaty with Hungary, by restricting more strongly worded measures found in the CSCE Copenhagen Document to the level of commitment found in the FCNM.[248]

In this context, it is also interesting to note how the ECtHR regarded the FCNM in its case law: In *Chapman v. UK*,[249] the applicant urged the ECtHR to take into account recent international developments, in particular the FCNM, in reducing the margin of appreciation accorded to states in light of the recognition of the problems of vulnerable groups, such as Roma. The ECtHR, however, observed that:

> there may be said to be an emerging international consensus amongst the Contracting States of the Council of Europe recognising the special needs of minorities and an obligation to protect their security, identity and lifestyle not only for the purpose of safeguarding the interests of the minorities themselves but to preserve a cultural diversity of value to the whole community. However, the ECtHR is not persuaded that the consensus is sufficiently concrete for it to derive any guidance as to the conduct or standards, which Contracting States consider desirable in any particular situation. The framework convention, for example, sets out general principles and goals but the signatory states were unable to agree on means of implementation. This reinforces the ECtHR's view that the complexity and sensitivity of the issues involved in policies balancing the interests of the general population, in particular with regard to environmental protection, and the interests of a minority with possibly conflicting requirements renders the ECtHR's role a strictly supervisory one.

This decision shows that there is still great reluctance to provide for positive minority rights, despite the commitments that have been made under the FCNM and, that the ECtHR cannot intervene when a Member State does not provide for the rights that have been recognised under the FCNM. With regards to the future accession of the EU to the ECHR under the Treaty of Lisbon, this is unfortunate. Not only has the FCNM not been permitted to become a protocol to the ECHR and therefore can neither become binding on the EU nor can rights under the FCNM be enforced by the ECtHR. The lack of justiciability has been the strongest criticism against the FCNM as international human rights instruments must include the possibility of a complaints procedure.

Nevertheless, it has to be recognised that the FCNM is the first multilateral legal instrument on this subject with a – however weak – enforcement mechanism; and the FCNM might initiate a process that leads gradually to more effective protection of minority rights, rather than providing immediate benefits. Regardless of its low level of protection, the FCNM has only been ratified by 11 of the old EU Member States. Accordingly, those Member States, which are not parties to the FCNM cannot be bound by it.[250] It is therefore questionable whether the FCNM can be taken into consideration in the context of any internal EU policy on minorities, unless the EU's accession to the ECHR under the Treaty of Lisbon leads to accession to other CoE conventions, such as the FCNM. Since this prospect is not even on the negotiation table yet, all EU Member States should at least be obliged to join, otherwise the reproach of double standards will not be silenced.

In the context of EU enlargement, the FCNM has played a significant role in the EU's pre-accession strategy, having progressively served as a key reference point in the EU's monitoring of candidate states' respect for and protection of minorities (see above under 4.4.1), while in the post-accession phase the EU lacks competence to monitor Member States' compliance with FCNM standards. The impact of the EU's pre-accession strategy on minority protection, and its contribution to enhancing the effectiveness of the FCNM, should not be overstated though. 'Respect for minorities has improved in those candidates that were prepared to listen to the Commission's suggestions. Indeed, while such improvement can be identified, it is difficult to establish a direct causal link with the EU minority conditionality. The latter's impact has to be related to numerous other factors which may have contributed to the overall progress in minority protection.'[251]

4.7 The European Charter for Regional or Minority Languages

The European Charter for Regional or Minority Languages of 1992,[252] drawn up by the CoE, proclaims that linguistic diversity 'contributes to the maintenance and development of Europe's cultural wealth and traditions'. The Charter's overriding purpose is cultural, designed to protect and promote regional or minority languages as a threatened aspect of Europe's cultural heritage. The Charter thus protects language rights without using the vocabulary of human rights. Indeed, the Charter's Explanatory Report specifies that the document's purpose is 'to protect and promote regional or minority languages', not linguistic minorities. For this reason it not only contains a non-discrimination clause concerning the use of these languages but also provides for measures offering active support: the aim is to ensure, as far as reasonably possible, the use of regional or minority languages in education and the media and to permit their use in judicial and administrative settings, economic and social life and cultural activities.[253] The Charter is divided into two main parts, a general one containing the principles applicable to all the Parties and all regional or minority languages (Part II), and a second part laying down specific practical commitments that may vary according to the state and the language (Part III). Part II sets out the main principles and objectives on which states must base their policies, legislation and practice, and which are regarded as providing the necessary framework for the preservation of the languages concerned.

The Charter does not establish any rights for the speakers of regional or minority languages. Nevertheless, the provisions of the Charter are clearly beneficial for linguistic minorities and promote an important part of minority protection, i.e. the promotion of a minority's mother tongue. Therefore, the European Charter for Regional or Minority Languages is of indirect relevance for the protection of minorities. However, as with the FCNM, it is not subject to any adjudicative mechanism, but has been given its own Advisory Committee to monitor States Parties' implementation of the Charter. It also has to be considered that not many EU Member States have ratified the Charter, namely Belgium, Bulgaria, Estonia, France, Greece, Ireland, Italy, Latvia, Lithuania, Malta, Poland, Portugal, and Romania are outside its remit. Nevertheless, the spirit of the Charter has been reflected in EU programmes such as LINGUA and the establishment of the EBLUL.

4.8 Protection under the ICCPR

The ECJ emphasised in *Nold*[254] that 'international treaties for the protection of human rights on which the Member States have collaborated or of which they are signatories, can supply guidelines for Community law'. This suggests that the protection of minorities under Article 27 ICCPR or other UN conventions may be taken into consideration with regard to EU policy for the protection of minorities. However, given the reservation of France to Article 27 of the ICCPR, this is uncertain ground.

When France joined the ICCPR it entered a reservation that Article 27 was inapplicable in view of Article 2 of the French Constitution, which assumes the indivisibility of the French Republic. Commenting on the declaration related to Article 27 ICCPR, the UN Human Rights Committee noted France's stated commitment to respect and ensure equal rights to all individuals, irrespective of their origin. The Committee disagreed with the government statement that France is a country in which there are no ethnic, religious or linguistic minorities and recalled that the act of granting equal rights to all individuals and stipulating that all individuals are equal before the law does not mean that there are no minorities in the country, and does not reduce the entitlement of the minorities to enjoy their culture, practise their religion or use their language in community with other members of their group.[255]

While France does not recognise minorities, the wording of its Constitution and the broader debate within Europe regarding the recognition of minorities makes it increasingly difficult for France to maintain its position within a united Europe of shared values and obligations. It is ever-more recognised that it is not for the state itself to define the limits of its human rights commitments based on a 'subjective' position, but that such a decision must be based on 'objective' criteria.

As all other EU Member States have ratified the ICCPR without a reservation to Article 27, this position has also received criticism from other countries, especially Germany.[256] However, until today France has not shown any signs of changing this policy. The difficulty of the French position has become evident around the debate about the wearing of the Muslim hijab and other religious symbols in state institutions, a debate which has divided French society, most noticeably along ethnic and religious lines. In the context of minority rights at EU level, France's attitude (together with Greece, which takes a similar approach) might become problematic; however, its signing of the Treaty of Lisbon which specifically states minority rights as one of the values on which the EU is founded, might signify a slow change of position.

The scope and meaning of Article 27 ICCPR as well as the case law regarding violations of this article will only be looked at briefly, as this has already been discussed elsewhere,[257] bearing in mind the potential inspirational character of this provision and its enforcement for the EU.

It was not until 1966 with the drafting of the ICCPR that the UN concerned itself with the situation of minorities. Article 27 establishes and recognises a right, which is conferred on individuals belonging to minority groups and which is distinct from, and additional to, all the other rights which, individuals in common with everyone else, are already entitled to enjoy under the ICCPR. The negative wording 'shall not be denied the right …' rather than 'shall enjoy' implies that there are no positive obligations for states, but rather a duty of tolerance, instead of recognition of rights. Thornberry suggests that Article 27 contains a 'programmatic element', it is a 'promotional … requirement' with a framework character which needs to be supplemented by a clearer statement of rights, and duties of minorities.[258] Thus, Article 27 ICCPR has been understood not to provide for positive rights of assistance, funding, etc., but rather as a negative right of non-interference. As a consequence, Article 27 has not stopped states from withholding funding for minority-language schools, abolishing traditional forms of local autonomy or even encouraging settlers to swamp minority territories.[259] However, in its General Comment on Article 27 ICCPR the Human Rights Committee came to the conclusion that Article 27 ICCPR '*may* require positive legal measures of protection and measures to ensure the effective participation of members of minority communities'.[260] In paragraph 6.1 of this General Comment the Committee states that:

> Although Article 27 is expressed in negative terms, that Article, nevertheless, does recognise the existence of a 'right' and requires that it shall not be denied. Consequently, a State Party is under an obligation to ensure that the existence and the exercise of this right are protected against their denial or violation. Positive measures of protection are, therefore, required not only against the acts of the State Party itself, whether through its legislative,

judicial or administrative authorities, but also against the acts of other persons within the State Party.

And in paragraph 6.2 it held:

> Although the rights protected under Article 27 are individual rights, they depend in turn on the ability of the minority group to maintain its culture, language or religion. Accordingly, positive measures by States *may* also be necessary to protect the identity of a minority and the rights of its members to enjoy and develop their culture and language and to practise their religion, in community with the other members of the group … as long as those measures are aimed at correcting conditions which prevent or impair the enjoyment of the rights guaranteed under Article 27, they may constitute a legitimate differentiation under the Covenant, provided that they are based on reasonable and objective criteria. Hence, the enjoyment of those rights may require positive legal measures of protection and measures to ensure the effective participation of members of minority communities in decisions which affect them.

Thus, the Human Rights Committee made it very clear that positive measures *may* be required under Article 27 ICCPR; however, the Committee has no means of enforcing this requirement against States Parties, as the ICCPR only provides for an individual complaints procedure under the First Optional Protocol. Nevertheless, the General Comments are part of soft law[261] and can be considered as an important 'guideline' – to quote from *Nold* – for EU policies as they have certainly influenced the drafting of the FCNM.

In some communications submitted to the Human Rights Committee, the rights protected under Article 27 have been confused with the right of peoples to self-determination proclaimed in Article 1 ICCPR. The right to self-determination is a right belonging to peoples and is dealt with in a separate part of the ICCPR, whereas Article 27 relates to rights conferred on individuals and does not prejudice the sovereignty and territorial integrity of a State Party. The minority rights issue under international law needs to be distinguished sharply from that of self-determination. Minorities as such do not have the right to self-determination, which only applies to peoples.[262] The right to self-determination in Article 1 ICCPR has traditionally been interpreted to include the right to form one's own state and was therefore mainly applied to former colonies, having the right to independence (in the process of gaining independence minorities should, however, participate in the self-determination process and not be excluded from it).[263]

Nonetheless, Article 27 allows for a complaints procedure to the Human Rights Committee to decide on cases concerning the protection of minorities, i.e. the protection of an individual as member of a minority group. In *Sandra Lovelace*,[264] a native Indian had been denied, by operation of the Canadian Indian Act, the legal right to reside on an Indian reserve because she had married a non-Indian, whom she later divorced. The Committee found a breach of Article 27 ICCPR and considered that for the purposes of Article 27 she must still be considered among 'persons belonging to the minority concerned'; and although the right to reside in the reserve was not as such guaranteed by Article 27, access to her native culture and language had, in fact, been denied to her in a way which the Committee held to be unjustified.

The applicant of the complaint in the case *Ivan Kitok v. Sweden*[265] was a member of an indigenous people, the Sami of Sweden, who make their living by reindeer breeding. With the aim of protecting the environment and preserving the Sami minority, the Swedish Parliament had restricted the number of reindeer breeders by imposing that the Sami would lose their reindeer-breeding rights under national law if he or she lost membership in a Sami village. Ivan Kitok lost his official membership in a Sami village due to his other economic activities outside the village. He claimed to be a victim of violations of both his right to self-determination and the right under Article 27 ICCPR to enjoy his culture in community with others. The Committee found that Article 27 ICCPR was applicable to the case, but found no violation. Nevertheless, the case is important for the protection of minority rights as it clarifies the scope of Article 27 ICCPR, by stating that traditional economic activities and ways of living may fall under its protection, as long as the conduct in question is closely related to the culture of a group and the activity is an essential element of cultural traditions.

In *Chief Bernard Ominayak and the Lubicon Band v. Canada*,[266] the applicant was the chief of an Indian band who lived to a large extent on fishing and hunting. Due to large-scale expropriations of land degradation of the environment, he claimed that members of the band were denied their right to self-determination and to dispose freely of their natural resources. The Committee decided that the applicant as an individual could not claim to be the victim of a violation of the right of self-determination because the procedure under the Optional Protocol provides exclusively for individuals to claim that their rights have been violated. Nevertheless, the Committee declared the case admissible based on Article 27 ICCPR, as the rights protected therein include the right of persons, in community with others, to engage in economic and social activities, which are part of the culture of the community to which they belong and, recognised that fishing and hunting were part of the way of life and the cultural tradition of the Lubicon Band and that Article 27 ICCPR had been violated by expropriation and the pollution. It is worth noting that these cases are similar to the decisions taken by the CoE's Commission of Human Rights in *Buckley v. UK* and *G and E v. Norway*, in which the Commission recognised the protection of a particular minority's lifestyle under Article 8 ECHR. In the case of *Länsman v. Finland*,[267] the Committee held that ethnic communities also have the right to use modern methods when carrying out their traditional trades.

The cases decided by the Human Rights Committee have been very clear in expressing the right to exercise one's culture as a basic right for minorities under international law to be protected by Article 27 ICCPR. Although this right has not been clearly defined in the Committee's decisions, as 'culture' may include a variety of aspects of a particular way of living, it appears that not only social but also economic activities form an important part of a minority's culture, which is not immediately obvious from the wording of Article 27 ICCPR. This aspect of minority culture can become very controversial when the minority culture does not harmonise well with certain interests of the majority, which is a problem that occurs in Europe in particular with regard to the Roma minority, whose particular way of living has caused many social problems and led to deplorable living conditions for them.

In a more recent decision, *Antonina Ignatane v. Latvia*,[268] which did not concern the violation of Article 27 ICCPR but was, however, a relevant case for minorities, the applicant claimed a breach of Articles 25 and 2(1) ICCPR regarding the right to be elected, without any of the distinctions mentioned in Article 2 ICCPR.[269] A member of the Russian-speaking minority in Latvia had passed a Latvian language test and was awarded a language certificate stating that she achieved the highest level of proficiency in the language. However, when she stood for local elections, she was struck off the list because of a decision by a different language authority that she did not have the highest level of language proficiency in the Latvian language required by law in order to stand for election. The Human Rights Committee noted that Article 25 ICCPR guarantees every citizen the right and the opportunity to be elected at genuine periodic elections without any of the distinctions mentioned in Article 2 ICCPR, including language. The Committee concluded that Mrs Ignatane had suffered specific damage in being prevented from standing for the local elections in the city of Riga in 1997, because of having been struck off the list of candidates on the basis of insufficient proficiency in the official language.

Minority members residing within the EU can use Article 27 and the individual complaints procedure under the First Optional Protocol to the ICCPR in order to enforce their rights, as has already happened in *Kitok v. Sweden.* However, only individuals who live in Member States that have ratified the First Optional Protocol to the ICCPR can benefit from this provision, i.e. citizens of the UK, which has not ratified the Optional Protocol and France, which has made a reservation with regard to Article 27 ICCPR, are excluded from this procedure. At the same time, the EU cannot act against international law provisions, i.e. commitments Member States have made under other international treaties such as the ICCPR. The fact that France submitted a reservation to Article 27 is not of relevance in this context since an EU obligation not to act against Article 27 ICCPR does not interfere with this reservation.

4.8.1 The UN Declaration on the Rights of Persons Belonging to National or Ethnic, Religious and Linguistic Minorities

In the light of the collapse of the Iron Curtain and in respect of the 'imprecision' of Article 27 ICCPR, the General Assembly of the UN adopted in 1992 the 'Declaration on the Rights of Persons Belonging to National or Ethnic, Religious and Linguistic Minorities',[270] which required the UN 14 years of preparation. The Declaration is formulated on the basis of individual and not group rights ('the Rights of Persons Belonging to … Minorities'). Although the rights provided for remain individual rights, their collective dimension is more elaborate than under Article 27 ICCPR and goes beyond the general concept of protecting individual human rights.

States are required 'to protect the existence and the national or ethnic, cultural, religious and linguistic identity of minorities within their respective territories and … encourage conditions for the promotion of that identity' (Article 1). More specifically, they undertake to 'take measures where required to ensure that persons belonging to minorities may exercise fully and effectively all their human rights and fundamental freedoms without any discrimination and in full equality before the law' (Article 4.1) and 'take measures to create favourable conditions to enable minorities to express their characteristics and to develop their culture, language, religion, traditions and customs' (Article 4.2). Also, Article 2(2) and (3) provides for participatory rights, at national and regional levels on matters that affect in particular minority groups.

This positive language requires states to adopt legislative and other measures in order to protect the existence and identity of persons belonging to minorities within their territory. The wording is similar to the wording of the FCNM, and even includes positive measures in Article 4.1 for achieving full equality before the law, whereas Article 27 ICCPR only requires states to desist from negative action.

The Declaration reflects a consensus that has been notoriously difficult to achieve within the international community and does show a certain trend for the recognition of collective rights.[271] It was also a response to the UN's inability to react more appropriately to the collapse of the Soviet Union and the ensuing violent conflicts. However, the Declaration is not a legal instrument and has no binding effect on states; it is simply a political statement.

The Declaration proclaims that it is 'inspired by' Article 27 ICCPR, that is to say, it seeks to be consistent with Article 27, but at the same time to build on it. There is undoubtedly scope for this, given three main factors: First, Article 27 is written in negative terms; second, the protection it provides is very modest in character; and third, it is clearly not an appropriate legal tool for the large-scale violations of minority rights witnessed as they occurred for example in the Balkans.[272] In addition, apart from protecting ethnic, religious and linguistic minorities – as provided for under Article 27 ICCPR – the Declaration adds 'national minorities' to the list. It is not entirely clear from this terminology whether it suggests that the guarantees only apply to 'citizens' or, whether 'national' is a variety of a minority, extending protection under the Declaration to as many persons as possible that can be 'ethnically defined'.[273]

Again, there is no definition of minorities at any point. It has to be acknowledged though, that the Declaration tries to reconcile the ambivalent attitude of the international community with its concern to protect minorities that are frequently confronted with the resurgence of nationalism, while at the same time avoiding the risks of the break-up of states, ethnic conflicts and secessionist trends.[274] Credit has to be given for its attempt to take a more defined stance for the position of minorities in contemporary international law. As mentioned above, since the Declaration does not contain legally enforceable rights, it can only be seen as a political declaration of intent that does not give any rights to members of minorities in Europe. However, as a non-binding instrument that lays down guidelines for future action, and through which states commit themselves politically to meeting certain objectives, it can be considered as being part of soft law.[275]

The Declaration was adopted by the General Assembly without the agreement of an implementation mechanism but concerted endeavours by a number of governments, mainly Nordic and Central European, have led to the establishment of a Working Group on Minorities in 1995, which is a Working Group of the UN Sub-Commission on the Promotion and Protection of Human Rights. One of its responsibilities included promotion of the implementation of the Declaration. At meetings of the Working Group (which were public as well as closed), governments made statements about their efforts in terms of constitutional arrangements, national legislation and other measures for protecting and accommodating minorities. Also representatives of minorities and NGOs highlighted actual trouble spots as well as positive developments. Members of the Working Group have played an active role in the deliberations by seeking clarifications and concrete proposals and responses from speakers and other representatives, promoting fruitful exchanges and actual dialogues between the participants. The Working Group ceased to exist in 2006 together with the Sub-Commission on the Promotion and Protection of Human Rights in 2007.

On 29 July 2005 the High Commissioner for Human Rights appointed Ms Gay J. McDougall as the first holder of the position of UN Independent Expert on minority issues, in accordance with the provisions of Commission on Human Rights.[276] The work of the Independent Expert on minority issues is a valuable source in informing the EU's approach to minority issues in relations with third countries. Her mandate was extended by the Human Rights Council on 27 March 2008[277] for a period of three years. Furthermore, the EU gives support to the Forum for Minority issues which was created by the Human Rights Council on 28 September 2007 as a follow-up body to the UN Working Group on Minorities under the former UN Sub-Commission for Human Rights.[278] The work of the Forum is to be guided by the Independent Expert in accordance with Resolution 7/6.

Despite the lack of an enforcement mechanism, the UN Declaration and the Working Group on Minorities have been influential for discussing the different aspects of minority protection, it remains to be seen whether the Forum for Minority Issues can make a similar impact.

Another human rights instrument of the UN system that could provide guidance for the EU on the question of minority rights is the CERD.

4.8.2 CERD

As already mentioned above, Article 2(2) of the Convention on the Elimination of All Forms of Racial Discrimination (CERD)[279] stipulates an approach that promotes the development and protection of certain racial groups:

> States Parties shall, when the circumstances so warrant, take, in the social, economic, cultural and other fields, special and concrete measures to ensure the adequate development and protection of *certain racial groups or individuals belonging to them*, for the purpose of guaranteeing them the full and equal enjoyment of human rights and fundamental freedoms. These measures shall in no case entail as a consequence the maintenance of unequal or separate rights for different racial groups after the objectives for which they were taken have been achieved [emphasis added].

The CERD is enforced by the Committee on the Elimination of Racial Discrimination, a body of independent experts that monitors implementation of the Convention by its State Parties. All States Parties are obliged to submit regular reports to the Committee on how the rights of CERD are being implemented. States must report initially one year after acceding to the Convention and then every two years. The Committee examines each report and addresses its concerns and recommendations to the State Party in the form of 'Concluding Observations'. The Committee may consider individual communications relating to States Parties who have made the necessary declaration under Article 14 CERD.[280] Individual complaints that have been considered by the Committee concerned cases of racial discrimination but not the denial or violation of specific minority rights,[281] and are therefore not relevant in this context.

CERD prohibits apartheid in Article 3 and in Article 4 the propaganda of racial hatred and discrimination. Article 5 provides a whole catalogue of human rights, whose enjoyment shall be available to everyone, without any distinction.[282] Article 6 requires States Parties to provide the possibility of redress through a judicial system and Article 7 requires the adoption of effective measures, particularly in the fields of teaching, education, culture and information, with a view to combating prejudices which lead to racial discrimination.

The content of these provisions clearly shows that the purpose of CERD lies in the prevention of ethnic and racial discrimination; it promotes the concept of non-discrimination rather than providing for specific minority rights. The ultimate goal is to achieve equality, as Article 2(2) provides: 'These measures shall in no case entail as a consequence the maintenance of unequal or separate rights for different racial groups after the objectives for which they were taken have been achieved'. Also, Capotorti commented that 'the aim of the special measures is to restore the balance between the respective positions of the various groups, including minority groups, but the ultimate objective of the Convention is uniform treatment of individuals to whatever group they belong'.[283]

Although one might argue that CERD appears simply to combat racism – as its title suggests – rather than promoting minority rights, the implementation procedure has shown that minority rights were often the subject of state reports (especially by Eastern European states) in particular regarding Roma, and consequently have been commented on by the Committee on the Elimination of Racial Discrimination in its Concluding Observations.[284]

CERD's broad field of application carries significant importance with regard to minorities, considering that States Parties are obliged to take special measures to support disadvantaged groups; these measures clearly go beyond the prohibition of discrimination, which is necessary for the promotion of minorities. However, an important argument against the application of CERD to minorities – as defined above – is the fact that these measures shall only apply temporarily until substantive equality is achieved, since this 'positive discrimination' would otherwise turn into prohibited discrimination. The approach taken by CERD in Article 1(4)[285] differs considerably from the approach taken by instruments that specifically promote minority rights, as for example the FCNM. Unlike affirmative action programmes, minority rights are not supposed to be temporary but require permanent regulations granting minorities a different legal status with regard to language rights, education or political participation in public life.

The activities at UN level and the case law under Article 27 ICCPR with respect to national minorities have so far been rather limited but can nevertheless be of inspirational character for the EU. In particular, cooperation with the UN Forum on Minority Issues can be beneficial for the new EU with its 27 Member States. Under the system of CERD the issue of minority rights has come up frequently in the considerations and recommendations of the Committee, which has been forthcoming in giving specific suggestions on what legal and practical measures states should take to fulfil their treaty obligations.[286] However, it has to be considered that the European institutions take a slightly different approach to minority rights. While the UN Human Rights Committee includes immigrants in the scope of protection of Article 27 ICCPR – regardless of their nationality – the CoE and the OSCE refer in the relevant documents exclusively to 'national minorities', which has been interpreted as not including immigrants, even though the FCNM's Advisory Committee has also accepted the protection of immigrants under the FCNM as long as they hold the nationality of the state in question. The protection currently provided by the OSCE might therefore be of more relevance to the EU and will be assessed in the next section.

4.9 Protection under the CSCE/OSCE

Unlike the EU, the OSCE had a political role from the outset and human rights were originally part of the Helsinki Process as an important element to promote peace and security in Europe. Both, the OSCE and the EU responded to the changes of 1989/1990 with restructuring the institutional framework of the organisation. Starting out as a process of conferences in 1975 the Conference on

Security and Cooperation in Europe (CSCE) evolved from being a process into an organisation and was christened the Organization for Security and Cooperation in Europe (OSCE) at the Budapest Summit in 1994. Although the OSCE has no legal status under international law, most of its instruments, decisions and commitments are framed in legal language and their interpretation requires an understanding of the principles of international law and of the standard techniques of the law of treaties.

Furthermore, the OSCE is considered to be a regional arrangement in the sense of Chapter VIII of the UN Charter and is therefore the primary instrument for early warning, conflict prevention, crisis management and post-conflict rehabilitation in its region. It provides active support for promoting democracy, the rule of law and respect for human rights throughout the OSCE area, giving priority to inter-institutional cooperation and coordination. Since crisis management is an area in which the EU has less experience, but aims to get involved with in the framework of its CFSP, close cooperation of these two organisations has developed over the last years. Especially in the Balkans, both organisations are present and engaged in peacekeeping and peace-building activities. Hence, a more efficient allocation of resources and the coordination of international efforts in conflict prevention has been put in place in order to guarantee political and operational coherence (as discussed in chapter 3).

Unlike the EU's complex institutional setup, the OSCE's political character and its relatively small institutional framework enable it to react quickly and flexibly in crisis situations. In addition, the OSCE does not operate in the spotlight of public attention; hence states are more willing to ask for the intervention of OSCE operations in crisis situations. Keeping the bureaucratic structure relatively small and financially efficient, maintaining its decentralised structures with autonomous field operations and institutions has proved to be a well-functioning concept. Furthermore, close cooperation with the international financial and economic institutions such as the European Bank for Reconstruction and Development (EBRD) and the EU is important, since the OSCE cannot back its activities with any economic incentives.

In the framework of the CSCE/OSCE, the end of communism created a new opportunity for the enforcement of rights in Europe and a reformulation of sovereignty that included an obligation of minority protection, which first appeared at the CSCE Copenhagen meeting of 1990 (which produced the already cited Copenhagen Document 1990),[287] after the CSCE had been largely ineffective in promoting human rights due to opposition from the states of the Soviet bloc.

Having considerably broadened since the collapse of the communist regimes of Eastern Europe, the human dimension of the OSCE activities now includes the upholding of human rights and fundamental freedoms, the promotion of the rule of law, protection of the rights of minorities, concern for migrants and the establishment, development and safeguarding of democratic institutions. The most comprehensive statement on the protection of minorities is contained in the Copenhagen Document, which was adopted unanimously by all CSCE participating states and therefore by all EU Member States at the time. Like all CSCE/OSCE documents, the Copenhagen Declaration is not binding on Member States. Though being merely a political undertaking, it is nevertheless considered as the 'European Charter of Minorities' with at least de facto effects, as it inspired other international instruments.

The specific human dimension mechanism which was set up at the Vienna Follow-Up Meeting in 1989 was also intended to apply to national minorities' issues. However, the effectiveness of this mechanism was questioned at the Copenhagen Conference in 1990; as a result, the Member States eventually decided to speed up the procedures and to set up a delegation of experts as well as a rapporteur group for on-site investigations and mediation purposes at the Moscow Conference in October 1991, the so-called 'Moscow Mechanism'.[288] The group of rapporteurs was meant to prevent the unilateral and abusive use of the mechanism, and to avoid its becoming deadlocked as a result of the requirements of consensus.

Since July 1992 there had only been four uses of the Moscow Mechanism, all of them in relation to minorities. These included the sending of a rapporteur mission to Croatia and Bosnia-Herzegovina, at the initiative of the UK, with the support of nine other EU countries. Furthermore there were self-initiated missions to Estonia and Moldova, i.e. the mechanism was activated by invitation of the countries concerned themselves, which was appraised as a very constructive use of the mechanism.[289] The activation of the human dimension mechanism by another participating state tends to be viewed as a politically unfriendly act, rather than a positive instrument which promotes interstate dialogue and cooperation on human dimension issues.[290]

The CSCE's Charter of Paris for a New Europe of 1990[291] declares under its section on Human Dimension the Member States' determination to foster the rich contribution of national minorities to the life of their societies, and initiated a special meeting of experts on national minorities to be held in Geneva from 1 to 19 July 1991.[292] However, the results of that meeting were rather unsatisfactory due to the opposing conceptions of Western European countries and Central and Eastern European countries. While states such as France and Greece refused to recognise the existence of minorities on their territory, others hesitated to grant rights to minorities on a general basis for fear of secessionist claims.

Dalton suggests that due to the continuing philosophical divide between states, which put the accent on non-discrimination and individual rights, and others, which also emphasise group rights and participation, the limits of what can be achieved by way of setting standards have, almost certainly, been reached.[293] This statement unquestionably also applies to the EU Member States, considering that some do not recognise the concept of minority protection and have not ratified the FCNM, while others subscribe to the approach being taken in the FCNM. As a means of encouraging observance of the principles of minority protection under the umbrella of the OSCE, mechanisms such as periodic reviews, including the Member States' behaviour under the human dimension mechanism, intergovernmental complaints procedure, and the High

Commissioner on Minorities (whose functions will be described below) contribute significantly to minority protection in Europe.

However, unlike the legally binding international treaties concluded under the auspices of the CoE, the protection of minorities in the framework of the CSCE/OSCE is manifested in non-binding but standard-setting instruments; these have inspired and served as a basis for the CoE's progress with the FCNM and the UN's Declaration on the Rights of Persons Belonging to National or Ethnic, Religious and Linguistic Minorities. In particular, the Copenhagen Document 1990 was a groundbreaking instrument as it combined minority protection with obligations concerning the rule of law and democratic institutions.

4.9.1 The role of the main political bodies

The Permanent Council (PC), composed of the permanent representatives of the OSCE states, has become the most important and regular OSCE body for political consultation and decision making. The Member States have decided that human dimension issues will be regularly dealt with by the PC[294] and that three informal supplementary human dimension meetings will be held each year by it. The OSCE has often sent ad hoc fact-finding missions, normally under the initiative and leadership of the Chairman in Office (CIO), to gather information, to establish initial contacts with the relevant state authorities, and also with the minorities involved. These contacts occasionally led to the establishment of long-term missions. An example is the fact-finding mission sent to Croatia in October 1995, which opened the ground for a long-term mission to this country.

The CIO, the Foreign Minister of the OSCE Member State who holds the annual OSCE Presidency, is vested with overall responsibility for executive action. Additional possibilities of dialogue with the parties to the tensions as well as political endorsement of the CIO's initiatives have been provided through the increasingly active role of the OSCE's troika, consisting of the acting, preceding and succeeding CIO. In addition, ad hoc steering groups have been established to monitor specific situations of tension and to help settling particular conflict situations, as, for example, the Minsk Group, which dealt with the Nagorno-Karabakh conflict.

4.9.2 The High Commissioner on National Minorities

Further conflict-prevention and crisis-management mechanisms were decided at the Helsinki Conference in 1992 and the post of the High Commissioner on National Minorities (HCNM) was established, prompted at the time by the difficulties in stopping the Yugoslav conflict. The HCNM's task is specifically designed to prevent conflicts involving national minorities at the earliest possible stage. Thus, he is not involved in all aspects of minority issues but is confined in his mandate to acting as an instrument of conflict prevention. The HCNM focuses primarily on those situations involving persons belonging to national/ethnic groups who constitute the numerical majority in one state but the numerical minority in another state (i.e. have a kin state), thus engaging the interest of governmental authorities in each state and constituting a potential source of interstate tension if not conflict. In addressing the substance of tensions involving national minorities, the HCNM approaches the issues as an independent, impartial and cooperative actor, who has been successful in conflict solving due to his 'quiet diplomacy'. The HCNM's role is to find compromises that are acceptable to all parties directly concerned and which answer to the requirements of the concrete situation.[295]

The mandate of the OSCE High Commissioner on National Minorities is contained in Chapter II of the 1992 Helsinki Document. According to the mandate, the HCNM will provide 'early warning' and as appropriate 'early action' at the earliest possible stage in regard to tensions involving national minority issues that have the potential to develop into a conflict within the OSCE area, affecting peace, stability or relations between participating states.[296] Though the tasks are framed in political terms and his tools are essentially tailored to deal with political issues, he can also refer to the whole body of international law on human rights and minority rights and associated documents.

The HCNM is not a supervisory mechanism but employs the international standards to which each state has agreed as his principal framework of analysis and the foundation of his specific recommendations. In this relation, it is important to recall the commitments undertaken by all OSCE participating states, in particular those of the 1990 Copenhagen Document of the Conference on the Human Dimension which, in Part IV, articulates detailed standards relating to national minorities. All OSCE states are also bound by UN obligations relating to human rights, including minority rights, and the great majority of OSCE states are further bound by the standards of the CoE. However, individual complaints of persons belonging to national minorities are explicitly excluded in paragraph 5(c) of the High Commissioner's mandate.

The first CSCE High Commissioner on National Minorities, Max van der Stoel, who operated in the early 1990s, a period of great changes in Eastern Europe, has intervened more than ten times in countries such as Albania, Estonia, Hungary, Kazakhstan, Kyrghyzstan, Latvia, Macedonia, Slovakia and the Ukraine.[297] In Estonia, the proposed introduction of the new Law on Aliens in 1993 inflamed opinions among the Russian-speaking community. President Yeltsin and other leading Russian politicians spoke rhetorically against the proposed law. After an intervention by Max van der Stoel, President Meri of Estonia agreed to modify the proposed law and opened round-table talks with the Russian community, which was a successful intervention for the benefit of the Russian minority in Estonia. The HCNM also intervened with positive effect in the disagreement between Albania and Greece in 1993 over the Greek minority in Albania. Furthermore the HCNM has investigated the situation of Roma in the OSCE area in cooperation with the Office for Democratic Institutions and Human Rights.[298]

The mandate provides the necessary freedom of initiative and allows the HCNM to operate with the essential amount of independence. On the one hand, it was deemed necessary to give this post a considerable amount of independence and flexibility, on the other hand, there was a reluctance on the part of many Member States with regard to an independent international official moving in a very sensitive area, who might trespass on state sovereignty.[299]

Although the HCNM's involvement does not require the approval of the Council of Senior Officials or Permanent Council (PC), the latitude of his/her independent activity cannot function properly without the political support of the participating states; the HCNM regularly briefs the PC, both formally and informally and, if the HCNM submits recommendations to a government, he or she will subsequently discuss them with the PC. As already mentioned, the HCNM first and foremost operates by means of quiet and confidential diplomacy. If in spite of the HCNM's involvement, a situation escalates towards conflict, then the HCNM will have to inform the Council of Senior Officials. If participating states will not let the HCNM enter or travel freely, the matter is to be discussed by the Council of Senior Officials.[300] With on-site investigations,[301] assessments and recommendations, the HCNM pays particular attention to the need for continual dialogue between the government and minorities.

In the absence of an OSCE definition of minorities, the first High Commissioner has simply stated that he will recognise a minority when he sees one;[302] in other words, the High Commissioner has interpreted 'national minority' quite broadly. Although the mandate seems to limit the HCNM to 'national' minorities and refers only to tensions affecting peace 'within' rather than 'between' states, the High Commissioner's missions have actually focused on a range of non-dominant groups, including groups which, lacking kin states, are less likely to provoke international tensions such as the Roma and Sinti.[303] In the context of autonomy arrangements, the HCNM has also pointed to the need for specific agreements and regulations on economic questions, such as land allocation and ownership, and the exploitation of natural resources as an element in the overall settlement of self-government regulations and respective division of competencies.[304] Furthermore, it is important to note that paragraph 5(b) of the mandate prevents the HCNM from entering into contact with leaders of militant minority movements, hence the HCNM has never become involved with the IRA in the UK or in the Basque country with ETA in Spain.[305]

While during the accession procedure the EU could rely to a large extent on the monitoring procedures of the OSCE and CoE, the CoE's experience with the FCNM has confirmed the need for and the usefulness of a continuing ongoing assessment of membership criteria after admission of new Member States, which is not taking place at EU level,[306] and which has been particularly criticised by the HCNM, who addressed the Irish Minister for Foreign Affairs during the latter's Presidency of the EU in 2004 requesting the continued validity of the Copenhagen Criteria.[307] The current HCNM, Knut Vollebaek, reminded the EU that the promotion of minority rights throughout the EU must not discontinue with completion of the accession rounds of 2004/2007, while cooperation between the EU's Directorate-General on Enlargement and the HCNM continues in view of the current applicant countries.

The HCNM has also contributed to standard setting by identifying certain recurrent issues and themes, which have become the subject of his attention in a number of states in his recommendations. The HCNM's recommendations are neither binding on states nor are they enforceable but aim to clarify the scope of specific minority rights and give states some practical guidance on respective policies. Among these are issues of minority education and the use of minority languages as matters of great importance for the maintenance and development of the identity of persons belonging to national minorities. With a view to achieving an appropriate and coherent application of relevant minority rights in the OSCE area, the HCNM requested the Foundation on Inter-Ethnic Relations – an NGO established in 1993 to carry out specialised activities in support of the HCNM – to bring together groups of internationally recognised independent experts to elaborate two sets of recommendations: the Hague Recommendations regarding the Education Rights of National Minorities (1996)[308] and the Oslo Recommendations regarding the Linguistic Rights of National Minorities (1998).[309] Both sets of recommendations have subsequently served as references for policy makers and law makers in a number of states.

A third recurrent theme, which has arisen in a number of situations in which the HCNM has been involved, is that of forms of effective participation of national minorities in the governance of states. In 1999 the HCNM, Max van der Stoel, published the Lund recommendations on the Effective Participation of National Minorities in Public Life,[310] which have been further developed by the 2001 Warsaw Guidelines to Assist National Minority Participation in the Electoral Process.[311] The most recent recommendations are the 2003 Guidelines on the Use of Minority Languages in the Broadcast Media[312] and the 2006 Recommendations on Policing in Multi-Ethnic Societies.[313] In 2008 the HCNM published the Bozen/Bolzano Recommendations on National Minorities and Inter-State Relations. The 19 individual recommendations are divided into four sections: general principles, state obligations regarding persons belonging to national minorities, benefits accorded by states to persons belonging to national minorities abroad and multilateral and bilateral instruments and mechanisms. They provide both normative and practical guidance to states in accordance with the general principles of sovereignty, human and minority rights and international responsibility.[314]

The HCNM's link to minority issues in the context of EU enlargement can be regarded as supplementary, as his/her mandate is confined to intervention in crisis situations. However, during the accession process with CEECs, the EU Commission cooperated closely with the HCNM and heavily relied on his expertise. The new Article 2 of the Lisbon Treaty brings the HCNM's mandate closer to the EU's field of activity. Unlike any of the EU institutions, the HCNM has sound expertise in dealing with minority rights related to the monitoring and implementing of laws as well as separatism and violent conflict. The activities of the HCNM in Europe are of diplomatic and persuasive nature, however, his/her efforts and the development of the mandate are an invaluable contribution for raising awareness and influencing minority policy in Europe that has been particularly effective in the new EU Member States.[315]

4.9.3 The Office for Democratic Institutions and Human Rights

The Office for Democratic Institutions and Human Rights (ODIHR) is not as active as the HCNM in bringing specific minority issues to the attention of the PC, but the ODIHR assists in long-term missions and acts as a contact point for Roma and Sinti issues. The ODIHR prepared two reports on human dimension issues for discussion by the PC, one of them was devoted to violence and discrimination against Roma.[316] The ODIHR is a useful source of information for Roma-related issues, but as a problem-solving actor its capacities are rather limited. The activities of the Contact Point for Roma and Sinti issues (CPRSI) include the recording of all reported instances of violence against Roma and Sinti, the provision of legal assistance, mainly through training programmes, the identification of national mediation bodies, support for the cooperation of Roma and Sinti associations, regular meetings on Roma and Sinti issues and the dissemination of information on the Roma and Sinti communities. These facilities and expertise should also be used by all EU Member States for addressing Roma issues within the EU.

These positive achievements notwithstanding, the lack of strictly legal guarantees of minority protection renders minority protection in the OSCE framework particularly fragile, as this protection can be easily counterbalanced by other security concerns. Moreover, the OSCE's political bodies tend to focus mainly on responding to emergency situations, and in particular, to gross violations of human/minority rights. However, as long as European states continue to be unable to agree on a solid and comprehensive system of international guarantees for minority protection that is capable of having an effect at the domestic level, the need for the OSCE's activities in this field remains crucial.

4.10 Conclusion

The minority issue in Europe is characterised by a large number of political declarations and a small number of legally binding rules. Having looked at the different international instruments for minority protection, we can conclude by saying that only those instruments which have no legally binding effect on the participating states contain the most far-reaching provisions for the protection of minorities. For example, the CSCE Copenhagen Document, the CoE's Recommendation 1201, and the UN Declaration on the Rights of Persons Belonging to National or Ethnic, Religious and Linguistic Minorities, as well as the various HCNM recommendations contain an extensive list for promoting minority rights. However, these documents are merely political declarations of intent and the political power to ensure compliance in this area is relatively weak.

Despite the EU's requirement of applicant countries to protect minorities, no specific framework for the protection of the rights of minorities has been provided by EC legislation. With the Copenhagen Criteria and the additional SAP conditionality, the EU addresses deficiencies in the applicant countries with a strong conditionality policy that goes beyond of what is required of the EU's old Member States and beyond the requirements for membership under the old Article 49 TEU. Even though there is no duty of reciprocity under international law and therefore no legal obligation that the EU or rather its already existing Member States have to fulfil the same accession criteria, the efficiency and legitimacy of this conditionality policy is questionable if the EU and its Member States are not protecting their minorities to the same standards as required of the new Member States. This perception of 'double standards' should be enough reason for the EU to find a more consistent common approach, in order to enhance its credibility.[317]

While civil and political rights have been relatively successfully promoted at international level, fears of secession in view of the conflicts in the Balkans, and the failure of the minority regime under the League of Nations, which was imposed by the Western victorious states on the Central Eastern European states, are still factors to be considered, which have prevented minority rights from having a stronger position. Old Member States might consider themselves as deep-rooted traditions of 'old democracies' which allows them to resolve minority-related issues without special instruments and arrangements. A similar approach could be observed in the minority treaties of 1919, which did not impose any obligations on countries such as Italy, France, Belgium, Denmark or even Germany; as one author puts it 'Minority safeguards were deemed unnecessary for politically mature Western European states that could be relied upon to fulfil the standard of civilisation.'[318] Also, the HCNM justified his non-involvement in minority conflicts in Northern Ireland and Spain[319] on account of sufficient democratic institutions in place, able to deal with minority conflicts. Still, it is remarkable that after the proclamation of the Copenhagen Criteria in 1993, neither the ToA nor the Treaty of Nice incorporated the protection of minorities, which only became a treaty provision under the Lisbon Treaty.

As minority protection has not been considered to be part of the EU's competences until Lisbon. Another reason for the invisibility of the EU in this area can be found in the 'principle of subsidiarity', enshrined in Article 5 TEC (Article 5(3) under the new TEU),[320] which prevents the EU from interfering in domestic affairs in areas that can be tackled more efficiently at national level. Under the principle of subsidiarity, the EU might be accused of overstepping its powers when getting involved in minority policies, as there is no clear competence for legislating in the area of minority rights. Member States are usually reluctant to confer new powers on the European level, upholding the principle of subsidiarity, which is often used to defuse fears of too much assimilation of national and regional specifications.[321] However, it is even debatable whether the minority issue can be better resolved at national level, which is the main argument for the subsidiarity principle. It is true that the internal situation in the Member States is so diverse that any attempt at a generally applicable minority protection model has been discouraged so far. Nevertheless, separatism and secession are on the European agenda, without the EU having a voice on these issues. Separatism has been advocated by political forces in parts of Spain (Basque country), Italy (northern Italy), Belgium (Flanders) and the UK (Northern Ireland). Even in cases of violent minority conflicts as in Northern Ireland, the Basque country or Corsica, the Member States have made slow progress in solving these problems and the EU has not been very active in increasing the prospects of a successful resolution. Neither have the instruments currently in force in Europe helped to remedy these problematic situations, as these instruments (such as the FCNM or the OSCE Copenhagen Document) mainly focus on cultural rights, which are not well suited to solving conflicts involving secessionist movements.

The analysis has shown, however, that despite the fact that there is no European consensus on what type of rights should be granted to national minorities, in particular with regard to territorial autonomy, and that the Member States as well as the EU prefer to provide protection only in so far as this protection furthers the non-discrimination principle, rather than granting specific minority rights, a positive trend towards more rights can be observed. As discussed (at section 4.4), in the recent past the EU has resorted more and more to means of soft law in order to promote minority rights. As the CoE considered itself competent to legislate in the area of non-discrimination (Article 13 TEC and the following Directives), including a prohibition of discrimination on the basis of ethnicity, it can be assumed that it is also competent to adopt legislation with regard to minority rights, in particular under the Treaty of Lisbon. Thus, the EU should further its strong competence based in Article 13 TEC/19TFEU, taking into account that the Treaty of Lisbon is of major relevance here, as it not only provides for a stronger mainstreaming provision in Article 10 TFEU, but also aims at introducing qualified majority voting as the ordinary legislative procedure.

5 Minority rights in the Member States

5.1 Introduction

In the context of enlargement to the East, the European Council set out its criteria for membership of the European Union at the Copenhagen Summit in 1993. One of the criteria was that 'the candidate country has achieved stability of institutions guaranteeing democracy, the rule of law, human rights, and respect for and protection of minorities'. It is in regard of this last criterion that a number of concerns have been raised on the applications for EU membership from the Eastern European States. Rules regarding economic liberalisation and rule-of-law reforms, have by way of contrast, been successfully emulated in the CEECs political/institutional system as they were considered beneficial to the emerging business community.[1] The question of whether the applicant countries (now new Member States) provided for strong institutional resources that were committed to the promotion of minority rights was not addressed by the Commission during the enlargement process, hence, other international monitoring mechanisms had to be relied on (in particular the relevant CoE institutions such as the Ad Hoc Committee for the Protection of National Minorities (CAHMIN)), in order to assess the actual minority situation in the Member States, as there is no EU post-accession monitoring by the EU.

The level of minority protection varies in every country as different factors such as the ethnic make-up of the country, territorial changes or historical/political aspects have to be taken into account. However, the Roma minority, which is the biggest and most marginalised minority in all Member States, old and new, has not profited much from the enlargement process. Despite the introduction of anti-discrimination legislation and a number of EU-sponsored policy initiatives (see, in particular, the EU's Network of Independent Experts proposal for a Roma Integration Directive),[2] only few real changes in the situation of the Roma throughout the EU can be accounted for. Also the Russian minority in Estonia and Latvia remains excluded from certain privileges due to their lack of citizenship which deprives them of a number of human rights.[3]

Central Eastern European countries (CEECs) revised the legal status of minorities in order to comply with the Copenhagen Criteria when seeking integration into the EU. Most applicant countries have acceded to the key international instruments for the protection of minorities, such as the European Framework Convention for the Protection of National Minorities (FCNM) and the European Convention on Human Rights (ECHR), which so far serve as the only reference point for the standard of protection that is required, while the actual implementation has not been under much scrutiny during the enlargement process. The different minority rights regimes differ in the CEECs but overall, their constitutional provisions do provide for a promising starting point for progressive minority laws and policies as most CEECs grant traditional minorities cultural, educational and language rights. By the same token, some states, such as the Czech Republic, Estonia and Slovenia, used citizenship legislation to exclude unwanted minorities after gaining their new statehood, which was eventually resolved by international pressure, also from the EU.

The fact that Eastern European applicant countries were held to a different standard than the Western Member States in their accession procedure has already been discussed in the preceding chapter.[4] The record of minority protection in the old Western Member States is mixed,[5] however, all have extensive legislation prohibiting discrimination on grounds of race or ethnicity. In the CEECs, the significance of the Anti-discrimination Directive 2000/43/EC became apparent after its adoption as CEECs had largely ignored anti-discrimination legislation until 2000. The imposition of anti-discrimination legislation on the applicant countries is the most obvious impact by the EU on minority rights in the region, while positive minority rights received less attention from the EU.[6]

To give a diverse picture of the minority situation in the EU, this chapter analyses the present minority situation in four CEECs, two of which were so-called 'first-wave' applicants (Estonia and Slovenia) and two of which were 'second-wave' applicants (Lithuania and Slovakia). While the first-wave applicants were more advanced than the second-wave applicants in their economic and political development when negotiations started, the EU not longer distinguished between first- and second-wave applicants after 2000. At the same time as, Estonia and Lithuania are two Baltic countries, which, despite a similar history, have different minority situations, Slovakia and Slovenia are two southern Central European countries that both underwent territorial changes and formerly belonged to a different state (Czechoslovakia and Yugoslavia) before their independence in the early 1990s. Although the type and the quantity of minorities differ in every country, the legal frameworks are similar. The situation in the old Member States, however, shows a different picture; while Germany provides for similar minority legislation as can be found in many CEECs for its traditional minorities, the UK embraces an entirely different approach. Since traditional minorities such as the Cornish, Irish, Scottish or Welsh are not seen as 'minorities' that suffer from discrimination, it is rather immigrants with different ethnic backgrounds that are considered to be a minority in the UK. In France, there are no officially recognised minorities; however certain minority cultures such as the Basque, Breton or Corsican receive support in some areas. As already discussed in the preceding chapter, the lack of an official definition of the term 'minority' also contributes to the different levels of protection in the Member States.

The situation of minorities will be assessed against eight criteria, which have been identified in chapter 4 as essential conditions for an adequate protection of minority rights. These criteria, which can also be found in FCNM, provide reference points for the analysis of national legislation on minorities, institutions and the practice in those countries. The following headings structure the analysis for assessing the status of minorities in the six chosen countries:

1 constitutional/statutory provisions;
2 institutions for the protection of minorities;
3 education;
4 language rights;
5 culture and media;
6 religion;
7 participation in public affairs; and
8 the situation of the Roma.

The assessment of minority law and policy in these seven different Member States is by no means exhaustive but rather focuses on some of the most important developments regarding the situation of their individual minorities.[7]

5.2 Estonia

5.2.1 Background

Estonia is situated between Latvia and Russia, bordering the Baltic Sea and the Gulf of Finland. It has 1,415,681 inhabitants, the current ethno-demographic situation in Estonia is as follows: Estonians comprise 65.27 per cent (1934: 88.2 per cent) thereof 81per cent have citizenship; Russians[8] 28.07per cent (pre-war: 6 per cent) thereof 14 per cent have citizenship and other national groups comprise 8.2 per cent (3.1per cent Ukrainians, 1.8 per cent Belorussians, 3.3per cent others).[9]

Estonians have lived in their present territory of fairly stable boundaries for more than 1,500 years. After being ruled by different nations for 700 years, the Estonians have been able to subsist as a distinct ethno-cultural entity. During the period of independence (1918–40), Estonia had several ethnic minorities as descendants of the former ruling nations, such as Swedes, Russians and Germans, which constituted 12 per cent of the population. After its incorporation into the Soviet Union, Estonia became the territory of massive population influx from the East as a result of the Soviet Union's idea of resettling people in non-Russian areas using internationalistic myths about the common Soviet people and their particular historical mission.[10] Thus, Estonia's current policy towards non-Estonians has grown out of a climate dominated by the restoration of Estonia's independence and its emergence from the Soviet regime. The possibility of controlling and regulating immigration did not arise for Estonia until July 1990 and with new independence Estonia halted the previously uncontrolled immigration, but could not change the results of half a century of continued influx.

The Estonian Republic considered the former Soviet Union as an illegal occupational regime and thus regards the period of its existence in the Soviet Union as colonisation and occupation. However, Estonia has responded to pressure from the EU and the Organization on Security and Cooperation in Europe (OSCE) by adopting measures to integrate the Russian minority, such as facilitating citizenship for stateless children and the restrictive language requirements in employment must now demonstrate a 'justified public interest'. The essence of ethnic conflicts today lies in changing the former social and political status of the groups concerned (Estonians and Russians) as well as in their efforts to maintain the privileges they had before. The 'ethnic division' has been particularly intertwined with the question of citizenship.

5.2.2 Constitutional and statutory provisions

According to Article 49 of the Constitution of Estonia[11] everyone has the right to preserve his or her national identity. A general non-discrimination clause is contained in Article 12(1) and, Article 51(2) provides for the use of minority language in areas with a minority population of more than 50 per cent: 'In localities where at least half of the permanent residents belong to an ethnic minority, everyone shall have the right to receive answers from state agencies and local governments in the language of the ethnic minority'. It is set out in Article 9 of the Constitution of Estonia that the rights, freedoms and duties of each and every person, as set out in the Constitution, shall be equal for Estonian citizens and for citizens of foreign states and stateless persons in Estonia. However, the most serious obstacle to integration is the fact that the majority of the Russian Estonians are without Estonian citizenship and therefore lack the political rights linked to citizenship, notably electoral rights in national elections. Citizenship is sometimes presented as 'the right to have rights', and serves as a criterion for the attribution of many rights.[12] The rules on the acquisition of nationality are relevant because the recognition of minority rights under international law, as opposed to human rights, is often made dependent on nationality.

5.2.2.1 Estonian citizenship law

As the local authorities had no control over the territory, Soviet Estonia did not have a citizenship law, which differed from that of the Soviet Union. Migrants from Russia, whose role was to strengthen the incorporation of Estonia into the USSR, moved under Soviet laws and did not factually come under – at the time – invalid Estonian laws.

The citizenship law of the pre-war republic (1938) was reintroduced with some amendments on 26 February 1992 with the 'Resolution on the Application of the Law on Citizenship'.[13] According to this law, all those who were citizens of Estonia on 16 June 1940, as well as their descendants, were automatically recognised as citizens. All other inhabitants of Estonia had to apply for citizenship and attain it through naturalisation, which affected most members of the Russian-speaking population. As a precondition for naturalisation, the applicant had to have his or her permanent place of residence in the Estonian territory for at least two years before and one year after the day of application (paragraph 5 of the Citizenship Resolution of 1992) and had to provide proof of knowledge of the Estonian language (Article 6 Law on Citizenship). The earliest date for establishing the permanent place of residence was set at 30 March 1990. The required time period was counted only from that day onwards, so that 30 March 1993 was the earliest date at which one could acquire Estonian citizenship through naturalisation. A large part of the population, especially Russians, did not have the right to vote or the right to be elected in the first parliamentary election of the new Estonia, which took place on 20 September 1992, and were thus excluded from political participation and from shaping the newly independent Estonia.

The new Law on Citizenship of 19 January 1995[14] that brought all citizenship regulations into one document changed the old residence requirements by extending the required period of residence from two years to five years on the basis of a permanent residence permit (Article 6). However, this provision does not apply to persons who had settled in Estonia prior to July 1990. A new requirement that applies to everyone is the proof of knowledge of the Estonian constitution and of the Law on Citizenship, which is assessed through an examination to be performed in Estonian language (Article 9).

The most intensively discussed problem for members of the ethnic minorities to attain Estonian citizenship is the language requirement. During Soviet times, most Russian speakers who migrated to Estonia could get along in their native tongue. Rather than having to learn the Estonian language, Russians continued speaking Russian, whereas Estonians were more or less compelled to become bilingual. In order to pass the language test for the citizenship application, the applicant had to either prove having received elementary, secondary or higher education in Estonian, or provide a certificate for having passed a 'level E' language exam. These requirements were very hard for ordinary Russian speakers, especially when they lived in a dominantly Russian environment where language instruction, which must usually be paid by the applicant, is hard to receive.[15]

In the period 1992–2000 about 114,000 people were naturalised. But the number of non-citizens among the Estonian inhabitants remains high and constitutes the focal point of the minority rights discussion in Estonia. In 1999, 50–70 per cent of stateless adults were not, in their opinion, able to fulfil the language requirements.[16] According to the Estonian Government Communication Office, on 31 May 2008, there were still 113,733 stateless persons in Estonia.[17]

Special provisions apply to the citizenship application of a minor. If the natural parents of the child have custody, an application can only be made if one of them holds Estonian citizenship. This means that in case where the parents are stateless, no one can initiate the naturalisation of the minor, which constitutes a violation of Article 24(3) International Covenant on Civil and Political Rights

(ICCPR) that gives every child a right to acquire a nationality. The UN fact-finding mission and the CSCE High Commissioner on National Minorities both had pointed out this conflict without receiving any swift feedback from the Estonian legislative.[18] However, new amendments to the Citizenship Act adopted by the Estonian government on 8 December 1998 now make it possible to obtain Estonian citizenship through naturalisation for children under the age of 15, who were born in Estonia after independence was reinstated and whose parents, single parent or adoptive parents have lived in Estonia for no less than five years, and who do not enjoy the citizenship of any state.

According to Article 21 of the Law on Citizenship, Estonian citizenship shall not be granted to a person 'who has been or is currently employed by the intelligence or security service of a foreign state' and (even more relevant) to a person 'who has served in a career position in the armed forces of a foreign state or has retired from such a position, nor to his or her spouse who entered Estonia in conjunction with this service'. Thus, former members of the Soviet troops in career positions and spouses who accompanied them to Estonia would have no possibility to acquire Estonian citizenship.

The granting of citizenship seems to be discretionary in all other cases, since the relevant provision, Article 20 of the Law on Citizenship states that the government of the Republic is in charge of the decision without mentioning on which grounds such decision has to be made.[19] Only an appeal to an administrative court (Article 36 of the Law on Citizenship)[20] can reveal if and where limitations to the government's discretion are to be found.

The Estonian claim that citizenship in Estonia is not derived from ethnicity is a very formal one when it is simply argued that everyone who came after 1940 has to apply for citizenship. No provision in the law grants citizenship merely on the basis of birth or a certain number of years of residence in the country. There is no doubt about the fact that ethnicity is the very motivation for the rules as they were drafted.[21] Or as Müllerson puts it, 'it was a desire to obtain or at least approximate ethnic purity … not consideration of legal consistency that led to such an approach towards the citizenship question in Estonia.'[22]

5.2.2.2 The Law on Aliens

The Law on Aliens of 8 July 1993[23] defines most of the Soviet-period immigrants and their descendants as aliens who have to apply for residence and work permits. Besides a number of provisions on the entry of aliens into the country and their sojourn, residence and employment, Article 20 and 21 of the Law on Aliens specifically concern 'aliens who settled in Estonia prior to July 1990', those aliens 'shall be guaranteed residence and employment permits if they meet the other requirements established in the law'.

However, according to §12(4) subparagraph 6–7, individuals who are presently or were formerly employed by the intelligence or security service of a foreign state, persons active in the armed forces of a foreign state and their family members, and persons who have retired from career positions in the armed forces of a foreign state and their family members who have entered Estonia in conjunction with such service are excluded from the possibility to receive residence permits.

This provision touched on vital interests of retired Russian military officers who stayed in Estonia and whose reintegration into Russia would have been very difficult. Thus Russia, despite earlier announcements to withdraw all troops from Estonia by August 1993, tried to link the withdrawal to social guarantees for military retirees living in the country. Eventually an agreement was reached 'On matters related to social guarantees for military pensioners of the Russian Federation on the territory of the Republic of Estonia'. Besides laying down the technical details of retirement payments and giving guarantees about property rights, housing, human rights and healthcare, the agreement also stipulated that they 'shall receive resident permits on the basis of a personal application'. This concession regarding residence permit for retired military personnel could be given on the basis of §12(5) of the Law of Aliens, which allows exemptions 'in accordance with procedures established by the government'. However, Russian military pensioners will not be able to become Estonian citizens. The legal and political debates have continued over the issue of residence permits of former military officers and their spouses and minor children, including in the light of amendments introduced to the Aliens Act in June 2002, which entered into force in January 2004, excluding explicitly the issuance of permanent residence permits to them.

5.2.3 Institutions for the protection of minorities

On 1 June 1999 the Office of the Legal Chancellor was established, to receive complaints from individuals on different legal issues.[24] The Legal Chancellor also acts as an Ombudsman, §1(5) of the Act provides: 'The Chancellor of Justice resolves discrimination disputes which arise between persons in private law on the basis of the Constitution and other Acts'. However, there is no specialised body that focuses on minority rights in Estonia.

In 1999 the Ombudsman received 100 applications from minorities and 158 in 2000, of which only five complaints concerned citizenship or language requirements.[25] The fact that only such few complaints regarding minority rights have been received by the Ombudsman is partly due to the fact that its mandate is not sufficiently defined in this respect and the Office is not easily accessible to the public; the European Commission criticised in its Regular Report of 2000 that public awareness of its existence and functions needs to be raised.[26] The total number of petitions submitted by citizens increased from 1,533 in 2000 to 2,530 (written and oral complaints) in 2001. This can be partly attributed to the positive fact that the Legal Chancellor has become better known. There are now three representative offices of the Legal Chancellor in northeast Estonia, in Narva, Jõhvi and Sillamäe. This should help ensure that the specific concerns of the significant proportion of non-Estonians in the region (such as those related to naturalisation and language) can be better dealt with.[27]

5.2.4 Education

In pre-war Estonia the educational policy of the state set bilingualism as an objective for educating children from minority groups. Apart from monolingual schools, there were mixed-language schools, where two or even three languages were used as a language of instruction (Estonian–Russian, Estonian–German, Estonian–Swedish, Latvian–Russian, Jewish–German–Russian schools).

The Second World War and the subsequent Soviet occupation resulted in the radical dismantling of the Estonian educational system. It was modified to fit the Soviet system of education and to serve the communist ideology. Estonian and Russian became the only languages of instruction. The official policy in Estonian language schools aimed at Estonian–Russian bilingualism, a compulsory requirement at graduation, while Russian children were educated in Russian-language schools oriented to monolingualism. An assimilation programme was introduced for children of other minority groups. Their minority language schools were closed down and children had to continue their studies in either Estonian- or Russian-language schools. It was not permitted to study one's minority language even as an optional subject.

For the above-mentioned reasons two distinct types of school developed in Estonia – the Estonian-language school and the Russian-language school, which differed from one another both as regards the language of instruction and the content of education. The Law on Basic and Upper Secondary Schools of 1993 stipulated the transition to Estonian instruction in all state and municipal upper secondary schools by the year 2000.[28] It thus proceeded from the assumption that by that time graduates of Russian basic schools will have sufficient knowledge to continue their education in upper secondary Estonian schools.

Today, the 1997 Law on Basic and Upper Secondary Schools establishes that all secondary schools would become 'Estonian language institutions' and that instruction in Estonian shall be started no later than 2007. Russian-speaking pupils would then be obliged to go to private schools where they can be taught in their mother tongue.[29] To achieve the goals of the reform, in January 1998, the Estonian government approved a policy document entitled 'The Development Plan for Russian-Medium Schools' outlining plans for the next ten years. The programme pays special attention to the teaching of Estonian as, according to the Basic and Upper Secondary Schools Act, by the year 2007 (§52), all graduates from non-Estonian language basic schools should have sufficient knowledge of Estonian to enable them to continue their studies in the Estonian language. However, the scaling back of Russian language education remains threatening to Russian speakers. As the envisaged start of the transfer to Estonian as the main language of instruction in upper secondary schools in the school year 2007/2008 was a major challenge, which has not yet been adequately prepared throughout Estonia, added flexibility was introduced by providing secondary schools with the possibility to apply for the exemption from the requirement to transfer to Estonian-language teaching. There is also a need to intensify the training and other efforts to ensure that teachers have adequate Estonian language and other skills, and that pupils and others involved are prepared for the transfer. To that end, the 'language immersion programme' has supported teaching Estonian to the minority groups. At the moment, approximately 7 per cent of students in schools where the language of instruction is Russian study according to the language immersion programmes. On 1 September 2007 the upper secondary schools with non-Estonian language of instruction started the transition to partial teaching of subjects in Estonian and by the 2011/2012 academic year the schools will guarantee Estonian-language instruction in at least 60 per cent of the minimum allowable educational content at the upper secondary school level. In the case of the remaining 40 per cent of the curriculum the schools themselves will determine the language of instruction.

Estonian legislation protects the right of all Estonian children to receive Estonian language pre-school education, but provides no similar right for Russian-speaking children. By law, a special Estonian-language group must be established to cater for a single Estonian-speaking child, even in regions where the Russian-speaking population is dominant and bilingual pre-schools are prohibited.[30]

5.2.5 Language rights

During the Soviet times the dominating position of the Russian language and the absence of cultural activities and institutions of other ethnic groups have caused one-sided dominance of the Russian language and culture. Russian has become a native language for 70 per cent of the non-Russian and non-Estonian ethnicities, at the same time, only 2.8 per cent of non-Estonians considered Estonian as their mother tongue. One of the first steps to re-establish the ethnic identity of Estonia was the adoption of the Language Law of 1989 (already undertaken by the ESSR Supreme Soviet),[31] which made Estonian the official language and put it under special protection. In its Article 4, this law requires all persons whose jobs involve 'communication with individuals' subject to certain requirements of Estonian language competence. At the same time, however, it was emphasised that the use of one's native language was the 'inalienable right of citizens of all other nationalities'.

The 1995 Law on Language[32] consolidates Estonian as the state language and further regulations define areas in which Estonian language must be used 'in the public interest'. A 1999 amendment to the Law on Language introduced a new system specifying three levels of linguistic proficiency[33] and required people who had not pursued their education in Estonian to take language exams by July 2002. Furthermore, a new regulation requires proficiency in Estonian for all public servants, service personnel, employees of companies, non-profit associations and foundations, and sole proprietors.[34]

In communication with public authorities Russian is generally tolerated, although the right to use minority languages as internal languages in local self-government has never been officially approved, despite its provision in Article 51 of the Constitution. The Law on Language allows in its Article 8 'persons not proficient in Estonian' to communicate orally with state authorities in a language both understand and Article 11 of the Law on Language provides that a minority language may be used alongside Estonian as the internal working language 'in local governments where the majority of permanent residents are non-Estonian speakers' with the approval of the central government. Although a number of local governments have made such requests, approval has never been given.[35] Adherence to the Law of Language, including the use of Estonian in public signs, advertisements and place-names, is monitored by a National Language Inspectorate under the Ministry of Education. The inspectorate conducts spot-checks, and has imposed administrative charges for violations. There have been improvements in some sectors in the practice of the Language Inspectorate and the Constitutional Court has made important references, *inter alia,* to the need to ensure that the measures taken to ensure language proficiency for employees are proportional in accordance with the Language Act. In an important decision, the Riigikogu amended Article 28 of the Language Act on 10 December 2003 in order to extend, indefinitely, the validity of the 'old' language proficiency certificates issued for occupational purposes. Furthermore, the Language Inspectorate is conscious of the fact that, in the private sphere, language proficiency of only those employees whose proficiency requirement is tightly linked to a public interest should be supervised.[36] Nevertheless, the establishment of a language inspectorate shows that Estonia takes the promotion of the Estonian language very seriously.

5.2.6 Culture and media

Article 50 of the Constitution stipulates that national minorities have the right, in the interests of national culture, to establish self-governing agencies under certain conditions and pursuant to procedure provided by the National Minorities Cultural Autonomy Act.[37]

The National Minorities Cultural Autonomy Act grants the right to form institutions for cultural self-government to all those minorities that fall under the definition of Article 1: 'This Law considers as national minorities citizens of Estonia who: – reside on the territory of Estonia; – maintain longstanding, firm and lasting ties with Estonia; – are distinct from Estonians on the basis of their ethnic, cultural, religious, or linguistic characteristics; – are motivated by a concern to preserve together their cultural traditions, their religion or their language which constitute the basis of their common identity.' This definition of minorities is almost identical with the definition given by the CoE's Parliamentary Assembly in its recommendation 1201 of 1993.[38] However, as only citizens of Estonia can profit from this law according to Article 1, Article 6 provides that 'Foreigners residing in Estonia *may participate* in the activities of cultural and educational institutions and religious congregations of national minorities, but they may not vote or be elected or appointed to the leadership of the institutions of cultural self-government.'

A national minority that is entitled to cultural autonomy can, by direct and uniform elections with a secret vote, elect their own cultural council, which is the highest organ of authority and representation within the frames of cultural autonomy. The cultural council of a national minority can form regional cultural boards according to their needs, appoint cultural deputies and found ethnic cultural institutions, schools, social and healthcare establishments, publishing houses, etc. (see Article 24 of the National Minorities Cultural Autonomy Act). Resources originate from specific allocations, partly from the state budget, partly from local budgets, as well as from membership fees and donations from enterprises, organisations and private persons. Presently the Union of Ingrian Finns and the Union of Slavic Education and Charity Societies have successfully applied for the status of cultural self-government and held elections for their cultural council in May 2004.

The CoE's FCNM Advisory Committee concluded, in its first Opinion, that the National Minorities Cultural Autonomy Act has not had a substantial impact in Estonia and that it should be revised or replaced with norms that are better adapted to the current minority situation in Estonia despite the fact that the law, while having finally led to the establishment of one national cultural autonomy, is generally considered to be ineffective and impractical, in particular as it only applies to Estonian citizens who have to be a group of at least 3,000 people.[39]

There are no special provisions that ensure Russian-language print or broadcast media. The Law on Language restricts in its Article 25 television broadcasting 'in foreign languages … without translation into Estonian … shall not exceed 10 per cent of the volume of the weekly production'. Estonian State Radio airs a channel broadcasting in Russian, Belorussian and Ukrainian (Radio 4) and there are three private radio stations broadcasting in Russian and two Russian TV channels (Ostankino and Russland TV) that can be received via cable. As regards print media, Article 45 of the Constitution (freedom of press and information) guarantees the right to publish in minority language. There are two Russian-language dailies and two local newspapers, five Russian language newspapers are published weekly.

5.2.7 Religion

According to Article 40 of the Constitution of Estonia, there is no state church in Estonia. Everyone may freely belong to churches and religious societies. Accordingly there is no enumeration in law of recognised religions. The Constitution affirms in Article 40 everyone's freedom to exercise his or her religion, unless this is detrimental to public order, health or morals.

5.2.8 Participation in public affairs

The right to citizenship, which includes the right to political participation in a state, is in many regards the core of the dispute on effective participation in public affairs. According to Article 48(1) of the Estonian Constitution, only Estonian citizens can found a political party. Estonia's National Minorities Cultural

Autonomy Act is limited to Estonian citizens, thus excluding the majority of members of the Russian communities who were denied citizenship.

In order to include more people into state and democracy building, some preconditions for equal participation have been provided through the right to vote in local government elections by all permanent residents and through the expansion of the right to cultural autonomy to ethnic groups (see Article 6 of the National Minorities Cultural Autonomy Act), however, to a limited extent. In addition, steps towards political self-organisation of the Russian community have been taken by the creation of their own political parties. In the national election of 1995 a coalition of two Russian parties, the United People's Party and the Russian Party of Estonia, won six out of 101 seats in Parliament. For the 1999 election two more Russian parties were established, the Russian Party of Unity and the Baltic-Russian Party and currently there are three ethnic Russian parties in Parliament with a total of four seats; another two seats are held by ethnic Russians affiliated with the 'Party of the Centre'.

The Law on Elections to Parliament[40] specifies detailed linguistic requirements for parliamentary and local councils' deputies and candidates to representative bodies. The European Commission criticised in its Regular Report of 2000 'these restrictions affect the right of non-Estonian speakers to choose their candidates, in particular at local level'.[41]

The 1997 amendments to the Language Act provided for language requirements of electoral candidates, in addition to the above-mentioned tighter language proficiency requirements for non-Estonians in the public and private sector. When this law was challenged on technicality grounds, the court reasoned that one of the duties of the state was to preserve the Estonian nation and culture and concluded that the language proficiency requirement for parliamentarian candidates was not unreasonable. Eventually, these language requirements were repealed in 2001 under pressure from the OSCE. Estonia addressed these concerns by removing the language proficiency requirements for candidates in parliamentary and local government elections through amendments, introduced on 21 November 2001, to the Riigikogu Elections Act and to the Local Government Council Election Act.

5.2.9 The situation of the Roma

The number of Roma living in Estonia is one of the lowest in Central Eastern Europe, which is one of the factors regarding their low level of protection. There are currently about 1,000–1,500 Roma in Estonia who suffer from discrimination on the employment sector (approximately 90 per cent of Roma are unemployed), only very few Roma attend school (according to European Commission against Racism and Intolerance (ECRI), out of 350 Roma children only 67 were registered in a school), many are being sent to schools for mentally disabled children. The Estonian print media often publish openly racist articles about Roma. In addition, there is little political initiative to address issues that are of concern regarding Roma, and projects that have been undertaken to assist

Roma have not sufficiently involved Roma representatives and therefore often resulted in failure.[42]

5.2.10 Conclusion

The main area of concern in Estonia is the citizenship law, including provisions on language and language education, which particularly disadvantage the Russian-speaking minority. Although there is no internationally accepted human right to obtain the citizenship of a particular state, minorities that do not possess the nationality of the country of their residence do not enjoy protection under international law[43] and are excluded from the democratic perspectives of the state. If Estonian citizenship becomes too difficult to obtain, the Russian minority might opt for Russian citizenship, which will not further their integration into Estonian society.

Consequently, also the definition of national minorities contained in the 1993 National Minorities Cultural Autonomy Act, which only applies to Estonian citizens raises concern. In the light of the significant number of non-nationals and stateless persons residing on the territory of Estonia, such a narrow definition may have the effect of transforming a policy of integration into a policy of assimilation. In addition, it clearly represents a violation of Article 27 ICCPR and Article 5(e) (vi) International Convention on the Elimination of All Forms of Racial Discrimination (CERD) with regard to the exercise of minority culture. Estonia has signed the Optional Protocol to the ICCPR on individual complaints, but no member of the Russian minority has so far alleged violation of Article 27 ICCPR.

5.3 Germany*

5.3.1 Background

Germany is situated in Central Europe and is bordered to the west by France, Luxembourg, Belgium and the Netherlands, to the north by the North Sea, Denmark and the Baltic Sea, to the east by Poland and the Czech Republic and to the south by Austria and Switzerland.

Germany has 82,218,000 inhabitants[44] of which 8.8 per cent are foreigners, more than one-quarter of them Turkish citizens,[45] and 9.5 per cent of all Germans come from an immigrant background,[46] who, however, are not considered as national minorities. Germany is a federal state with 16 *Bundesländer* (states), most of which have been formed after 1945.[47] There are four recognised national minorities in Germany which are protected under the FCNM, which Germany ratified in 1997: the Danish minority, the Friesian ethnic minority in Germany, the German Sinti, Roma and Sorbs. The Danes, Sorbs, Sinti and Roma are designated as national minorities whereas the Frisians, as requested by the group, are called the 'Frisian ethnic group'. Nevertheless the status remains equal to that of a national minority. The languages spoken by these minorities are Danish, North and Sater Friesian, Romani[48] and Lower and Upper Sorbian. All groups also speak fluent German. Until their disenfranchisement on 7 September 1939 there was also a Polish minority living in what was then called the German Reich. Today, all former German territories in which a Polish minority was resident belong to the territory of the Republic of Poland.

Three of the current recognised minorities are traditionally living in particular areas of Germany: since Denmark's defeat in 1864 approximately 50,000 German-national Danes have been a minority in the Schleswig region of the state of Schleswig-Holstein. Almost since records began the Friesians have been known as the people living close to the North Sea. They settled in North Friesia in about the seventh century, and in the Saterland region between 1100 and 1400. Today they can be found in three different areas: in the north of the Netherlands, as well as in the German states of Lower Saxonia and Schleswig-Holstein. Exact figures of the size of this minority are not available, though it is estimated that in Schleswig-Holstein alone about 50,000 people belong to the Frisian minority.

From the seventh century onwards, Sorbs settled in the region to the east of the Elbe and Saale Rivers; today there are about 20,000 Lower Sorbs living in Lower Lusatia (in the State of Brandenburg) and twice as many Upper Sorbs in Upper Lusatia (in the Free State of Saxony). The estimated 70,000 Sinti and Roma German nationals are not settled in a particular area but live throughout Germany in urban as well as more rural areas. They have lived in Germany at least since the fourteenth century when they were first mentioned in historical documents.

In the last century Germany underwent a number of changes to its boundary. Following the First World War, Germany lost control over some of its territory, as ruled in the Treaty of Versailles of 28 June 1919; Alsace-Lorraine was given to France, Eupen and Malmedy were given to Belgium, Northern Schleswig was given to Denmark, Hultschin was given to Czechoslovakia and finally West Prussia, Posen and Upper Silesia were given to Poland.[49]

After the Second World War, following four years of occupation by the allied forces of the UK, France, USA and the Soviet Union, two German states were founded in 1949: the Bundesrepublik Deutschland (referred to as West Germany) in the western part of Germany (plus the western parts of Berlin which had been occupied by allied forces from France, the UK and the USA) which was set up as a parliamentary democracy. The Deutsche Demokratische Republik (referred to as East Germany) in the Soviet occupation zone in the eastern part of Germany was set up as a communist regime, with the Soviet Union acting as a role model and exercising considerable control. The reunification of the two German States on 3 October 1990 was made possible by the collapse of East Germany, highly symbolised by the fall of the Berlin Wall on 9 November 1989.

5.3.2 Constitutional and statutory provisions

Germany has specific criteria as to what constitutes a minority in their country,[50] which includes: the requirement of German citizenship, that they differ from the majority population through a different identity, manifested by their own language, culture and history, have the wish to preserve this identity, are traditionally residents in Germany and live in traditional settlement areas.[51] Again this definition coincides the CoE's Recommendation 1201 of 1993. When challenged why the considerable numbers of migrants in Germany are not protected under the FCNM, the German government argued that the Convention does not specify any exact criteria of who should be classified as a minority. Their chosen restrictive definition would be within the overall spirit of protecting *national* minorities. Others would be protected by more general human rights instruments. Furthermore, under international law the recognition of minority rights tends to be dependent on nationality.[52] An argument that is hard to defeat in light of considerable European legislation for the protection of immigrants, in particular the anti-discrimination laws.[53]

5.3.2.1 Basic Law and federal laws

National minorities in Germany are protected by various legislations. Under Article 1(1) of the German Basic Law human dignity is inviolable,[54] and Article 3, a general non-discrimination clause states that all persons are equal before the law, and that no one can be discriminated on any grounds including '... parentage, race, language, homeland and origin'.[55]

Some more specific laws and regulations at a federal level exist, particularly the General Equal Treatment Act (*Allgemeines Gleichbehandlungsgesetz*) which was adopted in August 2006 in order to implement, *inter alia*, Directive 2000/43/EC,[56] and is mainly concerned with anti-discrimination in the areas of work and employment, but has yet to be assessed by the Advisory Committee to the FCNM. A much older law is the 1955 Declaration on the Rights of the Danish minority which enshrines their rights to use the Danish language in law, administration and education in Schleswig-Holstein, and to be represented politically in this state. According to Section 1 of the Declaration, they enjoy the same rights under the Basic Law as all other Germans.

The execution of federal laws is the responsibility of the *Länder*, within the boundaries set by the law.

5.3.2.2 Statutory provisions of the Länder

The freedom to declare oneself part of a national minority (as under Article 3 FCNM) is ensured by Article 5(1) of the Constitution of Schleswig-Holstein, and Article 37(2) of the Constitution of Saxony-Anhalt, under Article 1 of the Act on the Sorbs' Rights in the Free State of Saxony, as well as Section 2 of the Act on the Specification of the Rights of the Sorbs of Brandenburg. The prohibition of discrimination is also safeguarded by many of the *Länder*'s constitutions, including Article 4(1) of the North-Rhine/Westphalia constitution which expressly prohibits discrimination on the grounds of belonging to a national minority in that *Land*.

5.3.3 Institutions for the protection of minorities

5.3.3.1 Federal institutions

The Federal Ministry of the Interior is responsible for legislation developments and support of minorities. The Federal Commissioner for Matters Relating to Repatriates and National Minorities (the latter responsibility being added in 2002) is in charge of public information, chairing of consultative meetings at the Federal Ministry of the Interior and seeking to further improve relations between the majority population and minority groups. A similar post of Commissioner has been created by the government of Schleswig-Holstein (mainly for the benefit of the Danish minority), but minorities in Saxony and Brandenburg, and elsewhere have to address complaints to the Federal Commissioner.[57] Additionally a Consultative Committee for Issues of the Danish Minority exists at the Federal Ministry of Interior, which is chaired by the Federal Minister of Interior, and includes three members of the Danish minority, as well as two members from each of the parliamentary groups of the German Parliament (Bundestag). This Committee can bring minority issues to the attention of the federal government and the Bundestag. A similar consultative committee exists for the Sorbian people and the Frisian ethnic group, but not for the German Sinti and Roma. There are councils for Sorbian Affairs elected from the Parliaments of the *Länder* of Brandenburg and the Free State of Saxony which also contribute to increased participation by national minorities. The same applies to the appointment of a Commissioner for the border region of the *Land* of Schleswig-Holstein, who gives advice to the Minister-President of the *Land* on all matters relating to the Danish minority, the Frisians and the Roma/Sinti. Commissioners for Sorbian affairs have also been appointed by several municipalities in the areas traditionally inhabited by Sorbs and some of these even work on a voluntary basis.

The German Bundestag also runs a round-table discussion on National Minorities. However this has been criticised as a weak instrument, and there are demands that more official parliamentary hearings must be held.[58] The Secretariat for Minorities was established in response to the requirements of the FCNM.[59] The Secretariat represents all federal associations of national minorities and receives project funding from the federal government. It facilitates dialogue between the federal government and national minorities.

Furthermore, a system of collecting information on politically motivated crime was introduced in January 2001, as well as a national action plan to fight racism, xenophobia, anti-Semitism and related intolerance was developed in 2008. Brandenburg has also created a strategy against violence, right-wing extremism and xenophobia in 1998 which includes public discussion forums, counselling and mobile task forces.

5.3.3.2 Institutions run by the Länder *and the minority groups*

At *Land* level there are also institutions such as the Free State of Saxony's Ministry of Scientific Affairs and Arts which has a section for Sorbian Matters and

Memorials. In Schleswig-Holstein there is a Commissioner for Minorities and Culture, who advises the Minister-President on matters relating to the minorities in the *Land.* Saxony's Parliament elects a Council for Sorbian Affairs and Brandenburg a Council for Sorbian (Wendish) Affairs, each with five members. In the Schleswig-Holstein Parliament, there is a panel dealing with matters concerning the Frisian ethnic group, chaired by the President of the Parliament.

The Foundation of the Sorbian people was established in 1991, and is a legally autonomous organisation enabling Sorbs to organise their own interests and concerns. It receives funding from both federal and state level and was developed after signing an inter-state treaty between Brandenburg and Saxony in 1998. Another important organisation for the Sorbs is Domowina which was founded in 1912 in Hoyerswerda as the umbrella organisation of Sorbian societies and associations, which aims at defending the democratic and national interests of the Sorbs as well as maintaining Sorbian language and culture. The Umbrella organisation for the Frisians is the Inter-Frisian Council, which comprises three councils, but is no equivalent to the foundation for the Sorbian people. The Danish organisations work together and coordinate their joint activities in the Joint Council for the Danish Minority, an advisory body with no authority to issue binding Directives. The Central Council of German Sinti and Roma (an umbrella organisation of nine *Länder* associations, plus other regional and local ones) and the Documentation and Cultural Centre of German Sinti and Roma in Heidelberg have received government funding since 1991, and are recognised as public institutions. The Central Council of German Sinti and Roma focuses especially on an equal political standing for the minority. It must be noted that the Sinti Alliance of Germany (an umbrella of ten other associations) is not affiliated with the Central Council and Documentation Centre, but they also offer support for Sinti families in social matters.

Moreover, a Minority Council has been created, a discussion forum to maintain contact with the federal government, representing all of the national minorities, with the exception of some of the Sinti population since the Sinti Alliance of Germany is not a member.

5.3.4 Education

In the Federal Republic of Germany, education is the responsibility of the *Länder.* Non-discrimination in school education is expressed, *inter alia,* in section 1(1), 1(2), and 3(3) of the Hessian Schools Act and section 1(1) of the Schools Act of Baden-Württemberg. The Danish minority has a fully developed system of private schools, whose establishment is guaranteed under Article 7(4) and (5) of the Basic Law. There are 55 kindergartens and 48 schools run by the Danish Schools Association for South Schleswig, two of which enable students to reach the school-leaving certificate *Abitur* (equivalent to A-levels in the UK). There is also a historical network of Sorbian schools. Additionally, teacher training is available in Sorbian, along with classes in Sorbian language and culture at Leipzig University (at the Institute of Sorbian Language and Culture). There are three entirely Sorbian language students dormitories at different boarding schools. A Sorbian course for certified childcarers is also offered at the Sorbian College for Social Pedagogy. Nevertheless, there has been a threat of closure of some Sorbian secondary schools in Saxony. This was due to the decision that Sorbian schools would no longer be exempt from the requirement of a minimum of 20 pupils per class, and many of the schools operated with much smaller classes. These plans have been criticised by the Advisory Committee to the FCNM in its first opinion on Germany.[60]

State-run schools provide some instruction in the Frisian language, and this is also the case for a few nursery schools. Frisian is taught at some of the Danish minority schools, and there is a North Frisian Dictionary Institute at Kiel University since 1959, as well as a professorial chair of Frisian Philology since 1978. Lower Saxony has an education specialist for Saterfrisian since 2000.

Even though there is no discrimination regarding access to education, the Roma and Sinti population continues to be overrepresented in schools for underachievers (*Sonderschulen*).[61] There are no schools for the Roma and Sinti, and the group says it does not wish for any. In order to promote understanding of Roma and Sinti culture through the education system, teacher training has been enhanced, for example by running workshops for teachers in Baden-Württemberg on the integration of the Sinti and Roma minority in Germany. Special promotion of young Sinti and Roma is intended with a training strategy for those without the final high school certificate, which was developed in 2009 by the Regional Centre for Education, Integration and Democracy, Sinti associations from Baden-Württemberg and Schleswig-Holstein and Roma representatives from Hamburg. This will qualify the students to work in children and youth institutions and in schools, in order to improve the education and thus employment chances of the Roma and Sinti. Some associations have launched supplementary lessons for Sinti and Roma schoolchildren as well as adult education groups. Also, Roma/Sinti school mediators have been introduced in Schleswig-Holstein and Baden-Württemberg, a measure that was much welcomed by the CoE's Council of Ministers.[62]

5.3.5 Language rights

German is the only official language in Germany. However Article 2(1) of the Basic Law proclaims the right to free development of personality which includes learning and speaking one's own language, which is also protected by Article 5 of the Basic Law (providing for the freedom of expression). As Germany is also a signatory to the European Charter for Regional or Minority Languages (ECRML), Danish, North and South Frisian, Lower and Upper Sorbian and Romani, as well as the regional Low German are protected by the provisions of the ECRML.

There are separate specifications for each language since, due to the federal structure, the responsibility lies with the individual *Land*. All the above languages are protected under Part II of ECRML, and since Romani is dispersed throughout Germany it is protected under Part III, as well as Low German. This means extra safeguards must be given by choosing a minimum of 35 out of 64 undertakings listed in the ECRML. So far, the state of Hessen is the only one to have met these 35 requirements for Romani.[63] The language provisions and services vary in the different *Länder*, for example the website of Schleswig-Holstein offers visitors the option to listen to audio recordings of Danish, Frisian or Romani.[64]

5.3.5.1 Danish

Danish is well protected, because of the system of private schools (see above) and the proximity to Denmark. The Danish community has organised a Danish healthcare association which helps to treat the minority in their own language. Furthermore, the websites of district hospitals in Nordfriesland are available in Danish, and a number of the staff at the psychiatric clinic in the Schleswig region speak Danish.[65] As to administrative procedures, generally only German is admitted in courts and administrative courts in areas where Danish minorities live, but Danish is sometimes used in administrative relations if a Danish-speaking person is working there. Documents can be submitted to administrative authorities in the Danish settlement area in Danish, and there is the possibility of having civil marriages conducted in Danish in the town of Flensburg. It must be noted that all of the Danish minority are bilingual, as are the other minorities, and thus fluent in German.

Minority-led organisations are key in the development and protection of language rights. For example the Sydslesvigsk Forening (SSF) is dedicated to promoting, among other things, the Danish language, offering a wide range of activities such as theatrical performances and recreational facilities for senior citizens in Danish. Similarly the Danish Youth Association for South Schleswig offers sport activities and recreational facilities, where the use of Danish is encouraged. Lastly, the minority has its own library system run by the Danish central library for South Schleswig with seven branches. It also includes a research department and an archive for local history.

5.3.5.2 Sorbian

In German-Sorbian areas both languages can be used in relations with the administration of the Land and local governments. Sorbian is translated into German at the cost of the authority.[66] In addition to the freedoms guaranteed by the Basic Law for the entire territory of Germany, section 8 of the Act on the Specification of Rights of the Sorbs (Wends) in the Land of Brandenburg explicitly reaffirms the right to use the Sorbian (Wendish) language freely. Pursuant to the Saxon Constitution and section 8 of the Act on the Sorbs' Rights in the Free State of Saxony and a number of other laws and ordinances, the Sorbs in the Free State of Saxony have the right to communicate, orally and in writing, in their mother tongue. There are also bilingual signs in Sorbian areas for places, towns, public buildings, and so on. The *Länder* in question have given high priority to learning the Sorbian language at schools, and Sorbian organisations such as Witaj[67] (the Sorbian school association) have made sure that this option is available in some preschool centres. Overall the number of students studying the Sorbian language has increased, despite a decrease in student population, thanks to the efforts of organisations such as Witaj.[68] The Foundation of the Sorbian people also works for the preservation and development of Sorbian language.

5.3.5.3 Frisian

The Schleswig-Holstein Act on Promoting Frisian in the Public Sphere (Frisian Act) of 13 December 2004 includes specific rules to promote the Frisian language in various areas. In the academic year of 2006/2007, 23 teachers at 24 schools taught 159 hours of Frisian to over 1,000 pupils per week.[69] There is also a North Frisian Dictionary Institute at Kiel University since 1959, as well as a professorial chair of Frisian Philology since 1978. Linguistic and cultural activities of the Frisians have received considerable federal funding since 2000.[70] A dictionary of Saterland Frisian was published in 1980, with a second edition due in 2010. Schleswig-Holstein adopted the Act on Promoting Frisian in the Public Sphere in 2004 which promotes the use of the Frisian language. According to Section 1 of the Act, citizens can address administrative authorities in Frisian, including submitting documents in Frisian in the Nordfriesland district and Helgoland Island. The Frisian language is part of normal social life in Nordfriesland; there are Frisian street names and bilingual place name signs. Three of nine local idioms of Frisian are close to extinction, as they are spoken by fewer than 150 people.[71] Lastly, the Frisian ethnic group has various associations (such as the North Frisian Association or Association for a North Frisian Radio Station) who promote the importance of the preservation of Frisian language and culture.

5.3.5.4 Romani

There are no specific government bodies dealing with the protection and promotion of the Romani language, mainly as a result of many of the German Sinti and Roma associations who do not wish for the language to be taught in public schools, based on negative experiences of language researchers under the Nazi regime. The Sinti alliance also argues that by tradition, no one outside the community is allowed access to their language.[72] Most of the Roma and Sinti object to using their language with administrative officials who are not members of their own minority. Other groups wish for it to be taught by schools, and to develop a written form of the language. Diverse cultural demands in the community make action more difficult. Romani is offered more protection under the ECRML de jure than the other minority languages, but, in reality, implementation is difficult.

5.3.6 Culture and media

5.3.6.1 Culture

As with language rights, the right to exercise one's culture is encompassed by Article 2(1) of the Basic Law: the right to free development of personality, and thus preservation of culture is the freedom and right of every individual. Culture is the responsibility of the *Länder*. Explicit provisions on promoting and preserving the culture of national minorities can be found in the constitutions of five *Länder*.[73] Details of some of the institutions created for cultural promotion have been discussed (at section 5.3.2, above).

Cultural protection and promotion is primarily supported by the minority organisations for example the SSF who runs open-air festivals with parades and music, movies, discussions, etc. The Foundation of the Sorbian people also prides itself on preserving, documentation, publication and presentation of Sorbian art, culture and folklore. Local museums in the relevant areas collect items of Sorbian cultural heritage, and local authorities and administrative districts also support traditional festivals and customs observed by the numerous Sorbian associations. The Sorbian cultural tourism association (Verband Sorbischer Kulturtourismus e.v.) also works to increase tourism to Sorbian institutions and museums. Frisian culture is mainly promoted by the Nordfriisk Instituut (North Frisian Institute) which focuses on history, language and culture and receives most of its funding from Schleswig-Holstein and local authorities, e.g. the Andersen House, a Frisian cultural centre, has been renovated with substantial *Land* funds.

The Sinti Alliance of Germany aims to preserve a social and cultural system for example through history workshops. The Central Council of German Sinti and Roma and the Documentation and Cultural Centre of German Sinti and Roma are also important in preserving and promoting this minority's culture. The Free Hanseatic City of Bremen has funded projects to promote cultural identity, the Free Hanseatic City of Hamburg supports cultural initiatives for Roma and Sinti, and Lower Saxony has provided funding for Sinti music festivals.

5.3.6.2 Media

Freedom of expression is guaranteed by Article 5(1) of the Basic Law, which also includes the freedom of the media. The Advisory Committee to the FCNM has commented that access to the media, especially public service media is still limited.[74] Furthermore the Central Council of German Sinti and Roma have repeatedly complained about stigmatising and discriminative media coverage.[75] However, the freedom of expression and freedom of the press allows state intervention only under very strict and limited circumstances.

5.3.6.2.1 MEDIA SUPERVISORY BOARDS

Media supervisory boards have been widely discussed in connection with minorities. The first experience in Germany of a minority sitting on a supervisory body for private media was in Rhineland-Palatinate where a representative of the regional organisation of the German Sinti and Roma sat on the board. This positive measure has improved coverage on Roma in media productions.[76] Nevertheless, the German Federal Constitutional Court found that a minority national cannot claim a *right* to be on a supervisory body, since they are for the purpose of being trustees of public interest, and not to represent the interest of a minority.[77]

Other minority members have been elected onto supervisory boards, for example there is a Dane on the board of the public channel Zweites Deutsches Fernsehen (ZDF). The Friesian minority is not represented in the supervisory public-law bodies responsible for its settlement area. The Sorbian minority, however, is represented in a regional public-law broadcasting council.

5.3.6.3 Minority newspapers, radio and television

The national minorities have the right to create and use printed media, as much as anyone else in Germany. The daily Danish *Flensborg Avis* newspaper was founded in 1869, and is published in both German and in Danish, and includes weekly and monthly inserts of other printed material. The Sorbian minority has a total of seven printed publications, including one daily – the *Serbske Nowiny* – two weekly, three monthly and one quarterly publication. Four daily newspapers in the Frisian region include a page in Frisian and Low German about once a month and Frisian articles are published more irregularly in four other publications. Three publications entirely in Frisian come out a few times a year. Publication of printed media runs contrary to the belief of German Sinti, who believe the language must be used within family clans only. The Sinti Central Council regularly releases comments and statements in German to the press, and part of their state funding is allocated especially for press activities.

Public access broadcast stations, so-called open channels, have been created in all the *Länder* giving citizens the chance to air their own television and radio programmes. Eight training workshops have been held since 2003, to teach the Danish and Frisian minorities how to use recording and editing equipment.[78] There are three-minute weekly broadcasts in Frisian on NDR1 Welle Nord and there is a Danish-language news programme every weekday on Radio Schleswig-Holstein. Radio Sachsen currently airs 21.5 hours of programming in Upper Sorbian each week, and both Sorbian languages appear on regional TV for around 30 hours each week. There is one Sinti radio programme broadcast in Germany called *Latscho Dibes* (Good Afternoon), running one hour every three weeks.

5.3.7 Religion

Article 4(1) and (2) of the Basic Law provides for the freedom of faith and conscience, the freedom to profess a religious or philosophical creed, and the undisturbed practice of that religion. Furthermore, Article 3(3) sets out that no one shall be disfavoured because of faith or religious opinions. There is no state church in Germany, which means that all churches are autonomous organisations, independent of the state. No data of breakdown of religious affiliation by ethnicity are collected, but the national minorities have extensive church networks. The Evangelical Lutheran Danish Church in South Schleswig organises and supports Danish minority's church activities, with church services in about 70 parishes.[79] The Sorbian minority are either Catholic or one of the Protestant denominations. In Brandenburg, an increasing number of church services and Bible classes are held in the Sorbian language promoted by the Association for Sorbian-Language Church Service. Frisians are also both Protestant and Catholic, and there are occasional Frisian language church services. A Frisian language hymnbook has been published by the *Nordfriisk Instituut*. Sinti and Roma Germans are mainly Catholic, and they attend church services in the German language.

5.3.8 Participation in public affairs

Since the national minorities all hold German citizenship, full participation in public affairs is constitutionally guaranteed. Under Article 21 of the Basic Law there is a right to establish political parties freely, and political parties of national minorities are exempt from the 5 per cent threshold established by the Federal Electoral Act for Elections to the Bundestag. The Danish minority is represented by the Südschleswigscher Wählerverband, which won two seats in the *Land* Parliament in 2005.

The *Land* Brandenburg Parliament set up a Council for Sorbian Affairs (Rat für sorbische Angelegenheiten) dealing with all matters affecting Sorbian interests. This Council has the rights and the function of a parliamentary committee and thus is involved in legislative proposals concerning the Sorbs. The Freie Sorbische Wählervereinigung (FSWV) whose Sorbian name is Swobodne serbske wolerske zjednoćenstwo (Free Sorbian Voters' Association) nominated candidates for the new Bautzen district Parliament and won one seat. In 2008 Mr Stanislaw Tillich, a member of the Sorbian ethnic group, was elected Minister-President of the Free State of Saxony Parliament. He is the first Sorbian head of government in more than a thousand years of Sorbian-German coexistence in Saxony.

Schleswig-Holstein Frisians who are members of the Frisian association Friisk Foriining are politically represented by the South Schleswig Voters' Association SSW (Söödslaswiksche Wäälerferbånd), whose members are represented in local and district councils. The political association Die Friesen, which presents itself as a party for the Frisian minority, for the first time participated in the Lower Saxony *Land* elections on 27 January 2008. The *Land* election committee recognised it as a political party and authorised its participation in the elections.[80]

There are currently no Sinti or Roma representatives in either the federal or any *Land* Parliament, but some have been elected to municipal councils. Two federal associations of German Sinti and Roma and of German Sinti have participated in the implementation conferences on the FCNM at federal level but have not succeeded in finding a joint position, and an advisory committee, which exists for other national minorities, has not been requested for the German Sinti and Roma for this reason. However, Roma and Sinti may participate in Lower Saxony via its *Land* associations and the Counselling Bureau for Sinti and Roma and local advisory boards established in some cities.[81]

Eligibility for employment in public service is open to all national minorities, who are German nationals according to Article 33(2) of the Basic Law. This has been implemented by a variety of laws at both federal and *Länder* level.[82] A law on the promotion of Frisian in the public sector in the Land of Schleswig-Holstein was passed in 2004 and has been praised by the CoE.[83] In response to criticism concerning the lack of German Sinti and Roma participation in public affairs,[84] Germany's third report under the FCNM states that this is not only due to educational deficits but also because the minority group is opposed to putting their culture or language in the public spotlight.[85]

5.3.9 The situation of the Roma

The economic and social development of the Roma and Sinti minority lag behind all other national minorities. The UN Human Rights Committee also pointed out in its Concluding Observations to the ICCPR in 2004 that the Roma's suffering prejudice and discrimination in Germany gives reason for concern, particularly with regard to access to housing and employment.[86] The CoE also reiterated concerns, despite acknowledging that considerable efforts have been made.[87]

The Roma and Sinti were increasingly oppressed and persecuted from the end of the fifteenth century onwards. Despite improvements and gradual integration in the nineteenth century, and particularly later after the First World War, the population suffered great losses under the rule of the Nazi regime, which committed acts of genocide against the Roma and Sinti, including compulsory sterilisation, and brutal killing of up to 1.5 million people.[88] After 1945, great efforts have been made to improve the situation, including national state funding of counselling bureaus specifically for Roma and Sinti organisations,[89] and a statement from the German Bundestag confirming the need to improve the living conditions of the German Sinti and Roma and their integration into society.[90] In response to the second opinion of the FCNM's Advisory Committee[91] to address the continuing discrimination against Roma and Sinti by a national long-term strategy, Germany has claimed that measures can only be successful to the extent of participation of the individuals concerned and, that a national inclusion plan in a federal state was not feasible.[92] The labour market cannot be tailored for one individual minority, and they must also make commitments to the requirements of that market.[93] Furthermore, the promotion of only one particular group, the third report argues, could create a basis for social prejudice and is immensely difficult to draw up considering the minorities' dispersal in all of the *Länder*. Additionally there is unreliable information, partly due to the inherent freedom of declaring oneself a member of a national minority, as under Article 3 of the FCNM, but also due to Germany's failure to collect appropriate data. From consultations and working together with the German Sinti and Roma organisations, the report states, it is also clear that they do not want to be treated differently to the majority of the population albeit for the documentation of their history, in order to gain acceptance of the majority and to prevent further discrimination.[94]

Recommendations by the CoE's Council of Ministers[95] on the implementation of the FCNM include, *inter alia*, the creation and adoption of a strategy to improve substantially the situation of all Roma and Sinti in all areas, but especially for women and children. Moreover, consulting mechanisms should be improved, taking into consideration the diversity within the group of Sinti and Roma, more widespread participation in consultations is required. Efforts are being made with the Lower Saxony Counselling Bureau for Sinti and Roma which offers personal support and advice with the objective of social, cultural and economic integration, as well as public-relations work to raise awareness of relevant cultural and social concerns and counteract social exclusion. Other examples have been mentioned in light of education (see section 5.3.3, above). Nevertheless, there is still a problem of overrepresentation of Sinti and Roma in special schools, as well as a low level of participation of the minority in secondary and university education. A further problem is that Roma refugees, mostly from Eastern European countries do not have the same legal status as German Roma and Sinti and therefore do not fall under the protection of the FCNM.

As a result of negative reporting in the press of crimes committed by the Sinti and Roma a binding ordinance on the protection of minorities against the use of discriminating designations by police authorities[96] was passed. The membership of a minority may only be indicated in a police report if it is required to understand the case or to establish factual relationships. A system of registration of police checks to identify patterns of direct and indirect discrimination has been rejected, primarily since it would raise data protection issues.

The German government is making efforts to improve the situation of the Sinti and Roma minority, however, the results still remain dissatisfactory. This is due to reasons, including the freedom of press (no state intervention); the federal system (leaving decisions up to the *Länder*); the disparity within the minority itself and the German unwillingness to collect socio-economic data on the basis of ethnic or national criteria.

5.3.10 Conclusion

Germany has made thorough efforts to accommodate its national minorities and implement the FCNM. Unresolved issues remain the fact that there is no collection of socio-economic or other data on the basis of ethnicity or national minority group, and the fact that Sinti and Roma are still a very disadvantaged group while other minorities enjoy not only de jure but also de facto equality with the majority population, see in particular the recent election of a Sorb as Minister-President of Saxony. Germany's definition of a national minority is very restrictive, including only four groups and leaving out immigrants and in particular

'Germans with an immigrant background'. This group makes up 18.6 per cent of the overall population, in contrast to the national minorities which are overall a very small number.[97] However, the Advisory Committee to the FCNM has not been informed of specific demands from other groups, particularly those of immigrant origin, to benefit from the protection afforded by the FCNM.[98] Furthermore the Advisory Committee to the FCNM has stressed that 'the absence of reliable data on the situation of minorities obstructs the prevention of racial discrimination and the development of suitable policies to further the equal opportunities of persons belonging to minorities.'[99] It points out that socio-economic data can be collected with adequate data protection. Nevertheless, this is something that is contrary to the German beliefs of the post-Second World War era, and would thus be extremely difficult to implement. The situation of the Sinti and Roma minority remains dire in many aspects. In opinion polls conducted in Germany since the early 1960 Sinti and Roma are constantly the most unpopular group, for example in 2002 58 per cent of all Germans disliked the idea of having a Sinti or Roma family as neighbours.[100] Deep-rooted prejudices within the German population still hamper the progress of ending discrimination of this group.

5.4 Lithuania

5.4.1 Background

Lithuania is located between Latvia and Russia bordering the Baltic Sea. It has 3.4 million inhabitants and its ethnic groups comprise 83.4 per cent Lithuanian, 6.3 per cent Russian, 6.7 per cent Polish, 1.2 per cent Belarusian and 2,1 per cent other groups. Those other groups include about 257 Karaites (or 0.01 per cent of the total population), 0.1 per cent Tartars, 0.4 per cent Germans, 1.2 per cent Ukrainians and there is an estimated Roma population of 3,000 in Lithuania.[101]

During the First World War Lithuania was occupied by the Germans (1915–18). Lithuania regained independence after the defeat of Germany in the First World War when both Germany and Russia were ruined by revolutions and coups d'état. On 16 February 1918 the Council of Lithuania proclaimed the Republic of Lithuania. In 1940 the Soviet Union occupied and annexed Lithuania declaring it to be the Lithuanian Soviet Socialist Republic. During the Second World War, Lithuania was again occupied by Germany. In 1944 it was occupied by the Soviet Union for a second time and mass deportations of the Lithuanian population, which started back in 1940, were resumed. Approximately 250,000 Lithuanian inhabitants were deported to Siberia and circumpolar regions. On 11 March 1990 Lithuania became an independent state again.

5.4.2 Constitutional and statutory provisions

Article 29 of the Constitution of the Republic of Lithuania (1992) provides a general non-discrimination clause: 'All persons are equal before law, the court and other public institutions or officials. Human rights may not be restricted or accorded any privileges on the basis of a person's race, nationality, language, origin, social status, religion, convictions or beliefs.'[102] In addition, Article 37 of the Constitution stipulates: 'Citizens belonging to national communities shall have the right to foster their language, culture and customs.' Article 45 emphasises that: 'The national communities of citizens shall be independent in managing affairs related to their culture, education, charity and mutual assistance. The State shall provide support to national communities.'

Lithuanian legislation does not contain any definition of the concept of a national minority or a group of persons recognised to be a national minority, the term used in the Constitution is 'national community'. The above-mentioned provisions can be seen as rights against assimilation and to state support for fostering minority culture.

Article 1 of the Law on Ethnic Minorities (1989)[103] declares in Article 1: 'The Republic of Lithuania, in accordance with the principles of equality between nations and humanism, shall guarantee free development of all the national minorities residing on its territory and respect every nationality and language.' In addition to the general non-discrimination and equality provisions, the Law on Ethnic Minorities implements Articles 37 and 45 of the Constitution and gives, *inter alia*, members of minority groups the right to receive financial support from the state for developing their own culture and educational institutions (Article 2 (2), 1), the right to media and information in their mother tongue (Article 2(2), 3), the right to political representation on the basis of elections (Article 2(2), 7) and the right of free access to public service posts (Article 2(2), 7).

One of the most important factors for the preservation of the political stability and social cohesion in the country was the Law on Citizenship of 1989. On request, any non-Lithuanian, irrespective of the time or purpose for his or her arrival to reside in Lithuania, irrespective of the duration of his or her residence, was granted Lithuanian citizenship after independence and 90 per cent of all the inhabitants who were of different nationality received Lithuanian citizenship. However, in 1991 a more stringent citizenship law was introduced, which required 10 years of residence and permanent employment, as well as the passing of an exam testing knowledge of the Lithuanian language and provisions of the Constitution of Lithuania.[104]

5.4.3 Institutions for the protection of minorities

In 1992 the Parliament (Seimas) of the Republic of Lithuania set up a standing Committee for Human Rights to coordinate the drafting and implementation of legislation necessary for the public policy on national minorities. With the adoption of the Law on Ethnic Minorities a special Department for National Minorities was founded within the government. Its mandate includes the implementation of national and international obligations with regard to national minorities. The new body assumed some of the functions of an ombudsman by becoming responsible for monitoring the implementation of minority rights in

Lithuania but also prepared a new draft of the Law on Ethnic Minorities. Yet another body, the Council of National Communities was established within the Minorities Department, in 1995. This Council is composed of representatives of 17 national communities, including the Roma, and is charged with coordinating the activities of national minority communities. However, some Roma leaders have maintained that the concerns and recommendations they have expressed at meetings of the Council have not been taken into consideration when government policies and programmes were drafted.[105]

In 1994 the Ombudsman Office was set up under the authority of the Seimas. The Ombudsman investigates abuses and violations of the personal rights of all citizens, including those belonging to national, ethnic, religious and linguistic minorities. In 2000 many citizens, in particular Roma, were not aware of the Ombudsman institution, there was no complaint by a Romani person registered with the Ombudsman.[106] However, there were 52 complaints of violations of equal rights between men and women.[107] In 2005 the office received 18 complaints regarding ethnic or racial discrimination, 11 of which concerned Roma.[108]

5.4.4 Education

Article 2 of the Law on Ethnic Minorities stipulates that:

> the Republic of Lithuania, taking into account the interests of national minorities, shall guarantee them the right under the law and the procedures there under: to obtain aid from the state to develop their culture and education; to have schooling in one's native language, with provisions for pre-school education, other classes, elementary and secondary school education, as well as provisions for groups, faculties and departments at institutions of higher learning to train teachers and other specialists needed by ethnic minorities.

Article 10 of the Law on Education[109] states that:

> in the localities where a national minority resides or where there are many of its members, they shall be provided with facilities for having public, municipal or non-state pre-school establishments, schools of general education and lessons in the mother tongue, if the said individuals so request and if such request corresponds with an actual need. Parents (guardians of the child) shall choose for the children a pre-school establishment or a school of general education with instruction in an appropriate language.

The same Article also provides that for small ethnic communities, classes or optional courses as well as Sunday schools may be set up and municipal schools of general education for the purpose of learning or acquiring a better knowledge of the mother tongue. In accordance with Article 26 of the Law on

Education, the curricula of educational establishments of national minorities may be supplemented by elements of ethnic culture.

On the basis of these provisions, a satisfactory practice developed in Lithuania with regard to minority education: there are 2,246 schools of general education in the Republic of Lithuania, out of those 74 use Polish, 68 use Russian and one school uses Belorussian as the language of instruction, as well as 72 mixed schools that offer classes with minority language as the language of instruction. In addition there is the Herman Zuderman School in Klaipėda that could be referred to as a German school. Out of 586,294 pupils of the country, 41,162 study at schools with Russian as the language of instruction, 22,303 with Polish, 214 with Belarussian, 202 with Hebrew and 364 with German as the language of instruction.

Some national minorities, whose languages are not taught in public schools, such as the Ukrainians, Latvians, Armenians, Karaites, Tartars and Greeks study their mother tongue in Sunday schools. Sunday schools as well as classes at the schools of general education provide possibilities to study the mother tongue for small national minorities and those living in a disperse way.

There are no schools or classes that teach in Romani language. So far, Roma have not applied for funding for education in Romani. Since only very few Roma finish secondary education, many never learn the Lithuanian language well.[110]

5.4.5 Language rights

Article 14 of the Constitution of the Republic of Lithuania (1992) declares the Lithuanian language to be the official language of the Lithuanian state. The status of the official language is given a comprehensive definition in the Law on the State Language (1995)[111] establishing the most important areas of public life where the official language must be used, regulating its protection, control and legal responsibility for non-compliance with the provisions of the law.

The 1991 Law on Ethnic Minorities provides in its Articles 4 and 5 that minority language may be used in addition to Lithuanian in 'offices and organisations located in areas serving substantial numbers of a minority with a different language', however, it is not defined what constitutes a 'substantial number'. An attempt by the Polish minority to establish Polish as a second official language in areas where many Poles live, failed in Parliament. As regards the Roma minority, in practice, Roma are not able to use Romani language in communication with public authorities and only those Roma who speak Russian can benefit from an official interpreter, as there are Russian but no official Romani interpreters.

5.4.6 Culture and media

The Law on Ethnic Minorities declares that the Republic of Lithuania recognises the national identity and cultural continuity for all its citizens irrespective of their nationality and encourages national awareness and its expression. In Article 2, this law indicates that the state, having regard to the interests of national minorities, guarantees in the procedure laid down in the law 'the right to receive state support for the development of ethnic culture and education, the right to establish and join ethnic cultural organisations, the right to maintain cultural relations with representatives of their nationality residing outside the Republic'.[112]

National minorities are also free to set up cultural and educational institutions at their own expense. According to Article 6 Law on Ethnic Minorities 'Historical and cultural monuments significant for the national minorities and Lithuania shall constitute part of the culture of the Republic and shall be subject to the protection of the state.' Important cultural establishments of minorities are financially supported by the state, e.g. the House of National Communities which hosts ten minority organisations, the Russian theatre, the Jewish Museum, the Thomas Mann House and the Pushkin Museum for Literature.

Lithuania's 1st and 2nd programmes of the National Radio as well as the National Television include broadcastings in the languages of the national minorities of Lithuania. Since 1996 there have been four Russian and four Polish channels as well as two Belorussian channels.

According to Article 2 of the Law on Ethnic Minorities the right to have newspapers and publications and information in one's native language is guaranteed. There are 13 periodicals published in Russian, seven in Polish, five in Belorussian and four in German. The Jewish community publishes a monthly, *Lietuvos Jeruzalė*, in Yiddish, Lithuanian, English and Russian. The Tartar community publishes a monthly, *Lietuvos totoriai*, in Lithuanian. The Greek community publishes a paper, *Patrida*, in Russian, but the publication comes out irregularly. The Latvian community has a magazine, *Dabas speks* (Power of Nature), but the publication is irregular. There are no Romani publications, television or radio programmes in Lithuania.

5.4.7 Religion

The Law on Ethnic Minorities guarantees in Article 2 persons belonging to national minorities 'the right to profess any or no religion and to perform religious or folk observances in one's native language'. Lithuania does not have an official religion, which is enshrined in Article 43 of the Constitution. The Article stipulates that the state recognises the traditional churches and religious organisations of Lithuania in as much as they have support of the public and their teachings or rites do not contradict the law or morality. Article 5 of the Law on Religious Communities and Partnerships lists the following nine traditional religious communities and partnerships constituting part of Lithuania's historical, spiritual and social heritage: Roman Catholic, Greek Catholic, Evangelical Lutheran, Evangelical Reformed, Russian Orthodox, Old Believers, Judaism, Sunnite Muslims and Karaites. The recognition by the state means that the state supports the spiritual, cultural and social heritage of religious communities, also financially.

5.4.8 Participation in public affairs

The Republic of Lithuania guarantees equal political rights and freedoms to all its citizens regardless of their nationality. Article 33 of the Constitution provides that 'Citizens shall have the right to participate in the government of their state both directly and through their freely elected representatives, and shall have the equal opportunity to serve in a state office of the Republic of Lithuania.' In Lithuania, there are three political parties representing national minorities: the Election Action of the Lithuanian Poles (established in 1994), the Union of Lithuanian Russians (established in 1995) and the Alliance of Lithuanian National Minorities, which was established in 1996 and received three seats in the election of 1996 but no mandate in any further elections.

As citizens of the Republic of Lithuania, persons belonging to national minorities have the right to participate in the elections to the Seimas and to local authorities. National minority parties as well as all other parties have to comply with the 5 per cent (7 per cent for coalitions) election threshold according to Article 2 of the Law on the Elections to the Seimas, i.e. there are no special provisions for minorities, as for example in Germany.[113]

The Election Action of Lithuanian Poles is a political organisation of the Polish national minority. In the elections of 2000 to the Seimas, its two representatives were elected at the single-member constituencies. They also participated in the governing coalition. In the 2008 elections the Election Action of Lithuanian Poles gained three seats.

The Union of Russians of Lithuania is a political organisation of Russians. It took part in the elections to the Seimas in 2000 in the joint coalition of Social Democrats led by Algirdas Brazauskas and, as the result, received three mandates of the Seimas in the multi-member constituencies. In the 2000 elections to the municipal councils the Union of Russians of Lithuania received seven mandates in the Klaipėda City Council but no seats in the Seimas. In the Council of National Minorities, an advisory body to the government, one position is reserved for a Roma representative. However, Roma have been dissatisfied as they feel that their interests are not adequately represented.[114]

5.4.9 The situation of the Roma

Roma came to Lithuania in the fifteenth century via Poland and Belarus. For a long time they stuck to the nomadic lifestyle, but the territory of their travelling was not very large and they usually travelled only in summer. In 1956 the Supreme Soviet of the former Soviet Union issued an order prohibiting them from leading a nomadic lifestyle, demanding that they should get jobs and be registered. In the period from 1959 to 2000 the number of Roma in Lithuania fluctuated between 2,000 and 3,000. Their largest communities are concentrated in the major cities, such as Vilnius, Kaunas, Panevėžys and some other places.[115]

So far, the government has failed to achieve full integration of the Roma people into Lithuania's society. In response to this situation and as a reaction to international influences, in July 2000, the government of the Republic of Lithuania approved a Programme for the Integration of the Roma in Lithuanian Society for 2000–2004. The Minorities Department had the task of coordinating the implementation. The European Commission criticised this programme for not having consulted sufficiently with Roma representatives when developing the programme, including the Roma representative in the Council.[116] As a result, the programme does not entirely reflect the interests and concerns of the Roma community in Lithuania and has had no effect for the situation of the Roma.

Several Roma representatives expressed dissatisfaction about the degree to which they have been involved in the government's planning and implementing of projects that benefit the Roma community. In addition, the programme does not seem to acknowledge discrimination against Roma, which excludes them from employment, housing and other social services. There are no official data or monitoring systems on discrimination against Roma.[117]

The government also failed to address the educational problems of Roma children, which leads to illiteracy and low levels of education. Statistics provide a grim picture: in the academic year 1996/1997 there were 276 Roma pupils in Lithuanian public schools, 125 of whom dropped out during the school year. Post-primary level, no Romani pupil is known to have graduated from tertiary education and approximately five Roma are estimated to have completed secondary-level education.[118] Due to negative stereotypes against Roma and economic hardship, racism and discrimination of Roma persist in Lithuanian society.

5.4.10 Conclusion

Both Lithuania and Estonia declared restoration of their statehood instead of establishing it anew and, as a consequence only those persons who were citizens of these Baltic states before Soviet annexation in 1940, and their direct descendants, were recognised as 'initial' citizens. In Estonia this 'restored citizenship concept' excluded mainly the Russian minority group from political participation. Unlike Estonia, Lithuania granted the right to obtain citizenship by registration also to those persons who entered Lithuania between 1940 and 1990, and their descendants and thereby initiated a very liberal minority policy (until the coming into force of the new law in 1992), which was necessary for Lithuania's political stability after independence. The 'zero option' in the 1989 Law on Citizenship has enabled the majority of the population to obtain Lithuanian citizenship, and led to the construction of a more stable society.

Special administrative bodies (such as Lithuania's Department for National Minorities, the Council of National Communities and the Ombudsman Office and Estonia's Legal Chancellor and Ombudsman), which deal with minority cultural affairs, have been established in both Baltic states. However, the status of these bodies, their real authority, and the real amount of resources allocated at their disposal remains a crucial matter.

The right to exercise a minority language still represents an area that might need improvement, as minorities faced difficulties in establishing minority language as a second official language in areas predominantly inhabited by them. Although Lithuania's minority regime supports language rights for minorities, it is still affected by its historical legacy of 'ethnic insecurity' as the Lithuanian language had to defend itself against the influences of the Russian and Polish language in the past.[119] The Advisory Committee noted in its opinion on Lithuania of 2003:[120]

> further efforts are needed to remedy the legal uncertainty as regards the use of minority languages in relations between persons belonging to national minorities and the administrative authorities, and as regards local names, street names and other topographical information. In the field of education, it is essential to ensure that the changes in legislation currently in progress provide a clear and effective legal framework with respect to the instruction of and instruction in minority languages […] Despite recent initiatives by the authorities, certain Roma continue to be confronted with serious problems, including those of a socio-economic nature. Further efforts are essential to eliminate such difficulties.

5.5 Slovakia

5.5.1 Background

Slovakia is situated in Central Europe south of Poland and the Czech Republic. It has 5,422,366 inhabitants. According to a census conducted in May 2001 the Slovaks represent 85.7 per cent of the population, 9.7 per cent are Hungarian, 1.7 per cent Roma, 0.8 per cent Czech, 0.45 per cent Ruthenian and 0.2 per cent are of Ukrainian origin. Estimates however put the Roma minority, at up to 10 per cent of the overall population.[121]

In 1918 the Slovaks joined the closely related Czechs to form Czechoslovakia. Following the chaos of the Second World War, Czechoslovakia became a communist nation within Soviet-ruled Eastern Europe. Slovaks and the Czechs agreed to separate peacefully on 1 January 1993. Historic, political and geographic factors have caused Slovakia to experience more difficulty in developing a modern market economy than some of its Central European neighbours, in particular problems with the Roma community are more severe than in other CEECs and are therefore predominantly treated in this section. The expulsion of ethnic Hungarians after the Second World War, which was formally legalised with the infamous Beneš decrees became an issue for Slovakia (and the Czech Republic's) accession to the EU in 2002 when Hungary claimed the decrees to be incompatible with European values and basic legal principles. However, the EP eventually adopted a resolution stating that the decrees 'did not constitute an insurmountable obstacle to accession' but voiced its disapproval with certain provisions of the decrees.

5.5.2 Constitutional and statutory provisions

The Slovak Constitution of 1992 provides in its Article 34:[122]

> (1) The comprehensive development of citizens representing national minorities or ethnic groups in the Slovak Republic is guaranteed, particularly the right to develop their own culture, together with other members of the minority or ethnic group, disseminate and receive information in their mother tongues, associate in minority associations, and the right to create and maintain educational and cultural institutions. Details shall be laid down by law.
>
> (2) In addition to the right to master the state language, citizens belonging to national minorities or ethnic groups are also guaranteed, under conditions defined by law, the following:
> a) the right to education in their own language,
> b) the right to use their language in official contact,
> c) the right to participate in addressing matters concerning national minorities and ethnic groups.

These constitutional provisions for the protection of minorities are to be defined by law; what legislation has been undertaken so far on the basis of this provision – such as the Law on the Use of Minority Languages 1999 –[123] will be discussed below in the relevant sections.

There is no legal definition of the term national minority in the Slovak legislation at present. Equally, there is no formal system for the official recognition of national minorities. The belonging to a minority group is always deliberate; any kind of pressure leading to denationalisation is prohibited by Article 12(3) of the Constitution: 'Everyone has the right to freely decide his nationality. Any influence on this decision and any form of coercion aimed at assimilation are prohibited.'

The Slovak Constitution contains a general anti-discrimination provision in Article 12(2), which provides that 'Basic rights and liberties on the territory of the Slovak Republic are guaranteed to everyone regardless of sex, race, colour of skin, language, creed and religion, political or other beliefs, national or social origin, affiliation to a nation or ethnic group, property, descent, or another status. No one must be harmed, preferred, or discriminated against on these grounds.'

Specific anti-discrimination legislation transposing the EU's Council Directive 2000/43/EC was adopted in June 2004 (one month after EU accession).[124] However, in October 2005 (four months after the CoE's Council of Ministers had issued its recommendations on Slovakia's second State Report) Slovakia's Constitutional Court ruled the new anti-discrimination legislation unconstitutional because it 'violates full equality before the law'. The court ruling found Slovakia's anti-discrimination law and in particular its Article 5, which allows positive action, as unconstitutional.[125] Hence, in the course of 2007 and 2008 it underwent several amendments. Its second amendment, i.e. Act No. 85/2008, responded to the situation of the lack of legislative provisions on the so-called temporary positive measures by the provisions of paragraph 2 of the new §8a introducing temporary positive measures that may be adopted if: (a) there is demonstrable inequality; (b) the objective of such measures is to reduce or eliminate that inequality; and (c) they are adequate and necessary to attain the pursued objective. At the same time, the amendment defines the range of entities empowered to adopt such measures, i. e. state administration authorities, as well as the object of temporary positive measures, i. e. the elimination of various forms of social and economic disadvantages and disadvantages based on age or disability, with the aim of ensuring equal opportunities in practice.

5.5.3 Institutions for the protection of minorities

In 2001 the European Commission recommended that the Slovak government establishes an official body to 'promote non-discrimination, provide assistance to individual victims of discrimination, conduct surveys on discrimination and publish reports and recommendations on discrimination'. In December 2001, the Parliament eventually adopted the Act on the Ombudsman or 'public defender of rights'[126] and subsequently, in March 2002, elected the first office holder, an opposition candidate. According to the Act, the Ombudsman is to help protect fundamental rights and freedoms in cases where public administration bodies have violated the legal system or the rule of law. During its first three years of existence, the Ombudsman received 6,408 motions covering a range of sectors of relevance to persons belonging to minorities. Since 1 April 2006, the public defender of rights has the right to initiate proceedings before the Constitutional Court of the Slovak Republic if he finds that further application of legal provisions can endanger fundamental rights or freedoms or human rights or fundamental freedoms arising from an international treaty ratified by the Slovak Republic and promulgated as established by law.

It is also worth underlining the establishment, in 2003, of the Department of Equal Opportunities and Anti-discrimination within the Social Inclusion Division of the Ministry of Labour, Social Affairs and Family. This department has taken an active part in the implementation of the governmental strategies on the Roma and has, in this context, paid particular attention to Roma women.

In addition, the Slovak government established a number of official bodies to address issues related to minority protection in general, for example in 1998 it created the post of Deputy Prime Minister for Human Rights, Minorities and Regional Development. The Office of the Plenipotentiary of the Government of the Slovak Republic for Addressing the Issues of Roma was established following the 1998 elections, and mandated to coordinate fulfilment of the Strategy for Roma,[127] to mobilise Roma associations, initiatives and non-governmental organisations in support of the Strategy, and to prepare implementation reports. The Plenipotentiary was intended to act as a bridge between Roma communities and the government by raising Roma concerns with appropriate ministries and regional authorities, and identifying small-scale projects for government funding.

Since 2007 the role of the advisory and coordinating body of the government of the Slovak Republic for national minority policy is performed by the Government Council for National Minorities and Ethnic Groups. The Council is composed of the representatives of 12 officially recognised national minorities (Hungarian, Roma, Ruthenian, Ukrainian, Croatian, Czech, Moravian, Polish, Bulgarian, Russian and Jewish) appointed on a parity principle, each minority having one representative. The representatives of individual minorities are nominated by national minority associations, unions and societies. The Council is chaired by the Deputy Prime Minister – currently Dušan Čaplovič. The post of its vice-chairman is held by the Minister of Culture. Also invited to Council meetings are officials from central state administration authorities and independent experts (including one expert from Hungary and one expert from the Czech Republic). The Council deals with problem areas relating to persons belonging to national minorities – such as minority broadcasting of the Slovak Radio and Slovak Television, use of the grant scheme of the Ministry of Culture of the Slovak Republic to support the culture of national minorities in 2008, government activities in the area of combating extremism in 2007 and 2008, draft concepts and acts, such as the draft Medium-Term Concept of the Development of the Roma National Minority in the Slovak Republic, Concepts of Education and Instruction of Roma Children and Pupils including the Development of Secondary and Higher Education, Concepts of Education and Instruction of National Minorities, or the elaboration of the second periodic report on the implementation of the European Charter of Regional or Minority Languages in the Slovak Republic.[128]

5.5.4 Education

The Slovak Constitution provides in Article 42(1) 'everyone has the right to education'. In practice, Roma children are increasingly excluded from the Slovak school system. Those who attend school are cordoned off into separate classes and, increasingly, separate schools, including schools intended for mentally retarded children. Under these conditions, Roma children cannot be said to enjoy equal access to education or to skilled employment. In addition, there is a high drop-out rate, already in primary school, which according to some commentators is due to conditions of poverty and lack of parental education but also a reaction to discriminatory attitudes among the school authorities.[129] However, in theory, the School Act[130] provides in §3(d) the prohibition of all forms of discrimination and, in particular, of segregation. At the same time, §145(3) of the School Act stipulates: 'An applicant, a child, a pupil or a student who considers himself/herself wronged in his/her rights or lawfully protected interests by failure to apply the principle of equal treatment may pursue his/her claim by judicial process according to the specific legislation.'[131]

Teacher training is carried out, in addition to universities, via the State Pedagogical Institute and methodical centres, at which offices for the mother tongues of national minorities are established. In order to decrease the high number of unqualified teachers in primary schools, the Roma Culture Department of the Nitra Pedagogical University (now called the University of Constantine Philosopher) established a separate department in Spisska Nova Ves in the 1995/96 academic year. Under the coordination of the Romani Culture Department, this department secures, *inter alia*, the study of subjects such as 'Social and Educational Work' focused on Romani culture and training courses for young Romani women and unemployed Roma.

In October 2003, Parliament ratified an Act establishing the Selye János University in Komárno as a public institution with financial support from the state budget. Since September 2004, the three faculties of this higher education institution offer most of their courses in the Hungarian language. The Selye János University should, *inter alia*, greatly improve the training of teachers of primary and secondary schools providing instruction in the Hungarian language.

The Constitution guarantees minorities in Article 34(2)(b) the right to be educated in one's own language. The School Act, however, limits the exercise of this right to specific minorities only; Romani is not listed among the languages that can be used in primary and secondary school education: according to section 3(1) of the School Act 'Training and education are carried out in the state language. Citizens of Bohemian, Hungarian, German, Polish and Ukrainian (Ruthenian) nationality are ensured the right to education in their own language to an extent proportional to the interests of their national development.'

In its 2002 Programme on Education, the government committed itself to focusing on the creation of further opportunities for the Ruthenian and Roma minorities to receive education in their mother tongues. Due to joint efforts by the Plenipotentiary for the Roma communities and the Ministry of Education, the Roma language has been introduced in four pilot projects focusing on secondary education, and a considerable number of Roma language teachers graduated in spring 2005. To ensure the teaching of the Roma mother tongue in primary and secondary schools, the Ministry of Education approved 'Temporary positive measures with the aim of training the necessary number of teachers for teaching in the Roma language.'[132] The Roma language is now used as an auxiliary language of instruction in kindergartens, in preparatory grades of primary and special schools with a high concentration of Roma pupils, in the Secondary School of Fine Arts in Košice, in the private Gymnasium of Košice and in the Department of the Roma Culture at the University of Constantine the Philosopher in Nitra. Since 2002, at least three textbooks in the Roma language have been approved and subsequently published by the authorities. The national project on 'Improving the qualification potential of the Roma community by introducing a new course on Roma studies in the system of secondary schools' was carried out under the professional guidance of the National Institute for Education and financed by the European Social Fund.

5.5.5 Language rights

The constitutional right to use minority languages in contacts with public administration was elaborated in the 1999 Law on the Use of Minority Languages. The law provides in Article 1: 'Each citizen of the Slovak Republic who belongs to a national minority has the right to use, apart from the state language, the language of his national minority. The purpose of this law is to establish the rules for use of minority languages also in official state contacts.' Romani is a recognised minority language under the terms of the Language Law, although there was considerable opposition to its inclusion during the drafting process, with the justification that the Roma language has not been codified, despite the assertions of Roma leaders to the contrary.

The Law specifies in section 2(i) that 'the right to use minority languages may be employed in municipalities where a minority group constitutes at least 20 per cent of the population'; this requirement has left some municipalities with a combined minority population of over 100,000 outside the sphere of protection. The 2001 census results, however, reveal changes as regards the number of municipalities concerned with a decrease of the municipalities having the required share of the Hungarian, Roma and Ukrainian minorities and a substantial increase of the municipalities having the required share of the Ruthenian minority.

The single greatest obstacle to the enjoyment of minority language rights for Roma is the limited number of Romani speakers employed within the public administration. The FCNM Advisory Committee considered it essential to address the reported problems concerning its implementation, such as the lack of language skills in the offices concerned, and also Slovakia has to ensure that, as *lex specialis*, the Law on Minority Languages consistently takes precedence over the State Language Law.[133] In March 2009, the government approved a draft amendment to the State Language Law of 1995[134]on the state language of the Slovak Republic, which widens the possibility of using languages other than the state language (including national minority languages) in certain areas. Furthermore, on 29 June 2008 the 'Declaration of the Roma of the Slovak Republic on the Standardisation of the Roma Language in the Slovak Republic' was signed in Bratislava by the representatives of the Roma national minority. The aim of the standardisation of the Roma language is to officially recognise the Roma language as being equal to the languages of other national minorities living in Slovakia.[135] This can be contrasted with the situation of the Roma and Sinti in Germany who have opposed any standardisation of their language.

5.5.6 Culture and media

The Ministry of Culture uses a system of grants, on the basis of which it provides funds for selected projects. For the assessment system for projects for the development of minority cultures an expert commission was set up, which consists of 19 representatives of national minorities with the following structure: five representatives of the Hungarian national minority, three representatives of the Roma minority, two representatives of the Bohemian minority, and one representative of each the Ruthenian, Ukrainian, German, Croatian, Bulgarian, Polish, Jewish, Moravian and the Russian minorities. The expert commission's role is to determine the amount of finance from the total resources approved by the National Council for the development of minority cultures and its division among 12 minority cultures for the publication of periodical and non-periodical press and the organisation of cultural activities.

Slovak national radio is under the legal obligation to contribute to the culture of the national minorities living in Slovakia,[136] and Slovak public television is obliged to ensure broadcasting of minority language programs that promote minority interests and culture.[137] Act No. 16/2004 Coll. of 4 December 2003 on Slovak television now explicitly provides in its Article 5(1) that the main activities of the Slovak television include the broadcasting of programmes in the languages of national minorities or ethnic groups living in the territory of the Slovak Republic. A similar provision has been introduced by Act No. 619/2003 of 4 December 2003 as regards the main activities of the Slovak radio.

Minorities publish numerous periodicals, and have their own programmes (and programmes about them) broadcast by Slovak public television. The Ministry of Culture has provided funding for a number of Romani journals, particularly since 1999. Slovak public television produces the Roma magazine *Romale* every week, but relatively little time is devoted to radio programmes in the Roma language, with a single 20-minute weekly programme of news and cultural information for Roma on Presov Public Radio.

The Ministry of Culture also supports activities of national minority museums that operate as organic parts of the Slovak National Museum and several national minority museums are administered by self-governing regions.[138] The Slovak Republic has four national minority theatres: two Hungarian theatres (Thália Szinház Theatre, Košice; Jókai Theatre, Komárno); one Ruthenian–Ukrainian theatre (Alexander Duchnovič Theatre, Prešov) and one Roma theatre (Romathan Theatre, Košice).

5.5.7 Religion

The freedom of religion is enshrined in Article 24 of the Constitution and no particular problems have been reported in this regard. Article 24(3) provides that 'Churches and religious communities administer their own affairs. In particular, they constitute their own bodies, inaugurate their clergymen, organise the teaching of religion, and establish religious orders and other church institutions independently of state bodies.' Some religious organizations, however, complain about not receiving public financial support as they are not registered. In order to be registered, the signatures of at least 20,000 permanent residents adhering to this religion are necessary. Under the Church Act[139] the Ministry of Culture functions as a registration authority, i. e. it is responsible for the registration of churches and religious societies. As of 1 May 2008, Slovakia had 18 registered churches and religious societies. The churches that were registered as of the most recent date are: the Church of Jesus Christ of Latter-day Saints in the Slovak Republic (18 October 2006) and the Bahá'í community in the Slovak Republic (19 April 2007).

5.5.8 Participation in public affairs

Freedom of association is guaranteed by the Law on Association in Political Parties and Political Movements,[140] which provides in section 1(1) 'Citizens have the right to associate in political parties and political movements'. These rights and freedoms are also relevant for the assembly and association of persons belonging to national minorities and are fully applied by them. In the 1992 parliamentary elections, two Roma parties participated independently – the Roma Civic Initiative and the Party of Work and Security – but neither reached the required threshold of 5 per cent of votes. In 1994, the situation was repeated when the only running Roma party – the Roma Civic Initiative – again received less than 1 per cent of the vote. In 1998 no Roma political party stood independently. In all elections, Roma individuals have run for office with non-ethnic political parties but none has won a seat. By contrast, a coalition of parties representing the Hungarian minority (Hungarian Coalition party) – which, like the Roma minority, numbers approximately 500,000 – was able to negotiate a place within the government coalition following the 1998 elections, and plays a significant role in national politics. In the 2002 elections the Hungarian Party received 20 seats (as opposed to 14 seats in 1998) and was again voted in with 20 seats at the 2006 elections. Hungarian politicians earned the confidence of the Slovak electorate having positively contributed to political issues beyond their concerns for ethnic Hungarians.

On the local level, the situation is somewhat more favourable. In 1998 six mayors and 86 council members were elected from Roma political parties. However, one of those elections, in the town of Petrova (north-eastern Slovakia), was subsequently annulled due to the protests of non-Roma residents. Immediately after Marian Billy (the candidate for the Roma Civic Initiative) was elected mayor of Petrova, the local council called a vote of non-confidence on the basis of a door-to-door petition. A re-election in September 1999 returned a non-Roma mayor to office. The 2002 municipal elections have led to the election of a few Roma mayors and a considerable number of municipal councillors. Although limited, this progress recorded in the political participation of persons belonging to the Roma minority deserves to be welcomed and may pave the way for future improvements in this sphere. Following the administrative reform process, the regional office in Košice has recently been in a position to establish a commission dealing specifically with Roma issues. In the elections to municipal self-governing bodies – mayors and municipal councillors – the Hungarian Coalition Party won 1,952 seats of mayors and members of municipal councils. The Hungarian Coalition Party gained additional deputy seats as part of various coalitions. In all, 215 candidates of the Hungarian Coalition Party were elected as mayors of municipalities. The Roma Initiative of Slovakia gained 36 seats in municipal councils and six seats of mayors of municipalities. The role of the advisory body to the government on Roma issues continues to be performed by the Government Plenipotentiary for Roma communities who fulfils the tasks aimed at addressing the issues of Roma communities and carries out systemic measures designed to improve their situation and integration into society through the Office of the Government Plenipotentiary for Roma Communities.[141]

5.5.9 The situation of the Roma

According to the report of the CoE Commissioner on Human Rights of May 2001, the Roma community numbers between 400,000 and 500,000 people;[142] it is the poorest community, the one with the highest rate of unemployment, and the least educated, in addition to having the highest birth and death rates; there have been long-standing feelings of mistrust and prejudices between the Roma community and both the authorities and society in general, which have made it impossible to pursue a policy of integration and participation. The under-representation of Roma students in the education system has persisted, hand in hand with overrepresentation in schools for retarded children. Many Roma in Slovakia do not have residence permits and experience difficulties obtaining them when they move, either voluntarily or following evictions. Those without residence permits do not enjoy equal access to a wide range of social benefits. For example, without a permit, it is difficult to register children for school, and to exercise voting rights.

The government adopted a two-stage strategy in 1999–2000[143] to improve the situation of the Roma community. However, as of yet, there is no institutional mechanism for ensuring the Strategy's coherent implementation and evaluation. The Advisory Committee commented in its Second Opinion on Slovakia that the involvement of representatives of the Roma communities both in the assessment made of the 1999 and 2000 Roma Strategy does not seem to have been sufficient, despite the adequate representation of Roma staff members in the office of the Plenipotentiary for the Roma Communities. While bearing in mind that most measures envisaged to improve the socio-economic situation of the Roma require mid- and long-term efforts, the Advisory Committee noted that the impact of the 1999 Roma Strategy has not yet been up to the level of expectations in key sectors, such as education, housing and employment. For example, numerous concurring reports suggest that there has been no tangible improvement concerning the living conditions in most of the Roma settlements, where sub-standard living conditions continue to prevail.[144] Nevertheless, the office of the Government Plenipotentiary for Roma affairs has been strengthened, enabling it to function more effectively than in previous years. A regional office was opened in October 2001 in Eastern Slovakia, where the vast majority of Roma live. The new Plenipotentiary has significantly improved communication with the Roma community, the public and media, *inter alia*, by establishing an informal advisory board with a large number of representatives from the Roma community and civil society.

5.5.10 Conclusion

Despite positive steps that have been taken, especially since 1998 when the liberal pro-Western/pro-European opposition party came to power, the majority of persons belonging to the Roma community continue to be exposed to social inequalities, and continue to experience widespread discrimination in education, employment, the criminal justice system and access to public services. The gap between theory and practice is still wide and 'despite a marked increase in the efforts of the government, there remain problems in the implementation of the FCNM as concerns Roma … socio-economic differences between some of the Roma and the majority population are aggravated by the unsatisfactory status of Roma in the educational system'.[145] In Slovakia, necessary laws for the protection and promotion of minorities exist, but discriminatory attitudes and feelings of hostility towards members of the Roma community are deep rooted and widespread throughout the country, manifested by racially motivated crimes and incidents, which hinder every attempt of effectively putting these laws into practice. Although Slovakia has ratified all international human rights instruments that prohibit discrimination (including CERD and Article 14 on individual complaints), it has to intensify its efforts to ensure to everyone within its jurisdiction effective protection against any act of racial discrimination. However, from the above it can also be concluded that members of the Hungarian minority, who have benefited significantly from Hungary's advocacy (in particular the Treaty of 1995 between Slovakia and Hungary),[146] are being provided with minority rights according to international standards, and their condition is steadily improving while the Roma, who do not have a kin state, still suffer from discrimination.

5.6 Slovenia

5.6.1 Background

Slovenia is situated between Austria and Croatia, by the eastern Alps bordering the Adriatic Sea and has 1,932,917 (July 2002 est.) inhabitants. During the 1991 census 24 ethnic categories registered in Slovenia, only three exceeded 1 per cent of the total population of circa 2 million inhabitants. Most groups attain barely a few hundred and only in six cases are there more than 2,000 members (Italians, Hungarians, Albanians, Macedonians, Montenegrins, Roma) and in three cases there are more than 20,000 persons of the same ethnic group (Croats, Serbs and Muslims); the percentages are: Slovene 83.1 per cent, Croat 1.8 per cent, Serb 2 per cent, Bosniacs 1.1 per cent, Muslims 0.5 per cent, Bosnians 0.4 per cent, Hungarian 0.3 per cent, Albanians 0.3 per cent, Macedonians 0.2 per cent, Roma 0.2 per cent, Italians 0.1 per cent, Other 1.1 per cent.[147]

The Slovene lands were part of the Holy Roman Empire and Austria until 1918 when the Slovenes joined the Serbs and Croats in forming a new nation, renamed Yugoslavia in 1929. After the Second World War, Slovenia became a republic of the renewed Yugoslavia, which, though communist, distanced itself from Moscow's rule. Dissatisfied with the exercise of power of the majority Serbs, the Slovenes succeeded in establishing their independence in 1991. The EU recognised Slovenia's independence in January 1992, followed a little later by the USA, China and Russia. Historical ties to Western Europe, a strong economy, and a stable democracy made Slovenia a leading candidate for membership in the EU during the 2004 accession round.

However, when Slovenia split from Yugoslavia in 1991 issues of citizenship, similar to those of Estonia, surfaced as non-Slovene Yugoslavs (internal immigrants of the former Yugoslav Republics) were recognised neither as national nor as ethnic minorities; neither were they given Slovene citizenship, and 18,305 people were unlawfully omitted from the Register of Permanent Residents of Slovenia.

5.6.2 Constitutional and statutory provisions

The 1991 Constitution of the Republic of Slovenia[148] stipulates in Article 61 that 'Each person shall be entitled to freely identify with his national grouping or ethnic community, to foster and give expression to his culture and to use his own language and script.' In addition, the Constitution of Slovenia provides for special territorially based collective rights as well as individual rights for the autochthonous Italian and Hungarian national minorities. It specifies in Article 64 of the 1991 Constitution:

> the autochthonous Italian and Hungarian ethnic communities and their national symbols and, in order to preserve their national identity, the rights to establish organisations, to foster economic, cultural, scientific and research activities, as well as activities associated with the mass media and publishing. These two ethnic communities shall have, consistent with statute, the right to education and schooling in their own languages, as well as the right to plan and develop their own curricula ... The Italian and Hungarian ethnic communities and their members shall enjoy the right to foster contacts with their wider Italian and Hungarian communities living outside Slovenia, and with Italy and Hungary respectively. Slovenia shall give financial support and encouragement to the implementation of these rights.

As Slovenia's relationships with Italy and Hungary are politically less explosive than the relationship with countries of the former Yugoslavia, whose nationals represent a far bigger minority population (Croats, Serbs), the Italian and Hungarian minority members have been given a more elaborate status than other minorities and their rights have been defined in over 70 laws.[149] Both minorities are also directly represented at the local level and in the National Assembly (1991 Constitution, Article 64(3)).

As regards Slovenia's Roma, Article 65 stipulates: 'The status and special rights of the Roma living in Slovenia is regulated by a statute'. However, it took Slovenia over 16 years to pass such a law: the 2007 Roma Community Act[150] (see below).

Members of less numerous religious and linguistic communities living in Slovenia and immigrants from the former Yugoslav Republics, who settled in larger industrial centres predominantly following the Second World War, are not granted the status of a national minority, but in compliance with Article 61 of the Constitution, they are guaranteed the right to preserve their national identity, to foster their own culture and use their own language and script. Members of these groups are organised in associations involved mainly in cultural and information activities and they are also allocated funds from the state budget to finance their programmes, on the basis of annual invitations for applications which are issued by the Ministry of Culture. However, although not recognised as national minorities in the legal sense they represent the largest ethnic minority, and the intercultural dialogue, as required under Article 6 FCNM, takes place only to a very limited extent.

The EU's Anti-discrimination Directive 2000/43 has been implemented by the 2007 Implementation of the Principle of Equal Treatment Act,[151] prohibiting direct and indirect discrimination, victimisation, and harassment. The law also provides for the establishment of the 'Council for Fulfilling the Principle of Equal Treatment' and the 'Advocate of the Principle of Equal Treatment'.

The Law on Local Self-Government[152] guaranteeing a representative in a municipal council is in force in the areas predominantly inhabited by the Roma community. This provides the opportunity to incorporate Roma into the co-administration of local communities, but currently there is only one Roma representative in the Local Council of Murska Sobota. In practice, special Parity Commissions have started working in the municipalities, trying to settle promptly all open issues in the relations between the Roma and the majority population.

5.6.2.1 Citizenship law

When gaining its new statehood, Slovenia's citizenship policy was based on the residence principle (*jus domicile*) and the blood relation principle (*jus sanguini*). According to this policy, ethnic Slovenes automatically became Slovene citizens whereas others, who had immigrated from other (former) Yugoslav Republics had to apply for citizenship, unless they were registered in the Republican Book of Citizens of the Socialist Republic of Slovenia. Due to the anti-immigration sentiment at the time of new statehood many non-Slovenes either did not apply for citizenship as many were not correctly informed about the procedure or their applications were rejected,[153] or were erased from the Register of Permanent Residents on 26 February 1992, as a secret measure of the Ministry of Interior.[154] As a consequence, thousands were deprived of their right to reside in Slovenia, some even detained or deported. The lack of any legal status of the 'Erased' has been criticised by the CoE and the EU's reports during the accession period.[155] The Constitutional Court of Slovenia decided in 1999 and in 2003 that this situation should be remedied by reregistering all the persons concerned (approximately 18,305 people). However, this ruling met opposition from the government, and only 12,000 people were able to obtain permanent residence permit.[156]

5.6.3 Institutions for the protection of minorities

The Office for Nationalities within the government of the Republic of Slovenia is entrusted with coordinating and monitoring the implementation of constitutional obligations. The activities of the Office for Nationalities relate to the autochthonous national communities in the Republic of Slovenia, such as the Italian and Hungarian national communities and the Roma. The Office for Nationalities cooperates with all state authorities whose work concerns the protection of minorities, with self-governing communities of the Italian and Hungarian national communities and other minority institutions, with the Association of Romani Societies of Slovenia, with municipalities and other representatives of local authorities. The Office also cooperates with research institutions, which deal with research relating to minorities and inter-ethnic relations. In addition there is the Commission for the Protection of the Roma. The Commission, set up by the government, is composed of representatives of the ministries and government agencies involved in Roma issues, representatives of some municipalities where autochthonous Roma are present and a representative of the Alliance of Roma of Slovenia, however, only one of the members is of Roma origin.[157] The Commission offers a possibility for dialogue with the representatives of the national communities on all issues, relating to the implementing of the practical minority policy in the country.

The Human Rights Ombudsman is the superior body for lodging informal complaints in the state, as an unbiased form of informal protection of individuals in relation to state authorities, local self-government and bearers of public authority. The activities of the Human Rights Ombudsman are determined in the Human Rights Ombudsman Act.[158] In his reports, along with dealing with individual cases, he can also make proposals for amendments to legislation. Any person who believes that his/her human rights have been violated by an act or deed of a public body may lodge a petition with the Ombudsman to start the proceedings. The Ombudsman may also institute proceedings on his own initiative, e.g. lodging constitutional complaints on the consent of the person whose rights have been violated. However, the Ombudsman does not focus on ethnic discrimination.

In the year 2000 the Ombudsman visited two Roma settlements (Pušča and Žabjak) on his own initiative and further acquainted himself with Roma issues. He found that the main difficulties lay in regulating basic living conditions and employment. On occasion, however rarely, the Ombudsman has supported the enforcement of the rights and interests of certain Roma. For example in 2001 a Roma representative from Novo Mesto complained to the Ombudsman for compensation from the municipality because he had been denied the possibility of standing as the Roma representative on the municipal council at the last elections. The Ombudsman identified a discrepancy between the statute of the Municipality of Novo Mesto and the Local Government Act with regard to the representation of Roma on municipal councils[159] and in March 2001 the Constitutional Court ruled that the statute of the Municipality of Novo Mesto is in non-conformity with the Local Government Act since it does not provide that the Roma community shall have its own representatives on the municipal council. The Constitutional Court ruled that the autonomy of the Roma community in the area of Novo Mesto was undisputed and that therefore even on the basis of existing regulations the municipality was obliged to facilitate the election of a representative of the Roma community to the municipal council. In the same decision the Constitutional Court ruled that the Local Government Act is in non-conformity with the Constitution and ordered the National Assembly to remove the identified unconstitutionality within a year of the publication of the decision.[160]

The newly established Council for Fulfilling the Principle of Equal Treatment and the Advocate of the Principle of Equal Treatment have so far been ineffective in promoting and protecting the rights of Roma who suffered racist attacks and discrimination. The office holders have been uncritical of government policy as key positions in these institutions were filled with government officials.[161]

5.6.4 Education

In Slovenia, two models of bilingual education, Slovene–Italian and Slovene–Hungarian exist since 1950. In such ethnically mixed areas, educational institutions are obliged to provide competence in the other group's language. Italian is a compulsory subject in educational institutions with Slovene as a language of instruction. The same system applies in the mixed region of Prekmurje where the bilingual instruction is Hungarian and Slovene. Students of both nationalities attend classes together, and classes are held parallel in the Slovene and Hungarian languages. The educational system in the ethnically mixed areas in Slovenia as well as extensive cross border cooperation (see the Slovene–Italian Agreement of 1992)[162] contribute to the awareness of cultural and linguistic diversity in the region and at the same time promote the values of cultural pluralism and human rights.

Schools that integrate Roma pupils are granted additional classes by the Ministry of Education and Sport. These classes are held for Roma children in small groups. In the school year 1999/2000, the ministry granted 301 classes per week for Roma pupils in the first four grades of the primary school and 97 classes per week in grades five to eight. In 2004 the Ministry for Education and Sport adopted the 'Strategy for Education of Roma' which aims at improving the language skills of Roma children, special support for classes with Roma children and the inclusion of Roma culture and history in the educational programmes for teachers. Roma children are frequently segregated in the school system, with a disproportionate number attending 'special schools' for those with learning difficulties. The transfer from segregated to integrated classes is reportedly stressful and unpleasant for Roma children, as they often face hostility from non-Roma children. Even though this segregation of Roma children has been prohibited, non-Roma parents have strongly opposed this prohibition and the practice of undue placement of these children in 'special' schools has not been completely abolished.

5.6.5 Language rights

Article 11 of the Slovenian Constitution provides: 'The official language shall be Slovene. In those areas where Italian and Hungarian ethnic communities reside, the official languages shall also be Italian and Hungarian.' In ethnically mixed areas, the Italian and Hungarian languages are equal to the Slovene language. In the functioning of the judicial and state authorities and of the administration in ethnically mixed areas the use of national minority language is guaranteed, provided that one of the parties uses that language. Provisions on the equal use of the languages of both national minorities and provision on external bilingual status in ethnically mixed areas are included in laws and rules governing the functioning of the administration, state and judicial authorities (courts, public prosecutors' offices and notary offices) as well as the statutes of municipalities in ethnically mixed areas.[163]

The Law on Court Rules[164] provides in Articles 60–69 ('operation of courts in the territories in which the Italian and Hungarian national communities reside'), *inter alia*, for the different possibilities for ensuring the equal use of the Italian or Hungarian language. In the event that there is only one party to the proceeding, or if both parties use one language, the proceeding is conducted in that language. If there are two parties to the proceeding using a different language, the proceeding is conducted in two languages. In such event, the records and orders or decisions of the court are also bilingual.

The Public Administration Act[165] stipulates that in the ethnically mixed areas the administration shall conduct business, handle procedures and issue legal and other acts both in the Slovene language and in the language of the national community, if the party residing in this area uses the Italian or Hungarian language. In such event, the orders or decisions of the appellate court shall be in the same language or bilingual.

The Office for International Cooperation within the Ministry of Education and Sports, together with the Institute of Education, offers organisational and expert assistance in training teachers for teaching the mother tongue as a second/ or foreign language. Courses of Macedonian language are held on a reciprocal basis (children of Slovene nationality in Skopje are taught the Slovene language). Each side pays their teacher, and ensures provision of textbooks, while the other side provides the premises where classes are held. Courses in the Croatian language are organised according to the same principle as courses in the Macedonian language. The Ministry of Education and Sport also co-finances courses for the Albanian and Arabic languages.

5.6.6 Culture and the media

In ethnically mixed areas, the Italian and Hungarian national communities have established cultural organisations engaged in the preservation of their cultural identity and integrating their cultural activities.

The Office for Nationalities co-finances the publishing activity, radio and TV programmes for the Roma and for Italian and Hungarian minorities, and, within special programmes, also provides financial support through the Ministry of Culture, Ministry of Education, and the Public Relations and Media Office. The Roma community publishes a magazine *Romano them – Romani world*, with contributions in the Slovene and Romani languages. The publishing of this newspaper is co-financed by the Ministry of Culture. The Office for Nationalities co-finances radio programmes for the Roma on local radio stations in Novo Mesto and Murska Sobota. Radio programmes in the Romani and Slovene languages are intended for the education and informing of the Roma and for the presentation of their culture, as well as informing the wider society of their problems, and thereby fostering tolerance and coexistence.

The Ministry of Culture co-finances the publishing of the yearbook *Naptá* and the literary series *Murata* and supports the publishing of Italian newspapers and yearbooks such as *La Città*, *Il Mandracchio*, *Lassa pur dir*, *Il trillo* as well as the Hungarian weekly *Népújság*. Furthermore, Slovenia contributes around 20 per cent of the necessary means for the activities of joint institutions of the Italian minority also comprising the publishing house *Edit* in Rijeka which publishes newspapers in Italian language (*Voce del popolo*, *Panorama*), intended for the Italian minority in Slovenia and in Croatia. The remaining funds are provided by the Republic of Croatia; additional funds are also received from the parent country.

5.6.7 Religion

In the Republic of Slovenia, the church is separated from the state, and religious communities enjoy equal status. Article 7 of the Slovenian Constitution stipulates that 'The state and religious communities shall be separate. Religious communities shall enjoy equal rights; they shall pursue their activities freely'. Currently there are 31 registered religious communities in the Republic of Slovenia. A special Office for Religious Communities operates at governmental level; its activities relate to religious communities which are registered in Slovenia. Slovenia does not secure funds for the activities of religious communities since their activities are separated from the state.

5.6.8 Participation in public affairs

Members of the Italian and Hungarian national communities have the right to establish their own organisations and associations. The Constitution of the Republic of Slovenia, however, anticipates that they may also organise their self-governing national communities in the areas, where they live autochthonously (see Article 64).

The self-governing national communities are defined by law as public legal persons,[166] founded by members of the Italian and Hungarian national communities in the area where they live in order to be able to implement the special rights guaranteed to them by the Constitution, to assert their needs and interests and to take part in public affairs in an organised manner. Decisions and laws relating only to special rights of both minorities cannot be adopted without the prior consent of representatives of the minorities, as provided for in the Law on Self-Governing Ethnic Communities.

The most important form of co-decision guaranteed to the two ethnic communities in Slovenia is their right to have one deputy each in the National Assembly.[167] Deputies of both ethnic communities have the same status as all other deputies and, like the municipal councillors from the ranks of national communities, have the right to exercise the veto on those acts and regulations of the National Assembly, which refer solely to minority rights. No such law can be passed without their consent, which gives them the responsibility to solve possible disagreements in controversial cases during the preliminary deliberations; yet so far there has been no need for the two deputies to veto a statutory act. The two deputies partake in various working bodies of the National Assembly and have a special place in the National Assembly's Commission for National Communities, which consists of representatives of all parliamentary parties and is by tradition alternately presided by the minority delegates. No other minority group enjoys such privilege.

As regards the Roma's participation in public affairs, there is no representation of Roma in the Slovene Parliament. However, according to the Local Self-Government Act, 20 municipalities are designated to guarantee Roma representation in local councils, which so far has been implemented by 19 of these 20 councils.[168]

5.6.9 The situation of the Roma

Despite a number of efforts to improve the situation of the Roma, they still remain a marginalised minority that meets hostility and racist attitudes in society. In 2007 the xenophobia against Roma became so bad that the Slovene Ombudsman wrote a letter to the CoE's Commissioner for Human Rights who immediately undertook a visit to Slovenia to meet with government officials.[169] As to legal rights, the Roma minority is granted a significantly lower level of protection than the Italian or Hungarian minority. While the Italian and Hungarian minorities are recognised as a 'national minority', the Roma are considered as an 'ethnic minority'. Another issue regarding the Roma minority relates to the unjustified differentiation in the Constitution of 'autochthonous' and 'non-autochthonous' as only the former enjoyed minority rights in Slovenia, until in 2007 the Roma Act abolished this distinction.[170] Currently, the measures for achieving effective equality of the Roma community primarily encompass education of Roma children, the possibilities for cultural activities of the Roma, the development of services for providing information (radio broadcasts for Roma and Roma newspaper), and the right to be represented in the bodies of local self-government in the areas autochthonously inhabited by the Roma, as it is provided for the Italian and Hungarian minorities.

In November 1995 the government of the Republic of Slovenia adopted the 'Programme of Measures for providing aid to the Roma in the Republic of Slovenia'. In accordance with this programme, and in cooperation with the municipalities, the Ministry of Education and Sport has enabled Roma children to be included in the educational programmes in kindergartens at least two years prior to enrolment in the elementary school, and secures additional funds for carrying out such forms of education which promote their socialisation. In 2000 the 'Programme for the Employment of Roma in Slovenia' analysed the living conditions and the economic situation of Roma, and provided proposals for the inclusion of Roma in the workforce. Measures taken under these programmes include preparation for employment and training, establishment of Roma cooperatives, a public work scheme and subsidised employment. The programmes were prepared with the consultation of Roma representatives, however, a number of Roma leaders and other officials expressed doubts as to the effectiveness with which it has been implemented.[171]

So far, the Ministry of Education and Sport has not been very successful in sponsoring Roma students studying to become teachers, but in 2006 there were 30 'Roma coordinators' who help to facilitate interaction between the authorities and Roma members successfully finished their training. Nevertheless, like in most countries Roma are unwelcome neighbours and the local population opposes the settlements of the Roma in some villages, which sometimes led to the forced departure of Roma due to neighbourhood pressure.

5.6.10 Conclusion

In Slovenia, the Law of October 1994 on Self-Governing National Communities created territorial autonomies and a guaranteed seat in the national Parliament for its autochthonous Italian and Hungarian minorities. The protection of Hungarians and Italians minority offered by Slovenia includes provisions for bilingual administration, parliamentary representation and education. The Slovene Constitution recognises collective rights for the Italian and Hungarian minorities in its Article 64 and thereby follows a modern trend to combine individual and collective human rights. Also, the automatic representation of the Italian and Hungarian minorities in the National Assembly is an unusually high standard of minority protection. However, the same rights are not guaranteed to the Roma minority that is recognised as an ethnic minority in Article 65 of Slovenia's Constitution. While no progress has been made regarding Roma representation at national level, at local level there are 20 municipalities with Roma representation in local councils. The issue of the representation of other minorities in the Slovenian Parliament has to be addressed as they represent a higher percentage than the Italian and Hungarian minority.

Slovenia's declaration to the FCNM limits its definition of national minorities to 'the autochthonous Italian and Hungarian national minorities', but states that the provisions also apply to 'the members of the Roma community, who live in the Republic of Slovenia', while excluding its numerically largest minority group, the Croats and Serbs.[172] Most of these people from the former Yugoslavia (mainly Bosnia, Serbia and Kosovo) migrated internally to Slovenia during the decades leading to independence because of economic opportunities and are now faced with governmental and societal discrimination. Although the minority groups from the territories of former Yugoslavia greatly outnumber the traditional national minorities, they do not benefit from any special cultural rights. Unlike the Hungarian, Italian or Roma communities, ethnic Serbs, Croats, Bosnians or Kosovar Albanians are not protected by special provisions of the Constitution, except for Article 61, which provides that 'Each person shall be entitled to freely identify with his national grouping or ethnic community, to foster and give expression to his culture and to use his own language and script'. However, government engagement in this area remains limited, and the resources mustered are not commensurate with the needs.

5.7 United Kingdom

5.7.1 Background

The UK is a constitutional monarchy and at the same time a unitary state consisting of England, Northern Ireland, Scotland and Wales with a population of 59.8 million of which 50.1 million live in England, 5.1 million in Scotland, 2.9 million in Wales and 1.7 million in Northern Ireland.[173] Although the government seat is in London, since devolution there are three devolved administrations in Belfast, Cardiff and Edinburgh, while the Channel Islands Jersey and Guernsey and the Isle of Man are so-called Crown Dependencies. The process of devolution in the UK entailed considerable legislative and policy variation of relevance to minorities across the country. While the UK Parliament has exclusive power to legislate on human rights and equality issues for Great Britain, the Northern Ireland Assembly, during periods of devolution, is responsible for its own legislation in these fields (with the exception of criminal justice and policing). The Scottish Parliament also has legislative powers in a range of fields that are relevant to minorities, while the Welsh Assembly possesses important executive powers in these fields.[174] Devolution has helped to increase awareness and demand for the preservation and development of the cultures of the peoples of Wales, Scotland and Northern Ireland. The Scottish and Welsh administrations are responding to this by developing and overseeing the implementation of a range of language and other related policies. Progress developing such policies in Northern Ireland has been more limited, partly due to the suspension of the Northern Ireland Assembly from 2002 until May 2007.[175]

According to the definition of minorities in the CoE's Recommendation 1201 (1993) the Scots, Welsh and Northern Irish, together with the Cornish, and the

Travellers (who will be discussed in section 5.7.9 instead of the Roma) would have to be considered as traditional national minorities of the UK; however, the UK government has taken a very inclusive approach by considering ethnic minorities stemming from immigration to be protected under the FCNM, and maintaining its position that the scope of the FCNM is confined to the protection of 'racial groups' as defined in the Race Relations Act 1976, which, in turn, is a matter for the courts to interpret. This has allowed a wide range of groups to benefit from protection under the FCNM, including minority ethnic communities, the Scots, Irish and Welsh, Sikhs, Jews, Gypsies and Irish Travellers. Case law has determined that the Scots, Irish and Welsh, who originate from what were formerly independent nations, are defined as a racial group by virtue of their national origins, and has ruled that Roma Gypsies and Irish Travellers are protected by the 1976 Act.[176]

The term 'national minority' has no legal meaning in the UK and so there is no mechanism under any of the UK's legal jurisdictions to grant 'national minority status' to any particular group nor is it proposed to introduce such a mechanism. The UK's anti-discrimination laws (see section below) protect all individuals from being treated less favourably on racial grounds, whether they belong to a minority group or a majority group. Any individual who believes himself or herself discriminated against unlawfully can bring proceedings against the alleged discriminator. The UK therefore ratified the FCNM on the understanding that it would be applied with reference to 'racial groups' within the meaning of section 3(1) of the Race Relations Act 1976 (and the Race Relations (Northern Ireland) Order 1997), which is to say any groups defined by colour, race, nationality or national or ethnic origins. Under the Race Relations Act 1976 certain groups have not (or have not yet) been included in the definition of 'racial group', such as Muslims and other religious groups (although, in many cases, the latter are also members of minority ethnic communities, which are covered by the FCNM), as well as the Cornish. A percentage of Muslims are British converts to Islam, who are not covered by the FCNM, and many Muslims consider that their religious identity, rather than their ethnic identity, should be the basis for their inclusion.[177] In this context, some members of the UK's Parliament, as well as the Commission for Racial Equality (CRE), have questioned whether there is justification for interpreting the scope of the FCNM as confined to the protection of 'racial groups', resulting in the exclusion of British Muslims, for example, but not of Jews and Sikhs. Also, Scottish Gypsies/Travellers have been formally excluded from the FCNM's scope of application, which appears problematic, particularly in view of the inclusion of Gypsies and Travellers living in England and Wales.[178] No Scottish test case has ever established that Scottish Gypsies/Travellers are a racial or ethnic group for the purposes of the Act; the Scottish Executive[179] nevertheless treats them as such and has acknowledged that all Gypsy/Traveller communities in Scotland have specific needs and require the same protection from potential discrimination and abuse as do any of Scotland's minority ethnic communities. However, it is outwith the executive's remit to recognise Gypsies/Travellers as ethnic groups within equal opportunities legislation.[180]

Representations by the Cornish to become protected under the FCNM, which began as the submission of information concerning the Celtic identity and the specific history, language and culture of the Cornish, have gained in magnitude over the years, culminating most recently in an application for judicial review as the 'racial group' criterion appears to be too rigid to accommodate the situation of the Cornish, whose 'separate identity and distinctiveness' is recognised by the UK government in their second state report to the FCNM.[181]

Regardless of who qualifies for protection under the FCNM, the policies for protecting minorities in the UK focus mainly on equality and non-discrimination rather than positive rights. While the UK's first state report of 1999 to the FCNM mainly focused on aspects of racism, it stated in its second state report to the FCNM: 'The UK sees integration as a way of enabling people to practise their own culture and religion freely within the legal and democratic framework in the UK. There are values and responsibilities we should all share but within that framework all should be free to live their lives according to their own cultural background.'[182]

5.7.2 Constitutional and statutory provisions

The UK famously does not have a constitution as such; however, there are a number of different laws that provide for the protection of minorities. In its second state report under the FCNM the UK cited the Race Relations Act 1976 and its (Amendment) Act 2000, the Racial and Religious Hatred Act 2006, expanding on the existing offence of incitement to racial hatred in the Crime and Disorder Act 1998, which also includes statutory offences for racist crime, the Equality Act 2006, Part 2 of which prohibits discrimination on grounds of religion or belief in the provision of goods, facilities and services and public functions in Great Britain, as relevant UK laws for protecting minorities. Of course, there is also the Human Rights Act, which came into force in 2000 giving further effect in UK law to the rights and freedoms set out in the ECHR and providing for compliance of UK law with the ECHR. There are no provisions particularly tailored for specific minorities, but, as regards the Scots, Irish or Welsh, their protection is guaranteed by their own national administrations. Considering that the UK is an 'old' democracy, the above laws, except for the Race Relations Act 1976, have come into force in the rather recent past.

5.7.3 Institutions for the protection of minorities

The CRE is a statutory body established under the Race Relations Art 1976. Its functions are to work towards the elimination of racial discrimination, promote equality of opportunity, and good race relations, between persons of different racial groups generally; and keep under review the working of the Race Relations Act 1976 and to draw up and submit to the Secretary of State proposals for amending it. In addition to reviewing the Race Relations Act, the CRE legally assists complainants in cases of discrimination, tackles institutional discrimination by encouraging public and private sector leaders to commit themselves publicly to using their power and influence to end racial discrimination; raises public awareness of the problems of racism and advantages of multiculturalism through public education programmes and advertising campaigns.

The Equality Act 2006 established a Commission for Equality and Human Rights (CEHR) in Great Britain. The CEHR is supposed to promote the understanding of the importance of human rights, to encourage good practice in relation to human rights, the promotion of awareness, understanding and protection of human rights, and the encouragement of public authorities to comply with the Human Rights Act 1998.

The Northern Ireland Human Rights Commission (NIHRC) is an independent body with the statutory duty to review the adequacy and effectiveness of human rights law and practice in Northern Ireland. The NIHRC has an educational and advisory role, thereby providing a support mechanism for people in Northern Ireland.

The Department for Work and Pensions is committed to helping all those who are disadvantaged in the labour market, including Gypsies and Irish Travellers. The department's programmes are designed to help disadvantaged groups with the skills they need to find work, and are supposed to benefit those who have only basic skills and language problems. In 2002 it started the Ethnic Minority Outreach (EMO) programme.

The Scottish Executive's Equality Strategy and Race Equality Scheme of 2000 both identify Gypsies/Travellers as a minority group vulnerable to prejudice and discrimination and encouraged public bodies to include Gypsies/Travellers in their Race Equality Schemes and race equality work. In *Delivering for Scotland's Gypsies/Travellers* (June 2004) the Scottish Executive stated that all Scottish local authorities should give serious consideration to appointing a liaison officer to work with and support Gypsy/Traveller communities to ensure effective delivery of public services; and that all local authorities, with local police, should prepare strategies on working with Gypsies/Travellers. The Scottish Executive introduced legislation to establish a Scottish Commissioner for Human Rights on 7 October 2005, who is accountable to the Scottish Parliament.[183]

5.7.4 Education

Scots, Northern Irish and Welsh administer their own educational systems. As regards education in minority languages the introduction of the Gaelic Language (Scotland) Act 2005 secured the status of Gaelic as an official language of Scotland that commands equal respect to the English language, and established the Gaelic language development board.

In Wales, the languages of instruction are Welsh and English.

Due to the special conflict situation in Northern Ireland between Catholics and Protestants, the Department of Education has a statutory duty to encourage and facilitate integrated education, which brings together children, parents, teachers and governors from both Catholic and Protestant traditions in one school.

As regards children of Travellers, according to section 488 of the Education Act 1996, funding can be provided to projects undertaken by local authorities, (which is the case in Wales) to meet the needs of Gypsies and Travellers when accessing education.[184] The Scottish Executive Education Department (SEED) commissioned the Scottish Traveller Education Programme (STEP) to produce national guidance for schools and local authorities entitled *Inclusive Educational Approaches for Gypsies and Travellers within the Context of Interrupted Learning* in 2003. Other work funded by SEED through STEP has included the production and dissemination of three case studies in 2005, which highlighted good practice examples of working with young Gypsies and Travellers, and the production in 2006 of three leaflets for Gypsy/Traveller families containing targeted information on the education system in Scotland.

As to ethnic minorities stemming from immigration, the UK reported in its second state report to the FCNM that some minority groups, for example, 75 per cent of young people of Chinese origin achieved at least five A–C grades at GSCE and those of Indian origin also achieved significantly better than the national average. But children, particularly boys, from black African and Caribbean, Pakistani, Bangladeshi and Gypsy and Traveller groups are less likely to succeed and often do particularly poorly by the end of formal education.[185]

All local education authorities have to include in their educational development plans their strategies to raise the educational achievement of minority ethnic pupils including those pupils whose first language is other than English.[186] English is the language of instruction in schools (except in Wales, where the medium of instruction is English or Welsh), however, as there are about two hundred mother tongues represented in British schools, extra funds are provided by the government under section 11 of the Local Government Act 1966 for extra teaching posts to help children's development of English; section 11 funds may also be used to provide bilingual teachers and classroom assistants to provide mother tongue support, particularly in the early primary years, to ease the child's transition from home to school, especially for those children whose mother tongue is not English.[187]

5.7.5 Language rights

English is the language of the state and administration in England, Northern Ireland and Scotland. The Gaelic Language Act 2005, which came into force in 2006, establishes a body having functions exercisable with a view to securing the status of the Gaelic language as an official language of Scotland commanding equal respect to the English language, including the functions of preparing a national Gaelic language plan (which has been adopted by the Gaelic Committee in November 2007), of requiring certain public authorities to prepare and publish Gaelic language plans in connection with the exercise of their functions and to maintain and implement such plans, and of issuing guidance in relation to Gaelic education.[188] The Scottish Executive has also continued to provide financial backing (mostly through the Scottish Arts Council) to organisations that work to promote Scottish Gaelic and Scots.

The Welsh Language Act 1993 establishes in its preamble the principle that, 'in the conduct of public business and the administration of justice in Wales, the English and Welsh languages should be treated on a basis of equality'. Wales has 350 language schemes developed by public bodies already in operation. Besides developing and overseeing the implementation of Welsh language schemes by public bodies, the Welsh Language Board provides grants to voluntary sector organisations that work to promote the Welsh language.

In Northern Ireland the situation is less settled. The St Andrew's Agreement of 13 October 2006 places a duty on the Northern Ireland Assembly to adopt strategies on enhancing and protecting the development of Irish, and the Ulster Scots language, heritage and culture, however, the proposed Irish Language Act for Northern Ireland has to date not been adopted by the Northern Ireland Assembly. However, the Arts Council and the Irish Language Agency (Foras na Gaeilge), the body responsible for the promotion of the Irish language throughout the whole island of Ireland, provide funds for artists working in the medium of Irish and other educational and cultural initiatives. The Ulster Scots Agency plays the same role in promoting Ulster Scots, and has provided grants to groups undertaking educational, cultural and language initiatives. Both the Ulster Scots Agency and the Irish Language Agency receive funding from the UK and Irish governments under the terms of the 1998 Belfast (Good Friday) Agreement.

The UK ratified the Charter on Regional or Minority Languages in 2001. The government has to date recognised seven languages under Part II of the Charter: Welsh, Gaelic, Irish, Scots, Ulster Scots, Cornish and Manx. As regards the undertakings of Part III of the Charter, the government has only included Welsh, Gaelic and Irish and on that basis provides important financial backing to public bodies and voluntary sector organisations that work to promote the languages and cultures of the peoples of Wales, Scotland and Northern Ireland.

While considerable funding is also available for voluntary sector organisations representing minority ethnic communities (stemming from immigration), these funds are mostly available for projects aimed at promoting equality and mainstreaming rather than promoting minority cultures.[189]

5.7.6 Culture and media

The rights to freedom of expression and thought are guaranteed under the Human Rights Act. As regards the representation of minorities in public media, the public service broadcasters (the BBC, Channel 4 and S4C) are among the bodies subject to the general duty under the Race Relations (Amendment) Act to have due regard to the need to promote race equality in carrying out their public functions.[190] The BBC provides television and radio services in Wales, such as the television channel Sianel Pedwar Cymru (S4C) which broadcasts programmes in the Welsh language and receives an annual grant from the UK government. On radio, the BBC provides a radio service in Welsh called Radio Cymru which started broadcasting as an entirely Welsh language radio station on 1 January 1977. In Scotland, the Gaelic Broadcasting Committee, Comadaidh Craolaidh Gaidhlig, is an independent statutory body established under the Broadcasting Act, which is responsible for managing the Gaelic Broadcasting Fund (some £8.5m. per annum from the government) which finances through grants, the production of Gaelic programmes, training and research and other purposes related to Gaelic broadcasting.

In Northern Ireland, the Department of Culture, Art and Leisure (DCAL) ran a broadcasting training pilot project. This scheme, at a cost of around £250,000 trained a group of Irish speakers in TV and film production techniques. After evaluation of the project, it was agreed that the training scheme be included in the remit of the Irish Language Broadcast Fund, which began funding in June 2005.[191]

In addition, the Independent Television Commission has issued over 20 broadcasting licences for television services aimed at the Asian, Chinese, Japanese, Turkish, Iranian, and Afro-Caribbean communities. A number have been available on cable television since the late 1980s. For print media, the *Travellers' Times* magazine has to be mentioned.

5.7.7 Religion

The freedom of religion is guaranteed by the Human Rights Act, and the Equality Act which, among other things, prohibits discrimination on grounds of religion or belief in the provision of goods, facilities and services and public functions. However, the Church of England is the 'Established Church in England', or state church. The sovereign, who must be in communion with the Church of England, is Supreme Governor. As such, the Queen appoints bishops and senior dignitaries of the church, acting on the advice of ministers. In Wales, the (Anglican) Church was disestablished in the early part of this century, and no church is now established. A large part of the population of Wales has traditionally belonged to non-conformist denominations. There is no state religion or established church in Northern Ireland. The Church of Scotland is, however, a free church, meaning that it is not state-controlled and the sovereign is not the head of the church as is the case in the Church of England. Information on religious identity across the entire United Kingdom was collected for the first time in 2001, as illustrated in Table 5.1.

In 2001, the government amended the Crime and Disorder Act 1998, introducing specific religiously aggravated offences equivalent to the existing racially aggravated offences. In 2003, regulations were introduced in Great Britain making discrimination on the grounds of religion or belief unlawful in employment and vocational training.[192] The Racial and Religious Hatred Act 2006 makes it an offence in England and Wales to use threatening words or behaviour with the intention of stirring up hatred against a group of people on the grounds of their religious belief or lack of religious belief. The UK blasphemy laws have been criticised for being restricted solely to Christians, as they do not protect other religions.[193]

Table 5.1 Breakdown of religious identity in the UK (2001 census)*

UK	*Thousands*	*per cent*
Christian	42,079	71.6
No religion	9,104	15.5
Muslim	1,591	2.7
Hindu	559	1.0
Sikh	336	0.6
Jewish	267	0.5
Buddhist	152	0.3
Other religion	179	0.3
Not stated	4,289	7.3

* Second Report Submitted by the United Kingdom Pursuant to Article 25 (1) of the Framework Convention, ACFC/SR/II(2007)003, para. 245.

5.7.8 Participation in public affairs

Since devolution, the people of Wales, Scotland and Northern Ireland have a considerable say in their regional affairs, while the sovereignty of the UK Parliament is maintained in those matters which impact on the whole of the UK. Powers in certain clearly defined areas are devolved from the sovereign UK Parliament to the Scottish Parliament, the National Assembly of Wales and the Northern Ireland Assembly. For all other minorities the right to vote is restricted to British, qualifying Commonwealth and Irish citizens, who are eligible to vote at all elections, and to citizens of the EU, who may vote at European Parliamentary elections and local elections. EU citizens may also vote at elections for the National Assembly of Wales.

Since the presence of persons belonging to minority ethnic communities in legislative bodies is low, the government supports 'Operation Black Vote', an NGO which aims to promote greater participation of black and ethnic minorities in political life by organising internship opportunities with MPs and local councillors.

Under the Race Relations (Amendment) Act 2000, all the key public authorities in Great Britain must produce race equality schemes to show how they are fulfilling their statutory duty to have due regard to the need to eliminate unlawful discrimination and to promote equality of opportunity and good relations between persons of different racial groups (that does not apply to the private sector though which provides 75 per cent of employment). Among the public sector authorities, in particular the Crown Prosecution Service (which operates in England and Wales) made efforts to meet targets for recruitment, retention and progression of minority ethnic staff; also, efforts to encourage minority ethnic recruitment into the police, in England, Wales and Scotland have met with some success.[194] According to government figures, the national target for recruiting teachers from a minority background, established at 9 per cent, has been exceeded.[195]

There is an All Party Parliamentary Group (APPG) for Gypsy and Traveller Law Reform, which is committed to raising the social inclusion of Travellers and improving relations between the settled and Traveller community.

5.7.9 The situation of the Travellers

This section uses the term 'Travellers' to refer to a heterogeneous group of persons who associate themselves with a 'Gypsy' and/or 'Traveller' identity, including Romani Gypsies, Irish Travellers and Scottish Gypsies/Travellers. While the precise number of Gypsies and Travellers throughout the UK is not known, it is estimated that there are between 90,000 and 120,000 Gypsies and Travellers living in caravans in England, and up to three times as many living in conventional housing.[196] CRE estimates that there are currently 200,000–300,000 Travellers living in Great Britain.[197]

In terms of discrimination, the parallels with the Roma are obvious. Travellers have significantly less access to healthcare and education than the settled population, which makes it increasingly more difficult for them to be economically successful. When it comes to housing, Travellers are provided with sites for their caravans, but the number of sites in the UK is insufficient and they are often not wanted near settled areas where access to health, education and business facilities is available.

The courts have recognised that travelling and living in a caravan are a reflection of Gypsies' and Irish Travellers' cultural heritage, and not simply a choice of lifestyle that can be ignored. Yet the acute shortage of authorised public sites and difficulties getting planning permission for private sites have made it very difficult for Travellers to live according to their cultural heritage. Under the Housing Act 2004 local authorities have a new statutory duty to assess the need for Gypsy and Traveller accommodation in their area. According to this Act, authorities must make arrangements for Gypsy sites within a regional framework. The regional planning body, on the basis of local authorities' assessments of need, will determine how many pitches should be provided across the region, and specify in its regional strategy how many pitches need to be provided in each local authority area. Local planning authorities will have to identify sites in their development plans, in line with the regional strategy.

Before planning permission for a caravan site under UK law can be obtained, the applicant must establish that he or she falls within the statutory definition of Gypsy, that is, has Gypsy status. The leading case on Gypsy status before the Human Rights Act 1998 came into force was *R v. South Hams District Council, ex parte Gibb*.[198] The Court of Appeal considered whether the applicants were Gypsies for the purposes of the former duty to provide caravan sites according to the Caravan Sites Act 1968, which defined Gypsies as 'persons of a nomadic habit of life, whatever their race or origin'. The courts have also considered whether an individual can lose his or her Gypsy status, particularly in relation to cases where ill health has led to Gypsies or Travellers being unable to travel. In *R v. Shropshire CC, ex parte Bungay*[199] an aggrieved local resident who lived near a recently approved Gypsy site, challenged the local authority's decision that a Gypsy family who had not travelled for 15 years because they were caring for their elderly and infirm parents, were Gypsies. The judge held that a person could remain a Gypsy even if he or she did not travel, provided that his or her nomadism was held in abeyance and not abandoned.

However, this definition was overruled in *Wrexham CBC v. the National Assembly for Wales and Berry*;[200] it was held that Mr Berry was no longer a Gypsy because he had become too ill to continue to travel for work, Mr Berry appealed unsuccessfully to the House of Lords.[201] The effect of the Court of Appeal's decision is that Mrs Berry and her children lose their Gypsy status solely because their husband or father has become seriously ill and is unable to travel. This situation was eventually remedied in 2006 with a new government policy paper entitled 'Planning for Gypsy and Traveller Sites', Circular 1/06.[202]

Circular 01/06 provides in section 70:

> The provisions of the European Convention on Human Rights should be considered as an integral part of local authorities 'decision making' … Local planning authorities should consider the consequences of refusing or granting planning permission, or taking enforcement action, on the rights of the individuals concerned both Gypsies and Travellers and local residents, and whether it is necessary and proportionate in the circumstances.

There has been criticism from Traveller representatives regarding the often poor quality of the needs assessments conducted by local authorities. Concerns have also been expressed at the unwillingness of many local authorities to comply with the requirements of Regional Spatial Strategies once they are published owing to intense hostility among the local population.[203] However, there are a number of associations in support of Travellers, such as the Irish Traveller Movement in Britain, the London Gypsy and Traveller Unit (LGTU), the National Federation of Gypsy Liaison Groups, the Traveller Law Research Unit of Cardiff University, Canterbury Gypsy Support Group (International Gypsy and Traveller Affairs), and the Derbyshire Gypsy Liaison Group who work towards improving living conditions for the Travellers.

5.7.10 Conclusion

The UK is a special case, as its system of devolution provides for far-reaching rights regarding the Welsh, Scots and Irish. In addition, the UK government has taken a very inclusive approach and also considers ethnic minorities stemming from immigration to be protected minorities under the FCNM, which has allowed a wide range of groups to benefit from the FCNM, in particular, in the context of language use and education. The CRE has been active in promoting the employment of minority members in public offices; in addition, the CEHR established under the Equality Act 2006 has undertaken efforts to encourage good practice in relation to human rights, in particular in the workplace. As regards Travellers in the UK, attempts have been made to facilitate their obtaining permission for stopping sites for their caravans under the Housing Act 2004 and Circular 01/06. However, their participation in social life is affected by discrimination like in every other EU country.

5.8 France

5.8.1 Background

France officially denies the existence of minorities on its territory on the basis of Article 1 of the Constitution, which prohibits discrimination of inhabitants in France because of their membership in religious or ethnic groups. That makes it difficult to gather data on the population of foreign origin who are either of French nationality, or from abroad living legally on the territory; in fact, it is illegal in France to collect ethnic data.[204] However, France is a country of great cultural diversity and develops its effort to promote cultural integration within the limits envisaged by its republican laws. France is divided into 25 administrative regions (four of them overseas), excluding Corsica, which is considered to be a 'territorial collectivity' but practically it is a region. Corsica still aims to be separate from mainland France but the region has its own Parliament and language taught in schools. The French Constitutional Council refused in 1991 to recognise the existence of a 'Corsican people', arguing that there is only one French people.[205] Apart from Corsica, the regions of Brittany, Alsace/Lorraine and Languedoc-Roussillon have their own regional languages.

The regions were granted limited autonomy by the Law of 5 July 1972, which created the Regional Councils. Significant decentralisation occurred in France only in 1982, with the Law of 2 March 1982,[206] which prescribed the transfer of several competencies and resources from the state to the region. This decentralisation law gave greater autonomy in decision making by sharing administrative and budgetary tasks between central and local authorities; functions transferred from the central to the regional government included industrial development, regional economic planning, professional education, transport, and the delivery of health and social services, i.e. no particular cultural rights.

5.8.2 Constitutional and statutory provisions

Under French law, all citizens have equal rights, and the law is not intended to accord specific rights to 'groups' defined by their community of origin, culture, beliefs, language or ethnicity. France's legal and administrative texts avoid naming populations according to their ethnic origin, but this does not exclude recognition of an individual's social activities or lifestyle. The Constitution declares in Article 1 that 'France is an indivisible Republic, laic, democratic and social. It ensures equality, in the eyes of the law, for all the citizens, without distinction of origin, race or religion. It respects all beliefs. Its organisation is decentralised.' Hence, minorities in France do not have any particular cultural status (or other: legal, pertaining to worship, economic, etc.).

Immigrants have the same rights as the French, with regard to education, health and social security. If they are foreign, however, they cannot vote but can profit from cultural rights within the framework of the Law on Associations (1901),[207] which allows any foreigner or immigrant living in France, under certain conditions, to create associations, including religious organisations, with the proviso of respecting the Constitution (secularity, equality, freedom of conscience, etc.).

The preamble of the Constitution recalls the 1789 Declaration of the Rights of Man and of the Citizen, one of the first documents to recognise human rights. A recent anti-discrimination initiative was the introduction of the 2004 Anti-discrimination Law,[208] implementing EC Directive 2000/43/EC. The Act prohibits discrimination 'on the grounds of origin, gender, family/marital status, physical appearance, surname, state of health, disability, genetic characteristics, lifestyle, sexual orientation, age, political opinions, religious beliefs, union activities, and real or supposed membership or non-membership of an ethnic group, nation or race'. Under the provisions of this Act, the Independent High Authority for Equality and Against Discrimination (Haute Autorité de Lutte contre les Discriminations et pour l'Egalité, HALDE) was established (see below). Article 19 of the Act relating to discrimination on the grounds of ethnic origin, provides that if a prima facie case of discrimination exists, it shifts the burden of proof onto the defendant to prove that the challenged action or measure was justified by facts unrelated to any type of discrimination. Previously, a serious obstacle to the prosecution of discrimination cases was that the burden of proof lay solely with the plaintiff. In March 2006 a new law on equal opportunities[209] was adopted by the French Parliament following the outbreak of urban violence in French cities in autumn 2005. The law focuses largely on promoting employment opportunities in urban areas and enables HALDE to recommend that local government representatives impose administrative penalties on companies found guilty of discriminatory behaviour.

5.8.3 Institutions for the protection of minorities

Several national, inter-departmental or regional organisations and associations supervise and assist in the regulation of France's anti-discrimination and integration policy, for example: the Groupe d'étude et de lutte contre les discriminations (GELD), the Fonds d'action et de soutien pour l'intégration et la lutte contre les discriminations (FASILD) and the Association pour le développement des relations interculturelles (ADRI). FASILD finances operations in favour of the integration of immigrants. Another organisation working in this field is the National Agency for Social Cohesion and Equal Opportunities (ACSE).[210] There is also the Inter-Ministerial Committee to Combat Racism, Anti-Semitism and

Xenophobia, which is supposed to ensure coordinated policies and practices across ministries, recognising their interrelated mandates and the need for cooperation and holistic approaches to combat racism, and its impact on minorities, however, it has not been convened since 2005. In 2003 HALDE was established by the French government, headed by a senior civil servant, as part of the implementation of EC Directive 2000/43/EC. HALDE is an independent body with powers to mediate or refer discrimination cases for prosecution, conduct studies and promote non-discrimination programmes. It can intervene directly in court cases and can propose a settlement involving the payment of a fine. Unfortunately, it lacks enforcement powers with respect to non-payment of fines. The UN Independent Expert on Minorities criticised that targeted and more robust approaches are required to have a deeper and far-reaching impact on persistent discrimination experienced by minorities.[211]

5.8.4 Education

There are no particular provisions for minorities regarding the right to education, and the French educational system provides for the same rights for every citizen and foreigner. However, in some regions in France, it is possible to obtain education in the regional 'minority' language, such as the Seaska association of Basque schools (900 in Lapurdi, 300 in Nafarroa Beherea and 100 in Zuberoa), the Diwan school of Brittany and the Scola Corsa in Corsica. However, these schools are not part of the state education system.

As far as the higher level of education is concerned, only the Institut d'Etudes Basques (IEB) in Bayonne offers an entire programme of Basque studies. Basque is the main teaching language there. And the diploma of general university studies (*Diplôme d'études universitaires générales* – DEUG), a bachelor's degree (*licence*), a master's degree (*maîtrise*) and a competitive examination for a diploma in secondary education (*Concours d'Aptitude d'Enseignement dans le Secondaire* – CAPES) can be obtained in Basque at Bordeaux University.

5.8.5 Language rights

According to the Toubon Law[212] the use of the French language is mandatory in official government publications, in all advertisements, in all workplaces, in commercial contracts, in some other commercial communication contexts, in all government-financed schools and in some other contexts.[213] In Alsace, however, the German dialect can be used in local administration and in religious celebrations. Since 1919 electoral documents were distributed in two versions, in French and German (the written form of the Alsatian dialects), this has been forbidden for the municipal and cantonal elections in March 2008, and the State Council confirmed that supplementary documents in German, distributed and reimbursed, are illegal. Similarly, on 9 April 2006 the use of Polynesian in the French Polynesian Assembly was prohibited by the Constitutional Council.

In Catalan regions, the names of villages, streets and roads are written in the local and the national language, which is the same in Brittany, where Breton (Breizh) is spoken by approximately 250,000 people. Another linguistic minority present in Brittany are speakers of the Gallo language.

The Basque language is spoken in the *Département* of Pyrénées-Atlantiques. Basque has no legal status in the region's courts, although documents submitted in Basque are admitted. As far as use of the language during proceedings is concerned, French citizens may not use Basque, although Spanish citizens, by way of contrast, may address the court in Basque when appearing as witnesses or defendants.

The 1999 report written for the French government by Bernard Cerquiglini[214] identified 75 languages that would qualify for recognition under the government's proposed ratification of the European Charter for Regional or Minority Languages. Currently, the Charter is only signed but not ratified. A revision of the French Constitution creating official recognition of regional languages as part of the national heritage was implemented by Parliament in Congress at Versailles in July 2008.[215]

5.8.6 Culture and media

The programme of decentralisation, launched in 1982, has introduced a lot of autonomy for the management at regional level, and the revival of collective identities and internal diversities. As the French are fond of their history and genealogy, most regions are celebrating their particularisms, customs, rural habits and cultural memories even if these identities are sometimes folkloric and in opposition to the national state.[216]

According to the EBLUL Report addressed to the UN ESCR Committee, the use of regional languages in the media remains marginal and arbitrary.[217] In Alsace, regional language broadcasting is relegated to a middle-wave channel and is never heard on long-wave or FM channels. In Occitania,[218] only few local Radio France stations have regional language broadcasting, rarely more than one to two hours per week. The case of TV Breizh is highly emblematic: this private regional Breton television was created in 2000 on satellite with the aim of supporting Breton culture and the Breton language backed by financial resources. However, the three applications for authorisation to broadcast in the hertzian network were refused, notably in favour of an attribution of frequency to a station which did not exist.[219] Radio France-Pays Basque broadcasts an hour each day in Basque, five days a week, to around 60,000 listeners. Three private radio stations broadcast 105 hours per week in Basque, namely Gure Irratia in Lapurdi, Irulegiko Irratia in Nafarroa Beherea and Iberokobotza in Zuberoa. Lastly, the private station Lapurdi Irratia/Radio Labourg broadcasts 50 per cent of its programmes in Basque (six hours per day).

Three periodicals written entirely in Basque are on sale in the region: *Egunkaria* (circulation 400), *Herria* (3,000) and *Argia* (100). Three other weeklies use Basque, namely *Enbata*, with a circulation of 1,500, *Ekaitza* (1,500) and *Har Hitza*

(500). The regional daily newspaper *Sud-Ouest* publishes one article per week in Basque.

5.8.7 Religion

Even though the freedom of religion is guaranteed by the Declaration of Men and Citizens 1789, the relationship between government and religious organisations in France is defined by the 1905 Law Concerning the Separation of the Churches and the State[220] which states in its first section: 'The Republic assures freedom of conscience. It guarantees the free exercise of religious worship under the sole restrictions hereafter in the interest of public order. The Republic does not grant recognition nor pay nor subsidises any church.' The population of France is roughly 70 per cent Roman Catholic, 10 per cent Muslim and 20 per cent not religious. French insistence on the lack of religion in all things public (*laïcité* or secularism) is a notable feature in the French ideal of citizenship. Secularism has been debated during the first headscarf affair 1989 leading to the new Law on Secularity and Conspicuous Religious Symbols in Schools of 2004[221] inspired by the Commission on Secularism, prohibiting the wearing of any religious symbols in schools if they are too conspicuous. However, the French Council of the Muslim Faith plays an important role in a process of interfaith and inter-community dialogue. In addition, the innovative 'Marseilles Hope' initiative is a collective of religious leaders who meet together with local authorities to share information, views and issues, and to maintain positive and constructive communication and was consistently highlighted as an exemplary initiative of interfaith and community dialogue.[222]

5.8.8 Participation in public affairs

There are no special provisions for minorities regarding their participation in public affairs due to the strong principle of equality.

5.8.9 Situation of the Roma

As France does not recognise minorities, Gypsy and Traveller communities are denied recognition of their identity and possibilities to promote and preserve their culture, traditions, and other aspects of their identity. According to Article 9 of the Besson Law[223] Gypsies and Travellers cannot stop outside a designated area. However, regardless of the obligation imposed by municipal law, municipalities have not created sufficient halting areas.[224]

Persons without a fixed domicile or residence who live in vehicles, trailers or other mobile shelters are obliged to have in their possession special circulation documents. Persons unable to provide proof of their professional activities are required to present their circulation documents at the police station for validation every three months. Persons caught without circulation documents or who fail to present them for validation may be subject to penal sanctions, including prison.

Persons with circulation documents may only exercise their right to vote after a three-year period of 'attachment' to a selected municipality,[225] which makes it almost impossible for Travellers to vote. Other French citizens are able to vote already after a six-month period of residence in a given municipality. Furthermore, Gypsies and Travellers are excluded from other forms of political participation. Public officials often do not consult them directly, even when the issues at the forefront of public debate concern Travellers and Gypsies directly. Instead, they generally turn to 'intermediaries' who are considered to know and understand 'the Gypsies'. When consultative institutions are established in order 'to present a façade of consultation (such as the Departmental Consultative Commissions for Travellers established in each French Department), Travellers and Gypsies are in all or nearly all cases a small minority on these Commissions and their voices generally carry little weight'.[226]

5.8.10 Conclusion

France's model of immigration, the so-called republican model, rests on the demand that immigrants become culturally, intellectually and politically assimilated. Members of minority communities described an extreme pressure on them to alter their cultural and religious identities as a precondition for immigration and full inclusion and acceptance in French society.[227] Despite the recent recognition of regional languages in the Constitution, French language policy has endangered many regional languages. For example, in the 1950s more than one million people spoke Breton, today there are only 250,000 people left in the region who can speak Breton, most of whom are elderly; however, Alsatian and Corsican have resisted better. As regards the Roma minority, issues of concern include the failure to provide sufficient serviced parking areas for Travellers and Gypsies; access to identity cards and documentation issues, and obstacles to the right to vote and participate in political life.

Notes

Table of legislation

1 Publication in the Official Journal did not exist at the time of the Founding Treaties, for these documents see Office for Official Publications of the European Communities, Luxembourg.
2 Ibid.
3 Ibid.

Chapter 1

1 For the accession round on 1 May 2004 those states were: the Czech Republic, Estonia, Hungary, Latvia, Lithuania, Poland, Slovakia and Slovenia. Romania and Bulgaria joined in 2007.
2 See for example Andrew Williams, 'EU Human Rights Policy: A study in Irony'; Philipp Alston (ed.), 'The EU and Human Rights'; Andrew Clapham, 'Human Rights and the European Community: A Critical Overview'; Nanette A. Neuwahl and Allan Rosas (eds), 'The European Union and Human Rights'.
3 See for example the recent establishment of the Fundamental Rights Agency or the creation of the High Representative's Personal Representative for Human Rights in 2005.
4 See for example the preamble and Article 2 of the Treaty European Economic Community, Treaty of Rome establishing the European Communities, signed 25 March 1957, entered into force 1 July 1958.
5 ETS No. 005, concluded 4 November 1950, entered into force 3 September 1953.
6 Treaty of Rome establishing the European Communities, signed 25 March 1957, entered into force 1 July 1958.
7 Treaty of Maastricht, signed 7 February 1992, entered into force 1 November 1993, OJ C 191, 29.07.1992.
8 Treaty of Amsterdam, OJ C 340, 10.11.1997, signed 2 October 1997, entered into force 1 May 1999.
9 See e.g., *Stauder v. Ulm* Case 29/69 [1969] ECR 419; *Internationale Handelsgesellschaft v. Einfuhr und Vorratsstelle für Getreide und Futtermittel* Case 11/70 [1970] ECR 1125, [1972] CMLR 255; *Nold v. Commission*, Case 4/73 [1974] ECR 491, [1974] 2 CMLR 338; *Hauer v. Land Rheinland Pfalz*, Case 44/79 [1979] ECR 3727, [1980] 3 CMLR 42.
10 Opinion 2/94 of the Court of Justice on the Accession by the Communities to the European Convention for the Protection of Human Rights and Fundamental Freedoms, ECR 1996, I-1759 paras 27–28, 31 and 34–35.
11 EU Charter on Fundamental Rights, OJ C 364, 18.12.2002.
12 Treaty of Lisbon, OJ C 306 of 17 December 2007.

13 UN Charter, signed 26 June 1945, entered into force 24 October 1945.
14 Universal Declaration of Human Rights, adopted 10 December 1948, GA Resolution 217A (III), UN Doc. A/810 (1948).
15 International Covenant on Civil and Political Rights, adopted 16 December 1966, entered into force 23 March 1976, GA Resolution 2200 (XXI), 999 UNTS 171.
16 See chapter 4, section 4.8 for the relevant case law.
17 International Covenant on Economic Social and Cultural Rights, adopted 16 December 1966, entered into force 3 January 1976, GA Resolution 2200 A (XXI), 999 UNTS 171.
18 International Convention on the Elimination of All Forms of Racial Discrimination, concluded 21 December 1965, entered into force 4 January 1969, 666 UNTS 195.
19 International Convention on the Rights of the Child, adopted 20 November 1989, entered into force 2 September 1990, GA Resolution 44/25.
20 Convention for the Protection of Human Rights and Fundamental Freedoms, concluded 4 November 1950, entered into force 3 September 1953. ETS No. 005.
21 Framework Convention for the Protection of National Minorities, concluded 1 February 1995, entered into force 1 February 1998, ETS No. 157.
22 UN Declaration on the Rights of Persons Belonging to National or Ethnic, Religious or Linguistic Minorities, adopted 18 December 1992, GA Resolution 47/135.
23 Patrick Thornberry, 'International and European Standards on Minority Rights', in Hugh Miall (ed.), Minority Rights in Europe: The Scope of a Transnational Regime, p. 14–16.
24 Concluding Document of the Copenhagen Meeting of the Second Conference on the Human Dimension of the CSCE, 5 June–29 July 1990.
25 Conference for Security and Co-operation in Europe, Charter of Paris for a New Europe, adopted by Heads of State and Government of the participating States of the Conference on Security and Co-operation in Europe, Paris, 21 November 1990.
26 Conference for Security and Co-operation in Europe, Second Conference on the Human Dimension, Concluding Document of the CSCE, Document of the Copenhagen Meeting, 29 July 1990.
27 The High Commissioner on National Minorities, The Hague Recommendations, Education Rights of National Minorities, October 1996; The High Commissioner on National Minorities, Oslo Recommendations, Linguistic Rights of National Minorities, February 1998; The High Commissioner on National Minorities, Lund Recommendations, Effective Participation of National Minorities in Public Life, September 1999.
28 See e.g., Yoram Dinstein, 'Collective Human Rights of Peoples and Minorities'; Jack Donnelly, 'Human Rights, Individual Rights and Collective Rights', in Jan Berting et al. (eds), Human Rights in a Pluralist World: Individuals and Collectivities.
29 Even though the book does not assess the situation of minorities in Greece, the fact that Greece together with 'old' Western EU Members States such as Belgium, France and Luxembourg have not ratified the FCNM indicates opposition to a minority rights system in their national setup.

Chapter 2

1 Treaties of Rome, establishing the European Community and the European Atomic Energy Community, signed 25 March 1957, entered into force 1 July 1958.
2 Treaty of Maastricht, signed 7 February 1992, entered into force 1 November 1993, OJ C 191, 29.07.1992.
3 Treaty of Amsterdam, signed 2 October 1997, entered into force 1 May 1999, OJ C 340, 10.11.1997.

4 Treaty of Nice, signed 26 February 2001, entered into force 1 February 2003, OJ C 80, 10.03.2001.
5 Draft Treaty Establishing a Constitution for Europe, did not enter into force, OJ C 169, 18.07.2003.
6 Treaty of Lisbon, signed 17 December 2007, entered into force 1 December 2009, OJ C 115, 9.05.2008.
7 Convention for the Protection of Human Rights and Fundamental Freedoms, concluded 4 November 1950, entered into force 3 September 1953. ETS No. 005.
8 For a more detailed discussion of the ECJ's human rights case law, see Takis Tridimas, *General Principles of EC Law*, p. 209ff.
9 See the new Article 47 TEU.
10 ECSC Treaty, signed 18 April 1951, entered into force 23 July 1952, and expired 23 July 2002.
11 Above note 1.
12 Merger Treaty, signed 8 April 1965, entered into force 1 July 1967, OJ C 152, 13.07.1967.
13 These were at the time Belgium, France, Germany, Italy, Luxembourg and the Netherlands.
14 See Article 2 TEC, above note 1.
15 Single European Act, signed 17–28 February, entered into force 1 July 1987, OJ L 169, 29.06.1987.
16 See above note 2.
17 See above note 3.
18 See above note 4.
19 Above note 6.
20 Ex-Article 202 TEC. In the following the newly renumbered provisions of the Consolidated Version of the Treaty of Lisbon, OJ C 115, 9.05.2008 will be quoted.
21 For COHOM's mandate see www.consilium.europa.eu/uedocs/cmsUpload/COHOM_ mandates.pdf.
22 Articles 288–97 TFEU Consolidated Version of the Treaty on the Functioning of the European Union, OJ C 115, 9.05.2008, ex-Articles 249 to 253 TEC.
23 Article 14 TEU.
24 Articles 14(1) and 16(1) TEU, Articles 294, 310 TFEU, ex-Articles 192, 193, 251, 269, 276 TEC.
25 Articles 227, 228 TFEU, ex-Articles 194, 195 TEC.
26 Frederic Van den Berghe 'Double Standards and Minority Protection', p. 185.
27 An overview of the EP's main activities in the field of human rights in external relations can be found at www.europarl.europa.eu/comparl/afet/droi/default.htm.
28 For resolutions in 2008, see *EU Annual Report on Human Rights 2008*, p. 50.
29 See Article 263 TFEU.
30 Article 19 TEU.
31 Article 258 TFEU, ex-Articles 226, 227 and 230 TEC.
32 Ex-Article 225 TEC.
33 *Forcheri v. Belgium*, Case 152/82; *UEFA v. Jean-Marc Bosman*, Case 415/93, Opinion of the Attorney-General Lenz, para. 203.
34 Memorandum on Accession of the Communities to the European Convention for the Protection of Human rights and Fundamental Freedoms, Bulletin of the EC-S 2/1979.
35 Commission Communication SEC (90) 2087 of November 1990. On Community Accession to the European Convention for the Protection of Human Rights and fundamental Freedoms and some of its Protocols.
36 Ibid. p. 2.
37 *M & Co v. Federal Republic of Germany* [1990] ECHR (Ser. A).
38 *Matthews v. UK*, Reports 1999-I, 18 February 1999.

39 *Bosphorus Hava Yollari Turizm v. Ireland* (2006) 42 EHRR 1.

40 Opinion on the Accession by the Communities to the European Convention for the Protection of Human Rights and Fundamental Freedoms, 2/94, ECR 1996, I-1759, paras 27–28, 31 and 34–35.

41 Article 308 stipulates the following: 'If action by the Community should prove necessary to attain, *in the course of the operation of the common market*, one of the objectives of the Community and this Treaty has not provided the necessary powers, the Council shall, acting unanimously on a proposal from the Commission and after consulting the European Parliament, take the appropriate measures' [emphasis added].

42 Common Declaration [1977], OJ C 103/1, 05.04.1977. On 5 April 1977, the Presidents of the European Parliament, the Council and the Commission of the European Communities signed a joint declaration in Luxembourg affirming that they will do their utmost to protect the fundamental rights enshrined in both the Constitutions of the Member States and ECHR.

43 *Internationale Handelsgesellschaft v. Einfuhr-und Vorratsstelle für Getreide und Futtermittel* Case 11/70 [1970] ECR 1125 [1972] CMLR 255.

44 *Hauer v. Land Rheinland Pfalz* Case 44/79 [1979] ECR 3727.

45 Report of the Court of Justice on Certain Aspects of the Application of the Treaty of the European Union; No. 15/95, p. 5.

46 See *A v. Commission*, Case T-10/93 [1994] ECR II-179, para. 49.

47 *Portugal v. Council*, Case C 268/94 [1996] ECRI-6184, paras 23–24.

48 Unlike the EU, the EC has the power to conclude international treaties in the area of trade and development with third countries, Article 300 (1) TEC provides:

> Where this Treaty provides for the conclusion of agreements between the Community and one or more States or international organisations, the Commission shall make recommendations to the Council, which shall authorise the Commission to open the necessary negotiations. The Commission shall conduct these negotiations in consultation with special committees appointed by the Council to assist it in this task and within the framework of such directives as the Council may issue to it.

However, under the new Article 47 TFEU Lisbon Treaty the EU is awarded legal personality.

49 The Lomé Convention is an agreement between the EC and African, Caribbean and Pacific States on cooperation in the development of all economic sectors, and in matters of cultural, social and regional cooperation and the protection of the environment. In the field of trade cooperation, the Lomé Convention aimed at developing trade relations between the ACP states and the EC, among ACP states and neighbouring countries in the region, and industrialisation and development of the agricultural sector. The Fourth Lomé Convention was signed on December 15, 1989 between 68 ACP states and 12 EEC members. The Convention, which was concluded for a period of ten years, provided for ACP–EC cooperation in the following areas: Cooperation on issues dealing with the environment, agricultural cooperation and food security, development of services, industrial development, cultural, social and regional cooperation; finance structural adjustment support, debt, investment and development financing; trade agreements, commodities and the stabilisation of export earning, including mining products. At the start of Lomé IV, however, it was agreed that a mid-term review would take place and that the Financial Protocol could be renewed for the second-half of the term. Negotiations finally closed in Mauritius in November 1995. By that time, three new countries had joined the Convention – Finland, Sweden and Austria – while provisions were made for the accession of South Africa and Somalia to the grouping.

50 For further details on Lomé I-III, see Andrew Williams, *EU Human Rights Policies: A Study in Irony*, p. 25ff.
51 International Covenant on Civil and Political Rights, adopted 16 December 1966, entered into force 23 March 1976, GA Resolution 2200 (XX), 999 UNTS 171.
52 Fourth ACP–EEC Convention signed at Lomé on 15 December 1989, OJ L 229/3, 17.08.1991.
53 For the specific human rights content of Lomé IV, see Gillian White, 'Structural Adjustment with a Human Face and Human Rights in Development: New Approaches in the Fourth Lomé Convention', in R. S. and R. P. Dhokalia (eds), *International Law in Transition – Essays in Memory of Judge Nagendra Singh*, p. 56ff.
54 Communication from the Commission to the Council on Human Rights, Democracy and Development Cooperation, EC-Bulletin 3–1991, 122–23.
55 Vienna Convention on the Law of Treaties, concluded 23 May 1969, entered into force 27 January 1980, 1155 UNTS 331.
56 Agreement amending the fourth ACP–EC Convention of Lomé signed in Mauritius on 4 November 1995, OJ L 156, 29.05.1998.
57 See Anette Windmeißer, 'Der Menschenrechtsansatz in der Entwicklungszusammenarbeit', pp. 377–87.
58 Signed in Cotonou on 23 June 2000, OJ L 317, 15.12.2000.
59 Article 96(2) of the Agreement stipulates:

> If, despite the political dialogue conducted regularly between the Parties, a Party considers that the other Party has failed to fulfil an obligation stemming from respect for human rights, democratic principles and the rule of law referred to in paragraph 2 of Article 9, it shall, except in cases of special urgency, supply the other Party and the Council of Ministers with the relevant information required for a thorough examination of the situation with a view to seeking a solution acceptable to the Parties … The term 'cases of special urgency' shall refer to exceptional cases of particularly serious and flagrant violation of one of the essential elements referred to in paragraph 2 of Article 9, that require an immediate reaction … The Party resorting to the special urgency procedure shall inform the other Party and the Council of Ministers separately of the fact unless it does not have time to do so … It is understood that suspension would be a measure of last resort.

60 For more detail, see Olufemi Babarinde and Gerrit Faber 'The EU and the Developing Countries: The Cotonou Agreement'.
61 Council Decisions 2001/131/EC, 2001/510/EC, 2002/148/EC and 2001/334/EC. For more details, see also Elena Fierro, *The EU's Approach to Human rights Conditionality in Practice*, p. 321ff.
62 Article 11 of the Cotonou Agreement (OJ L 317, 15.12.2000, pp. 3–353, as amended by OJ L 209, 11.8.2005, pp. 27–53).
63 Above note 59, pp. 384–387.
64 Marjorie Lister, *The European Community and the Developing World*, p. 215.
65 EP Resolution of 8 May 2008 on the Annual Report on Human Rights in the World 2007.
66 GSP Regulation 980/2005.
67 An overview of agreements containing a human rights clause is available at the Treaties Office of the Commission: http://ec.europa.eu/world/agreements/default.home.do.
68 EIDHR, OJ L 120 of 08.05.1999, laying down the requirements for the implementation of development cooperation operations which contribute to the general objective of developing and consolidating democracy and the rule of law and to that

of respecting human rights and fundamental freedoms; see also at http://europa.eu.int/comm/europeaid/projects/eidhr/eidhr_en.htm.

69 Regulation 1889/2006 of 20 December 2006.

70 The PHARE programme ran out in 2000 and has been replaced by CARDS, which stands for Community Assistance for Reconstruction, Development and Stabilisation, it is the EU's main instrument of financial assistance to the western Balkans, covering specifically the countries of Croatia, Bosnia and Herzegovina, Serbia, Montenegro, the Former Yugoslav Republic of Macedonia and Albania. It was created in 2000 by Council Regulation 2666/2000.

71 Lenz Report on setting up a single coordinating structure within the European Commission responsible for human rights and democratisation, PE 220.735/fin, 4.12.97, p. 9; Imbeni Report on the report from the Commission on the implementation of measures intended to promote observance of human rights and democratic principles (for 1995), COM (96) 0672–C4–0095/97, PE 223.610/fin, 02.12.97; Roubatis Report on 'the European Union and the External Dimension of Human Rights Policy: From Rome to Maastricht and Beyond', COM (95) 0567–C4–0568/95, PE 228.009fin, 06.11.98.

72 See at http://europa.eu.int/comm/europeaid/projects/eidhr/pdf/programming_document.pdf.

73 Ibid. Annex 4.

74 Article J.3 TEU provided: '1. The European Council shall define the principles of and general guidelines for common foreign and security policy, including for matters with defence implications. 2. The European Council shall decide on common strategies to be implemented by the Union in areas where the Member States have important interests in common'.

75 Article J.4 TEU provided: 'The Council shall adopt joint actions. Joint actions shall address specific situations where operational action by the Union is deemed to be required. They shall lay down their objectives, scope, the means to be made available to the Union, if necessary their duration, and the conditions for their implementation.'

76 Article J.5 provided: 'The Council shall adopt common positions. Common positions shall define the approach of the Union to a particular matter of a geographical or thematic nature. Member States shall ensure that their national policies conform to the common positions.'

77 Council Decision of 6 December 1993 on a Joint Action adopted by the Council on the basis of Article J.3 of the Treaty on European Union concerning support for the transition towards a democratic and multi-racial South Africa, 93/678/CFSP, OJ L 316, 17.12.1993.

78 Council Decision of 19 April 1994 on a Joint Action adopted by the Council on the basis of Article J (3) of the Treaty on European Union, in support of the Middle East peace process, 94/276/CFSP, OJ L 119, 07.05.1994.

79 Joint Action adopted by the Council on the basis of Article J.3 of the Treaty on European Union on the Great Lakes Region, 96/669/CFSP, OJ L 312, 02.12.1996.

80 Joint Action of 1 October 1996 adopted by the Council on the basis of Article J.3 of the Treaty on European Union on anti-personnel landmines, 96/588/CFSP, OJ L 260, 12.10.1996.

81 Kapteyn and VerLoren van Themaat, *Introduction to the Law of the European Communities: From Maastricht to Amsterdam*, p. 1274.

82 Council Decision of 24 October 1994 concerning the Common Position adopted by the Council on the basis of Article J.2 of the Treaty on European Union on the objectives and priorities of the European Union vis-à-vis Rwanda, 94/697/CFSP, OJ L 283, 29.10.1994.

83 Common Position of 28 November 1994 defined by the Council on the basis of Article J.2 of the Treaty on European Union on the objectives and priorities of the European Union towards Ukraine, 94/779/CFSP, OJ L 313, 06.12.1994.

84 Common Position of 25 June 1996 defined by the Council on the basis of Article J.2 of the Treaty on European Union, concerning East Timor, 96/407/CFSP, OJ L 168, 06.07.1996.

85 Common Position adopted by the Council on the basis of Article J.2 of the Treaty on European Union on Myanmar (Burma), 96/635/CFSP, OJ L 287, 08.11.1996.

86 Common Position defined on the basis of Article J.2 of the Treaty on European Union concerning the imposition of an embargo on arms, munitions and military equipment on Sudan, 94/165/CFSP, OJ L 75, 17.03.1994.

87 Toby King, 'Human Rights in European Foreign Policy: Success or Failure for Post-Modern Diplomacy', in EJIL 10 (1999) p. 325.

88 Manfred Nowak, 'Human Rights Conditionality in the EU', in Philip Alston (ed.), *The EU and Human Rights,* p. 688.

89 Affirming fundamental rights in the European Union. Time to act. Report of the Expert Group on Fundamental Rights of 1999, pp. 9–10.

90 Anthony Arnull, *The European Union and its Court of Justice*, p. 219.

91 Report by Martti Ahtisaari, Jochen Frowein and Marcelino Oreja, 8 September 2000 at www.mpg.de/pdf/commentsStatements/berichtOesterreich_en.pdf.

92 *P v. Sand Cornwall County Council,* Case C-13/94 [1996] ECR I-2143.

93 Ibid. para. 22.

94 *K. B. v. NHS,* Case C–117/01 [2004] ECRI-541.

95 *Grant v. South West Trains* (especially para. 42), Case C-249/96 [1998] ECR I-621.

96 *D v. Council,* Case C-122 and 125/99 [2001]ECR I-4319.

97 For more detail, see Mark Bell, *Anti-Discrimination Law and the EU* (Oxford University Press, 2002)

98 Council Directive 2000/43/EC of 29 June 2000.

99 See Europa Press Release of 27/06/2007, MEMO/07/263, available at http://europa.eu/rapid/pressReleasesAction.do?reference=MEMO/07/263& format = HTML& aged = 1& language = EN& guiLanguage = fr.

100 For more detail, see Padraig Flynn, 'The Implications of Article 13 E C – After Amsterdam: Will Some Forms of Discrimination Be More Equal than Others?' in 36 CMLR [1999], pp. 1151–52.

101 European Parliament Report on Countering Racism and Xenophobia in the European Union, final A5–0049/2000, para. 8, at 14.

102 See ex-Article 35 TEU.

103 The Geneva Convention of 28 July 1951 on refugees is now mentioned in the first-pillar provisions under Article 63 TEC, regarding measures on asylum.

104 See Steve Peers, 'Human Rights and the Third Pillar', in Philip Alston (ed.), *The EU and Human Rights,* p. 171.

105 Common Position of 25 May 1998 concerning human rights, democratic principles, the rule of law and good governance in Africa, 98/350/CFSP, OJ L 158, 02.06.1998.

106 Joint Action of 22 December 1998 adopted by the Council on the basis of Article J.3 of the Treaty on European Union in support of the democratic process in Nigeria, 98/735/CFSP, OJ L 354, 30.12.1998.

107 Council Common Position of 14 May 2001 on Nigeria, 01/373/CFSP, OJ L 132, 15.05.2001; Council Common Position 2002/401/CFSP of 27 May 2002 on Nigeria repealed Common Position 2001/373/CFSP in order to implement an even more positive and constructive approach towards Nigeria, OJ L 139, 29.05.2002.

108 Council Common Position on Myanmar (Burma) adopted by the Council on the basis of Article J.2 of the Treaty on European Union, 96/635/CFSP, OJ L 287, 08.11.1996.

109 'Regulation' is defined in Article 249 TEC:

> In order to carry out their task and in accordance with the provisions of this Treaty, the European Parliament acting jointly with the Council, the Council and

the Commission shall make regulations and issue directives, take decisions, make recommendations or deliver opinions. A *regulation* shall have general application. It shall be binding in its entirety and directly applicable in all Member States. A directive shall be binding, as to the result to be achieved, upon each Member State to which it is addressed, but shall leave to the national authorities the choice of form and methods. A decision shall be binding in its entirety upon those to whom it is addressed. Recommendations and opinions shall have no binding force.

110 Council Regulation (EC) No 1081/2000 of 22 May 2000 prohibiting the sale, supply and export to Burma/Myanmar of equipment which might be used for internal repression or terrorism, and freezing the funds of certain persons related to important governmental functions in that country, OJ L 122, 24.5.2000, p. 29 and Regulation (EC) No 1211/2003, which amends Regulation 1081/2000, OJ L 169, 08.7.2003, p. 24.
111 Council Common Position of 16 June 2003, OJ L 150, 18.6.2003, p. 67.
112 December 2007 (16395//07), January 2008 (5922/08 and June 2008 (10832/08)).
113 Declaration 7918/08, http://ue.eu.int/cms3_applications/applications/newsRoom/loadBook.asp?BID=73&LANG=1&cmsid=359,.
114 Declaration 12535/1/09 REV1, http://ue.eu.int/cms3_applications/applications/newsRoom/loadBook.asp?BID=73&LANG=1&cmsid=359,.
115 Declaration 11280/09, http://ue.eu.int/cms3_applications/applications/newsRoom/loadBook.asp?BID=73&LANG=1&cmsid=359,.
116 See also: Commission of the European Communities, Communication from the Commission: A Long-term Strategy for China–European Relations, COM (95) 279 final, 5 July 1995, pp. 1–10.
117 See EU Annual Report on Human Rights 2008, 14146/2/08 REV 2, p. 29.
118 See *Commission v. Council* (Air Transport Visas) [1998], Case C–170/96, ECR I-2763.
119 Article 60 TEC provides: '1. If, in the cases envisaged in Article 301, action by the Community is deemed necessary, the Council may, in accordance with the procedure provided for in Article 301, take the necessary urgent measures on the movement of capital and on payments as regards the third countries concerned.' Article 301 TEC provides: 'Where it is provided, in a common position or in a joint action adopted according to the provisions of the Treaty on European Union relating to the common foreign and security policy, for an action by the Community to interrupt or to reduce, in part or completely, economic relations with one or more third countries, the Council shall take the necessary urgent measures. The Council shall act by a qualified majority on a proposal from the Commission.'
120 See Annex IV to the Treaty of Nice, Doc. SN 533/1, pp. 71 and 78, to be found at www.europa.eu.int/futurum/documents/offtext/declaration_de.pdf.
121 Ibid. pp. 79–81.
122 Member States may make use of the mechanism in the fields covered by the TEC (the first pillar) and as regards matters concerning police and judicial cooperation in criminal matters. The conditions and procedures for closer cooperation are laid down in Articles 40 and 43–45 of the TEU and in Article 11 TEC. These conditions provide for a right of veto for every Member State that opposes closer cooperation, even if that Member State does not wish to participate. Furthermore, the current provisions require a majority of members to start closer cooperation. The provisions on closer cooperation have so far not been used in practice. Under the Treaty of Nice the possibility of establishing closer cooperation will in future also be possible within the 'second pillar', i.e. CFSP, in order to implement a joint action or Common Position. It may not, however, involve matters with military or defence implications; a minimum of eight Member States is required to form closer cooperation and the veto mechanism has been abolished. Whether these new provisions will promote the human rights policy within the EU remains to be seen; at least in theory enhanced cooperation offers the opportunity for more committed Member States to include

human rights in joint actions or Common Positions more often than it would have been possible with the participation of all Member States. With the enlargement to a total of 27 Member States enhanced cooperation might become a useful instrument for the further promotion of human rights. It has not yet acquired any significance in the EU's human rights policy.

123 See at www.europa.eu.int/comm/justice_home/unit/charte/en/about-status.html.

124 For a detailed account of the genesis of the Charter, see Mats Lindfelt, p. 103ff.

125 See Annex IV to the conclusions of the Presidency of the Cologne European Council of 3 and 4 June 1999, http:/www.europarl.eu.int/dg7/summits/en/kol2.htm#UP. The Charter itself can be found in OJC 306, 14.12.2007.

126 E.g. by the ICCPR, ECHR, the Convention against Torture or the Convention on Elimination of Discrimination against Women, all of which create obligations for states to protect the fundamental human rights of their citizens.

127 Joseph Weiler, 'European Citizenship and Human Rights', in Jan A. Winter et al. (eds), *Reforming the Treaty on European Union: the Legal Debate*, pp.79–81.

128 See for example A. G. Toth, 'Human Rights as General Principles of Law, in the past and in the future', in U. Bernitz and J. Nergelius (eds), *General Principles of European Union Law*, pp.73–92.

129 *Affirming fundamental rights in the European Union. Time to Act. Report of the Expert Group on Fundamental Rights*, 1999, p. 12.

130 Article 51 states:

> 1. The provisions of this Charter are addressed to the institutions and bodies of the Union with due regard for the principle of subsidiarity and to the Member States only when they are implementing Union law. They shall therefore respect the rights, observe the principles and promote the application thereof in accordance with their respective powers. 2. This Charter does not establish any new power or task for the Community or the Union, or modify powers and tasks defined by the Treaties.

131 Treaty establishing a Constitution for the European Union, OJC 310 of 16 December 2004.

132 See Xavier Groussot, *Development and Impact of the General Principles of Community law: Towards a Jus Commune Europaeum?* pp. 171–72.

133 Koen Lenaerts and Eddy De Smijter, 'A Bill of Rights for the European Union', in CMLR, vol. 38, pp. 273–300, p. 289.

134 *European Parliament v. Council of the European Union*, Case 540/03.

135 The Directive stipulates the conditions for family reunification by third-country nationals who reside lawfully in a Member State.

136 Above note 134, para. 38.

137 Ibid.

138 *Reynolds Tobacco Holdings v. Commission*, Case C-131/03 [2006] ECR I-7795.

139 See for example AG Colomer in Case C–466/00 *Kaba v. Secretary of State for the Home Department* [2003] ECR I-2219, para. 74 and Case C-208/00 *Überseering v. NCC* [2002] ECR I-9919, para. 59. Or AG Tizanno in Case C–173/99 BECTU [2001] ECR I-4881, para. 4883.

140 *max.mobil Telekommunikation Service GmbH v. Commission*, Case T-54/99 [2002] ECR II-313.

141 *Jégo-Quéré v. Commission*, Case T–177/01} [2002] ECR-II-02365, paras 42–47.

142 COM (2005) 172 final.

143 See below section 2.5.7, for more details on impact assessments.

144 Still the Charter was not legally binding as it only entered into force with the Treaty of Lisbon 1 December 2009. See also Mats Lindfelt, *Fundamental Rights in the European Union: Towards Higher Law of the Land?*, p. 237 and fn 712–13.

145 The reports can be accessed at http://ec.europa.eu/justice_home/cfr_cdf.

146 See at http://ec.europa.eu/justice_home/cfr_cdf/doc/report_eu_2005_en.pdf.
147 For further critique, see Andrew Williams 'The Indifferent Gesture: Article 7 TEU, the Fundamental Rights Agency and the UK's Invasion of Iraq' in *European Law Review* (2006) 31.
148 See http://ec.europa.eu/external_relations/enp/index_en.htm.
149 *EU Annual Report on Human Rights 2005*, p. 105.
150 EP Report on the Annual Report on Human Rights in the World 2005 and the EU's policy on the matter, p. 23.
151 See Article 27 Treaty of Nice:

> Enhanced co-operation in any of the areas referred to in this Title shall be aimed at safe-guarding the values and serving the interests of the Union as a whole by asserting its identity as a coherent force on the international scene. It shall respect: the principles, objectives, general guidelines and consistency of the common foreign and security policy and the decisions taken within the framework of that policy … Enhanced co-operation pursuant to this Title shall relate to implementation of a joint action or a common position. It shall not relate to matters having military or defence implications.

152 For further reference, see Thomas Jaeger, 'Enhanced Co-operation in the Treaty of Nice and Flexibility in the Common Foreign and Security Policy', in *European Foreign Affairs Review* (2002), 7: 297–316.
153 Helen Toner, 'Impact Assessments and Fundamental Rights Protection in EU Law', in 31 *European Law Review* (2006), 316–41, at 318.
154 International Association for Impact Assessment website www.iaia.org.
155 Ibid.
156 See the Communication 'Compliance with the Charter of Fundamental Rights in Commission legislative proposals. Methodology for systematic and rigorous monitoring', COM(2005) 172 final, 27 April 2005.
157 See Impact Assessment Guidelines, SEC(2005) 791, 15 June 2005, table 3 (social impacts), 31–32, available online at http://europa.eu.int/comm/secretariat_general/impact/docs/SEC2005_791_IA%20guidelines_annexes.pdf.
158 For further details, see Gabriel Toggenburg, 'The EU's Evolving Policies vis-à-vis Minorities: A Play in Four Parts and an Open End', EUR.AC research August 2008, pp. 15–17.
159 Evaluation of the Commission's Impact Assessment System, Final Report, April 2007, p. 45, at http://ec.europa.eu/governance/impact/key_docs/docs/tep_eias_final_report.pdf.
160 Ibid. p. 42.
161 Impact Assessment Board Report for 2008, Third Strategic Review of Better Regulation in the European Union, COM(2009) 15 final, p. 10.
162 Above note 159, p. 16.
163 For more detail see Oliver De Schutter, 'Mainstreaming Human Rights in the European Union', in Alston and De Schutter (eds), *European Law*, pp. 52–54.
164 See OJC 310/47 of 16 December 2004; this treaty was never ratified.
165 See also Paul Craig, 'The Treaty of Lisbon, Process, Architecture and Substance', in *European Law Review* (2008), 33(2), p. 139.
166 For further reference, see Tridimas, *General Principles of EC Law*, p. 366.
167 The Charter rights are only limited by Article 53 (1) which states that 'Any limitation on the exercise of the rights and freedoms recognised by this Charter must be provided for by law and respect the essence of those rights and freedoms. Subject to the principle of proportionality, limitations may be made only if they are necessary and genuinely meet objectives of general interest recognised by the Union or the need to protect the rights and freedoms of others.' The ECHR, by way of contrast, provides

every right with a limitation in the same provision in its second subsection, see for example Article 9 which provides:

> 1. Everyone has the right to freedom of thought, conscience and religion; this right includes freedom to change his religion or belief and freedom, either alone or in community with others and in public or private, to manifest his religion or belief, in worship, teaching, practice and observance. 2. Freedom to manifest one's religion or beliefs shall be subject only to such limitations as are prescribed by law and are necessary in a democratic society in the interests of public safety, for the protection of public order, health or morals, or for the protection of the rights and freedoms of others.

168 'Accession of the European Union to the European Convention on Human Rights', Reflection paper prepared by the Secretariat, for consideration at the meeting of the GR–EU on 14 February 2001, DG-II(2001)002.

169 Article 6 (1) TEU stipulates:

> The Union recognises the rights, freedoms and principles set out in the Charter of Fundamental Rights of the European Union of 7 December 2000, as adapted at Strasbourg, on 12 December 2007, which shall have the same legal value as the Treaties. The rights, freedoms and principles in the Charter shall be interpreted in accordance with the general provisions in Title VII of the Charter governing its interpretation and application and with due regard to the explanations referred to in the Charter, that set out the sources of those provisions. The provisions of the Charter shall not extend in any way the competences of the Union as defined in the Treaties.

170 Declaration No. 1 concerning the Charter of Fundamental Rights of the European Union, Treaty of Lisbon.

171 Protocol on the Application of the Charter of Fundamental Rights of the European Union to Poland and to the United Kingdom, Treaty of Lisbon.

172 Above note 165, p. 163.

173 COM (2007) 412.

174 For criticism see, e.g. Koen Lenaerts, 'Fundamental Rights in the European Union', in *European Law Review* (2000) 25; J. H. H.Weiler and N. Lockhart 'Taking Rights Seriously: The European Court and Its Fundamental Rights Jurisprudence' in (1995) 32 CMLR, pp. 51 and 597; Andrew Williams, *EU Human Rights Policies: A Study in Irony*.

175 The issue of international organisations violating human rights is little explored; see Guilliermo Verdirame 'Breaches of the European Convention on Human Rights Resulting from the Conduct of International Organisations' in (2008), EHRLR, 2, 209–13.

176 Articles 230ff. TEC regulate the procedures before the ECJ.

177 Meinhard Hilf, 'Ein Grundrechtskatalog für die Europäische Gemeinschaft', in (1991), *Europarecht*, 26, 24–27 and see Report of the Commission of 4 February 1976, EC Bulletin, Supplement 5/76.

178 *See Stork & Co v. High Authority*, Case 1/58 [1959] ECR 17, para. 26; *Präsident Ruhrkohlen-Verkaufsgesellschaft GmbH v. High Authority*, Case 36/59 [1960] ECR 423, para. 438.

179 See *van Gend en Loos v. Netherlands Inland Revenue Administration*, Case 26/62 [1963] ECR 1 and *Alfons Lütticke GmbH v. Hauptzollamt Sarrelouis* Case 57/65 [1966] ECR 205.

180 For more details on direct effect, see Erika Szysczak and Adam Cygan, *Understanding EU Law*, p. 103ff.

181 *Internationale Handelsgesellschaft v. Einfuhr und Vorratsstelle für Getreide und Futtermittel.* Case 11/70 [1970] ECR 1125, [1972] CMLR 255.

182 See also earlier case *Stauder v. Ulm*, Case 29/69 [1969] ECR 419, para. 425. The case turned on the interpretation of the different language texts of a Commission decision: the Commission decision had a requirement that recipients of the EC's cheap surplus butter had to prove their entitlement to welfare benefit. The German and Dutch texts both required the person to give a coupon indicating their name whereas the French and Italian texts simply required that a coupon be given referring to the person concerned. Stauder argued that it was a breach of his fundamental rights to have to reveal his name to those selling the cheap butter. The ECJ followed the liberal interpretation of the French and Italian text and thereby avoided any possibility of a breach of fundamental rights, the ECJ established its acceptance of the concept by saying: 'Interpreted in this way the provision at issue contains nothing capable of prejudicing the fundamental human rights enshrined in the general principles of Community law and protected by the Court.'

183 See above note 181, para. 3, the claimant's argument was that the obligation to import or export resulting from the issue of licenses, together with the deposit system attached thereto, constitutes an excessive intervention in the freedom of disposition in trade, as the objective of the regulations could have been obtained by methods of intervention having less serious consequences, thereby violating in particular articles 2 (1) and 14 of the German Basic Law.

184 *Staatsanwaltschaft Freiburg v. Franz Keller*, Case 234/85 [1986] ECR 2897, [1987] I CMLR 875.

185 Article 12(1) of the German Basic Law provides: 'All Germans shall have the right to choose freely their occupation or profession, and their place of training.'

186 See *Hauer v. Land Rheinland Pfalz*, Case 44/79 [1979] ECR 3727, paras 3744–50, where the ECJ referred to the German, Italian and Irish Constitutions in establishing the scope of the right to property.

187 For a more detailed discussion of this issue, see Bruno de Witte, 'Direct Effect, Supremacy and the Nature of Legal Order', in *The Evolution of EU Law*, p. 201.

188 *Re Wünsche Handelsgesellschaft* [1987] 3 CMLR 225.

189 See *Solange I BverfGE* 37, 271 of 29.05.1974 *and Solange II BverfGE* 73, 339 of 22.10.1986. See also Craig and de Búrca, 'EU Law', ch. 10, on the different Member States' perspectives.

190 *Nold v. Commission*, Case 4/73 [1974] ECR 491, [1974] 2 CMLR 338.

191 Common Declaration [1977], OJ C 103/1, 05.04.1977.

192 *Rutili v. Minister for the Interior* Case 36/75 [1975] ECR 1219.

193 *Hauer v. Land Rheinland Pfalz*, Case 44/79 [1979] ECR 3727, [1980] 3 CMLR 42.

194 Article 1 of the First Protocol to the ECHR provides: 'Every natural or legal person is entitled to the peaceful enjoyment of his possessions. No one shall be deprived of his possessions except in the public interest and subject to the conditions provided for by law and by the general principles of international law'.

195 *Wachauf v. Bundesamt für Ernährung und Forstwirtschaft*, Case 5/88 [1989] ECR 2609.

196 *Kremzow v. Austrian Republic*, Case C–299/95 [1997] ECR I-2629, paras 15ff. and 19. Kremzow had been found guilty of murder and was sentenced to life imprisonment by the Austrian courts. The ECtHR, however, found a violation of Article 6(3) ECHR in Kremzow's case. Following that decision, Kremzow initiated various proceedings in Austria for unlawful detention, furthermore he asked for a preliminary ruling of the ECJ on grounds that his freedom of movement protected under the TEC has been violated.

197 The Community interest mainly can be seen in the establishment of a common market, an economic union and the promotion of economic and social cohesion and solidarity among Member States (see Article 2 TEC).

198 See preamble of the ECHR and *Soering v. UK*, Series A 161, (1989), para. 87.

199 *Prais v. Council*, Case 130/75 [1976] ECR 1589, [1976] 2 CMLR 708.

200 Article 9 provides:

> 1. Everyone has the right to freedom of thought, conscience and religion; this right includes freedom to change his religion or belief and freedom, either alone or in community with others and in public or private, to manifest his religion or belief, in worship, teaching, practice and observance. 2. Freedom to manifest one's religion or beliefs shall be subject only to such limitations as are prescribed by law and are necessary in a democratic society in the interests of public safety, for the protection of public order, health or morals, or for the protection of the rights and freedoms of others.

201 Above note 186, para.18.

202 *Oyowe and Traore v. Commission*, Case 100/88, [1989] ECR 4285.

203 Article 10 provides:

> 1. Everyone has the right to freedom of expression. This right shall include freedom to hold opinions and to receive and impart information and ideas without interference by public authority and regardless of frontiers. This Article shall not prevent States from requiring the licensing of broadcasting, television or cinema enterprise. 2. The exercise of these freedoms, since it carries with it duties and responsibilities, may be subject to such formalities, conditions, restrictions or penalties as are prescribed by law and are necessary in a democratic society, in the interests of national security, territorial integrity or public safety, for the prevention of disorder or crime, for the protection of health or morals, for the protection of the reputation or rights of others, for preventing the disclosure of information received in confidence, or for maintaining the authority and impartiality of the judiciary.

204 *Schmidberger v. Austria*, Case 112/00 [2003] ECR I-5659.

205 *Omega Spielhallen und Automatenaufstellungs GmbH v. Stadt Bonn*, Case 36/02, [2004] ECR I-9609.

206 *Kadi v. Council and Commission*, Case T-315/01, [2005] ECR II-0000; *Yussuf and Al Barakaat International v. Council*, Case T-306/01, [2005] ECR II-0000.

207 P. Allot, 'Epilogue: Europe and the Dream of Reason', in Weiler and Wind (eds), *European Constitutionalism Beyond the State*, p. 217.

208 Above note 205, para. 49. For further discussion of the relationship between economic freedoms and fundamental rights, see Tridimas, *General Principles of EC Law*, pp. 337–41.

209 *Funke v. France*, Series A, No 256 A (1993), para. 44 of the judgment.

210 *Niemitz v. Germany*, Series A, No. 251 (1992).

211 *Hoechst AG v. Commission*, Case 46/87, [1989] ECR 2859, [1991] 4 CM3LR 410.

212 Article 8 ECHR provides:

> 1. Everyone has the right to respect for his private and family life, his home and his correspondence. 2. There shall be no interference by a public authority with the exercise of this right except such as is in accordance with the law and is necessary in a democratic society in the interests of national security, public safety or the economic well-being of the country, for the prevention of disorder or crime, for the protection of health or morals, or for the protection of the rights and freedoms of others.

213 Above note 210, para.31.

214 *Roquette Frères SA v. Directeur de la Concurrence*, Case 94/00 [2002] ECR I-9011.

215 *Orkem v. Commission*, Case 374/87, [1989] ECR 3283, [1991] 4 CMLR 502.

216 See above note 209. The applicant was convicted of an offence of failing to produce bank statements relevant to investigations into customs offences that might have been

committed by him. The ECJ held that, by attempting to compel him to produce incriminating evidence, the state had infringed his right to remain silent.

217 *Orkem v. Commission*, Case 374/87, Opinion of Advocate-General Darmon on 18 May 1989, paras 139–40.

218 *Danzer v. Council*, Case T- [2006] ECRII-1779.

219 *Emesa Sugar v. Aruba*, Case 17-/98 [2000] ECR I 555.

220 *Vermeulen v. Belgium*, [1996] ECHR Case 19075/91, para.33.

221 *Open Door Counselling Ltd and Dublin Well Women Centre v. Ireland*, Series A No. 246 (1992) 15 EHRR 244.

222 *SPUC v. Grogan*, Case C–159/90, [1991] ECRI-4685.

223 *Elliniki Radiophonia Tileorassi AE v. Dimotiki Etairia Pliroforissis and Sotirios Kouvelas*, Case C-160/89 [1991] ECR I-1281.

224 *Informationsverein Lentia and Others v. Austria*, Series A, No. 276 (1993).

225 Koen Lenaerts, 'Fundamental Rights in the European Union', in *European Law Review* (2000) 25, p. 580.

226 S. O'Leary, 'Accession by the European Community to the European Convention on Human Rights – The Opinion of the ECJ', in *European Human Rights Law Review*, vol. 4, 1996.

227 See the cases of *Schmidberger*, *Omega Spielhallen* or *Grant v. South West Trains, P v. Sand Cornwall County*.

228 This issue will not be discussed here. See Laurance Helfer, 'Redesigning the European Court of Human Rights: Embeddedness as a Deep Structural Principle of the European Human Rights Regime', in (200) EJIL, 19(1), pp. 125–59.

229 *Pafitis and Others v. Greece*, Reports 1998-I, 26 February 1998.

230 Ibid. para. 95 of the judgment.

231 *Matthews v. UK*, Reports 1999-I, 18 February 1999.

232 See in particular the joint dissenting opinion of Judges Freeland and Jungwiert on the question of whether the ECJ can pronounce itself on acts of the EC.

233 See para. 33 of the judgment.

234 Ibid.

235 Ibid. para. 32.

236 *Bosphorus Hava Yollari Turizm v. Ireland* (2006) 42 EHRR 1.

237 Ibid. para. 156

238 *M & Co. v. Germany*, [1990] ECHR (Ser. A), p. 138.

239 See Cathryn Costello, 'The *Bosphorus* Ruling of the European Court of Human Rights: Fundamental Rights and Blurred Boundaries in Europe', in (2006) HRLR, 6(1), pp. 87–130, p. 94.

240 Article 230(4) TEC (now Article 263 TFEU) states: 'Any natural or legal person may, under the same conditions, institute proceedings against a decision addressed to that person or against a decision which, although in the form of a regulation or a decision addressed to another person, is of direct and individual concern to the former.'

241 Above note 236, see concurring opinion, para. 2

242 Another recent case that illustrates the ECtHR's perspective on human rights competences among international organisations was *Behrami* (*Behrami and Others v. France, Germany and Norway*, decision of 2 May 2007). In form of an admissibility decision, the Strasbourg judges had to assess whether some Member States could be held liable under the ECHR for actions committed under UN military mandates in Kosovo. Here, the ECtHR ruled rather cautiously, after investigating the conditions of the challenged mandates, the structure of command and the possibility of attributing the actions to the UN, it decided that the responsibility for the possible human rights violation was not with the Member State but with the UN mandate. Hence, the ECtHR declined jurisdiction *ratione personae*, because the ultimate authority and control over the missions remained with the UN Security Council. See also above note 206, *Al Barakaat* case, C 415/05 *Al Barakaat International Foundation v. Council of the*

European Union and Commission of the European Communities, Opinion Advocate-General Poiares Maduro of 23 January 2008, para. 24.

243 See R. Macdonald, 'The Margin of Appreciation', in R. Macdonald et al., *The European System for the Protection of Human Rights*, p. 83.

244 *Brannigan and Mc Bride v. UK*, Judgment of 26 May 1993, Series A, No. 258-B; (1994) 17 EHRR 539.

245 The presence of a judge representing the EC/EU would be justified on the same grounds as the presence of a judge appointed in respect of each State Party (representation of every legal system in the ECJ). Election of a full-time judge to represent the EC/EU would not require amendments to Articles 20 or 22 ECHR which already uses the term 'High Contracting Parties' and not 'States' in the applicable provisions. Article 20 ECHR provides that the number of judges shall be 'equal to that of the High Contracting Parties'.

246 See Tridimas, *General Principles of EC Law*, p. 352.

247 Protocol Relating to Article 6(2) of the Treaty on European Union on the Accession of the Union to the European Convention on the Protection of Human Rights and Fundamental Freedoms, Treaty of Lisbon.

248 Declaration No. 2 on Article 6(2) of the Treaty on European Union, Treaty of Lisbon. For the current EU–CoE dialogue, see chapter 3.

249 See also Study of Technical and Legal Issues of a possible EU/EC accession to the European Convention on Human Rights. Report adopted by the Steering Committee for Human Rights (CDDH) at its 53rd meeting, DG-II (2002) 006.

250 A valuable detailed analysis can be found in Steve Peers, 'Statewatch Analysis of the EU Reform Treaty', available at www.statewatch.org/.

251 See the Council Regulation (EC) No. 168/2007 of 15 February 2007, in OJ L 53, 22.02.2007.

252 The Member States' NHRIs are inspired by the so–called 'Paris Principles' established by a resolution issued by the UN General Assembly in 1993.

253 See Article 4(2) of the Proposal for a Council regulation establishing a European Union Agency for Fundamental Rights COM (2005) 280.

254 For further discussion see Gabriel Toggenburg, 'The Role of the new EU Fundamental Rights Agency: Debating the Sex of Angels or Improving Europe's Human Rights Performance?', in *European Law Review* (2008), 33(3), p. 390ff.

255 Ibid. p. 394.

256 See the EPs' legislative Resolution of January 17, 2008 (P6 TA(2008)0014) which is based on the Cashman report A6–0514/2007 as of 20 December 2007, Amendment 11 of the Parliament's Resolution. For the Commission Proposal (which was hardly changed by the Council), see Commission Proposal for a Council decision implementing Regulation (EC) No. 168 (2007) as regards the adoption of a Multi-annual Framework for the European Union Agency for Fundamental Rights for 2007–12 COM(2007) 515 final.

257 For more details on FRA–CoE cooperation, see chapter 3, at section 3.7.1.3.

258 See above note 204, para. 74.

259 Tridimas, *General Principles of EC Law*, p. 340.

Chapter 3

1 Martine Fouwels, 'The EU's Common Foreign and Security Policy and Human Rights', in NQHR 3/1997, p. 324. Enzo Cannizzaro, (ed.), *The European Union as an Actor in International Relations*, pp. 297–302; Andrew Clapham, 'Where is the EU's Human Rights Common Foreign Policy, and How is it Manifested in Multilateral Fora?' in Philip Alston et al. (eds), *The EU and Human Rights*, pp. 627–83.

2 The book will not address the security aspect of the CFSP, but the 'common foreign policy' will be abbreviated with 'CFSP'.
3 Member States such as the UK, Italy and Spain as well as the new Member State Poland supported the military intervention, which was fiercely opposed by other Member States.
4 Karen E. Smith, 'The EU, Human Rights and Relations with Third Countries: Foreign Policy with an Ethical Dimension?', in Karen E. Smith and Margot Light (eds), *Ethics and Foreign Policy*, p. 186.
5 See chapter 2, section 2.3.1.
6 COM (95) 216 final, 23 May 1995, On the Inclusion of Respect for Democratic Principles and Human Rights in Agreements between the Community and Third countries; and COM (2001) 252 final, 8 May 2001, The European Union's Role in Promoting Human Rights and Democratisation in Third Countries.
7 Edward Carr, 'The Twenty Years Crisis 1919–39: An Introduction to the Study of International Relations', p.87.
8 Above note 4, p. 188.
9 Roy H. Ginsberg, 'Foreign Policy Actions of the European Community: the Politics of Scale', p. 3.
10 David Allen, 'Who speaks for Europe?', in John Peterson and Helene Sjursen (eds), *A Common Foreign Policy for Europe? Competing visions of the CFSP*, p.56.
11 Andrew Clapham, 'Human Rights and the European Community: A Critical Overview', p. 76.
12 See Renzo Imbeni, Rapport sur les droits de l'homme dans le monde en 1993/1994 et de la politique de l'Union en matière des droits de l'homme, Commission des Affaires étrangères, de la sécurité et de la politique de la défense, Documents de Séance, A4–0078/95, 12 April 1995, p. 8.
13 Despite Russia's interventions in Chechnya in 2004, that entailed grave human rights violation, suspension of the cooperation agreements with Russia has not been seriously considered.
14 No suspension of aid followed the military coup in 1999. The invasion of Georgia by Russia in August 2008 divided EU Member States which gave varied responses to the crisis and disagreed on who was to blame. Some Member States (UK, Estonia and Lithuania) called for the suspension of the new partnership agreement of 2008 with Russia, however, France, the holder of the EU Presidency at the time, refused to condemn either side and succeeded in brokering a ceasefire with the help of the OSCE.
15 See in particular the EU's list of sanctions against third countries on the Council's website, where, apart from China, no economically important country appears, at http://ec.europa.eu/external_relations/cfsp/sanctions/measures.htm.
16 See Anette Windmeißer, *Der Menschenrechtsansatz in der Entwicklungszusammenarbeit*, pp. 377–87.
17 Above note 6. See also the *Comité des Sages* report, which argued for an informed, consistent and credible human rights policy for the EU. *Leading by Example – A Human Rights Agenda for the European Union for the Year 2000 – European University Institute* (October 1998– Report commissioned by the EC on the occasion of the 50th anniversary of the UDHR. Available at www.iue.it/AEL/events.htm).
18 Ibid. pp. 5–6.
19 Above note 1, p. 296.
20 J. Koppel and A. O'Neill, 'The European Court of Justice: Taking Rights Seriously', 29 (1992) CMLR 669; Andrew Williams, *EU Human Rights Policy – A Study in Irony*, chapters 2–4.
21 Takis Tridimas, *Principles of EU Law*, p. 299.
22 The Badinter Commission, Joint Statement, 28 August 1991, 24 EC Bulletin, No. 7/8, p. 115 (1991).

23 'EC – Guidelines on the Recognition of New States in Eastern Europe and in the Soviet Union, EC Foreign Affairs Council', 16 December 1991, reprinted in UKMIL 1991 (1991) 62 BYIL 559.
24 Conference on Yugoslavia, Arbitration Commission, Opinion No. 1, 29 November 1991: 92 ILR 162, p. 163.
25 Conference on Yugoslavia, Arbitration Commission, Opinion No. 2, 11 January 1992: 92 ILR 167, pp. 168–69.
26 See Will Kymlicka, 'The Evolving Basis of European Norms of Minority Rights', in Mark Weller et al. (eds), *The Protection of Minorities in the Wider Europe*, p. 14.
27 For more details, see Roland Rich, 'The Recognition of States: The Collapse of Yugoslavia and the Soviet Union', 4 (1993), EJIL, pp. 36–65.
28 Presidency Conclusions of the European Council, Luxembourg, 28–29 June, 1991; Annex V, para. 7. SN 151/2/91.
29 Council Declaration of 11 May 1992 concerning relations of the EC with CSCE States (1992), 5 Bulletin EC para.1.2.13. Presidency Conclusions of the European Council, Luxembourg, 28–29 June, 1991; Annex V, para. 7. SN 151/2/91.
30 Conclusions of the Presidency of the European Council, Copenhagen 21–22 June 1993.
31 See Annex III to Council Conclusions, Luxembourg 29–30 April 1997, in EU Bulletin, 4(1997).
32 For more details on enlargement policy and minorities, see chapter 4, section 4.4.1.
33 See Karen E. Smith, 'The Making of EU Foreign Policy: The Case of Eastern Europe', pp.136–37.
34 Political scientists have tried to build theories around the idea that all action is fundamentally 'rational' in character and that people calculate the likely costs and benefits of any action before deciding what to do. This approach to theory is known as rational choice theory, as embodied particularly in realist theory.
35 Karen E. Smith, 'The Making of EU Foreign Policy: The Case of Eastern Europe', pp. 12–13.
36 For the cost of enlargement and the 'adjustment strains', see Agenda 2000 (COM (97) 15 July 1997 (2000 Vol. II)), in Bulletin of the European Union, Supplement 97/05.
37 Jürgen Habermas, *The Inclusion of the Other*, p. 14.
38 Arnold Wolfers, *Discord and Collaboration: Essays on International Politics*, p. 93.
39 Robert Keohane, *After Hegemony*, p. 123, fn 9.
40 Helene Sjursen and Karen E. Smith, 'Justifying EU Foreign Policy', ARENA Working Papers WP 01/01, p. 9.
41 This is particularly manifested by the frequent appearances of the High Representative of CFSP, Javier Solana, at crucial points of international conflict.
42 For further reference see S. R. Rock, *Why Peace Breaks Out. Great Power Rapprochement in Historical Perspective.*
43 Lily Gardner Feldman, 'Foreign Relations and Enlargement of the EU', in Thomas Banchoff and Mitchell P. Smith (eds), *Legitimacy and the European Union: The Contested Polity*, p. 69.
44 Ibid. p. 70.
45 Will Kymlicka, 'The Evolving Basis of European Norms of Minority Rights', p. 14.
46 James Hughes and Gwendolyn Sasse, 'Monitoring the Monitors: EU Enlargement Conditionality and Minority Protection in the CEECs', in JEMIE 1/2003; see in particular Andrew Williams, *EU Human Rights Policy – A Study in Irony.*
47 In fact, the lack of cooperation has been criticised by Tudyka, who claims that the secretariats of international organisations are characterised by jealousy, competition and dominance, rather than cooperation. K. P. Tudyka, *Die Vernetzung der Europäischen Institutionen*, OSZE Handbuch, p. 89.
48 See chapter 2, section 2.5.4.
49 Arrangement between the Council of Europe and the European Community, concluded on 16 June 1987.

50 See at http://ec.europa.eu/external_relations/coe/index.htm.
51 See Document 15595/08 (Presse 325).
52 Joint Declaration at www.jp.coe.int/Upload/91_Joint_Declaration_EF.pdf.
53 Ministers' Deputies Document, 'Action Plan' CM (2005) final 17 May 2005. See in particular, the ten guidelines on the relationship between the EU and the CoE in appendix 1 of this action plan.
54 Memorandum of Understanding between the Council of Europe and the European Union, Recommendation 1743 (2006).
55 For a complete list of the current joint programmes, see www.jp.coe.int/docs/default.asp?Link=0.
56 Currently, a key priority for the EU and CoE cooperation is the promotion of democratic stability and peace, both in the western Balkans (Albania, Bosnia and Herzegovina, Croatia, Serbia, including Kosovo, Montenegro and FYROM) and in the south Caucasus region (Armenia, Azerbaijan and Georgia). The Joint Programmes aim to support the participation of these countries in the EU's SAP, or ENP, thus facilitating closer association and integration with the EU.
57 See Gabriel Toggenburg, 'The EU's role vis-à-vis Minorities after the Enlargement Decade', in Mark Weller et al. (eds), *The Protection of Minorities in the Wider Europe*, p. 116; and DSP(2004) 21, European Commission/Council of Europe Joint Programmes, Scoreboard Report October 2004.
58 The European Commission for Democracy through Law, better known as the Venice Commission, is the CoE's advisory body on constitutional matters. Established in 1990, the Commission has played a leading role in the adoption of constitutions that conform to the standards of Europe's constitutional heritage.
59 Agreement on Cooperation, OJL L 186/7, 15.7.2008.
60 Council of Europe Convention on Action Against Trafficking in Human Persons 2005 ETS No.197.
61 For criticism of this practice, see speech by Serhiy Holovaty, chairperson of the Parliamentary Assembly of the CoE's Committee on Legal Affairs, to the 26th Conference of European Ministers for Justice, April 2005.
62 The transfer of sovereignty, which is the distinctive feature of the EU institutions, does not allow international organisations, which are not contracting parties to EC treaties, to participate in internal deliberations.
63 See Emma J. Stewart, 'Capabilities and Coherence? The Evolution of European Union Conflict Prevention', (2008), *European Foreign Affairs Review*, 13(2), pp. 229–53.
64 Emma J. Stewart, 'Restoring EU–OSCE Cooperation for Pan-European Conflict Prevention', *Contemporary Security Policy*, 29(2), pp. 266–84; see also Council of the European Union, 'EU–OSCE Cooperation in Conflict Prevention, Crisis Management and Post-Conflict Rehabilitation', 17 November 2003.
65 See *Council Decision of 20 December 1993 concerning the joint action adopted by the Council on the basis of Article J.3 of the Treaty on European Union on the inaugural conference on the stability pact*, 93/728/CFSP, in OJL 339, 31.12.1993 and Council Decision of 14 June 1994 on the continuation of the joint action adopted by the Council on the basis of Article J.3 of the Treaty on European Union on the inaugural conference on the Stability Pact, 94/367/CFSP, in OJL 165, 01.07.1994.
66 Conference on Security and Cooperation, Concluding Document of the Inaugural Conference for a Pact of Stability in Europe, Paris 26/27 May 1994, para. 1.5.
67 Treaty on Good-neighbourly Relations and Friendly Cooperation between the Republic of Hungary and the Slovak Republic of 19th March 1995, reprinted in 36 ILM 340 (1997).
68 Treaty on Understanding, Cooperation and Good Neighbourliness between Hungary and Romania of 16 September 1996, 36 ILM 340 (1997).
69 See Conclusions of the 3rd Ministerial Council Meeting, Stockholm, December 1992, Chapter 3.

70 For a detailed analysis of the EU's involvement in management of ethnic conflict, see Stefan Wolff and Annemarie Peen Rodt in Marc Weller et al. (eds), *The Protection of Minorities in the Wider Europe*, pp. 128–153.

71 *Common Position of 17 May 1999 adopted by the Council on the basis of Article 15 of the Treaty on European Union, concerning a Stability Pact for South-Eastern Europe* 1999/345/CFSP, in OJ L 133 28.05.1999.

72 'The European Union and the Organization for Security and Cooperation in Europe: The Shape of Future Cooperation', Address by Javier Solana to the Permanent Council of the OSCE, Vienna, 25 September 2002. Available at www.consilium.europa.eu/uedocs/cmsUpload/72254.pdf.

73 The conference was organised by the Swedish Presidency with the support of the European Commission and on request by the UN Secretary General for improvement of cooperation between international/regional organisations for conflict prevention.

74 Stewart, 'Restoring EU–OSCE Cooperation for Pan-European Conflict Prevention', p. 276.

75 Ibid.; also Dermot Doyle 'EU and OSCE, Natural Born Partners', *European Security Review*, 14 September 2002.

76 Council Conclusions on EU–OSCE cooperation in conflict prevention, crisis management and post-conflict rehabilitation, Council of the EU, Brussels, 10 November 2003, 14512/03, to be found at http://register.consilium.europa.eu/pdf/en/03/st14/st14527-re01.en03.pdf.

77 Stewart, 'Restoring EU–OSCE Cooperation for Pan-European Conflict Prevention', p. 276.

78 Similarly, the OSCE Mission in Croatia had to close down in 2007, as the country became an EU candidate country.

79 Above note 73; see also Council Conclusions of 17 November 2003, 'EU–OSCE cooperation in conflict prevention, crisis management and post-conflict rehabilitation'.

80 See e.g., CFSP Declaration 13648/05 on the election campaign in Azerbaijan in 2005.

81 See OSCE Annual Report 2003, p. 100.

82 Above note 79 Council Conclusions of 17 November 2003, para. 8.

83 See OSCE Annual Report 2008, at p. 98.

84 Ibid.

85 See OSCE Annual Report 2008, p. 98.

86 See in particular above note 46.

Chapter 4

1 The last accession round took place in 1995 with Sweden, Finland and Austria.

2 See Human Rights Watch Report of 9 October 2005 'Serbia Fails to Curb Violence Against Minorities', at www.hrw.org/en/news/2005/10/09/serbia-fails-curb-violence-against-minorities.

3 See for example fingerprinting of Roma in Naples, Italy since June 2008. Also, see the discussion on a Roma Directive in Network of Independent Experts in Fundamental Rights 2003 (CFR–CDF) 'Report on the Situation of Fundamental Rights in the European Union and its Member States'.

4 See in particular the First EU Roma Summit of 16 September 2008 http://ec.europa.eu/news/employment/080916_1_en.htm, and 'NGOs Want Results from First EU Roma Summit', published Tuesday 16 September 2008 at www.euractiv.com/en/socialeurope/ngos-want-results-eu-roma-summit/article-175412; and 'The European Roma Rights Centre Calls on the EU to Reaffirm Human Rights Standards in Policies on Roma' last updated: 19 September 2008 at www.errc.org/cikk.php?cikk=2983.

5 See below section 4.3.2, on specific minority rights.

6 See Miriam J. Aukerman, 'Definitions and Justifications: Minority and Indigenous Rights in a Central/East European Context', in HRQ 22 (2000), p. 1
7 Jennifer Jackson Preece, 'Minority Rights', p. 5.
8 Ibid. p. 6.
9 GA Resolution 2200 A (XXI) of 16 December 1966, entered into force 23 March 1976. 999 UNTS 171.
10 ETS No. 157, concluded 1 February 1995, entered into force 1 February 1998.
11 Jacob Robinson et al., *Were the Minority Treaties a Failure?*, p. 3.
12 For example Hungarians were split among Slovakia, Romania, Ukraine and Serbia.
13 Above note 11, p. 21.
14 Patrick Thornberry, *International Law and the Rights of Minorities*, p. 41.
15 Ibid. pp. 42–43.
16 Ibid. p. 37.
17 Ibid. p. 47.
18 Gilbert Murray, 'National Tolerance as an International Obligation', in *Problems of Peace, Fifth Series: Lectures delivered at the Geneva Institute of International Relations*, p. 182.
19 See e.g., Security Council Resolution 724 (1991) Socialist Federal Republic of Yugoslavia (15 December 1991), and 1031 (1995) on implementation of the Peace Agreement for Bosnia Herzegovina and transfer of authority from the UN Protection Force to the multinational Implementation Force (IFOR) (15 December 1995).
20 See e.g., Security Council Resolution 1203 (1998) on the situation in Kosovo (24 October) and 1244 (1999) on the situation relating Kosovo (10 June).
21 See e.g., Security Council Resolution 1345 (2001) on the letter dated 4 March 2001 from the Permanent Representative of the Former Yugoslav Republic of Macedonia to the United Nations addressed to the president of the Security Council (S/2001/191) (21 March 2001).
22 *UN General Assembly Resolution GA/10708. May 15, 2008.*
23 See OSCE High Commissioner on National Minorities, Mandate, in Chapter II of the 1992 Conference for Security and Cooperation in Europe, 'The Challenges of Change', Summit, Helsinki 9–10 July 1992.
24 For problems of minority protection and security in Europe see e.g., Kinga Gál, 'Protection of National Minorities and Stability in Central and Eastern Europe', in particular pp. 21–31; Alisdair M. Stewart, 'Migrants, Minorities and Security in Europe'; Robert Zaagmann, 'Minority Questions, Human Rights and Regional Instability: The Prevention of Conflict'.
25 Will Kymlicka, 'The Evolving Basis of European Norms of Minority Rights', in Marc Weller et al. (eds), *The Protection of Minorities in the Wider Europe*, p. 12.
26 For a detailed analysis of the EU's involvement in management of ethnic conflict, see Stefan Wolff and Annemarie Peen Rodt in Marc Weller et al. (eds), *The Protection of Minorities in the Wider Europe*, pp. 128–153.
27 Minority Schools in Albania, PCIJ, Ser. A/B, No. 64, 1935, p. 4f.
28 The Sub-Commission was the main subsidiary body of the Commission on Human Rights. It was established by the Commission at its first session in 1947 under ECOSOC authority. In 1999 ECOSOC changed its title from Sub-Commission on Prevention of Discrimination and Protection of Minorities to Sub-Commission on the Promotion and Protection of Human Rights, which eventually ceased to exist. Pursuant to GA Resolution 60/251 of 15 March 2006 entitled 'Human Rights Council', all mandates, mechanisms, functions and responsibilities of the Commission on Human Rights, including the Sub-Commission on the Promotion and Protection of Human Rights, were assumed, as of 19 June 2006, by the Human Rights Council.
29 Francesco Capotorti, 'Study of the Rights of Persons belonging to Ethnic Religious and Linguistic Minorities', UN DOC E/CN.4/Sub.2/384/Rev.1, 1979.
30 Ibid. p. 96.

31 See for example the Bretons in France who have maintained their distinctive culture and language despite France's official denial of the existence of 'minorities' on French territory.

32 Jules Deschênes, 'Proposal Concerning a Definition of the Term Minority', UN Doc. E/CN.4/sub.2/1985/31.

33 Council of Europe's deliberations from 1973, recorded in Francesco Capotorti 'Study on the Rights of Persons Belonging to Ethnic, Religious and Linguistic Minorities', 1977, published as a separate volume by the UN in 1991, Sales No. E.91.XI.2, paras 196–201.

34 General Assembly Resolution 47/135 on the Declaration on the Rights of Persons Belonging to National *or* Ethnic, Religious and Linguistic Minorities.

35 Asborn Eide, 'Final Text of the Commentary to the Declaration on the Rights of Persons belonging to National, Ethnic, Religious and Linguistic Minorities' (1998), UN Doc. E/CN.4/sub.2/AC.5/2001/2.

36 General Comment No. 23, 50th session, 1994, paras 5.1 and 5.2.

37 Under EU law immigration is dealt with under the first pillar, Title IV, Article 61ff. TEC; Title V, Article 67ff. TFEU under the Treaty of Lisbon.

38 See Annual Report of the Human Rights Committee, 1989, UN-Doc. A/44/40, p. 53.

39 Recommendation 1201 (1993) on an additional protocol on the rights of national minorities to the ECHR.

40 See Recommendation 1255 (1995). The Parliamentary Assembly has reasserted the need for a protocol to the European Convention on the rights of national minorities in 2001, see Council of Europe Press Service, press release, 24 January 2001.

41 See the report 'The Protection of Minorities in the European Union', at http://ec.europa.eu/justice_home/cfr_cdf.

42 This Resolution is based on the report A6–0140/2005 prepared by Claude Moares (henceforth quoted as the Moares Report, see its para. 7).

43 For a summary of the relevant *travaux préparatoires* to the Convention, see CoE documents DH-MIN (97)7, DH-MIN (93)4 and CAHMIN (94) 5, paras 5 and 14.

44 See Comments by the Federal Republic of Germany on the opinion of the Advisory Committee on the implementation of the Framework Convention in the Federal Republic of Germany, in GVT/COM/INF/OP/I(2002)008. Apart from Germany, the following Member States have made declarations with respect to the FCNM, clarifying which group qualifies as a 'national minority' within the meaning of the FCNM: Austria, Belgium, Denmark, Estonia, Luxembourg (declaring that there is no national minority on its territory), Poland, Slovenia and Sweden. See at http://conventions.coe.int/Treaty/Commun/ListeDeclarations.asp?NT=157&CV=1&NA&PO=999&CN=999&VL=1&CM=9&CL=ENG.

45 Jochen Abr. Frowein, Roland Bank, 'The Effect of Member States' Declarations Defining "National Minorities" upon Signature or Ratification of the Council of Europe Framework Convention for the Protection of National Minorities', in *Zeitschrift für Ausländisches Öffentliches Recht und Völkerrecht* 59 (1999), pp. 649–75.

46 Explanatory Report European Framework Convention for the Protection of National Minorities, General Considerations, para. 12.

47 It is also worth mentioning that the Roma are recognised by the Slovenian constitution in Article 65 as an ethnic minority and therefore do not necessarily need to have Slovenian nationality for benefiting from minority protection.

48 Opinion on Cyprus, ACFC/INF/OP/I(2002)004, 21.02.2000, paras 18–21.

49 Article 6 FCNM states 'The Parties shall encourage a spirit of tolerance and intercultural dialogue and take effective measures to promote mutual respect and understanding and cooperation among all persons living on their territory, irrespective of those persons' ethnic, cultural, linguistic or religious identity, in particular in the fields of education, culture and the media'.

50 See Rainer Hofmann, 'The Future of Minority issues in the CoE and the OSCE', in Marc Weller et al. (eds), *The Protection of Minorities in the Wider Europe*, p.183
51 See chapter 5, section 2.
52 See W. Kemp, 'Quiet Diplomacy in Action: The OSCE High Commissioner on National Minorities'.
53 For further details on affirmative action see Gabriel Moens, 'Affirmative Action. The New Discrimination', St Leonards, Centre for Independent Studies, 1985.
54 For two other approaches, 'the self-determination approach' and the 'subsidiarity approach' see Kinga Gál, 'The Implementation of Minority Rights', in Erwin Müller et al. (eds), *Menschenrechtsschutz*, pp. 163–64.
55 Human Rights Committee's General Comment No. 12 (21) on Article 1, CCPR/C/21/Rev.1 19 May 1989.
56 Ad Hoc Committee for the Protection of National Minorities. Report of First Meeting. CAHMIN/Gr (94).
57 PACE Recommendation 1492 on the rights of national minorities (2001).
58 CAHMIN Explanatory Report to the Framework Convention for the Protection of National Minorities (1995), CAHMIN H (1995) 010, at para. 13.
59 South West Africa Case ICJ Reports 1966, 4, pp. 284–316.
60 John Packer, 'On the Definition of Minorities', in John Packer and Kristian Myntti (eds), *The Protection of Ethnic and Linguistic Minorities in Europe.*
61 Natan Lerner, 'The Evolution of Minority Rights in International Law', in Catherine Brölmann et al. (eds), *Peoples and Minorities in International Law*, p. 91.
62 Yoram Dinstein, 'Collective Human Rights of Peoples and Minorities', 25 (1976) ICLQ, p. 102.
63 Bruno de Witte, 'Politics Versus Law in the EU's Approach to Ethnic Minorities', EUI Working Paper, RSC No. 2000/4, p. 12.
64 See Jennifer Jackson-Preece 'Minority Rights'; also Arend Lijphart, *The Politics of Accommodation: Pluralism and Democracy in the Netherlands.*
65 See chapter 5 for provisions of the Estonian and Slovenian Constitutions.
66 Convention (No. 169) concerning Indigenous and Tribal Peoples in Independent countries, concluded 27 June 1989, entered into force 5 September 1991. 28 ILM 1382 (1989).
67 GA Res. 2106A(XX) of 21 December 1965, entered into force 4 January 1969. 660 UNTS 195.
68 Theodor Meron, 'The Meaning and Reach of the International Convention on the Elimination of all Forms of Racial Discrimination', AJIL 1985, p. 305.
69 See e.g., the Opinion on Austria, ACFC/INF/OP/I/(2002)009, at paras 24–27; or the (second) Opinion on the Czech Republic, ACFC/INF/OP/II(2005)002, at paras 60–67.
70 Opinion on Finland, ACFC/INF/OP/I(2001)002 at paras 21–23; Opinion on Norway, ACFC/INT/OP/I(2–3)003, at para. 38; Opinion on Sweden ACFC/INT/OP/I(2003)006, at paras 30–32.
71 Opinion on the UK, ACFC/INF/OP/I(2002)006 at paras 40–42; Opinion on Ireland, ACFC/INF/OP/I (2004)003, at paras 48–55.
72 Opinion on Germany, ACFC/INF/OP/I(2002)008, at paras 29–32.
73 The CSCE Copenhagen Document at para. 31, Article 4 para. 1 of the FCNM, Article 3 of the UN Declaration, Article 26 ICCPR and Article 14 ECHR.
74 Rosalyn Higgins, 'Minority Rights: Discrepancies and Divergences between the International Covenant and the Council of Europe System', in *Liber Amicorum for Henry Schermers*, p. 199.
75 See Rainer Hofmann, 'The Future of Minority Issues in the CoE and the OSCE', in Marc Weller et al. (eds), *The Protection of Minorities in the Wider Europe*, pp. 185–86.
76 Ibid.
77 See at www.osce.org/documents/hcnm/1998/02/2699_en.pdf. Paragraph 3) provides: 'In areas inhabited by significant numbers of persons belonging to a national

minority and when there is sufficient demand, public authorities shall make provision for the display, also in the minority language, of local names, street names and other topographical indications intended for the public'.

78 Rainer Hofmann, 'The Future of Minority Issues in the CoE and the OSCE', in Marc Weller et al. (eds), *The Protection of Minorities in the Wider Europe*, p.189, in particular fn 65.
79 Ibid. fn 70–75.
80 See at www.osce.org/documents/hcnm/1996/10/2700_en.pdf.
81 Rainer Hofmann, 'The Future of Minority Issues in the CoE and the OSCE', in Marc Weller et al. (eds), *The Protection of Minorities in the Wider Europe*, p.191 and fn 81–82.
82 See Opinion on Austria, ACFC/INF/OP/I(2002)009, paras 61–65; Opinion on Estonia, ACFC/INF/OP/I(2002)00, para. 51; and Opinion on Switzerland ACFC/INF/OP/I(2003)007, para. 72.
83 Rainer Hofmann, 'The Future of Minority Issues in the CoE and the OSCE', in Marc Weller et al. (eds), *The Protection of Minorities in the Wider Europe*, p.188 and fn 56.
84 Guidelines on the Use of Minority Language in the Broadcast Media, accessible at www.osce.org/hcnm/documents/.
85 Opinion on Denmark, ACFC/INF/OP/I(2001)005, para. 29; Opinion on Finland, ACFC/INF/OP/I(2001)002, para. 29.
86 Opinion on the UK, ACFC/INF/OP/I(2002)006, paras 57–61.
87 Wolf Mannens, 'The International Status of Cultural Rights for National Minorities', in Cumper and Wheatley (eds), *Minority Rights in the New Europe*, p. 186.
88 Will Kymlicka, 'The Evolving Basis of European Norms of Minority Rights', in Marc Weller et al. (eds), *The Protection of Minorities in the Wider Europe*, p. 23.
89 See at www.osce.org/hcnm/publications.html.
90 See at www.osce.org/publications/odihr/2001/01/12347_129_en.pdf.
91 See also the right to free transboundary contacts, provided for under Article 17 FCNM and Paragraph 32 Copenhagen Document.
92 Rainer Hofmann, 'The Future of Minority Issues in the CoE and the OSCE', in Marc Weller et al. (eds), *The Protection of Minorities in the Wider Europe*, p. 187.
93 Under the League of Nations System, minority clauses were included in the treaties with a dozen new, enlarged, and defeated states in Eastern Europe. These documents contained identical stipulations on civil, political and religious rights, new language and educational rights as well as a minimal degree of cultural protection. Most important, all were placed under the guarantee of the League's petition procedure.
94 See Jacob Robinson et al., *Were the Minority Treaties a Failure?* pp. 236–37.
95 Rudolf Bernhardt, 'Federalism and Autonomy', in Yoram Dinstein (ed.), *Models of Autonomy*, p. 26.
96 Asbjon Eide, 'The Universal Declaration in Space and Time', in Jan Berting (ed.), *Human rights in a Pluralistic World: Individuals and Collectives*, p. 25.
97 See Bengt Broms, 'Autonomous Territories', in *Encyclopedia of Public International Law*, vol. I, p. 308.
98 James Crawford, *The Creation of States in International Law*, pp. 211–12.
99 For example China granted autonomy to Tibet, which meant at the same time that Tibet had to submit to the rule of the Communist Party and to align its regional features to the Chinese way of living.
100 Bengt Broms, 'Autonomous Territories', p. 311.
101 See above note 95.
102 See above note 39.
103 See Opinion of the Venice Commission on the Interpretation of Article 11 of the Draft Protocol to the European Convention on Human Rights appended to Recommendation 1201, Council of Europe 1996.
104 UN Doc. A/RES/61/295, adopted by General Assembly Resolution 61/295 on 13 September 2007; see in particular Articles 3, 4, 14, 26 and 34.

105 See Will Kymlicka, in Marc Weller et al. (eds), *The Protection of Minorities in the Wider Europe*, p. 21.

106 According to these criteria, membership requires that the candidate country:

> Has achieved stability of institutions guaranteeing democracy, the rule of law, human rights, and respect for and protection of minorities; the existence of a functioning market economy as well as the capacity to cope with competitive pressures and market forces within the Union, and has the ability to take on the obligations of membership ('acquis communitaire'), including adherence to the aims of political, economic and monetary Union.

107 Adam Biscoe, 'The European Union and Minority Nations', in Cumper and Wheatley (eds), *Minority Rights in the New Europe*, p. 90.

108 Protocols 2 and 3 to the Treaty of Accession, OJ C 241/352, 29.08.1994.

109 See also the case ECtHR, Appl. No. 25781/94, *Cyprus v. Turkey*, judgment of 10 May 2001.

110 See Bruno de Witte, 'The Constitutional Resources for an EU Minority Policy', in Gabriel Toggenburg (ed.), *Minority Protection and the Enlarged European Union: The Way Forward*, p. 109; Frederic Van den Berghe 'The European Union and the Protection of Minorities: How real is the alleged double standard?' in *The Yearbook of European Law* 2003, vol. 22, pp. 155–202.

111 Common Declaration of 17 December 1991 laying down 'Guidelines on the Recognition of New States in Eastern Europe and in the Soviet Union', EC Foreign Affairs Council, 16 December 1991.

112 http://europa.eu/legislation_summaries/enlargement/2004_and_2007_enlargement/e50004_en.htm.

113 See at http://europa.eu.int/comm/enlargement/pas/phare/statistics/commit_sector.pdf.

114 See Council Regulation (EC) No. 2666/2000 of 5 December 2000.

115 See Article 5 of the CARDS Regulation 2666/2000, in OJ L 306/1, 7.12.2000.

116 Commission Regulation (EC) No. 718/2007 of 12 June 2007 implementing Council Regulation (EC) No. 1085/2006 establishing an instrument for pre-accession assistance (IPA), OJ L 170, 29.06.2007, p. 1.

117 European Council Meeting in Essen, December 1994, Presidency Conclusions, to be found at www.consilium.europa.eu/ueDocs/cms_Data/docs/pressData/en/ec/00300-301.EN4.htm.

118 Enlargement of the European Union, White Paper on Enlargement, to be found at www.europarl.europa.eu/enlargement/index_en.htm.

119 http://ec.europa.eu/enlargement/how-does-it-work/index_en.htm.

120 See Gabriel Toggenburg, 'The EU's evolving policies vis-a-vis minorities: a play in four parts and an open end', EUR.AC.research, August 2008, p. 6.

121 See Article 78(2) of the Europe Agreement with Lithuania in OJL 51/22, 20.02.1998. Similar provisions can be found in the Agreements with Latvia and Estonia.

122 Council Regulation (EC) No. 622/98 of 16 March 1998 on Accession Partnerships.

123 Council Decision 2008/212/EC of 18 February 2008, in OJL 80/32, 19.3.2008, p. 36

124 The same is true for the Commission's regular reports that assess the candidate's progress.

125 Similar stipulations can be found in the Accession Partnerships with Turkey and Croatia, see Council Decision 2008/119/EC of 12 February 2008 in OJL 42/51, 16.2.2008 and Council Decision 2008/157/EC of 18 February 2008 in OJL 51/4, 26.2.2008.

126 See Annex III to Council Conclusions, Luxembourg 29/30 April 1997, in EU Bulletin, 4(1997), point 2.2.1.

127 Regular Reports, at http://ec.europa.eu/enlargement/archives/key_documents/reports_2005_en.htm.
128 Enlargement Strategy Paper, COM(2002)0700 final.
129 COM(2007) 663 final, Brussels, 06.11.2007.
130 For this criticism, see e.g. James Hughes and Gwendolyn Sasse, 'Monitoring the Monitors: EU Enlargement Conditionality and Minority Protection in the CEECs', in JEMIE 1/2003.
131 Above note 120, p. 8.
132 Note, however, the graduated approach (SAP Conditionality) under the Council Conclusions, Luxembourg 29/30 April 1997, Annex III in EU Bulletin, 4(1997).
133 See e.g. Regular Report from the Commission on Bulgaria's Progress towards Accession, 1998, p. 5: 'The Commission also used assessments made by the Member States, particularly with respect to the political criteria for membership and the work of various international organisations, and in particular the contributions of the Council of Europe, the OSCE and the IFIs as well as that of non-governmental organisations in preparation of the regular reports.'
134 Above note 120, p. 12–13.
135 See Regular Report on Hungary of 2001, p. 22 and Report of 2002, p. 30.
136 See James Hughes, Gwendolyn Sasse, 'Monitoring the Monitors: EU Enlargement Conditionality and Minority Protection in the CEECs', in JEMIE 1/2003, p. 15–19.
137 See 2001 and 2002 Reports on the Czech Republic, Slovakia, Estonia.
138 Comprehensive monitoring report of the European Commission on the state of preparedness for EU membership of the Czech Republic, Estonia, Cyprus, Latvia, Lithuania, Hungary, Malta, Poland, Slovenia and Slovakia, SEC (2003) 1200–1209.
139 Christophe Hillion 'The Framework Convention for the Protection of National Minorities and the European Union', *Conference Report on Enhancing the Impact of the Framework Convention*, 9–10 October 2008, p. 8.
140 According to rule 48 of its rules of procedure the EP can table resolutions that are political statements, aimed at persuading the Council to take action on the issue at hand.
141 A3–0000/93, page 6, para. K.1; see also Maria Amor Martin Estebanez, 'The Protection of National, Ethnic, Religious and Linguistic Minorities', in Nanette Neuwahl and Allan Rosas (eds), *The European Union and Human Rights*, p. 138.
142 A3–0042/94, OJ C 61/111 1994, p. 110.
143 ETS No.148.
144 See Consideration L of the Resolution.
145 See para. 4 of the Resolution.
146 See in OJ C 76 E, 374. 2004.
147 The Treaty of Lisbon addresses only this last postulation (majority voting in the area of culture).
148 See above note 42, in OJ C 124, 04.05.2006.
149 Council of the European Union: EU Annual Report on Human Rights 2003, p. 22, 3.1.4.
150 See para. 7 of the Resolution; see also above section 4.3 on the definition.
151 See para. 8 of the Resolution.
152 See para. 45 of the Resolution.
153 See para. 49 of the Resolution.
154 See European Parliament Legislative Resolution on the proposal for a 2005 European Parliament resolution on the situation of the Roma in the European Union (see OJ C 45E, 2006, p. 129) and later again by the Committee on Womens Rights and Gender Equality in the 2006 European Parliament resolution on the situation of Roma women in the European Union (see P6_TA(2006)0244, 1.06.2006).

Finally end of January 2008 the European Parliament agreed on a resolution on a 'European strategy on the Roma' (see P6_TA(2008)0035, 31.01.2008).

155 For more detail see Gabriel Toggenburg, 'A Rough Orientation Through a Delicate Relationship: The European Union's Endeavours for (its) Minorities', European Integration Online Papers 16 (2000).

156 Case relating to certain aspects of the laws on the use of languages in education in Belgium (Merits), judgment of 23 July 1968, Series A, vol. 6.

157 Council of the European Union: EU Annual Report on Human Rights 2003, p. 22, 3.1.4.

158 Kristin Henrard, 'Equal Rights Versus Special Rights?', report published by the European Commission, DG Employment, Social Affairs and Equal Opportunities, 2007.

159 See Council Directive 2000/78/EC of 27 November 2000, establishing a general framework for equal treatment in employment and occupation.

160 Directive 1976/207/EEC on the implementation of the principle of equal treatment for men and women as regards access to employment, vocational training and promotion, and working conditions. See Article 2(4) 'provisions contrary to the principle of equal treatment, when the concern that originally inspired them is no longer well founded, shall be revised'.

161 See Article 141(4) TEC: 'With a view to ensuring full equality in practice between men and women in working life, the principle of equal treatment shall not prevent any Member State from maintaining or adopting measures providing for specific advantages in order to make it easier for the under-represented sex to pursue a vocational activity or to prevent or compensate for disadvantages in professional careers.'

162 For a definition of affirmative action see Asbjørn Eide in UN Doc. E/CN.4Sub.2/1993/34,172: 'Affirmative action is preference, by way of special measures, for certain groups or members of such groups (typically defined by race, ethnic identity or sex) for the purposes of securing adequate advancement of such groups or their individual members in order to ensure equal enjoyment of human rights and fundamental freedoms.'

163 Case C-450/93 *Kalanke* [1995] ECR I-305.

164 Case C-409/95 *Marschall* [1997] ECR I-6363.

165 Case C-409/98 *Katarina Abrahamson and Leif Anderson v. Elisabeth Fogelquist* [2000] ECR I-39.

166 Individual assessment in this context could mean that it would relate to different minority groups individually or separately.

167 Article 149(1) TEC provides: 'The Community shall contribute to the development of quality education by encouraging cooperation between Member States and, if necessary, by supporting and supplementing their action, while fully respecting the responsibility of the Member States for the content of teaching and the organisation of education systems and their cultural and linguistic diversity.'

168 See Rachael Craufurd Smith 'From Heritage Conservation to European Identity: Article 151 EC and the multi-faceted nature of Community cultural policy', *European Law Review* (2007), 32(1), pp. 48–69.

169 The aim of the Culture 2007 programme, which combines the old Raphaël, Kaleidoscope, the Ariane and Culture 2000 programme, is to develop a common cultural area by promoting cultural dialogue, knowledge of the history, creation and dissemination of culture, the mobility of artists and their works, European cultural heritage, new forms of cultural expression and the socio-economic role of culture. 'Culture 2000' supports transnational cooperation projects which involve cooperation between creative artists, cultural operators and the cultural institutions of the countries participating in the programme. See Decision No. 1855/2006/EC of the EP and of the Council of 12 December 2006 establishing the Culture Programme (2007–2013).

170 The fact that Greece and France have obstructed the official funding of EBLUL shows the different approaches to regional cultural diversity and underlines the uncertain status of minorities in the EU.

171 Life Long Learning Programme, see at http://ec.europa.eu/education/lifelong-learning-programme/doc78_en.htm.

172 Communication from the Commission to the Council and the European Parliament on 'A Special Support Programme for Peace and Reconciliation in Northern Ireland', COM (94) 607 final, p. 3.

173 Above note 120, p. 12.

174 See Sven Hölscheidt, 'Artikel 22', in Jürgen Meyer (ed.), *Kommentar zur Charta der Grundrechte der Europäischen Union*, pp. 290–98.

175 S. McInernney, 'The Charter of Fundamental Rights of the European Union and the Case of Race Discrimination' (2002) 27 El. Rev. 490.

176 For a brief analysis of what provisions in the Treaties might represent restrictions for minority rights, see Frederic Van den Berghe 'The European Union and the Protection of Minorities: How real is the alleged double standard?' in *The Yearbook of European Law* 2003, vol. 22, p. 186–89.

177 *Groener v. Minister for Education and the City of Dublin*, Case C-379/87 [1989] ECR 3967.

178 The principal aim of Regulation 1612/68 is to ensure that in each Member State workers from other Member States receive treatment which is not discriminatory by comparison with that of national workers by providing for the systematic application of the rule of national treatment as far as all conditions of employment and work are concerned. It is not the purpose of that Regulation to create rights by virtue of insurance periods completed in another Member State if such rights, in the case of nationals of the host state, do not derive from national provisions.

179 Bruno de Witte, 'Free Movement of Persons and Language Legislation of the Member States of the EU, Some Reflections after the Recent Judgment in Bickel and Franz', in *European Academy, EURAC research*, Academia Nr: 18 (März–Juni /marzo–giugno 1999).

180 Case 137/84 Mutsch [1985] ECR 2681.

181 Case C-274/96 Bickel/Franz [1998] ECR I-7637.

182 Ibid. para. 12.

183 See Article 5(2)(b) of the Founding Regulation, Council Regulation (EC) No. 168/2007 of 15 February 2007, in OJ L 53, 22.02.2007.

184 In the European Parliament Resolution on Promotion and Protection of Fundamental Rights (P6_TA(2005)0208, 26 May 2005, paras 39 and 40), it was pointed out that 'the Roma issue and minority rights and respect for cultural, religious and linguistic diversity should be part of the Agency's work since protecting national minorities in an enlarged EU is a major issue that will not be achieved simply by fighting against xenophobia and discrimination.' See in OJ C 117 E, p. 242,18.5.2006.

185 See above note 42, para. 3.

186 Further information on these projects and activities can be obtained at www.fra.europa.eu/fraWebsite/home/home_en.htm.

187 Council regulation (EC) No. 168/2007 of 15 February 2007, in OJ L 53, 22.2.2007.

188 Agreement on Cooperation, OJL L 186/7, 15.7.2008.

189 The Network of Independent Experts established by the Directorate-General Freedom, Security and Justice of the European Commission, and which has been invited to support the work of the FRA, had produced a report on Minority Protection in the Member States: Thematic Comment No. 3; the Protection of Minorities in the European Union; CFR–CFF.ThemComm2005.

190 See above note 120, sponsored by the Sixth Framework Programme FP6, an EU programme for research and technological development, see at http://ec.europa.eu/research/fp6/index_en.cfm. The report 'The European Union's Policies Vis-à-Vis Minorities: A Play in Three Parts and an Open End', is available at www.eurac.

edu/Org/Minorities/IMR/Partner/rof_toggenburg#publications. See in particular, pp.15–20.

191 Ibid. p. 17.

192 See at http://ec.europa.eu/social/main.jsp?catId=101&langId=en.

193 Ibid.

194 Employment guideline No. 9 in 1999 and 2000.

195 Employment guideline No. 7 in 2001 and 2002.

196 Employment guideline No. 7 in 2003 and 2004.

197 1999 Joint Employment Report, Part I: the European Union, adopted by the Joint Council (Labour and Social Affairs/ECOFIN) at its session on 29 November 1999, pp. 29 and 46.

198 Some Member States (UK, Netherlands) use a broad definition to encompass 'visible minorities' (i.e. people who appear to be of foreign origin, irrespective of their nationality), while others restrict the scope either to non-nationals or non-EU nationals (Germany, Sweden) or to national minorities (Ireland, Finland, Austria).

199 Above note 120, p. 18.

200 See Council Doc. 7169/08, 03.03.2008.

201 See the Commission decision of 20 January 2006 establishing a high-level advisory group on social integration of ethnic minorities and their full participation in the labour market (2006/33/EC), in OJ L 21, 2006, p. 20.

202 Ibid. Article 2.

203 http://ec.europa.eu/employment_social/spsi/vulnerable_groups_en.htm.

204 See the 'Report on Social Inclusion 2005: An analysis of the National Action Plans on Social Inclusion (2004–6) Submitted by the 10 New Member States', available at http://ec.europa.eu/employment_social/spsi/joint_reports_en.htm#2005_2.

205 Above note 120, p. 24.

206 Decision No. 771/2006/EC of the European Parliament and the Council establishing the European Year of Equal Opportunities (2007), in OJ L 146, 2006, p. 1.

207 Decision No. 1983/2006/EC of the European Parliament and the Council concerning the European Year of Intercultural Dialogue (2008), in OJ L 412, 2006, p. 44.

208 Communication from the Commission to the Council, the European Parliament, the European Economic and Social Committee and the Committee of the Regions of 1 June 2005 – Non-Discrimination and Equal Opportunities for All – A Framework Strategy, COM(2005)224 in OJ C 236, 24.09.2005.

209 Erica Howard, 'The European Year of Equal Opportunities for All – 2007: Is the EU moving away from a formal idea of equality?' (March 2008) *European Law Journal* 14 (2), pp. 168–85.

210 Above note 208, p. 2.

211 Ibid. at p. 6.

212 The 12th Protocol to the ECHR, ETS No. 177 of 4 November 2000 amended Article 14 and made it a free-standing non-discrimination article (before the 12th Protocol, another article of the Convention had to be violated before Article14 could apply) guaranteeing that no one shall be discriminated against on any ground by any public authority. Nonetheless, the protection of minorities has not been addressed explicitly in the 12th Protocol and therefore does not improve the scope of protection of minorities.

213 Note that the Commission no longer exists since the coming into force of the 11th Protocol to the ECHR, ETS No. 155 of 11 May 1994, entered into force 1 November 1998.

214 *Belgian Linguistics* case, relating to certain aspects of the laws on the use of languages in education in Belgium, Series A, No. 6 (1968).

215 *Airey v. Ireland*, Series A, No. 32 (1979).

216 ECtHR, Appl. Nos 43577/98 and 43579/98, *Nachova and Others v. Bulgaria*, judgment of 6 July 2005.

217 ECtHR, Appl. No. 15250/02, *Bekos and Koutropoulos v. Greece*, judgment of 13 December 2005.

218 ECtHR, Appl. Nos 41138/98 and 64320/01, *Moldovan and Others v. Romania*, judgment of 12 July 2005.

219 ECtHR, Appl. No. 46317/99, *Ognyanova and Choban v. Bulgaria*, judgment of 23 February 2006.

220 ECtHR, Appl. No. 43233/98, *Osman v. Bulgaria*, judgment of 16 February 2003.

221 ECtHR Appl. No. 57325/00, *D. H. and Others v. the Czech Republic*, judgment of 7 February 2006.

222 European Commission of Human Rights, Appl. Nos 9278/81, 9415/81, 3.10.1983.

223 European Commission of Human Rights, Appl. No. 20348/92, 19 EHRR, CD 20 (1995).

224 *Buckley v. UK*, Reports 1996-IV, 25 September 1996.

225 *Chapman v. the United Kingdom*, Reports 2001-I, 18 January 2001, paras 93–100. The case concerned applications brought by applicants from five British Gypsy families. Sally Chapman bought land in 1985 in the Three Rivers District in Hertfordshire on which to station her caravan, without obtaining prior planning permission. They were refused planning permission for a caravan, and also permission to build a bungalow. It was acknowledged in the planning proceedings that there was no official site for Gypsies in the area and the time for compliance with the enforcement order was for that reason extended. The applicants complained that measures taken against them to enforce planning measures concerning the occupation of their own land in their caravans violated Articles 8 and 14 ECHR.

226 For more case law, see Geoff Gilbert, 'The Burgeoning Minority Rights Jurisprudence of the European Court of Human Rights' (2002) HRQ, 24(3), August.

227 *United Communist Party of Turkey and Others v. Turkey*, Reports 1998-I, 30 January 1998.

228 *Sidiropoulos and Five Others v. Greece*, Reports 1998-IV, 10 July 1998.

229 Ibid. paras 41 and 44.

230 ECtHR Appl. No. 74989/01, *Ouranio Toxo and Others v. Greece*, judgment of 20 October 2006.

231 *United Macedonian Organization Ilinden and Others v. Bulgaria*, Appl. No. 59491/00, 19 January 2006

232 ECtHR, Appl. No. 25803/04, *Herri Batasuna v. Spain*, decision of 30 June 2009.

233 ECtHR, Appl. No. 2581704, *Batasuna v. Spain*, decision of 30 June 2009.

234 ECtHR, Appl. No. 44158/98, *Gorzelik and Others v. Poland*, judgment of 17 May 2001.

235 Ibid, para. 70.

236 Ibid. para. 62.

237 *Informationsverein Lentia & Others v. Austria*, Series A, No. 276 (1993).

238 *Incal v. Turkey*, Reports 1998-IV, 9 June 1998.

239 See Article 53 ECHR which provides: 'The High Contracting Parties undertake to abide by the decision of the Court in any case to which they are parties'.

240 *Marckx v. Belgium*, Series A, No. 31 (1979), para. 58.

241 See Articles 24–25 FCNM.

242 For a detailed description of the monitoring system under the FCNM, see Rainer Hofmann, 'The Framework Convention for the Protection of National Minorities: An Introduction', in Marc Weller (ed.), *The Framework Convention for the Protection of National Minorities: A Commentary*.

243 Article 3 (1) FCNM states: 'Every person belonging to a national minority shall have the right freely to choose to be treated or not to be treated as such and no disadvantage shall result from this choice or from the exercise of the rights which are connected to that choice.'

244 All opinions by the Advisory Committee can be found at on the CoE's website at www.coe.int/t/e/human_rights/minorities/Country_specific_eng.asp#P829_44467.

245 See section 4.3 for specific minority rights with references to the FCNM.

246 Rainer Hofmann, 'The Future of Minority Issues in the Coe and the OSCE' in Marc Weller et al. (eds), *The Protection of Minorities in the Wider Europe*, p. 182; see also the Explanatory Report of the Advisory Committee, above note 46.

247 See First Opinion on the UK, ACFC/INF/OP/I(2002)006.

248 Jane Wright, 'The Protection of Minority Rights in Europe: From Conference to Implementation', (1998) IJHR 2(1).

249 See also *Jane Smith v. UK*, Appl. No. 25154/94. 18.01.2001. *Lee v. UK*, Appl. No. 25289/94. 18.01.2001. *Coster v. UK*, Appl. No. 24876/94. 18.01.2001.

250 All new Member States have ratified the FCNM. Belgium and Luxembourg have not ratified the FCNM, France and Greece have not even signed it.

251 The Framework Convention for the Protection of National Minorities and the European Union, Report prepared by Christophe Hillion, p. 10.

252 ETS No. 148 concluded 5 November 1992, entered into force on 1 March 1998.

253 See European Charter for Regional or Minority Languages, Explanatory Report, para. 11, at http://conventions.coe.int/Treaty/en/Reports/Html/148.htm.

254 *Nold v. Commission*, Case 4/73 [1974] ECR 491; see chapter 2.

255 For the text and interpretation of this reservation, see Martin Nowak, *CCPR Commentary*, pp. 485 and 755.

256 Ibid.

257 See for example above note 14.

258 Above note 14, pp. 180–86.

259 See Will Kymlicka, 'Politics in the Vernacular: Nationalism, Multiculturalism and Citizenship'; and above note 25, p. 17.

260 HRC General Comment 23 in Compilation of General Comments and General Recommendations adopted by Human Rights Treaty Bodies, HRI/GEN/1/Rev.7, 12.05.2004, at p. 165, para. 7.

261 For the emergence of soft law, see Peter Malanczuk, *Akehurst's Introduction to International Law*, p. 54.

262 See Human Rights Committee's General Comment No. 23(50) on Article 27, CCPR/C/21/Rev.1/Add.5, 26 April 1994, para. 3.1. See also section 4.3.1.

263 See Human Rights Committee's General Comment No. 12 (21) on Article 1, CCPR/C/21/Rev.1 19 May 1989.

264 Sandra Lovelace, Communication No. R.6/24 (29 December 1977), UN Doc. Supp. No. 40 (A/36/40) at 166 (1981).

265 *Kitok v. Sweden*, Communication No. 197/1985 and also *Ominayak v. Canada*, Communication No. 167/1984.

266 *Chief Bernard Ominayak and the Lubicon Band v. Canada*, Communication No. 167/1984.

267 *Länsman v. Finland*, Communication No. 511/1992, CCPR/C/52/D/511/1992.

268 *Antonina Ignatane v. Latvia* 25 July 2005, Communication No. 884/1999, CCPR/C/72/D/884/1999.

269 Article 2 (1) ICCPR provides: 'Each State Party to the present Covenant undertakes to respect and to ensure to all individuals within its territory and subject to its jurisdiction the rights recognized in the present Covenant, without distinction of any kind, such as race, colour, sex, language, religion, political or other opinion, national or social origin, property, birth or other status.' Article 25 ICCPR states:

> Every citizen shall have the right and the opportunity, without any of the distinctions mentioned in article 2 and without unreasonable restrictions:
>
> (a) To take part in the conduct of public affairs, directly or through freely chosen representatives;

(b) To vote and to be elected at genuine periodic elections which shall be by universal and equal suffrage and shall be held by secret ballot, guaranteeing the free expression of the will of the electors;

(c) To have access, on general terms of equality, to public service in his country.

270 Declaration on the Rights of Persons Belonging to National or Ethnic, Religious and Linguistic Minorities. UN General Assembly Resolution 47/135, 18 December 1992.

271 Patrick Thornberry, 'The Declaration on the Rights of Persons Belonging to National or Ethnic, Religious and Linguistic Minorities: Background, Analysis and Observations', in Alan Philips and Allan Rosas (eds), *The UN Minority Rights Declaration*, p. 54.

272 Rosalyn Higgins, 'Minority Rights: Discrepancies and Divergences between the International Covenant and the Council of Europe System', in Liber Amicorum for Henry Schermers, p. 199.

273 General Comment No. 23 of the Human Rights Committee found that individuals designed to be protected by Article 27 ICCPR need not be citizens/nationals of the State Party, nor even permanent residents.

274 Florence Benoît-Rhomer, *The Minority Question in Europe*, p. 23.

275 For the emergence of soft law, see Peter Malanczuk, *Akehurst's Introduction to International Law*, p. 54.

276 See Commission on Human Rights Resolution E-CN.-Res/2005/79.

277 Commission on Human Rights Resolution A-HRC-Res-7/6 of 27 March 2008.

278 Human Rights Council Resolution 6/15 of 28 September 2007.

279 GA Res. 2106A(XX) of 21 December 1965, entered into force 4 January 1969. 660 UNTS 195.

280 So far only the following countries have made an Article 14 Declaration: Austria, Belgium, Bulgaria, Cyprus, Czech Republic, Denmark, France, Germany, Hungary, Ireland, Italy, Luxembourg, Malta, Poland, Portugal, Romania, Slovakia, Slovenia, Spain and Sweden.

281 See *Yilmaz Dogan v. the Netherlands*, Communication No. 1/1984: an employer had dismissed the claimant on racial grounds; *Demba Talibe Diop v. France*, Communication No. 2/1989: the claimant was denied a licence to practise law, allegedly on racial grounds; *L. K. v. the Netherlands*, Communication No. 4/1991: the claimant had not been properly protected against harassment and insults by a xenophobic mob.

282 Article 5 CERD stipulates:

> States Parties undertake to prohibit and to eliminate racial discrimination in all its forms and to guarantee the right of everyone, without distinction as to race, colour, or national or ethnic origin, to equality before the law, notably in the enjoyment of the following rights: (a) The right to equal treatment before the tribunals and all other organs administering justice; (b) The right to security of person and protection by the State against violence or bodily harm, whether inflicted by government officials or by any individual group or institution; (c) Political rights, in particular the right to participate in elections – to vote and to stand for election – on the basis of universal and equal suffrage, to take part in the Government as well as in the conduct of public affairs at any level and to have equal access to public service; (d) Other civil rights, in particular: (i) The right to freedom of movement and residence within the border of the State; (ii) The right to leave any country, including one's own, and to return to one's country; (iii) The right to nationality; (iv) The right to marriage and choice of spouse; (v) The right to own property alone as well as in association with others; (vi) The right to

inherit; (vii) The right to freedom of thought, conscience and religion; (viii) The right to freedom of opinion and expression; (ix) The right to freedom of peaceful assembly and association; (e) Economic, social and cultural rights, in particular: (i) The rights to work, to free choice of employment, to just and favourable conditions of work, to protection against unemployment, to equal pay for equal work, to just and favourable remuneration; (ii) The right to form and join trade unions; (iii) The right to housing; (iv) the right to public health, medical care, social security and social services; (v) The right to education and training; (vi) The right to equal participation in cultural activities; (f) The right of access to any place or service intended for use by the general public, such as transport hotels, restaurants, cafes, theatres and parks.

283 Francesco Capotorti, 'The Protection of Minorities under Multinational Agreements on Human Rights' in Italian Yearbook on International Law, 1976, p. 9.
284 See for example CERD's Concluding Observations on Italy CERD/C/ITA/CO/15; Estonia CERD/C/EST/CO/7; Czech Republic CERD/C/CZE/CO/7; Latvia CERD/C/63/CO/7; Poland CERD/C/62/CO/6; Slovakia CERD/C/65/CO/7 or Sweden CERD/C/SWE/CO/18.
285 Article 1(4) CERD provides:

> Special measures taken for the sole purpose of securing adequate advancement of certain racial or ethnic groups or individuals requiring such protection as may be necessary in order to ensure such groups or individuals equal enjoyment or exercise of human rights and fundamental freedoms shall not be deemed racial discrimination, provided, however, that such measures do not, as a consequence, lead to the maintenance of separate rights for different racial groups and that they *shall not be continued after the objectives for which they were taken have been achieved* [emphasis added].

286 See the Concluding Observations of CERD's Committee on the Elimination of Racial Discrimination at www.ohchr.org/english/bodies/cerd/cerds72.htm.
287 Concluding Document of the CSCE Human Dimension Conference in Copenhagen of June 1990.
288 See paras 1–16 of the Moscow Concluding Document of 1991.
289 See Concluding Document of the Budapest Review conference in 1994.
290 Maria Amor Estebanez Martin, 'Minority Protection and the OSCE', in Peter Cumper and Steven Wheatley (eds), *Minority Rights and the New Europe*, p. 36.
291 Charter of Paris for a New Europe, adopted by Heads of State and Government of the participating States of the Conference on Security and Cooperation in Europe, Paris, 21 November 1990, reprinted in 30 ILM 190.
292 Conference on Security and Cooperation in Europe, Meeting of Experts on National Minorities, Geneva, 1 to 19 July 1991.
293 Richard Dalton, 'The Role of the CSCE', in Hugh Miall (ed.), *Minority Rights in Europe.*
294 See Budapest Decisions 1994, para. 5.
295 The Role of the High Commissioner on National Minorities in OSCE Conflict Prevention, Foundation on Inter-Ethnic Relations, p. 18.
296 Helsinki Summit Decisions 1992, Chapter II, para. 3.
297 See Report of the High Commissioner on National Minorities in the CSCE Region, OSCE Communication No. 240 of 14 September 1993.
298 See section 4.9.3, below.
299 Robert Zaagman, 'The CSCE High Commissioner on National Minorities: An Analysis of the Mandate and the Institutional Context', in Arie Bloed (ed.), *The Challenges of Change, The Helsinki Summit of the OSCE and its Aftermath*, p. 117.

300 Ibid.

301 The authorisation for on-site investigations is provided for in Chapter II, part 26 B of the Helsinki Document.

302 Max van der Stoel, Keynote Address to the OSCE Human Dimension Seminar on Case Studies on National Minority Issues; cited in Jane Wright, 'The OSCE and the Protection of Minority Rights', (1996) HRQ 18, pp. 193–96.

303 See Report of the High Commissioner on National Minorities on Roma and Sinti in the OSCE Region, Communication of 10 March 2000.

304 Maria Amor Estabanez Martin, 'The High Commissioner on National Minorities: Development of the Mandate', in Michael Bothe et al. (eds), *The OSCE in the Maintenance of Peace and Security*, p. 156.

305 In a keynote lecture at the London School of Economics, 'The International Politics of Minority Issues: Could the Early 1990s Return?', lecture by Knut Vollebaek at the London School of Economics, 7 May 2009, recording on file with the author,the HCNM gave another reason as to his non-involvement in Western Europe in general and stated that conflicts in Western Europe, such as the Basque or Irish conflict, are taking place in countries where competent institutions were already in place to deal with the conflict at hand; while his office focuses on intervention in countries that lack a strong democratic institutional setup.

306 Krysztof Drzewicki, 'Enlargement of the European Union and the OSCE High Commissioner on National Minorities', in Marc Weller et al. (eds), *The Protection of Minorities in the Wider Europe*, p. 163; A. Drzemczewski, 'Monitoring by the Council of Europe', in G. Alfredsson et al. (eds), *International Human Rights Monitoring Mechanisms: Essays in Honor of Jacob Th. Möller*, p. 525–32.

307 Letter of 14 January 2004 by Rolf Ekeus OSCE HCNM to H. E. Mr Brian Cowen, Minister for Foreign Affairs of Ireland.

308 See at www.osce.org/documents/hcnm/1996/10/2700_en.pdf. Last accessed on 30 November 2009.

309 See at www.osce.org/hcnm/item_11_31527.html. Last accessed on 30 November 2009.

310 See at www.osce.org/hcnm/item_11_31545.html. Last accessed on 30 November 2009.

311 See at www.osce.org/hcnm/item_11_31627.html. Last accessed on 30 November 2009.

312 See at www.osce.org/hcnm/item_11_31598.html. Last accessed on 30 November 2009.

313 See at www.osce.org/documents/hcnm/2006/02/17982_en.pdf. Last accessed on 30 November 2009.

314 See at www.osce.org/hcnm/item_11_33388.html. Last accessed on 30 November 2009.

315 For a complete overview of the HCNM's activities, see www.osce.org/hcnm/.

316 According to the Budapest Document of 1994: 'the ODIHR, in consultation with the Chairman in Office, will, acting in an advisory capacity, participate in discussions of the Senior Council and the Permanent Council, by reporting at regular intervals on its activities and providing information on implementation issues the director of the ODIHR may propose further action.'

317 The imposition of certain criteria on new Member States (or candidate countries) that are not equally required from old Member States is not only the case for minority rights, also the implementation of the Schengen *acquis* or the fulfilment of EMU requirements are not equally imposed on old Member States who enjoy the privilege to opt out.

318 Jennifer Jackson-Preece, '*Minority Rights in Europe: From Westphalia to Helsinki*', (1997) *Review of International Studies*, 23, p. 82.

319 See above note 305.

320 The new Article 5(3) TEU provides: 'Under the principle of subsidiarity, in areas which do not fall within its exclusive competence, the Union shall act only if and in so far as the objectives of the proposed action cannot be sufficiently achieved by the Member States, either at central level or at regional and local level, but can rather, by reason of the scale or effects of the proposed action, be better achieved at Union level.'
321 See above note 176, p. 191.

Chapter 5

1 Wojciech Sadurski, 'Minority Protection in Central Europe and Accession to the EU', in Marc Weller et al. (eds), *The Protection of Minorities in the Wider Europe*, p. 214.
2 Available at http://ec.europa.eu/justice_home/cfr_cdf/doc/thematic_comments_2005_en.pdf, at p. 52.
3 In 2007 17 per cent of the Russian minority in Estonia have not obtained citizenship (Estonian Ministry of Foreign Affairs 2008) and in Latvia 9 per cent remain non-citizens (Naturalisation Board of Latvia 2008).
4 Article 49 TEU on accession does not include the requirement to provide for minority protection as the Copenhagen Criteria do.
5 For minority rights in Austria, Belgium, Germany, Great Britain, France, Italy and Spain, see Jochen Abr. Frowein et al. (eds), *Das Minderheitenrecht europäischer Staaten*, Teil 1; for minority rights in Greece, see Jochen Abr. Frowein et al. (eds), *Das Minderheitenrecht europäischer Staaten*, Teil 2. For a systematic account of the various minority groups in Europe, see Klemens Ludwig, *Ethnische Minderheiten in Europa, Ein Lexikon* and Manfred Straka (ed.), *Handbuch der Europäischen Volksgruppen*.
6 Bernd Rechel, 'The Way Forward', in *Minority Rights in Central and Eastern Europe*, pp. 227–28.
7 More detailed information can be found for example in the Member States' reports submitted pursuant to Article 25 FCNM, see at www.coe.int/t/dghl/monitoring/minorities/default_en.asp.
8 The 'Russian minority' referred to includes all Russian-speaking people who are not always ethnic Russians but stem from other parts of the former Soviet Union.
9 Sources: Statistical Office of Estonia; Citizenship and Migration Board, at www.stat.ee.
10 Klara Hallik, 'Human Rights and Minorities in the New European Democracies: Educational and Cultural Aspects', p. 42.
11 Constitution of Estonia, RT 1992, 26, 349; all Eastern European laws cited in this chapter can be found on www.minelres.lv/NationalLegislation/natleg.htm.
12 See Erika Schlager, 'The Right to Have Rights: Citizenship in Newly Independent OSCE Countries', in Helsinki Monitor 19.
13 Resolution on the Application of the Law on Citizenship, RT, 1938, 39, 357.
14 Law on Citizenship, RTI 1995, 12, 122.
15 M. H. Wiegandt, 'The Russian Minority in Estonia' (1995) *International Journal on Group Rights* 3, p. 121.
16 UNDP, Estonian Human Development Report, 1999, section 2.3, at www.undp.ee/nhdr99/en/2.3.html.
17 www.valitsus.ee/brf/index.php?id=293886&tpl=1007&external=0&search=&-aasta=2008-.
18 Conference on Security and Cooperation in Europe, The High Commissioner on National Minorities (1993), p. 218 (para. 4).
19 Article 20 of the Law on Citizenship provides: '(1) Decisions on the grant or resumption of Estonian citizenship shall be taken by the Government of the Republic'.
20 Article 36 of the Law on Citizenship stipulates: 'If a person believes that his or her rights provided for in this Act have been violated or his or her freedoms restricted by legislation or a measure of the Government of the Republic or the government

agency authorised by the Government of the Republic or an official thereof, the person has the right to file an action with an administrative court pursuant to the procedure provided for in the Code of Administrative Court Procedure.'

21 See above note 15, p. 125.

22 Rein Müllerson, 'International Law, Rights and Politics, Developments in Eastern Europe and CIS', pp. 147–87.

23 Law on Aliens, RT1 I 1999, 44, 637; consolidated text RT I 1997, 50, 548.

24 The Legal Chancellor's Act, RT I 1999, 29, 406.

25 See Communication from the Legal Chancellor's Office of 5 January 2001, No. 1–14/328.

26 2000 Regular Report on Estonia, p. 21.

27 For the most recent activities of the Legal Chancellor/Ombudsman, see at www.oiguskantsler.ee/?menuID=55.

28 The Law on Basic and Upper Secondary Schools of 1993, RT I 1993, 63, 892; consolidated text RT I 1999, 42, 497, §52 provides: '(1) By the year 2007, the curricula and organisation of study of non-Estonian language basic schools shall ensure all graduates of basic schools a level of Estonian language skills which enables them to continue studies in Estonian. (2) Transition to instruction in Estonian shall be started in state and municipal upper secondary schools not later than in the academic year 2007/2008.'

29 Law on Private Schools, RTI 1993, 35, 7, consolidated text RT I 1998, 57, 859

30 Article 8 of the Kindergarten Act, RT I 1999, 27, 387.

31 Reproduced in Flanz/Ruchti (1992) Estonia, in A. P. Blaustein and G. H. Flanz (eds), *Constitutions of the Countries of the World*, p. 209.

32 Law on Language, RT I 1995, 23, 334.

33 Regulations on State Language Knowledge Levels, 1999, RT I 1999, 66, 656.

34 Regulations on State Language Knowledge Levels, 2001, RT I 2001, 48, 269.

35 The central government has twice rejected the application by the city council of Sillimäe, which is an area with 95 per cent Russian-speaking inhabitants, see in 'Monitoring the EU Accession Process: Minority Protection 2001', Open Society Program, Budapest 2001, p. 192.

36 ACFC/INF/OP/II(2005)00, para. 162.

37 National Minorities Cultural Autonomy Act, RT I 1993, 71, 1001.

38 See chapter 4, section 4.3.

39 Second opinion on Estonia, ACFC/INF/OP/II(2005)00, paras 8 and 68.

40 Law on Elections to Parliament, RT I 1999, 1, 1.

41 In the Tallinn City Council, ethnic Russians have 25 per cent of the seats, although the number of ethnic Russian residents approaches 50 per cent.

42 ECRI's Third Report on Estonia, paras 138–41.

43 Most instruments on minorities, such as the FCNM include the nationality criterion; an exception is Article 27 ICCPR.

* This section was researched by Sabine Zanker and Francisca Zanker.

44 See Federal Statistical Office (Statistisches Bundesamt Deutschland) at www.destatis.de/jetspeed/portal/cms/Sites/destatis/Internet/EN/Navigation/Statistics/Bevoelkerung/Bevoelkerungsstand/Bevoelkerungsstand.psml.

45 On demographics in Germany, see at www.zdwa.de/zdwa/artikel/diagramme/20060215_59194914_diagW3DnavidW2666.php.

46 Federal Statistical Office 2008 at www.destatis.de/jetspeed/portal/cms/Sites/destatis/Internet/DE/Presse/pm/2008/03/PD08–105–12521templateId=renderPrint.psml.

47 This is relevant for the legislative competence in the area of minority rights in Germany.

48 The Romani spoken by the Sinti is derived from Sanskrit, whereas the Romani used by the Roma is closer to the Romani elsewhere in Europe.

49 Article 27 Peace Treaty of Versailles, 28 June 1919.

50 Third Report Submitted by Germany Pursuant to Article 25, Paragraph 1, of the Framework Convention for the Protection of National Minorities, ACFC/SR/III (2009)003; A.2.1, para. 005.
51 With the exception of Sinti and Roma minority.
52 Comments by the Federal Republic of Germany on the Opinion of the Advisory Committee on the Implementation of the FCNM in the Federal Republic of Germany, GVT/COM/INF/OP/I(2002)008, p. 5.
53 See discussion in chapter 4.
54 Basic Law for the Federal Republic of Germany (Grundgesetz, GG), English version available at www.iuscomp.org/gla/statutes/GG.htm#1.
55 Article 3(3) German Basic law.
56 Council Directive 2000/43/EC of 29 June 2000 implementing the principle of equal treatment between persons irrespective of racial or ethnic origin.
57 World Directory of Minorities and Indigenous People, Overview on Germany, www.minorityrights.org/1723/germany/germany-overview.html
58 OSCE – 2007 Human Dimension Implementation Meeting HDIM.DEL/20/07 24 September 2007, section 4.
59 Resolution CM/ResCMN(2007)4 on the implementation of the Framework Convention for the Protection of National Minorities by Germany, section 1(a).
60 ACFC/INF/OP/I(2002)008, at paras 59–60.
61 Above note 59, section 2.
62 Ibid.
63 For more detail, see Germany's Third Periodical Report submitted according to Article 15 of the Charter, MIN-LANG/PR 2007–1.
64 www.schleswig-holstein.de/.
65 Above note 50, Part B.10.1.2.1, para. 10010.
66 Above note 50, Part B.10.2.2.1, para. 10032.
67 www.witaj.de/index.html.
68 Above note 50, Part B.5.1.7.2, para. 05073.
69 Ibid. Part B.10.1.2.3, para. 10019.
70 Ibid. Part B.5.1.7.3.2, para. 05091.
71 Ibid. Part B.10.1.2.3, para. 10017.
72 On their homepage, the Sinti Alliance explicitly asks to refrain from any national or international protection measures that would have an impact on the private nature of their language, see www.sintiallianz-deutschland.de/kulturundsprache.html
73 Article 25 of the Constitution of Brandenburg; Article 18 of the Constitution of Mecklenburg-Western Pomerania; Article 5(2) and Article 6 of the Constitution of Saxony; Article 37(1) of the Constitution of Saxony-Anhalt; and Article 5 of the Constitution of Schleswig-Holstein.
74 Above note 59, section 1(b).
75 Above note 50, Part B.4.1.2, para. 04009.
76 Above note 59, section 5.
77 German Federal Constitutional Court, Decision of 25 August 1998, 109-BVerfG-Az-1-BvR-248794.
78 Above note 50, Part B.9.3.3, para. 09044
79 Above note 50, Part B.5.1.7.1, para. 05057
80 Ibid. at para. 15021.
81 Ibid. at para. 15023.
82 At federal level for example: section 8 (1) of the Act on Federal Public Officials (*Bundesbeamtengesetz*) and section 67 of the Federal Personnel Representation Act (*Bundespersonalvertretungsgesetz*).
83 Advisory Committee on the Framework Convention for the Protection of National Minorities, Second Opinion on Germany, ACFC/OP/II (2006)001, para. 100.
84 Ibid. at para. 16.

85 Above note 50, Part B.5.1.7.4.1, para. 05108.
86 Concluding Observations of the Human Rights Committee: Germany CCPR/CO/80/DEU, section 21.
87 Above note 59, section 1(b).
88 See above note 57.
89 Above note 50, Part B.4.2.2, para. 04025.
90 Bundestag Resolution of 16 June 1986.
91 Comments by the government of Germany on the second opinion of the Advisory Committee on the implementation of the Framework Convention for the Protection of National Minorities, GVT/COM/II(2006)003, at para. 39.
92 Above note 50, Part B.4.2.2, para. 04029 and para. 04030.
93 Ibid, para. 04034.
94 Ibid, para. 04031.
95 Above note 59.
96 See above note 50 Part B Article 4, at para. 04012 for the full text of the ordinance.
97 See http://culturalpolicies.net/web/germany.php?aid=421.
98 Above note 52, para. 10.
99 Ibid. at para. 12.
100 'Sinti and Roma als Feindbilder' (Sinti and Roma as perceived enemies), Information for political education No 271/2005: Prejudices, p. 56 (in German).
101 Lithuanian Department of Statistics 2001.
102 Constitution of Lithuania, approved by the citizens of the Republic of Lithuania in the Referendum on 25 October 1992.
103 Law on Ethnic Minorities of 1989, as amended on 29 January 1991.
104 See Article 12 of the Law on Citizenship, 5 December 1991, as amended on 6 February 1996.
105 'Monitoring the EU Accession Process: Minority Protection 2001', Open Society Program, Budapest 2001, p. 337.
106 Ibid. p. 335.
107 See Annual Report of the Office of Equal Opportunities of Men and Women, Ombudsman, 15 March 2000–14 March 2001 and for the most recent activities of the Ombudsman at http://ombuds.lrs.lt/.
108 See above note 6, p. 158.
109 Law on Education, 25 June 1991, No I-1489, as amended on 26 June 1997, No VIII-306.
110 See above note 105, p. 331.
111 Law on State Language, 31 January 1995, No.I-779.
112 Article 2 provides:

> The state shall provide equal protection for all the citizens of the Lithuanian SSR, regardless of ethnicity. The Lithuanian SSR, taking into account the interests of all ethnic minorities shall guarantee them the right under the law and the procedures thereunder: to obtain aid from the state to develop their culture and education; to have schooling in one's native language, with provision for preschool education, other classes, elementary and secondary school education, as well as provision for groups, faculties and departments at institutions of higher learning to train teachers and other specialists needed by ethnic minorities; to have newspapers and other publications and information in one's native language; to profess any or no religion, and to perform religious or folk observances in one's native language; to form ethnic cultural organizations; to establish contact with persons of the same ethnic background abroad; to be represented in government bodies at all levels on the basis of universal, equal, and direct suffrage; and to hold any post in the bodies of state power or government, as well as in enterprises, institutions or organisations.

113 Law on Elections to the Seimas, as amended on 27 June 1996, No. I-1408.
114 See above note 105, p. 331.
115 See Report Submitted by Lithuania Pursuant to Article 25 (1) of the Framework Convention for the Protection of National Minorities, ACFC/SR(2001)007, under Article 3, para. 7.
116 See Lithuania's 2000 Regular Report, at p. 21.
117 Some monitoring of violation of rights is carried out by the Ombudsman, however, he does not monitor the frequency of discrimination on the basis of ethnicity or minority rights per se.
118 Above note 105, p. 321.
119 Above note 6, p. 152.
120 First Opinion on Lithuania, ACFC/INF/OP/I (2003) 008.
121 Slovakia's 2002 Regular Report by the EU Commission, p. 30.
122 Constitution of the Republic of Slovakia, available at www.minelres.lv/National Legislation/Slovakia/Slovakia_Const_excerpts_English.htm
123 Law on the Use of Minority Languages of July 11, 1999.
124 Act No. 365/2004 Coll. On Equal Treatment in Certain Areas and Protection Against Discrimination.
125 A summary of the decision can be found at www.slovensko.com/news/2521. Last accessed on 2 December 2009.
126 Ombudsman Act, Law No. 564/2001.
127 Government Resolution No. 821/1999 – Strategy of the Government of the Slovak Republic for the Solution of the Problems of the Roma National Minority and the Set of Measures for Its Implementation (1999) and Government Resolution No. 294/2000 – Elaboration of the Government Strategy for Addressing Problems of the Romani National Minority into a Package of Concrete Measures for year 2000 – Stage II (2000), at http://pdc.ceu.hu/archive/00002779/01/strategia_II_eng.pdf. Last accessed on 2 December 2009.
128 See Third State Report submitted by the Slovak Republic Pursuant to Article 25 (1) of the Framework Convention for the Protection of National Minorities, ACFC/SR/III(2009)008, p. 6.
129 See above note 105, p. 443.
130 Act No. 245/2008 Coll. on education and instruction
131 That specific legislation is Act No. 365/2004 Coll. on equal treatment in certain areas and protection against discrimination and on amending and supplementing other relevant acts as amended, see above.
132 No. CD-2004-7613/14980–81:097 of 28 June 2004.
133 In its first opinion ACFC/OP/II(2005)004 the Advisory Committee drew attention to certain provisions in the State Language Law of 1995, such as Article 5(6), that could lead to undue limitations on the freedom to receive and impart information and ideas in minority languages, and invited the authorities to address this issue.
134 Act No. 270/1995 Coll.
135 Above note 128, p. 44.
136 Article 6 (d) Law 255/1991 Coll. Of May 1991 on Slovak Radio as amended.
137 Act on Slovak Television No. 254/ 1991 Coll. as amended.
138 Above note 128, p. 20–21.
139 Act No.308/1991 Coll. on freedom of religion and the status of churches and religious societies as amended by Act No. 394/2000 Coll. and Act No. 201/2007 Coll.
140 Law on Association in Political Parties and Political Movements, Act No. 424/1991 Coll.
141 Above note 128, p. 57.
142 Other sources claim 10 per cent of the population and not 1.7 per cent as claimed by the Slovak government. See e.g. Fionnuala Sweeney (16.04.2004) 'Slovakia Seeks

Help on Roma Issue' CNN available at http://edition.cnn.com/2004/WORLD/europe/04/14/eu.slovakia.roma/.

143 See above note 127.

144 ACFC/OP/II(2005)004, paras 45–46.

145 ACFC/INF/OP/I (2001)001.

146 Treaty on Good-neighbourly Relations and Friendly Cooperation between the Republic of Hungary and the Slovak Republic of 19 March 1995, official translation at www.htmh.hu/dokumentumok/asz-sk-e.htm.

147 Statistical Office of the Republic of Slovenia 2007.

148 Constitution of the Republic of Slovenia, Official Gazette No. 1–4/91.

149 See Wojciech Sadurski, above note 1, p. 216.

150 Official Gazette No. 33/2007.

151 Official Gazette No. 93/2007.

152 Law on Local Self-Government, Official Gazette No. 72/93.

153 Jelka Zorn, 'Ethnic Exclusion in a Model of Accession' in *Minority Rights in Central and Eastern Europe*, p. 213.

154 Ibid.

155 See 2001 Regular Report on Slovenia by European Commission, p. 19; Second Opinion on Slovenia ACFC/INF/OP/II(2005)005 at paras 54–61.

156 Above note 153, p. 220.

157 Above note 105, p. 524.

158 Ombudsman Act, Official Gazette 7/1993 and 15/1994.

159 See Ombudsman Annual Report of 2001, at www.varuh-rs.si.

160 Constitutional Court of Slovenia, Ljubljana, 22 March 2001, Sajnovič case, Decision No. U-I-416/98.

161 Above note 153, p. 219.

162 The 1992 Agreement on ensuring the special rights of Slovenians in Hungary and of the Hungarian ethnic population in Slovenia.

163 See Law on the Office of the State Prosecutor of 29 September 1994 and Notary Act of 21 February 1994.

164 Law on Court Rules of 24 March 1994.

165 Public Administration Act of 20 October 1994.

166 Law on Self-Governing Ethnic Communities of 5 October 1994.

167 Members of national communities have two votes. With the first they take part as all other citizens in the general elections to municipal councils and to the Parliament, and with the second they elect their representative from a special list of candidates. The right to vote and the right to be elected is held by those members of national communities who live in the ethnically mixed area and enter their names into a special electoral register.

168 In 2007 the Grosuplje municipality refused to include a Roma representative in the local council.

169 See the letter by the Human Rights Commissioner to the Slovene Prime Minister at https://wcd.coe.int/ViewDoc.jsp?id=1100865&BackColorInternet=FEC65B&BackColorIntranet=FEC65B& BackColorLogged=FFC679.

170 Slovene legislation distinguishes two categories of minorities and Roma, respectively 'non-autochthonous' and 'autochthonous'. Regardless of the existence of this legal distinction, there is no legal definition of the term 'autochthonous', and it is not found in the text of the constitutionally guaranteed protection of the Roma community. This distinction entails serious disadvantages for 'non-autochthonous' Roma. According to the Slovene Constitution, only 'autochthonous' minorities ('autochthonous' Roma, Hungarian and Italian national minorities) enjoy the special minority protection accorded by domestic and international standards, whereas members of all other ethnic minorities enjoy only individual rights and freedoms. The problems of 'non-autochthonous' Roma, such as lack of Slovene citizenship and personal

documents, receive no special attention, indeed the distinction between 'autochthonous' Roma and 'non-autochthonous' Roma may give rise to further discrimination.

171 See above note 105, p. 525.

172 Slovenia, Declaration of 25 March 1998 on the application of the FCNM, available at www.interculturaldialogue.eu/web/files/33/en/CFCNM-R.pdf. Last accessed on 2 December 2009. According to the 1991 census, there were 81,220 Serbo-Croat speakers, and 52,110 Croat speakers, but only 9,240 Hungarian speakers, 4,009 Italian speakers, and only 2,847 Romani speakers. See www.ecmi.de/emap/slo_stat.html.

173 www.statistics.gov.uk/geography/uk_countries.asp.

174 First Opinion on the UK, ACFC/INF/OP/I(2002)006, para. 4.

175 In May 2007, an important power-sharing agreement was reached between Northern Ireland's leading nationalist and loyalist parties, marking the resumption of Northern Ireland's devolved government, established in 1998 under the historic Belfast (Good Friday) Agreement. Significant efforts are being made in Northern Ireland to promote integration between Protestants and Catholics, although housing estates and schools still tend to be split along sectarian lines.

176 First Report Submitted by the United Kingdom Pursuant to Article 25(1) of the Framework Convention ACFC/SR(1999)013, para. 47.

177 Second Opinion on the UK, ACFC/OP/II(2007)003, para. 34.

178 Ibid. para. 35.

179 The Scottish government was known as the Scottish Executive when it was established in 1999 following the first elections to the Scottish Parliament. The current administration was formed after elections in May 2007.

180 Second Report Submitted by the United Kingdom Pursuant to Article 25 (1) of the Framework Convention, ACFC/SR/II(2007)003, para. 120.

181 Above note 177, paras 33–34.

182 Above note 180, para. 4.

183 Above note 180, para. 121

184 Section 488 Education Act 1996 provides: Grants for Education of Travellers and Displaced Persons:

> (1) Regulations may make provision for the payment to local education authorities of grants in respect of expenditure incurred or to be incurred by them in making provision the purpose (or main purpose) of which is to promote and facilitate the education of persons to whom this section applies.
>
> (2) This section applies to a person if—(a) by reason of his way of life (or, in the case of a child, his parent's way of life) he either has no fixed abode or leaves his main abode to live elsewhere for significant periods in each year; (b) he fell within paragraph (a) within a prescribed period immediately preceding the making of the provision in question; or (c) he is for the time being resident in a camp or other accommodation or establishment provided for refugees or for displaced or similar persons.

185 Above note 180, para. 309,

186 Ibid. para. 310.

187 Above note 176, at para. 194.

188 See preamble of the Act, www.opsi.gov.uk/legislation/scotland/acts2005/asp_20050007_ en_1#pb1-l1g1.

189 Above note 177, para. 16.

190 Above note 174, para. 103.

191 Above note 180, para. 264.

192 Ibid. para. 247.

193 Above note 174, para. 60.
194 Above note 177, para. 237.
195 Ibid. para. 238.
196 See 'Common Ground. Equality, Good Race Relations and Sites For Gypsies and Irish Travellers', Report of the Commission for Racial Equality inquiry in England and Wales, 15 May 2006.
197 See Commission for Racial Equality at www.cre.gov.uk.
198 *Regina v. South Hams District Council, ex parte Gibb and Another, Regina v. Gloucester CC, ex parte Davies* [1995] QB 158.
199 *Regina v. Shropshire County Council, ex parte Bungay* [1991] 23 HLR.
200 *Court of Appeal in Wrexham County Borough Council v. (I) The National Assembly of Wales (2) Michael Berry(3) Florence Berry* [2004] J.P.L 65.
201 *Wrexham County Borough Council v. Berry* [2003] UKHL 26.
202 ODPM Circular 01/2006, Office of the Deputy Prime Minister. Circular 1/06 introduced a more appropriate definition in section 15: 'For the purposes of this Circular "gypsies and Travellers" means "Persons of nomadic habit of life whatever their race or origin, including such persons who on grounds only of their own or their family's or dependants' educational or health needs or old age have ceased to travel temporarily or permanently, but excluding members of an organised group of travelling show people or circus people travelling".'
203 Above note 177, para. 98.
204 See the *Guardian* of 23 March 2009 'French Plan to Break Taboo on Ethnic Data Causes Uproar' at www.guardian.co.uk/world/2009/mar/23/france-race-sarkozy-ethinic-minorities. Last accessed on 3 December 2009.
205 'La Constitution ne reconnaît que le peuple français, composé de tous les citoyens français, sans distinction d'origine, de race ou de religion' ('the constitution recognises only the French people, comprised of all French citizens, irrespective of origin, race or religion').
206 La loi relative aux droits et libertés des communes, des départements et des regions, 2 Mars 1982.
207 Law of July 1, 1901 relating to the contract of association (Official Journal of 2 July 1901), Law N°81–909 of 9 October 1981, Official Journal of 10 October 1981.
208 Act No. 2004–1486 of 30 December 2004.
209 Law No. 2006–396 of 31 March 2006.
210 Created by Law n° 2006–396 of 31 March 2006, published in the Official Journal on 2 April 2006.
211 Report of the Independent Expert on Minority Issues, Mission to France 19–28 September 2007, A/HRC/7/23/Add.2, p. 3.
212 Law 94–665 of 4 August 1994 relating to usage of the French language.
213 In 2006 a French subsidiary of a US company was fined €500,000 plus an ongoing fine of €20,000 per day for providing software and related technical documentation to its employees in the English language only.
214 Bernard Cerquiglini 'Les Langues de la France', avril 1999.
215 Loi constitutionnelle de modernisation des institutions de la Ve République, Article 41.
216 Catherine Wihtol de Wenden, 'Debating Cultural Difference in France', in Gino G. Raymond and Tariq Modood (eds), *The Construction of Minority Identities in France and Britain*, p. 52.
217 The International Covenant on Economic, Social and Cultural Rights Third periodic report of France – pre-sessional working group, 21–25 May 2007, 'Regional and Minority Languages in France and Cultures are Outlaws', p. 6.
218 The southern half of France: Provence, Drôme-Vivarais, Auvergne, Limousin, Guyenne, Gascony, southern Dauphiné and Languedoc is also called Occitania, where Occitan is spoken.

219 Above note 218.
220 Loi concernant la séparation des Eglises et de l'Etat.
221 The full title of the law is Loi n° 2004–2228 du 15 mars 2004 encadrant, en application du principe de laïcité, le port de signes ou de tenues manifestant une appartenance religieuse dans les écoles, collèges et lycées publics (literally Law No. 2004–2228 of 15 March 2004 concerning, as an application of the principle of the separation of church and state, the wearing of symbols or garb which show religious affiliation in public primary and secondary schools).
222 Founded in 1989 as a response to growing urban violence, the body promotes intercommunity understanding and 'social peace' through a range of activities including interfaith symposiums.
223 Law No. 2000–2614 of 5 July 2000 relating to the Welcome and Housing of Travellers as amended by subsequent legislation.
224 National authorities confirmed that while an estimated 40,000 such sites are required, only 8,000 currently exist. Of the existing places, less than half meet the legal requirements pertaining to infrastructure provision and environmental adequacy. Municipal authorities reportedly prefer to pay penalties than comply with the law.
225 According to Article 10 of Law No. 69-3 of 3 January 1969 relating to the exercise of ambulatory activities and to the regime applicable to persons circulating in France without a fixed domicile or residence.
226 European Roma Rights Centre (ERRC) Report 'Always Somewhere Else: Anti-Gypsyism in France', p. 16.
227 Above note 212, p. 2.

Bibliography

Books

Allen, David, 'Who speaks for Europe?' in John Peterson and Helene Sjursen (eds), *A Common Foreign Policy for Europe? Competing Visions of the CFSP* (European Public Policy Series, London, 1998).

Allot, P. 'Epilogue: Europe and the Dream of Reason', in Joseph Weiler and Marlene Wind (eds), *European Constitutionalism Beyond the State* (Cambridge: Cambridge University Press, 2003).

Alston, Philip (ed.), *The EU and Human Rights* (Oxford: Oxford University Press, 1999).

Arnull, Anthony, *The European Union and its Court of Justice* (Oxford: Oxford University Press, 1999).

Babarinde, Olufemi and Faber, Gerrit (eds), *The EU and the Developing Countries: The Cotonou Agreement* (London: Sweet & Maxwell, 2005).

Bell, Mark, *Anti-Discrimination Law and the EU* (Oxford: Oxford University Press, 2002).

Benoît-Rhomer, Florence, *The Minority Question in Europe: Towards a Coherent System of Protection for National Minorities* (Strasbourg: International Institute for Democracy, 1994).

Bernhardt, Rudolf, 'Federalism and Autonomy', in Yoram Dinstein (ed.), *Models of Autonomy* (New Brunswick/London: Tel Aviv University Press, 1981).

Biscoe, Adam, 'The European Union and Minority Nations', in Peter Cumper and Steven Wheatley (eds), *Minority Rights in the New Europe* (The Hague: Martinus Nijhoff Publishers, 1999).

Broms, Bengt, 'Autonomous Territories', in *Encyclopedia of Public International Law*, vol. I (Amsterdam: North-Holland Publishing Company, 1992).

Cannizzaro, Enzo (ed.), *The European Union as an Actor in International Relations* (The Hague: Kluwer Law International, 2002).

Carr, Edward Hallett, *The Twenty Years Crisis 1919–39: An Introduction to the Study of International Relations* (London: Macmillan, 1964).

Craig, Paul and de Búrca, Gráinne, *EU Law, Text, Cases and Materials* (New York: Oxford University Press, 4th edn, 2007).

Clapham, Andrew, *Human Rights and the European Community: A Critical Overview*, vol. 1 (European University Institute, Florence, Baden Baden: Nomos, 1991).

——, 'Where is the EU's Human Rights Common Foreign Policy, and How is it Manifested in Multilateral Fora?', in Philip Alston (ed.),: *The EU and Human Rights* (Oxford: Oxford University Press, 1999).

Crawford, James, *The Creation of States in International Law* (Oxford: Clarendon Press, 1979).

Cumper, Peter and Wheatley, Steven (eds), *Minority Rights in the New Europe* (The Hague: Martinus Nijhoff Publishers, 1999).

Dalton, Richard, 'The Role of the CSCE', in Hugh Miall (ed.), *Minority Rights in Europe: The Scope for a Transnational Regime* (London: Royal Institute of International Affairs, 1994).

Dehousse, Renaud and Weiler, Joseph, 'EPC and the Single Act: From Soft Law to Hard Law?', in Martin Holland (ed.), *The Future of European Political Cooperation: Essays on Theory and Practice* (London: Macmillan, 1991).

De Schutter, Oliver, 'Mainstreaming Human Rights in the European Union', in Alston, Philip and De Schutter, Oliver (eds), *European Law* (Oxford: Oxford University Press, 2005).

De Witte, Bruno, 'Direct Effect, Supremacy and the Nature of Legal Order', in P. Craig and G. de Búrca (eds), *The Evolution of EU Law* (Oxford: Oxford University Press, 1999), pp. 177–213.

——, 'The Constitutional Resources for an EU Minority Policy', in Gabriel Toggenburg (ed.), *Minority Protection and the Enlarged European Union: The Way Forward* (Budapest: OSI/LGI, 2004).

Donnelly, Jack, 'Human Rights, Individual Rights and Collective Rights', in Jan Berting et al. (eds), *Human Rights in a Pluralist World: Individuals and Collectivities* (Middleburg: Roosevelt Study Center, 1990).

Drzemczewski, A., 'Monitoring by the Council of Europe', in Gudmundur Alfredsson et al. (eds), *International Human Rights Monitoring Mechanisms: Essays in Honor of Jacob Th. Möller* (The Hague: Martinus Nijhoff Publishers, 2001).

Drzewicki, Krysztof, 'Enlargement of the European Union and the OSCE High Commissioner on National Minorities', in Mark Weller et al. (eds), *The Protection of Minorities in the Wider Europe* (Basingstoke: Palgrave Macmillan, 2008).

Eide, Asbjørn, 'The Universal Declaration in Space and Time', in Jan Berting et al. (eds), *Human Rights in a Pluralist World: Individuals and Collectivities* (Middleburg: Roosevelt Study Center, 1990).

Estebanez Martin and Maria Amor, 'The Protection of National, Ethnic, Religious and Linguistic Minorities', in Nanette Neuwahl and Allan Rosas (eds), *The European Union and Human Rights* (The Hague/London/Boston: Kluwer Law International, 1995).

——, 'The High Commissioner on National Minorities: Development of the Mandate', in Michael Bothe et al. (eds), *The OSCE in the Maintenance of Peace and Security* (The Hague/London/Boston: Kluwer Law International, 1997).

——, 'Minority Protection and the OSCE', in Peter Cumper and Steven Wheatley (eds), *Minority Rights in the New Europe* (The Hague: Martinus Nijhoff Publishers, 1999).

Fierro, Elena, *The EU's Approach to Human Rights Conditionality in Practice* (Dordrecht: Martinus Nijhoff Publishers, 2003).

Flanz, Gisbert, 'Estonia', in Albert P. Blaustein and Gisbert H. Flanz (eds), *Constitutions of the Countries of the World*, Release 92–2 (Dobbs Ferry, NY: Oceana Publications, 1992).

Frowein, Jochen Abr., Hofmann, Rainer and Oeter, Stefan (eds), *Das Minderheitenrecht europäischer Staaten*, Teil 1 and Teil 2 (Max Planck Institut für ausländisches öffentliches Recht und Völkerrecht: Springer-Verlag, 1993 and 1994).

Gál, Kinga, *Protection of National Minorities and Stability in Central and Eastern Europe*, Berghof Research Center for Constructive Conflict Management (Berghof Occasional Paper No. 6, September 1996).

——, 'The Implementation of Minority Rights', in Erwin Müller et al. (eds), *Menschenrechtsschutz, Demokratie, Sicherheit, Frieden durch Recht III*, 143 (Baden-Baden: Nomos, 2002).

Gardner Feldman, Lily, 'Foreign Relations and Enlargement of the EU', in Thomas Banchoff and Mitchell P. Smith (eds), *Legitimacy and the European Union, The Contested Polity* (London/New York: Routledge, 1999).

Ginsberg, Roy, *Foreign Policy Actions of the European Community: The Politics of Scale* (Boulder, CO: Lynne Rienner; London: Adamantine Press, 1989).

Groussot, Xavier, *Development and Impact of the General Principles of Community Law: Towards a Jus Commune Europaeum?* (Lund: Lund University, 2005).

Habermas, Juergen, *The Inclusion of the Other: Studies in Political Theory*, Ciaran Cronin and Pablo de Greif (eds) (Cambridge, MA: MIT Press, 1998).

Hallik, Klara, 'Ethnicity and Cultural Transition, Human Rights and Minorities in the New European Democracies: Educational and Cultural Aspects', in Cesar Birzea and General Rapporteur, *Report on the Workshop Held at Lohusolu (Estonia)* (Strasbourg: Council of Europe Publications, 1996).

Heraclides, Alexis, *Helsinki II and its Aftermath: the Making of the CSCE into an International Organisation* (London/New York: St Martin's Press, 1993).

Higgins, Rosalyn, 'Minority Rights: Discrepancies and Divergences Between the International Covenant and the Council of Europe System,' in *Liber Amicorum for Henry Schermers* (Lawson and de Blois eds.), vol. III, 195–209 (Dordrecht: Martinus Nijhoff Publishers, 1994).

Hofmann, Rainer, 'The Framework Convention for the Protection of National Minorities: an Introduction', in Marc Weller (ed.), *The Framework Convention for the Protection of National Minorities: A Commentary* (Oxford: Oxford University Press, 2005).

——, 'The Future of Minority issues in the CoE and the OSCE', in Mark Weller, Denika Blacklock and Katherine Nobbs (eds), *The Protection of Minorities in the Wider Europe* (Basingstoke: Palgrave Macmillan, 2008).

Hölscheidt, Sven 'Artikel 22', in Jürgen Meyer (ed.), *Kommentar zur Charta der Grundrechte der Europäischen Union* (Nomos: Baden-Baden, 2003).

Hull, Andrew, 'International Society and the Study of Regimes: A Reflective Approach', in Volker Rittberger (ed.), *Regime Theory and International Relations,* (Oxford: Clarendon Press; New York: Oxford University Press, 1993).

Jackson-Preece, Jennifer, *Minority Rights* (Cambridge: Polity Press, Key Concepts series, 2005).

Kemp, W. (ed.), *Quiet Diplomacy in Action: The OSCE High Commissioner on National Minorities* (The Hague: Kluwer Law International, 2001).

Keohane, Robert, *After Hegemony – Cooperation and Discord in the World Political Economy* (New Jersey: Princeton University Press, 1984).

Kymlicka, Will, 'Politics in the Vernacular: Nationalism, Multiculturalism and Citizenship' (Oxford: Oxford University Press, 2001).

——, 'The Evolving Basis of European Norms of Minority Rights', in Mark Weller et al. (eds), *The Protection of Minorities in the Wider Europe* (Basingstoke: Palgrave Macmillan, 2008).

Lerner, Natan, 'The Evolution of Minority rights in International Law', in Catherine Brölmann et al. (eds), *Peoples and Minorities in International Law* (Dordrecht/London: Martinus Nijhoff Publisher, 1993).

Lindberg, Leon, The Political Dynamics of European Economic Integration (Stanford, CA: Stanford University Press, 1963).

Lijphart, Arend, *The Politics of Accommodation: Pluralism and Democracy in the Netherlands* (Berkeley, CA: University of California Press, 1968).

Lindfelt, Mats *Fundamental Rights in the European Union: Towards Higher Law of the Land?* (Åbo: Åbo Akademi University Press, 2007).

Lister, Marjorie, *The European Community and the Developing World* (Aldershot: Avebury, 1988).

Ludwig, Klemens, *Ethnische Minderheiten in Europa, Ein Lexikon* (Munich: Beck, 1999).

Macdonald, R. 'The Margin of Appreciation', in R. Macdonald et al. (eds), *The European System for the Protection of Human Rights* (Dordrecht: Kluwer Academic Publishers, 1993).

Malanczuk, Peter, *Akehurst's Modern Introduction to International Law* (London/ New York: Routledge, 8th edn, 2001).

Mannens, Wolf, 'The International Status of Cultural Rights for National Minorities', in Peter Cumper and Steven Wheatley (eds), *Minority Rights in the New Europe* (The Hague: Martinus Nijhoff Publishers, 1999).

Müllerson, Rein, *International Law, Rights and Politics, Developments in Eastern Europe and CIS* (London: Routledge, 1994).

Murray, Gilbert, 'National Tolerance as an International Obligation', in Geneva Institute of International Relations (ed.), *Problems of Peace, Fifth Series: Lectures delivered at the Geneva Institute of International Relations, August 1930* (Geneva, 1931).

Napoli, Daniela, 'The European Union's Foreign Policy on Human Rights', in Nanette A. Neuwahl and Allan Rosas (eds), *The European Union and Human Rights* (The Hague/ Boston/London: Martinus Nijhoff Publications 1995).

Neuwahl, Nanette, 'The Treaty on European Union: A Step Forward in the Protection of Human Rights?', in Nanette A. Neuwahl and Allan Rosas (eds), *The European Union and Human Rights* (The Hague/Boston/London: Martinus Nijhoff Publications 1995).

Neuwahl, Nanette and Rosas, Allan (eds), *The European Union and Human Rights* (The Hague/Boston/London: Martinus Nijhoff Publications, 1995).

Nowak, Manfred, *The UN Covenant on Civil and Political Rights, CCPR Commentary* (Strasbourg: Engel Verlag, 1993).

——, 'Human Rights Conditionality in the EU', in Philip Alston (ed.), *The EU and Human Rights* (Oxford: Oxford University Press, 1999).

Open Society Institute, *Monitoring the EU Accession Process: Minority Protection 2001* (Budapest: Open Society Program, 2001).

Packer, John, 'On the Definition of Minorities', in John Packer and Kristian Myntti (eds), *The Protection of Ethnic and Linguistic Minorities in Europe* (Åbo/Turku: Åbo Akademi University Press, 1993).

Peers, Steve, 'Human Rights and the Third Pillar', in Philip Alston (ed.), *The EU and Human Rights* (Oxford: Oxford University Press, 1999).

Raymond, Gino G. and Modood, Tariq (eds), *The Construction of Minority Identities in France and Britain* (Basingstoke: Palgrave Macmillan, 2007).

Rechel, Bernd (ed.), 'The Way Forward', in *Minority Rights in Central and Eastern Europe* (London: Routledge, 2008).

Robinson, Jacob, Karbach, Oscar, Laserson, Max M., Robinson, Nehemiah and Vichniak, Marc, *Where the Minority Treaties a Failure?* (New York, NY: Institute of Jewish Affairs, 1943).

Rock, Stephen R., *Why Peace Breaks Out: Great Power Rapprochement in Historical Perspective* (Chapel Hill, NC/London: University of North Carolina Press, 1989).

Sadurski, Wojciech, 'Minority Protection in Central Europe and Accession to the EU', in Marc Weller et al. (eds), *The Protection of Minorities in the Wider Europe* (Basingstoke: Palgrave Macmillan 2008).

Smith, Karen E., *The Making of EU Foreign Policy: the Case of Eastern Europe* (New York: St Martin's Press, 1998).

——,'The EU, Human Rights and Relations with Third Countries: Foreign Policy with an Ethical Dimension?', in Karen E. Smith and Margot Light (eds), *Ethics and Foreign Policy* (Cambridge: Cambridge University Press, 2001).

——, Stewart and Alasdair M., *Migrants, Minorities and Security in Europe* (London: Research Institute for the Study of Conflict and Terrorism, 1992).

Straka, Manfred (ed.), *Handbuch der Europäischen Volksgruppen* (Vienna/Stuttgart: Wilhelm Braumüller Universität Verlagsbuchhandlung GmbH, 1970).

Szysczak, Erika and Cygan, Adam, *Understanding EU Law* (London: Sweet & Maxwell, 2008).

Taylor, Paul, *The European Union in the 1990s* (Oxford: Oxford University Press, 1996).

Thornberry, Patrick, *International Law and the Rights of Minorities* (Oxford: Clarendon Press, 1991).

——, 'The Declaration on the Rights of Persons Belonging to National or Ethnic, Religious and Linguistic Minorities: Background, Analysis and Observations', in Alan Philips and Allan Rosas (eds), *The UN Minority Rights Declaration* (Turku/Åbo: Åbo Akademi University Press, 1993).

——'International and European Standards on Minority Rights', in Hugh Miall (ed.), *Minority Rights in Europe: The Scope of a Transnational Regime* (London: Pinter, 1994).

Toggenburg, Gabriel, 'The EU's Role Vis-à-Vis Minorities after the Enlargement Decade', in Mark Weller et al. (eds), *The Protection of Minorities in the Wider Europe* (Basingstoke: Palgrave Macmillan, 2008).

Toth, A. G., 'Human Rights as General Principles of Law, in the Past and in the Future', in U. Bernitz and J. Nergelius (eds), *General Principles of European Union Law* (The Hague: Kluwer Law International, 2000).

Tridimas, Takis, *General Principles of EC Law* (Oxford: Oxford University Press, 2006).

Tudyka, Kurt P., *Die Vernetzung der Europäischen Institutionen*, OSZE Handbuch (Opladen: Leske + Budrich, 2002).

Weiler, Joseph, 'European Citizenship and Human Rights', in Jan A. Winter et al. (eds), *Reforming the Treaty on European Union – The Legal Debate* (The Hague: Kluwer Law International, 1996).

Weiler, Joseph and Wessels, Wolfgang, 'EPC and the Challenge of Theory', in Alfred Pijpers et al. (eds), *European Political Cooperation in the 1980s: A Common Foreign Policy for Western Europe?* (Dordrecht: Martinus Nijhoff Publishers, 1998).

White, Gillian, 'Structural Adjustment with a Human Face and Human Rights in Development: New Approaches in the Fourth Lomé Convention', in R. S. Pathak and R. P. Dhokalia (eds), *International Law in Transition – Essays in Memory of Judge Nagendra Singh* (Dordrecht: Martinus Nijhoff Publishers, 1992).

Windmeißer, Anette, 'Der Menschenrechtsansatz in der Entwicklungszusammenarbeit', in Manfred Nowak and Hannes Tretter (eds), *Studienreihe des Ludwig Boltzmann Instituts für Menschenrechte* (Verlag Österreich 2002).

Williams, Andrew, *EU Human Rights Policies, A Study in Irony* (Oxford: Oxford University Press, 2005).

Wihtol de Wenden, Catherine 'Debating Cultural Difference in France', in Gino G. Raymond and Tariq Modood (eds), *The Construction of Minority Identities in France and Britain* (Basingstoke: Palgrave Macmillan, 2007).

Wolff, Stefan and Peen Rodt, Annemarie, 'The EU and the Management of Ethnic Conflict', in Marc Weller et al. (eds), *The Protection of Minorities in the Wider Europe* (Basingstoke: Palgrave Macmillan, 2008).

Wolfers, Arnold, *Discord and Collaboration: Essays on International Politics* (Baltimore, MD: Johns Hopkins University Press, 1962).

Zaagman, Robert, 'The CSCE High Commissioner on National Minorities: An Analysis of the Mandate and the Institutional Context', in Arie Bloed (ed.), *The Challenges of Change, The Helsinki Summit of the OSCE and its Aftermath* (Dordrecht: Martinus Nijhoff Publishers, 1994).

——, Minority Questions, Human Rights and Regional Instability: the Prevention of Conflict (Vienna: Conference on Security and Co-operation in Europe, 1994).

Zorn, Jelka, 'Ethnic Exclusion in a Model of Accession', in Bernd Rechel (ed.), *The Minority Rights in Central and Eastern Europe* (London: Routledge, 2008).

Articles

Amato, Guiliano and Batt, Judy, 'Minority Rights and EU Enlargement to the East', EUI Working Paper, RSC No. 98/5.

Auckerman, Miriam J., 'Definitions and Justifications: Minority and Indigenous Rights in a Central/East European Context', (2000) HRQ 22(4), November.

Buergenthal, Thomas, 'The Copenhagen CSCE Meeting: A New Public Order for Europe', 1990 HRLJ.

Capotorti, Francesco, 'The Protection of Minorities under Multinational Agreements on Human Rights', (1976) Italian Yearbook on International Law.

Christiansen, Thomas, Jorgensen, Knud Erik and Wiener, Antje, 'The Social Construction of Europe', (1999) *Journal of European Public Policy* vol. 6.

Costello, Cathryn, 'The *Bosphorus* Ruling of the European Court of Human Rights: Fundamental Rights and Blurred Boundaries in Europe', (2006) HRLR 6(1).

Craig, Paul, 'The Treaty of Lisbon, Process, Architecture and Substance', (2008) *European Law Review* 33(2).

Craufurd Smith, Rachael, 'From Heritage Conservation to European Identity: Article 151 EC and the Multi-faceted Nature of Community Cultural Policy' (2007) *European Law Review* 32(1).

De Witte, Bruno, 'Politics Versus Law in the EU's Approach to Ethnic Minorities', EUI Working Paper, RSC No. 2000/4.

——, 'Free Movement of Persons and Language Legislation of the Member States of the EU, Some Reflections after the Recent Judgement in *Bickel* and *Franz*, in European Academy', in EUR.AC research, Academia Nr. 18 (März–Juni /marzo–giugno 1999).

Dinstein, Yoram, 'Collective Human Rights of Peoples and Minorities', (1976) ICLQ 25.

Doyle, Dermot, 'EU and OSCE, Natural Born Partners', (2002) *European Security Review* 14, September.

Flynn, Padraig, 'The Implications of Article 13 EC – After Amsterdam: Will Some Forms of Discrimination Be More Equal than Others?', 36 (1999) CMLR.

Fouwels, Martine, 'The EU's Common Foreign and Security Policy and Human Rights', 3 (1997) NQHR.

Frowein, Jochen Abr. and Bank, Roland, 'The Effect of Member States' Declarations Defining 'National Minorities' upon Signature or Ratification of the Council of Europe Framework Convention for the Protection of National Minorities', (1999) *Zeitschrift für ausländisches öffentliches Recht und Völkerrecht* 59.

Gilbert, Geoff, 'The Burgeoning Minority Rights Jurisprudence of the European Court of Human Rights', (2002) *HRQ* 24(3), August.

Hilf, Meinhard, 'Ein Grundrechtskatalog für die Europäische Gemeinschaft', 26 (1991) *Europarecht* 24–27.

Hillion, Christophe 'The Framework Convention for the Protection of National Minorities and the European Union', *Conference Report on Enhancing the Impact of the Framework Convention*, Strasbourg 9–10 October 2008, Council of Europe.

Howard, Erica, 'The European Year of Equal Opportunities for All – 2007: Is the EU Moving Away from a Formal Idea of Equality?', (2008) *European Law Journal* 14(2), March.

Hughes, James and Sasse, Gwendolyn, 'Monitoring the Monitors: EU Enlargement Conditionality and Minority Protection in the CEECs', (2003) *JEMIE* 1.

Jackson-Preece, Jennifer, 'Minority Rights in Europe: from Westphalia to Helsinki', (1997) *Review of International Studies* 23.

Jaeger, Thomas, 'Enhanced Co-operation in the Treaty of Nice and Flexibility in the Common Foreign and Security Policy', (2002) *European Foreign Affairs Review* 7.

King, Toby, 'Human Rights in European Foreign Policy: Success or Failure for Post-Modern Diplomacy', (1999) *EJIL* 10.

Koppel, J. and O'Neill, A., 'The European Court of Justice: Taking Rights Seriously', 29 (1992) *CMLR* 669.

Lenaerts, Koen, 'Fundamental Rights in the European Union', 25 (2000) *European Law Review*.

Lenaerts, Koen and De Smijter, Eddy, 'A Bill of Rights for the European Union', 38 (2001) *CMLR* 273.

McInernney, S., 'The Charter of Fundamental Rights of the European Union and the Case of Race Discrimination', 27 (2002) *European Law Review*.

Mearsheimer, John, 'Back to the Future: Instability in Europe after the Cold War', (1990) *International Security* 15(4), pp. 5–56.

Meron, Theodor, 'The Meaning and Reach of the International Convention on the Elimination of all Forms of Racial Discrimination', 79 (1985) *AJIL* 283.

Moens, Gabriel, 'Affirmative Action. The New Discrimination', St Leonards, Centre for Independent Studies, 1985.

Moravscik, Andrew, 'Preferences and Power in the European Community: A Liberal Intergovernmentalist Approach', (1993) *Journal of Common Market Studies* 31(4), December.

O'Leary, S. 'Accession by the European Community to the European Convention on Human Rights – The Opinion of the ECJ', (1996) *EHRLR* 4.

Peers, Steve, Statewatch Analysis of the EU Reform Treaty (2007), available at www.statewatch.org.

Rich, Roland, 'The Recognition of States: The Collapse of Yugoslavia and the Soviet Union', 4 (1993) *EJIL*.

Roth, Stephen, 'The CSCE Charter of Paris for a New Europe,' (1999) *HRLJ*.

Schlager, Erika, 'The Procedural Framework of the CSCE, from the Helsinki Consultations to the Paris Charter, 1972–1990', 12 (1991) *HRLJ*.

——, 'The Right to Have Rights: Citizenship in Newly Independent OSCE Countries', (1997) *Helsinki Monitor* 8(1).

Sjursen, Helene and Smith, Karen E., 'Justifying EU Foreign Policy', ARENA Working Papers WP 01/01.

Stewart, Emma J., 'Capabilities and Coherence? The Evolution of European Union Conflict Prevention', (2008) *European Foreign Affairs Review* 13(2).

——, 'Restoring EU–OSCE Cooperation for Pan-European Conflict Prevention', (2008) *Contemporary Security Policy* 29(2), pp. 266–284.

Toner, Helen, 'Impact Assessments and Fundamental Rights Protection in EU Law', (2006) *European Law Review* 31.

Toggenburg, Gabriel, 'A Rough Orientation Through a Delicate Relationship: The European Union's Endeavours for (its) Minorities', (2000) European Integration Online Papers 16.

——, 'The EU's Evolving Policies Vis-à-Vis Minorities: A Play in Four Parts and an Open End', (2008) EUR.AC Research, August.

——, 'The Role of the New EU Fundamental Rights Agency: Debating the Sex of Angels or Improving Europe's Human Rights Performance?', (2008) *European Law Review* 33(3).

Tretter, Hannes, 'Human Rights in the Concluding Document of the Vienna Follow-Up Meeting of the CSCE', (1989) *HRLJ*.

Van den Berghe, Frederic, 'Double Standards and Minority Protection, The European Union and the Protection of Minorities: How Real is the Alleged Double Standard?', (2003) *Yearbook of European Law*, vol. 22 (Oxford: Oxford University Press, 2004), pp. 155–202.

Verdirame, Guillermo, 'Breaches of the European Convention on Human Rights Resulting from the Conduct of International Organisations', 2 (2008) *EHRLR*.

Wendt, Alexander, 'Anarchy is What States Make of it: the Social Construction of Power Politics', (1992) *International Organisation* 46(2), spring.

Weiler J. H. H. and Lockhart, N., 'Taking Rights Seriously: The European Court and Its Fundamental Rights Jurisprudence', 32 (1995) *CMLR*.

Wiegand, M. H., 'The Russian Minority in Estonia', (1995) *International Journal on Group Rights* 3.

Williams, Andrew, 'Enlargement of the Union and Human Rights Conditionality', (2000) *European Law Review* 25.

——'The Indifferent Gesture: Article 7 TEU, the Fundamental Rights Agency and the UK's Invasion of Iraq', 31 (2006) *European Law Review*.

Wright, Jane, 'The OSCE and the Protection of Minority Rights', (1996) *HRQ* 18(1), February.

——, 'The Protection of Minority Rights in Europe: From Conference to Implementation', (1998) *IJHR* 2(1).

Index